Capoeira Connections

CAPOEIRA
CONNECTIONS

A MEMOIR IN MOTION

KATYA WESOLOWSKI

UNIVERSITY OF FLORIDA PRESS
Gainesville

Frontis: Camarão (the author) and Naldo (Ronaldo Cavalcanti) playing capoeira in a street roda, Rio de Janeiro. Illustration by Julia Illana.

Publication of this open monograph was the result of Duke University's participation in TOME (Toward an Open Monograph Ecosystem), a collaboration of the Association of American Universities, the Association of University Presses, and the Association of Research Libraries. TOME aims to expand the reach of long-form humanities and social science scholarship including digital scholarship. Additionally, the program looks to ensure the sustainability of university press monograph publishing by supporting the highest quality scholarship and promoting a new ecology of scholarly publishing in which authors' institutions bear the publication costs. Funding from Duke University Libraries made it possible to open this publication to the world.

Publication of this work is made possible by a Sustaining the Humanities through the American Rescue Plan grant from the National Endowment for the Humanities.

All photographs are by the author unless otherwise indicated.

28 27 26 25 24 23   6 5 4 3 2 1

Library of Congress Cataloging-in-Publication Data
Names: Wesolowski, Katya, author.
Title: Capoeira connections : a memoir in motion / Katya Wesolowski.
Description: Gainesville : University of Florida Press, [2022] | Includes
  bibliographical references and index.
Identifiers: LCCN 2022026752 (print) | LCCN 2022026753 (ebook) | ISBN
  9781683402732 (hardback) | ISBN 9781683403203 (paperback) | ISBN
  9781683403463 (ebook) | ISBN 9781683403630 (pdf)
Subjects: LCSH: Wesolowski, Katya. | Capoeira (Dance)—History—Biography.
  | Capoeira (Dance)—Personal narratives. | Capoeira (Dance)—Brazil—Rio
  de Janeiro—Personal narratives. | Martial arts—Biography. | BISAC:
  SOCIAL SCIENCE / Anthropology / Cultural & Social | HISTORY / Latin
  America / South America | LCGFT: Personal narratives. | Autobiographies.
Classification: LCC GV1796.C145 W47 2022 (print) | LCC GV1796.C145
  (ebook) | DDC 793.3/1981—dc23/eng/20220624
LC record available at https://lccn.loc.gov/2022026752
LC ebook record available at https://lccn.loc.gov/2022026753

University of Florida Press
2046 NE Waldo Road
Suite 2100
Gainesville, FL 32609
http://upress.ufl.edu

UF PRESS

UNIVERSITY
OF FLORIDA

For Orin

In Memory of Mark, Daddy, and Tourinho.
Saudades.

CONTENTS

LIST OF FIGURES   IX

OPENING SENSATIONS   XI

Introduction: "Everything the Mouth Eats"   1

1. Entering the Roda: Rio de Janeiro, 1995–1996   19

2. Authenticity and Loss: Bahia, 1996   45

3. An Anthropologist in the Roda: Rio de Janeiro, 1997   84

4. "Only Intellectuals Like Misery": Rio de Janeiro, 2001–2004   115

5. Imagining Brazil in Africa: Angola, 2002   158

6. Global Convivência: Brussels, Venice, Accra, Havana, 2008–2018   181

7. Return to Roots: Angola, 2019   199

8. Bringing It All Home: Durham, North Carolina, 2021   220

ACKNOWLEDGMENTS   239

LIST OF CAPOEIRISTAS   243

GLOSSARY   247

NOTES   255

REFERENCES   265

INDEX   273

FIGURES

Figures follow page 146.

1. Roda in a Favela
2. Mestre Beiçola
3. Mestre Sardinha and Fernandinho playing in a street roda
4. Mestre Touro playing with a *navalho* (razor)
5. Mestre Dentinho at Mestre Touro's monthly roda
6. Jorginho
7. Mestre Camisa
8. Parafuso
9. Tourinho
10. Cascão with berimbau at the Cristo Redentor
11. Bacurau and Chá Preto playing at the foot of the Cristo Redentor
12. Kids class in Dona Marta favela, Rio de Janeiro
13. Hamster at the top of Santa Marta Hill
14. Pirulito playing capoeira in the street
15. Naldo doing a flip
16. Maria Preta dancing jongo
17. Cafeína playing berimbau
18. Maestrinha
19. Camarão (author) playing in a street roda
20. Playing locally made instruments in Benguela, Angola
21. Cabuenha. Still image taken from video
22. Camarão (author) playing with son Lucien in a roda

OPENING SENSATIONS

I heard, saw, and felt capoeira for the first time when I was eighteen years old.

Berkeley, California, my hometown, 1988. Pulsing, percussive music spills out of an auditorium into the street. The skin on my forearms goose bumps as a chorus of voices swells over the drum like a cresting wave. When I enter, the sound amplifies and materializes into tumbling bodies riding the wave. Though on a stage and at a distance from me, the circular embrace of musicians and singing-clapping participants around two flying bodies generates a palpable energy. I want to join.

Taking my seat in the audience as the sensorial abundance settles, I begin to focus on the movement: the spinning kicks and feints demonstrate the efficacy of martial arts and elegance of modern dance; acrobatics rival the most virtuoso breakdancing; shuffling steps and rhythmic breaks echo tap dance; and the momentary conjoining of bodies in a back-and-forth waltz channels the beauty of tango. Movement appears improvised yet coordinated. Two players sway around each other in a circular ebb and flow, at times fitting together like puzzle pieces, and other times stealing space and knocking each other over like chess pieces. The corporeal dialogue is both competitively cooperative and aggressively playful. Fierce, beautiful, and exhilarating, capoeira mesmerizes and seduces. I immediately begin training.

I cannot now remember, after thirty years, what capoeira felt like for the first time. Now, I swing in the *ginga,* capoeira's side-to-side step, as instinctively as I walk and go upside down on my hands as easily as bending over. But I watch my students and know that my first ginga was also awkward and hesitant, like a toddler's first steps. I have been a dancer and athlete all of my life, and yet capoeira at first felt completely foreign. Beyond building strength and agility, I had to forge a new perception of space and my body and other bodies in it. Turning upside down and moving on the ground while keeping my partner-opponent always in sight, disoriented and confused. As challenging was capoeira's mix of play and combat.

Like a couple's social dance, capoeira required reading and responding to a partner while yet staying vigilant to attack, and finding opportunities to unbalance my opponent. Capoeira's intersubjectivity—melding physical, mental, and emotional relationality—was unlike anything I had known in dance or life. It continues to challenge me. Learning, improving, discovering more in the game has kept me coming back again and again to the circle, to the *roda*.

Capoeira's call, however, sounds far beyond the ephemeral moments of play. For me, capoeira has been a medium for exploring my evolving interior and exterior self. The practice has shaped my physical and perceptual body, my intellectual and emotional life, and my social world. Around the time that I was intensifying my involvement in capoeira, traveling to Brazil to train and meet my extended capoeira family, I entered graduate school to study anthropology. Although not my initial intention, within my first year of studies the two projects merged, and I found myself returning to Brazil as both capoeirista and anthropologist. This book is the story of my long engagement with capoeira as a practitioner, researcher, and now teacher.

Capoeira Connections is both memoir and ethnography. As a memoir it chronicles my own transformation into a capoeirista and what the practice has meant in my life. As an ethnography—the descriptive and analytic writing anthropologists do—it traces the transformations in capoeira over the last three decades and what the practice has meant in the lives of some of the many capoeiristas I have moved with over the years. In weaving our stories together, I hope to convey an intimate look into the diversity of individuals who embrace capoeira and through their practice discover meaning, connection, and potentiality.

Capoeira was created by and for Brazilians of African descent. Emerging out of the long nightmare of the Transatlantic Slave Trade and the forced displacement of millions of Africans from their homelands that created what we know today as the African diaspora, capoeira has always been global and mobile: "conceived in Africa and birthed in Brazil," as some practitioners say. With few resources beyond their bodies and voices, enslaved and free African men in Brazil (women would become involved only much later) came together to play, to sing, to fight. Today, capoeira spans six continents, taught in health clubs from Japan to Italy; in schools from Angola to Nepal; from kibbutz in Israel to refugee camps in Palestine; from sprung-floor dance studios in Australia to elite university classrooms in the United States. As it crosses geographic, national, race, class, gender, and sexual borders, capoeira comes to mean and do different things for different people. It forges avenues to professionalization and transnational mobility for Brazilian capoeiristas—and new ways of engaging Brazil for foreign capoeiristas. For some practitioners, capoeira is a part-time activity to stay in shape and socialize; for others it is a full-time vocation for consciousness-raising and social activism. Diverse people pursuing a common passion can produce disagreement, misunderstanding, and conflict. Yet, capoeira's demand for proximity, dialogue, and cooperation also fosters a space of movement in which to connect and create belonging across difference.

My transformation into a capoeirista (and anthropologist) has not been easy. My body and ego have been bruised, and at times I have doubted my place in capoeira as a white, middle-class, non-Brazilian woman. And I have questioned my ability to merge the personal and professional, to focus my anthropologist's analytical tools on my capoeirista's embodied experience. Along the way, I have, at times, almost abandoned the project and capoeira altogether. But, as I tell fellow capoeiristas who chuckle in agreement, "*ela não me deixa*" (she doesn't let me). Despite the doubt, hurt, and insecurity that capoeira sometimes engenders in me, it has been an enduring joy in my life. This book, then, is also a love letter to capoeira: an attempt to understand my passion and what work such love might do in knowing, being, and acting in the world.

My changing relationship to capoeira over the years has kept my engagement alive and fresh: from a novice thirsty for knowledge and experience; to a researcher with a critical eye; to an instructor attempting to transmit all I have learned from capoeira to my students. Along the way I have trained and played in different styles with different communities of practitioners on four continents. And I continue to find novelty, depth, and challenge in my practice.

Still, after all these years, when I approach a good roda alive with music and energy, my skin goose bumps, my heart races, and I think, *cheguei*, I have arrived.

INTRODUCTION

"Capoeira is everything the mouth eats."

In the capoeira world, Mestre Pastinha's often quoted aphorism leaves much to interpretation. The famous capoeira teacher seemed to suggest that, like food, capoeira sustains the body. That it is life-giving energy, or perhaps life itself, resonates with how many capoeiristas experience and speak about their practice; more than a physical or aesthetic activity, capoeira is an artful way-of-being in the world.

For me, "capoeira is everything the mouth eats" attests to its transformative potential. We take the world inside us when we eat, and the act changes us, physically, emotionally, socially. Around the world, eating brings people together to nourish, to celebrate, to mourn, to mark life transitions, to create bonds, and even to compete. Capoeira brings people together in similar ways.

The conjoining of food, sociality, and capoeira was driven home to me by a *mestre* in Rio de Janeiro.[1] As a novice capoeirista and anthropologist, I began asking my teachers "what is capoeira?" Like the moving target of capoeiristas in play, definitions were elusive, shifting, and paradoxical: game, fight, dance, play, self-defense, art, sport, expression, resistance, liberation, education, culture, history, identity, energy, philosophy, a gathering, a dialogue, a prism, a vice, a way of life. One teacher, Mestre Touro, told me, "capoeira is you coming to my house and eating my rice and beans one week and me going to your house and eating your rice and beans the next week."

I first interpreted Mestre Touro's definition literally. Capoeira is a gathering and a social event. The *roda* (wheel or circle) refers to both the physical space, or ring, in which capoeira is played as well as to the event of bringing capoeiristas together to "play." Capoeiristas do not "fight" or "dance," but "play" (*jogar*), and a match between two capoeiristas is "a game" (*jogo*). A roda can last a half hour or four hours; be preplanned or spontaneous; occur in public or private spaces; be closed only to friends or open to strangers;

stay friendly or turn rough. In one of the Rio de Janeiro capoeira networks in which I move, each group—consisting of a mestre and students—hosts a monthly roda.

For at least the last twenty-five years, as long as I have known him, Mestre Touro has held his roda without fail, unless he is traveling, every first Saturday of the month at 5:00 p.m. Held on the cement patio in front of his house, the roda lasts one to two hours and is followed by food and drink: *churrasco,* the famous Brazilian barbecue, grilled and served by older students, and plenty of beer and *guaraná,* the national soda, distributed by younger students. Conversations and fraternizing continue until the circulation of meat and drink—determined by Mestre Touro's cash flow that month—slows. A close comrade of Touro's until his death in 2011, Mestre Nacional held his roda in a samba school rehearsal space on the last Sunday of the month and always served *angu* (corn grits) and beef stew. So, one weekend Touro and his students along with mestres and students of other groups would be at Nacional's "house" playing in his roda and eating his food; and the next weekend Mestre Nacional and the others would be at Mestre Touro's house. And so it goes year-round, playing and eating together.

Mestre Touro's definition thus appears to refer to the great reciprocal potlatch, or kula ring, of the monthly rodas.[2] Hosting a roda is a way to display and share "wealth" in the capoeira world. At rodas, reputations are made and unmade, stories birthed, and bonds of sociality woven. However, Mestre Touro referred to "rice and beans" rather than the beer and meat I and others have enjoyed plenty of at his rodas over the years. Rice and beans are the iconic Brazilian *everyday* food. On any morning, walk into any house in Brazil—rich or poor, rural or urban—and good chances are you will see, smell, or hear beans (black or red depending on the region) steaming in a pressure cooker for the midday meal. While generally prepared in the same simple way, with plenty of garlic, every pot of beans tastes slightly different depending on the kitchen and cook.

Defined as food sharing, capoeira becomes a practice of "making kin."[3] Nourishment is essential work of kinship, and sharing food creates belonging and obligation. A capoeira group is a supportive (if also hierarchical and at times dysfunctional) family. Mestre Touro, like many of the capoeira mestres in Rio's peripheral neighborhoods and *favelas* where they live and teach,[4] rarely receives payment from his students, at least in cash: a student who is a baker brings fresh morning rolls to the mestre's house, while one with a motorcycle runs errands. Unremunerated for most of its history, capoeira is primarily a gift and a tool, a pleasure and release, an act of protest and camaraderie.

As a tool and gift, capoeira cultivates corporal skills and creates social relationships. Gifts, French sociologist Marcel Mauss taught us, produce reciprocity.[5] Bonds between mestres and their disciples create group loyalty, build reputations, and manufacture cultural capital. As a pleasure and release, capoeira is a way to unwind from a day filled with hard labor and stress—and at times hunger and violence—and enjoy the presence of friends. As an act of protest and camaraderie, capoeira transmits a sense of pride in and ownership of a practice that was repressed for much of its history and can spark political consciousness and mobilization around social injustice. Teaching and practicing capoeira is a kind of "body work" that enhances possibility for action on the world.[6]

What then does the work and pleasure, joy and release, of capoeira look and feel like?

Playing Capoeira

"Capoeira is flying to the moon."

I knew exactly what the ten-year-old Brazilian capoeirista meant the day I mastered the *aú de frente*. I had been working for months on this particular cartwheel (*aú*), which orients the body forward rather than sideways, legs shooting over the top, the chest lifting last as the eyes gaze toward the ground. The forward thrust of the hips had eluded me until it didn't anymore, and suddenly, I popped up onto my feet instead of crashing to the ground. I shouted, clapped my hands, and repeated the move over and over until dizzy and breathless. For the brief moment when my feet reached for the ground as my hands left the floor, I felt airborne and free, my body no longer an obstacle but an enabler.

"Flying to the moon" captures not only the momentary, gravity-defying freedom one might feel when executing the more spectacular acrobatic moves or *floreios* (flourishes) as they are known: "*vai, vai, vai voa!*" (go, go, go fly!) young Brazilians chant when a player is showing particular skill flipping around the roda. "Flying to the moon" also communicates the aspirational possibilities of capoeira—and of even occasionally achieving the impossible—as I felt at my first *aú de frente*.

This sense of achievement occurs by means of what is often considered, ironically, an "unproductive" activity. Capoeira is play. In Portuguese, "to play" translates into three verbs: *jogar* refers to game play; *tocar* to musical play; and *brincar* to the spontaneous, creative play among children or adults during moments of pleasure and release.[7] Capoeira incorporates all three forms of play. As a physical game, capoeira, like all play, exists outside of ordinary life, bounded in its own time and space, and is voluntary, with no goal other than the absorbing pleasure of play itself.[8] Historian Johan Huizinga argued that culture emerged out of the creativity and innovation of humans at play. Developmental psychologist Jean Piaget argued that child's play is important for imagining worlds and possibilities, experimenting with social roles and rules, and learning empathy. Freud argued that play creates the "illusion of mastery," of being in control of feelings, actions, and the world itself.[9] In positive psychology this illusion of mastery is described as the ideal play state, or "flow," where awareness and action merge to temporarily free one from time and space.[10] In capoeira, flow is the momentary liberation "from the poverty of everyday life and ultimately even from the constraints of the human body."[11] Or as the young capoeirista told me, "flying to the moon."

Flow in capoeira is what capoeiristas call *axé*. Like athletes "in the zone" and jazz musicians "in the groove," capoeiristas, and a roda, flowing right, are full of axé. Described by players as good energy, axé is sensation and emotion: it is the goose-bumping of the flesh at the rise of a chorus; tears that fill the eyes at the soulful lament of a single voice and berimbau; the undistracted presence when one finds unison with a partner; the pleasure of a game well played. A Yoruba term (*asë*) and an important concept in the Afro-Brazilian religious arena, axé also embodies a theory of action: "the power-to-make-things-happen, the key to futurity and self-realization."[12] As a novice anthropologist, I once asked a mestre what capoeira could do for people. "It is not what capoeira can do," he told me, "but what people do with capoeira." In the space of the roda, axé is the ability to take control of the game and make things happen. Axé is capacity-building. But axé also depends on flow for all. As capoeiristas say, "capoeira cannot be played alone": an individual singer is only as good as the responding chorus, and a player is at her best when in harmony with another.

Capoeira's play and axé link it to other expressive and ritual practices of the African diaspora. As an "art in motion," capoeira is a fluid exchange between participants and spectators, musical call-and-response, and improvisation.[13] Movement is accompanied by percussive music: the thump of an *atabaque* (drum), the trill of *pandeiros* (tambourines), the ring of the *agogô* (clapperless bell), the clack of the *reco-reco* (scraper), and the twang of the *berimbau* (one-string musical bow). The musicians, who will also take turns moving inside the roda, riff off of one another's rhythms and cadences. A good instrument player maintains the beat, never crosses the rhythm, yet finds spaces to improvise and embellish. Like much music with African roots, the singing is call-and-response—one voice calls and others answer.

The lead singer may improvise verses by borrowing and weaving in lines from other songs or inventing new lyrics on the spot. These spontaneous verses can comment, humorously or critically, on the game or players in the roda.

Like the music, movement is call-and-response, or as capoeiristas say, a dialogue. One player "asks a question" and the other "responds." While movements can be performed on their own (during training or as solos in performances) they only take on meaning when played with another in an improvised exchange. Each movement is contingent on the previous one and influences the following one. The greater mastery a player has, the greater movement-vocabulary and dexterity she has in maneuvering and manipulating the conversation to affect the outcome of the game. As a "game of chess played with the body," capoeira is about claiming, defending, and stealing space. In less competitive moments, a game unfolds like a puzzle, bodies negotiating and sharing space, fitting together in a moving mosaic.

Creating dialogue is more important than "scoring a point." Still, there is an objective to unbalance or knock one's partner to the ground: a foot may sweep a standing leg; a head strike the chest or ribs; the legs "scissor," twist, and drop a body to the ground; and a well-placed kick knock a partner out of the roda. The moves must be carefully timed and not too frequent to maintain the flow and aesthetics of the game. Sometimes attacks are embellished with theatrics and humor, heightening tension and excitement. But there are no declared winners or losers. Games seamlessly enfold one another: two new capoeiristas beginning afresh at the foot of the lead berimbau or one player "buying" a game (*comprando o jogo*) by entering the roda and replacing one already playing. Like the movement of the ocean's tides, an image invoked in many capoeira songs, games ebb and flow.

Convivência and Malandragem

Gathering people together in collective creativity—to play, to express, to dialogue—capoeira, I have come to understand, is above all else *convivência*. A Portuguese term with no singular translation, convivência connotes connection, coexistence, and companionship. We can have convivência with each other, with places, experiences, and spiritual entities. Convivência is the flip side of *saudades,* another difficult to translate Portuguese word and often-evoked sentiment in Brazil. Saudades is an intense missing, longing or nostalgia for a person, place, or time. Saudades marks absence; convivência "being-with."

In capoeira, one has convivência with the practice itself and with fellow capoeiristas. This convivência exists on multiple levels: in the evanescent relationship of bodies in play in the roda; in the day-to-day togetherness of practitioners in local groups; and in the growing "imagined community" of capoeiristas around the globe. Convivência makes one legible in the world, to oneself and to others, on a visceral level: experiencing one's own and others' bodies through play and knowing others' day-to-day lives, or in other words, eating their rice and beans. As the Bantu people of West Central Africa, capoeira's deep ancestors, say: "food tastes good only if one can taste and feel the mind and heart of the person who cooked it."[14]

Convivência translates most literally as "conviviality." There are certainly moments of capoeira conviviality—a good roda full of axé and the food shared afterward can overflow with lively friendliness and good-will. But convivência does not assume or depend on harmony. Nor does it necessarily arise spontaneously or effortlessly; convivência takes time, effort, and dedication. We may think of capoeira "conviviality" as *how we might live together in this moment*. As theorized by cultural studies scholar Paul Gilroy, "conviviality" is a "radical" and always risky openness to difference. Convivial spaces such as global cities—in which capoeira increasingly circulates—encourage living "with alterity without becoming anxious, fearful or violent." Conviviality allows difference to become "unruly," challenging regimentation of space along notions of culture and social worth.[15] Conviviality can be messy but is necessary for moving toward a more egalitarian and shared world.

Imagining the futures made possible through conviviality, anthropologist Francis Nyamnjoh suggests that it "encourages us to recognize our own incompleteness" and dependency on others.[16] Conviviality, he writes, "challenges us to be open-minded and open-ended in our claims and articulations of identities, being and belonging . . . to reach out, encounter and explore ways of enhancing or complementing ourselves with the added possibilities of potency brought our way by the incompleteness of others."[17] Playing in the roda reminds us that only when we are in motion together may we experience something close to completion.

Axé creates the conditions for convivência, and the possibility of momentarily experiencing completeness in unison with others. But axé operates in a field of multiple players, all jockeying to make things happen so that outcomes are uncertain.[18] According to dance scholar Yvonne Daniel, in the Afro-Brazilian religious arena, axé is divine energy that manifests in worshipping dancers "to push forward individuality and independence" but also demonstrates "our need for social exchange, solidarity, acknowledgement, and love."[19] A similar tension between the individual and social exists in the roda: capoeiristas desire harmony and flow but also strive to display singular virtuosity, to "show off" while maintaining a keen sense of self-preservation.

Looking out for oneself is a fundamental attitude that capoeira cultivates alongside physical skills and collective belonging. This approach to life, captured in the term *malandragem,* helps capoeiristas to act within and beyond the roda. Another word with no singular translation, malandragem is glossed as cunning, trickery, dishonesty, and opportunism. Malandragem is the code by which the *malandro* (rogue or scoundrel) lives. Emerging in post-abolition Brazil and popularized by samba lyrics in the early twentieth century, the malandro is an Afro-Brazilian folk figure who survives on the edges and interstices of society through his wit, charm, good looks, and skill at conning those with greater social and economic capital. Today in Brazil, malandragem, no longer the exclusive domain of the malandro, is a social tactic for anyone willing to take advantage of others in order to get ahead. In the roda, malandragem manifests as strategic cunning and humorous theatrics deployed to outplay one's partner and demonstrate greater skill. Derision, laughter, and feigned detachment, all tactics of malandragem, display capoeira's "aesthetics of cool" common across African diasporic performance genres.[20] Turning again to a food metaphor, capoeiristas say malandragem is capoeira's *dendê,* the rich palm oil that gives certain Brazilian dishes their distinctive taste.

Positively valued in the capoeira roda and ambiguously valued in other contexts, malandragem is a kind of cultural agency for moving through a society that prides itself on its "cordiality" and racial harmony even though it is one of the world's most unequal nations. Malandragem, however, is not simply a performative or feigned threat. There are often moments in a game that push the boundary between play and fight, the performative and the real. Play, like conviviality, can be explosively unruly. Capoeiristas call these moments *jogo duro* (hard or rough play). Rough games must be carefully controlled so that they do not break the "play-frame" altogether and slip into a *briga,* or fight.[21] Some players seek out the danger and excitement of jogo duro as an opportunity to test their skills. Whether surfacing or not, the possibility of jogo duro raises the stakes of the game, lending it gravitas. A good capoeirista who deploys malandragem must be ready to back it up with jogo duro.

Both malandragem and jogo duro are responses to the hardships of everyday life, or as they say in Brazil, *a luta que é a vida* (the fight that is life). Distrust, dissimulation, and aggression—alongside camaraderie, creativity, and playfulness—can be survival tactics. Jogo duro is a way to *desabafar* or release pent-up frustrations and emotions; and malandragem can provide a sense of control and agency over situations. Ultimately, these tactics may only provide an "illusion of mastery" as structural inequalities remain in place. Yet they do important work in witnessing and communicating—in different registers—suffering and discontent with the world as it is. And they remind us that convivência is always incomplete in a world so fractured by the divides of race, class, and geography.

First Ginga

Berkeley in the 1980s and 1990s was a hotbed of progressive politics and multiculturalism. With its Tibetan jewelry stores, Indian meditation ashrams, Irish fiddle jams, and Afro-Cuban drum circles, the city was a playground inviting white people to discover "cultural elsewheres."[22] The perfect location for capoeira to land in its migration from Brazil to the world. I will not deny that I, too, was captivated by capoeira's "virtuosic difference" of otherness.[23] The pull of capoeira was both visual and aural. I felt the call of an African-inspired rhythm that had been working on me since childhood.

I was introduced to Africa by a neighbor, South African archaeologist Glynn Isaac. I associated my deep affection for him, his wife, two daughters, and home full of artifacts, with Africa: the earthy smell of the low-slung leather chairs; the scrape of rough-hewn wood against my knuckles and plonk of stones in the Mancala board; the taste of hot milk and bedtime tales of the great gray-green, greasy Limpopo River. When I was ten, they took my older sister on a dig in Kenya. I was deeply envious and promised myself I would go to Africa someday.

Black music came via my father. Saturday mornings he took my brother and me to dance at the enormous drum circle on UC Berkeley's campus, congas and bongos reverberating from Lower Sproul Plaza to Telegraph Avenue. At home we'd put on his swing and bebop 45s, and my father would do his version of Howard Sims's "sand dance," one foot hovering above the floor, his big toe a fulcrum to swivel back and forth while snapping his fingers low. I learned to appreciate his John Coltrane and Miles Davis LPs mixed in with my mother's Bach and Beatles. When I managed to catch glimpses of *Soul Train,* during my strictly allotted television time, I was mesmerized by the music and beautiful Black dancers in spectacular clothing-costumes showcasing signature swivel-hip, high-kick moves.

Capoeira also attracted the tomboy in me. It was still a male-dominated practice with only a sprinkling of women in the 1980s. I was comfortable moving in male spaces as they had defined my childhood. My brother Mark, older by two years, had been my best friend and constant companion. We rode bikes, played sports, and created complicated imaginative worlds to-gether. Garbage Can Alley—inspired by the "bike gang" who hung out on undersized BMX bicycles in the park by our house—involved practicing acrobatic fighting skills. I never took up martial arts in real life, having fol-lowed my older sister into ballet. I loved the big jumps but wasn't as flexible or well-groomed as the other girls. I was much happier (as was my father) when I took up tap. I liked the music, wearing street clothes, making rhythm with my feet, and the possibility of someday being good enough for the Soul Train Line.

Capoeira offered the possibility of becoming the fierce warrior dancer of my childhood dreams, but also drew me for its participants: diverse in age, race, nationality, and gender, at least as I witnessed it in the Bay Area. At that first roda, a father played with his two-year-old son, his miniature down to his short dreadlocks, wide grin, spunky cartwheel, and astonishing head spin. Mestre Beiçola had recently arrived from Brazil, and it was with him that I began training.

We trained in whatever no-rent spaces we could find: parks, school play-grounds, and in an Oakland nightclub, first sweeping away cigarette butts and broken glass to protect our bare feet. A long mirror in the club gave the dim place a semblance of a dance studio. But we never looked in the mirror, our gaze glued to the powerful grace of our teacher. Beiçola's invit-ing and mocking smile, especially while upside down, coaxed us through difficult and disorienting movement. Though muscular, he was remarkably lithe, sweeping from the ground in a slow handspring, stopping in a hand-stand, and melting into a headspin; he bounced and bounded in a circu-lar parade of surprises. He was unexpected outside of the roda as well. He showed up one day with a new haircut to honor his dedication to the Hare Krishna religion: he had shaved off all his dreadlocks except for a small circular patch at the back of his head, "so God can pull me up to heaven when I die," he teased.

We were a small group, and Beiçola often instructed us one-on-one. Play-ing extensively with each of us, he'd offer various "responses" to "questions," and demonstrate how a single move could be used differently depending on context or intent. As a drummer might teach a rhythm pattern by build-ing in complexity over time, Beiçola's pedagogy was what anthropologist Greg Downey calls a type of scaffolding mimesis.[24] Our teacher was less interested in technique or form and more concerned with expanding our movement-vocabulary and understanding of the game. Once committed to muscle memory the movements became ours, and he infrequently critiqued our style or execution. We also did lots of repetition—one hundred spinning kicks!—calisthenic and strengthening exercises, leftovers from Beiçola's time as a sergeant in the Brazilian military.

This pedagogy was foreign to my dancer's body. I was used to following choreography to counts while looking in a mirror. Now, with no choreography and no reflection, I had to *feel* the movement in my body and gauge my partner's reaction to know whether I had it right. Moving upside down and on a circular rather than straight axis, I frequently lost my sense of direction. The game altered both my proprioception, or sense of my own body in space, as well as my orientation to others around me.

While struggling with all this, I had also to attend to aesthetics. I longed to slow down my cartwheel, languorously shifting weight from one hand to the other at the top like a southern drawl elongating a vowel. Simultaneously, I had to keep track of my partner/opponent, maneuvering him or her into a space where I could deliver a sweep or headbutt. Most challenging, capoeira demanded an embodied attitude: a theatrical playfulness that was mocking, ironic, aggressive, cunning, and opportunistic. Capoeira's intersubjectivity—one iteration of convivência—is both intimate and provocative. I found this challenging game ephemeral and tactile, elusive and animating.

An integral part of training with Beiçola was time together after class. After Sunday morning trainings, we sometimes went to the Berkeley Hare Krishna Temple for chanting and a meal. Other times we just sat where we were, on a patch of grass or curb, chatting about life. When Beiçola moved with his family to a suburb on the Peninsula, the only place open after 10:00 p.m. was a supermarket. Still in our uniforms, we would gather in the parking lot sharing food and occasionally bursting into song or a quick capoeira game, to the bewilderment of the employees and late-night shoppers.

I discovered over the months and then years of training with Mestre Beiçola that certain things are not explicitly taught. A fellow student—a large, lumbering, middle-aged man who drove a UPS delivery truck—begged Beiçola to teach him the "secret" of the ginga. He told us he had been practicing the swinging side-to-side step in front of a mirror at home at night "to get it right." Another student was scornful: "You can't learn that from the mirror!" Our teacher just laughed and shrugged, "everyone does the ginga differently."

The ginga carries the DNA of a capoeirista's lineage but is also, like a fingerprint or footstep, unique to each. While the basic step is the first thing a student is taught, it takes years of practice and exploration to make it an expression of self. Practitioners observe that a capoeirista's personality, including otherwise hidden qualities, comes out in the ginga and the roda: a serious and reserved person becomes animated and playful; an easygoing and accommodating person becomes fiercely competitive; and a large, heavy-footed person becomes remarkably light and graceful in the roda. While the ginga is an intimate expression of the self, it is also the medium through which one connects to the music, history, and one's partner.[25] As a kinesthetic and interpersonal encounter, a medium for self-expression *and* interaction, the ginga encourages discovery of self and other.[26] Developing our ginga and game, we established convivência with our bodies and histories, desires and fears, limitations and capabilities.

"Who is your mestre?" is one of the first questions capoeiristas ask of each other. Knowing and claiming one's lineage is a way to respect and honor one's ancestors. This is not always easy. Rifts occur between teachers and students, and I would come to know over the years that capoeira can make kin and also unmake kin. My own capoeira trajectory has been an eclectic movement through different styles and groups: from the playful roughness of what I call *fundo de quintal,* or backyard, capoeira; to the more athletic and disciplined *capoeira regional;* and eventually the syncopated playfulness and cunning of *capoeira angola.* While struggling to physically embody these stylistic changes I have also, at times, felt challenged to define (or defend) my capoeira identity.

Ancestry in capoeira is not just knowing one's immediate lineage. It is also knowing the deep history of struggle, suffering, and loss, and the creative resilience out of which the practice emerged: it is honoring the enslaved Africans who created capoeira in the late eighteenth century, and the "old guard" (*velha guarda*)—like Mestre Pastinha whose words began this chapter—who kept the practice alive through the early twentieth century despite racism and poverty. This history is encoded in capoeira music and movement and transmitted through players' bodies. I cannot play, teach, think, or write capoeira without engaging its history. This deep history is the warp of the book; the weft is my own journey with others to understand and embody an unfamiliar way of moving through the world that has become an essential part of me.

An Anthropologist in the Roda

A fellow graduate student once asked how I could possibly study something so close to me. She was a yoga practitioner and couldn't imagine writing about it as an anthropologist. At first, I took this as an indictment of excessive proximity to my topic. In the early years, as anthropologists struggled to have their discipline accepted as an objective science, critical distance was considered essential for good participant-observation, the key methodology of fieldwork. An ethnographer accused of "going native" and becoming too close to the subject of study (perhaps trading in life in the Ivy Tower for village life!) lost academic authority.

Yet even early on, pioneering female anthropologists pushed back against the presumption that ethnographic research was only valid if conducted with detachment and presented in scientific language. These women, who embraced research and writing as intimate, personal, and embodied projects, are crucial figures in my intellectual genealogy. As with my capoeira ancestors, I honor and thank them for giving me license to write from the body and heart.

Zora Neale Hurston, Ella Cara Deloria, and Ruth Landes studied with Franz Boas and Ruth Benedict at Columbia University, who in the early twentieth century were defining American anthropology as the relativistic study of cultures. Hurston and Deloria wrote about their own communities—Black American Southerners and South Dakota Sioux—producing ethnographies and novels based on fieldwork.[27] Ruth Landes, a Jewish New Yorker and nonnative in her field site of Brazil, melded travel memoir and ethnography in a beautifully rendered study of female religious leaders in Salvador, Bahia. Based on fieldwork conducted in the late 1930s and published in 1947, *City of Women* was panned by the anthropological establishment for being unscientific and too personal.[28] The poor reception of her work affected her career, and she never secured a tenured professorship. Years later, in a challenge to the Cartesian mind/body split, Landes would write "fieldwork serves an idiosyncrasy of perception that cannot separate the sensuousness of life from its abstractions, nor the researcher's personality from his [sic] experiences."[29]

Two pioneering Black women who embodied the impossibility of separating "the sensuousness of life from its abstractions" were Katherine Dunham and Pearl Primus. Primarily remembered as modern American dancers, Dunham and Primus were also both trained anthropologists whose fieldwork informed their intellectual, artistic, pedagogical, and activist lives.[30] In the same decade that Landes went to Brazil, Dunham traveled through the Caribbean with a visiting card that read "anthropology and the dance" because she could not "separate the two callings."[31] *Island Possessed,* the memoir she wrote thirty years after her fieldwork into Haitian Vodou, is saturated—with the attuned eye of a dancer—with detailed descriptions of the movements and gestures of others, as well as her own embodied sensations. Trinidad-born Pearl Primus burst onto the New York dance scene a few years after Dunham with her athletic style and magnificent leaps. Her multiyear research on dance in various African and Caribbean countries was foundational to the development of African dance performance and pedagogy in the United States. Dunham and Primus are the godmothers of the field of dance ethnography that blossomed in the 1990s and shaped my graduate studies.[32]

The innovative ethnographies of these pioneering women, while certainly displaying some of the problematics of anthropological studies of the time, were nonetheless prescient of the "crisis of representation" and "self-reflexive turn" the field would take later in the century.[33] While underappreciated at the time, their work inspired later generations of feminist anthropologists, also many of color, who occupied "in-between" spaces. As both academics and members of studied cultural groups, anthropologists like Kirin Narayan, Lila Abu-Lughod, Ruth Behar, and Virginia Domínguez theorized the category of "native" in new ways, blurring the objective/subjective, and self/other divide that had shaped the field of anthropology. Kirin Narayan argues that we all carry various positionalities in the field as do our interlocutors, such that the "native" label is never total or fixed. Instead of drawing lines between insider and outsider, Narayan suggests that we "focus our attention on the quality of relations with the people we seek to represent in our texts."[34] Virginia Domínguez argues that love is the most "closeted" feeling in our scholarship and yet may be the most "enabling." By showing our affection, our readers will likewise come to care about the people we write about.[35] Furthermore, Black feminists have taught us that love is not just an emotion but a political practice that encourages us to recognize our deep connections to one another and our "collective inhabitation of the social world."[36] As an ethnographic tool, love reminds us to center relationality and response-ability in our work.[37]

Today an increased global circulation of cultural practices creates new insider/outsider positionalities and responsibilities. As a capoeirista, I was, to a certain extent, a "native anthropologist." Yet in Brazil I was also a white, female, American, relatively wealthy graduate student from a prestigious university. These identities afforded me immediate privilege in Brazil. This unnerved and infuriated me, such as when a good friend of mine, Senegalese and a PhD student like myself, was frequently told to ride the service elevator in apartment and office buildings. Alain suffered an overt racism in Brazil to which he was unaccustomed in Senegal; in contrast, I experienced the same—if more blatant—white privilege I live with every day in the United States.

In the capoeira arena, I was embraced as a native *and* an outsider. In the 1990s before capoeira's transnational explosion, a foreign, female capoeirista in Brazil was still rather exotic, at least in certain circles. Furthermore, my academic credentials in a country of vast educational inequality—another source of discrimination—granted me credibility and certain privileges. I could visit different groups, train in various styles, and play in multiple rodas in a way that was not available to most Brazilian capoeiristas. I was not held to the same standard of loyalty, and perceived "betrayals" were (usually) overlooked. I was also seen as a valuable resource for goods from, or even immigration to, the United States. At times, I felt claimed by certain groups or individuals in struggles over legitimacy, visibility, and opportunity.

In the end, mobility shaped my fieldwork. With capoeira's growing popularity, capoeiristas were in motion within and beyond the roda. So, I moved with them. Over the course of my multiyear fieldwork, I traveled all over Rio de Janeiro from community centers in favelas to a television soap opera set in the nouveau-riche neighborhood of Barra da Tijuca. I traveled to other Brazilian states to attend capoeira events and a national meeting that gathered hundreds of practitioners to debate polemic legislature to professionalize capoeira.[38] Eventually my research took me beyond Brazil to Angola and Europe. My fieldwork had become, in anthropological parlance, multisited.

And like many anthropologists today who work on transnational multisited projects, I never really left the field. When I returned to the Bay Area to write my dissertation, my practice continued almost at the same intensity as during my time in Rio. I integrated into a local group affiliated with the one I had been working with in Brazil and trained three or four nights a week. As my writing progressed, I came to understand my colleague's question about being too close to my topic differently: did intellectualizing my practice detract from the embodied pleasure of doing it? To some extent it did. Different from the descriptive field notes I had written every morning in Rio de Janeiro, the analytic writing I was now doing demanded a critical distance that disrupted my personal practice. I got distracted while training, spinning dangerously off into thought. And my analytic lens laid bare my own complicated desires in practicing and studying capoeira that didn't seem to have an appropriate outlet in the dissertation. In *writing* capoeira, I temporarily stopped *doing* capoeira. And in the writing, my own capoeira story went largely untold.

Now, my story has returned. It provides the narrative arc of this book because it is the story I can tell best, and because through it I can most closely capture and share the visceral, emotional, and intellectual experience of capoeira convivência. Anthropologist Kathleen Stewart suggests that "the authority to narrate comes of having been somehow marked by events, in mind if not in body."[39] For me, events *have* been marked on my body. A torn MCL from a capoeirista landing on my leg from an airborne kick still makes my knee ache from time to time; the thin, curved scar on my big toe is the sign of a surgery after years of barefoot ginga; and a bump just above my right ankle bone that appeared after a particularly hard sweep has been with me for twenty-five years. These scars are my body's memories.

Deeper than the marks of injury, is my capoeira "habitus," or what sociologist Pierre Bourdieu defined as the dispositions, habits, perceptions, and expressions that dictate everyday action. Habitus is invisibly inculcated in individuals through historical, socioeconomic, and gendered practices but is also learned through such things as sport, dance, or martial arts.[40] In the case of capoeira, along with acquiring new movement skills—such as walking on one's hands—training transforms the physical and perceptual body.[41] As my body grew leaner and stronger from daily practice, I acquired new ways of moving through my environment: using peripheral vision, gauging space, reacting quickly, falling with control, moving on the ground. Such dispositions are invaluable in a city like Rio with its fast-moving traffic, broken pavement, and pickpockets.

I also move, now, with an inner rhythm. When I lecture about capoeira, my body sways and dips as I describe movement. I cannot think or speak capoeira without feeling its generative beat. This rhythm, while specific to capoeira, is also the percussive, syncopated beat of the African diaspora. While habitus is individually experienced in the present, it is collectively and historically engendered.[42] My capoeira habitus is the embodied history of my own training, and more deeply, the history of capoeira and the African diaspora. Black performance scholars Thomas DeFrantz and Anita Gonzalez theorize diaspora as a skin, "porous and permeable, flexible and self-repairing, finely spun and fragile," that protects and connects, and allows us "to see each other in skins that go together or sometimes belong apart."[43] Expressive practices of the diaspora, like capoeira, invite belonging and connectivity but also remind us of the complexity, fragility, and limitations of convivência.

My long-term being and moving with capoeira has allowed me to feel the embrace of its diasporic skin. This skin warms and connects and demands accountability and responsibility toward the practice and to others who share it with me. Yet, of course, I experience capoeira convivência differently from the many capoeiristas who daily live the precarity and violence of structural racism and poverty. I will never know what it feels like to play in a roda with hunger in my gut, rage in my heart, and hopelessness in my soul. But I can consider the ways in which race and class privilege have also shaped my embodied dispositions and social experiences. Through our shared practice we can envision futures that move beyond the historically entrenched inequalities that shape our bodies, everyday lives, and interpersonal relationships.

And through stories, I hope to share the connection with others—and the unity through difference rather than sameness—that convivência, such as the one I live with capoeira, can enable.

If the storyteller's authority comes from having been marked by events, then it is the writer's job to bring those events to life on the page. Clifford Geertz reminds us that the anthropologist must convince her readers that she was actually there; and "being there" in the authorial sense, "palpably on the page," is just as, if not more, difficult as "being there" in the flesh.[44] By emplotting my own capoeira journey, I hope to place my readers there with me. For those of you who have been "marked" by capoeira in your own ways, I hope my story percusses in your body so that you sway, dodge, and leap along with me. For those of you unfamiliar with capoeira, I strive to dance an image before your eyes, syncopate a rhythm in your chest, and invite you in.

But how to bring sensations alive on the page?

A Capoeirista on the Page

Ethnography is an embodied methodology; we take our bodies into the field where they are our tools for participant-observation—that paradoxical method that demands both immersive doing and critical reflection. In translating experiences of the field to the page, however, the physical and emotional quality of doing fieldwork often disappears.[45] Ethnographers of dance, sport, and performance are particularly attuned to the body as a methodological tool and site of knowledge production.[46] Yet even in studies that privilege the body, the language sometimes fails to convey the sensual richness of experience. Social scientists often still feel beholden to rationalist ways of understanding and presenting "data." But capoeira knowledge is largely created and transmitted body-to-body rather than through written texts; through feelings and intuition rather than empirical facts; and through memories, stories, and gossip rather than official history. Privileging these alternate ways of knowing through storytelling is what brings me, and I hope my readers, closest to the sensuousness of experience.

My capoeira convivência has put me in motion not only with different capoeiristas over the years but also with distinctive urban spaces. Cities, with personalities as complex and contradictory as people, have particular rhythms and sensations. Learning to navigate urban landscapes while at the same time training a movement practice situated in that landscape can open up the senses to the politics and poetics of place.[47] Through capoeira I experienced the segregation of urban space as well as the creative ways people navigate, traverse, and challenge divisions.

Increasingly, the borders capoeiristas cross are transnational. Capoeira is now a global "kinetoscape" connecting people and places through practices of the body.[48] My narrative follows the global flow of capoeira from California to Rio de Janeiro, New York City to Salvador, Bahia, and Luanda, Angola, to Venice, Italy. It is based on field notes, interviews, journals, vivid and fragmented memories, and thousands of hours training, playing, watching, and talking capoeira. Through centering intercorporeality—bodies in motion together—in my writing, I hope to blur the line between memoir and ethnography in order to convey the intimacies and entanglements of a global expressive practice.[49]

Once I realized the narrative I had to follow was my own, stories and dialogue populated my head and flowed onto the page. Later I confirmed, modified, and adjusted while consulting field notes, journals, interviews, and the internet. There was no internet in my early capoeira years; today just about everything capoeira can be found online, from how to make and play a berimbau or execute the hardest acrobatic movements, to the life histories and music of legendary mestres. Above all else, the internet is a video library of games that are widely circulated, studied, and discussed. I sometimes turned to these videos to reconstruct the particular style of individuals. Translating movement into words is challenging; attempting this transcription from a conjured memory in the mind is even more difficult. I am thus immensely thankful (while wary) of the living capoeira archive the internet provides.

For sections of my early narrative, there are no records or methods for re-creation. Diaries from my first visits to Brazil do not contain the wealth of detail that my later field notes do, and so I rely on memory. But memories shift and change over time. Nonetheless, similar to an anthropologist revisiting field notes and interview transcripts to produce ethnography, a memoirist revisits memories to see where they take her in the present. So, while there may be misremembered people, places, and events in the following pages, I hope that some "truth" emerges from my trying to make sense of it all.

In sharing the stories of the many capoeiristas—some well-known in the capoeira world and others not—who all contribute to making capoeira what it is today, I do not shy away from moments of disagreement and conflict. Writing from a place of love means showing people in their complexity and, thus, not treating them with "kid gloves."[50] I, too, as will be seen in these pages, have not always been treated gently. I do not use pseudonyms, a long held but changing convention in ethnography. Instead, I introduce people with their capoeira nicknames because that is how we know and call each other, and because nicknames convey our affection and convivência. For those capoeiristas who also wanted their full name to appear, I have provided an appendix. All photographs, except where noted, were taken by me.

Writing, anthropologist Michael Jackson suggests, is "a 'tool of conviviality,' a means of bridging the gulf that lies between oneself and others, subsuming the singular in the plural."[51] Writing is a lonely process; yet through writing we connect to others. Sitting alone at my desk, I have reconnected in my mind and on the page with capoeiristas with whom I share convivência. Sometimes the convivência was but fleeting: an intense game with a stranger on the street whom you may never play with or even see again; a game, nonetheless, that fills your heart with joy, or perhaps disappoints and haunts. Sometimes it is circumstantial and temporary: living in the house of a mestre for three months, training alongside his kids and eating his rice and beans. And sometimes these convivências stretch over a lifetime, infrequent in hours spent together but deep in feeling; friendships that *moram no meu coração* (live in my heart).

1

ENTERING THE RODA

RIO DE JANEIRO, 1995–1996

Nossa Senhora da Penha stands on a small hill above the flat expanse of the Zona Norte. The church welcomes me each time I arrive in Rio de Janeiro. In a private ritual of return, I look for it from the air when descending to Galeão; and then again while racing or crawling, depending on traffic, along the Linha Vermelha between the international airport and city center. The church has a simple, narrow elegance: two steeples rise tall, pale-yellow whitewash and blue trim gleam against the granite rock on which it stands. This rock (*penha*) gives the church and the cluster of neighborhoods below it—Penha, Vila da Penha, and Penha Circular—their names.

Our Lady of the Rock, oral history tells, was first built in the seventeenth century by a Portuguese hunter in honor of the Virgin Mary, who saved him from a giant snake while he was out walking in the outskirts of the colonial city.[1] Today the church is famous for its 382 stairs that pilgrims climb, the most devout on their knees, to hang little plastic heart, kidney, knee, or arm *ofertas*—supplications for their own miracles.

My eyes linger on the church every time I arrive and depart Rio thinking not of *its* history, but of *my* history with the church and this majestic city. Most visitors to Rio are first seduced by the glamorous and breezy Zona Sul (South Zone). The white sand beaches of Copacabana, Ipanema, and Leblon and sweeping vistas of Guanabara Bay from the rock and jungle mountains of Corcovado and Pão de Açúcar certainly enchant. Rio's natural beauty makes it a visually stunning city. Visitors may eventually venture to the historic center and ports; or take an "adventure tour" in a safari jeep to one of the hillside favelas that dot the Zona Sul.[2] Few visitors, however, make it out to the peripheral suburbs of the Zona Norte (North Zone) or the farther outlying cities of the Baixada Fluminense that comprise Rio's greater metropolitan area of thirteen million people.

Rio's *subúrbios* are not the quiet, tree-lined bedroom communities of U.S. suburbs. Zona Norte suburbs are a noisy, polluted, and chaotic mix of retail businesses, factories, working classes houses, government subsidized apartment complexes, and favelas. The Baixada Fluminense that stretches beyond the Zona Norte is a low-lying area between the city and the mountains that was historically a transportation hub between Rio's port and the coffee plantations and gold mines in the interior. Today it is a densely populated tangle of urban centers, informal housing, garbage dumps, industry, and motorways. Far from the ocean breezes and jungled mountains, the Zona Norte and Baixada are claustrophobically hot, flat, concrete sprawls. Yet these metropolitan areas teem with a life and rhythm as vibrant as the Rio of postcards. And it was here, in the periphery, that I first came to know, and eventually love, this city and its inhabitants, or *cariocas,* as they call themselves.

Sensations of Place

My movement in Rio was counter to the usual visitor flow because I first came to Brazil not as a tourist or anthropologist, but as a capoeirista.[3] My trip was fueled by a desire to root capoeira more deeply in my body and to make new connections. I met people who became my capoeira kin, increased fluency in my new physical language, and opened myself to new "sensations of place."[4] Some of these sensations were tropical: sticky, sensual heat against the skin; fresh coconut sweetness on the tongue; fecund jungle humidity in the nose; and the melancholic descent on the psyche of a swift, equatorial nightfall. Some were Global South sensations: the smell of burning rubbish; the sound of street vendors' cries; the sight of raw sewage; and the presence of street kids and elderly beggars, some disfigured by polio and other treatable afflictions. Still other sensations were particular to Rio de Janeiro: the sensed solidarity on crowded, long bus rides when seated passengers hold bags for standing passengers; stumbling upon small, narrow favelas sandwiched between high-rise luxury condominiums; climbing steep staircases in cramped favela homes to emerge onto a *laje,* or rooftop terrace, to the pleasures of meat grilling, beer bottles clinking, live *pagode* music playing, and glimpses of the Cristo Redentor through laundry dancing on a line.

These carioca sensations—intoxicating and troubling—arise out of an urban geography shaped by intense socioeconomic and racial inequality. Visible signs of de facto segregation lace the natural landscape with precarity and unease. In his ethnographic memoir, *Tristes Tropiques,* Claude Lévi-Strauss recollects an "off-putting" sensation upon arriving by ship in 1935. His descriptive metaphors mix nature and human: Guanabara Bay "eats right into the heart of the city"; the dramatic rock eminences punctuate the bay like "stumps sticking up here and there in a toothless mouth"; and the steep hills are "fingers bent in a tight, ill-fitting glove."[5] Nature devours the manmade, while human imperfection mars natural beauty. A Brazilian joke delivers a similar message: in making the world, God populates Brazil with beautiful beaches, forests, savannas, and mountains all rich with resources. The angels, concerned with equity, ask "but what about the other countries?" God chuckles, "wait until you see the people I put here!"

Named by Portuguese explorer Gaspar de Lemos, who mistook the bay he sailed into in January 1502 for the mouth of a river, Rio de Janeiro (January River) was for most of its early history an outback trading post. Focused on sugar production around the colony's first capital in the northeastern state of Bahia, the Portuguese did not invest in Rio until the eighteenth century when gold and diamond deposits were discovered in the interior state of Minas Gerais. With its strategic location on the coast not far from the mines, Rio became the colony's new capital and main port for exportation of resources and importation of enslaved people. Hemmed in by sea and mountains, the city was a dirty warren of neighborhoods clustered around the ports.

A 2011 urban renewal project to revitalize the port district revealed the stratum in Rio's "palimpsestic landscape," known in the nineteenth century as both the Corte Imperial (Imperial Court) and Cidade Negra (Black City).[6] In 1808, fleeing Napoleon's invasion of the Iberian Peninsula, Portugal's royal court moved to Rio (elevated figures boast ten thousand people filling thirty-six ships). Shocked to find that the capital of Portugal's prized colony lacked everything from plumbing to police force, Dom João VI established infrastructure, law enforcement, schools, museums, and gardens, transforming Rio into an Imperial Court in the tropics. When the royalty returned to Portugal in 1825, Brazil transitioned to independent Empire, ruled first by João VI's son Pedro I and then his grandson Pedro II.

In 1843 a dock was built in the port district to welcome Princess Teresa Cristina's arrival from Europe to marry Dom Pedro II. A square and commemorative column marking the spot had been known since then as the Empress Wharf. Excavation during the urban renewal uncovered another deeper layer, the remains of the Valongo Wharf. An estimated two million enslaved Africans, almost half the total number brought to Brazil, disembarked at the Valongo Wharf and were processed through what was the largest slave market in South America.[7] Most of these Africans were destined for the diamond and gold mines. Yet quite a few remained in Rio, so that by 1821 Africans made up 46 percent of the population of what would become known as the Black City.[8]

Rio's mixed demographic, enslaved and freed Africans, lower-class European immigrants, Brazilian-born elites, and European visitors jostled together in the cramped city in a self-policing social hierarchy. Capoeira first appears in the historical record in individual and collective acts of resistance to this social order. In 1826, an English visitor was shocked to witness two well-dressed servants standing idle by a carriage suddenly and ruthlessly attack a shoeless Black man walking by just for the fun of humiliating him. Passive at first, the victim then sprang to action and, with what appears to have been capoeira skills, "in a flash of lightening [sic]" headbutted the coachman and kicked the footman with such force he "stretched him lifeless."[9]

Collective resistance by the enslaved against their enslavers included running away to the *quilombos,* or fugitive enclaves, that existed in rural areas throughout Brazil. Unsubstantiated myths abound of capoeira utilized in guerrilla warfare to fight off the *capitães do mato,* or slave catchers, who raided the quilombos. What written documentation of capoeira that does exist in police records, court cases, and newspaper articles focuses on Rio's infamous *maltas,* or capoeira gangs.[10] Consisting of enslaved and free Black men and recently immigrated European laborers (also near the bottom of Rio's social ladder), the maltas were hierarchical and ritualized organizations that defended the territory in which their members worked as street vendors, shoe-shiners, and porters. Sworn to loyalty and secrecy, the *capoeiras* (as these early capoeiristas were known) used codes (slang, whistles, nicknames, and dress) and rituals of provocation to distinguish themselves from, and threaten, rival gangs.[11] Though their aggression was directed mainly against other maltas and civilians who fell prey to their petty crime, these Black-controlled spaces were seen as a social threat and persecuted by the authorities.[12] A 1789 court report records the case of Adam, an obedient and "timid slave," who, after being hired out to work as a porter, takes up with other *capoeiras.* He becomes "wanton" and brashly independent, ending up in jail and sentenced to five hundred whip lashes.[13]

Civilians also feared *capoeiras,* but with a mix of awe and admiration: Sunday afternoon rumbles between maltas became a spectator sport, and *capoeiras* were hired as bar bouncers and thugs.[14] Chico-Juca, from the nineteenth-century satirical novel *Memoirs of a Police Sergeant,* is perhaps the earliest literary description of a *capoeira.* Always dressed in "a white jacket, full-legged pants, black slippers and a small white hat ever tipped at a rakish angle," Chico-Juca "made a living from ruffianism" and is hired by the novel's protagonist to start a brawl at the wedding of a former lover.[15] A later realist novel by Aluísio Azevedo, the action of which takes place in a *cortiço* (beehive), as Rio's tenement houses were known, stars a *capoeira* who causes a riot at a rival cortiço after seducing someone's girlfriend.[16] So admired were some of these *capoeiras* for their style, valor, and popularity with women, that some Brazilian elites began to practice capoeira "not only for self-defense but also as an expression of physical elegance."[17]

By the end of the nineteenth century, after a prolonged and failed war with Paraguay, political unrest grew among the Conservatives who supported the Empire and the Liberals who fought for abolition and a new Republic. In 1888, in a last-ditch concession, Princess Isabel, daughter of Emperor Pedro II, signed the golden law of abolition, and Brazil became the last country in the Americas to end slavery. Nonetheless by 1889 the Republicans had won and were flying their new flag—a blue orb emblazoned with the message *Ordem e Progresso* (Order and Progress). Rio was targeted in projects to sanitize and modernize the nation. Public health and urban renewal campaigns sought ways to remove Rio's large emancipated Black population, now viewed as a threatening blight, from the city center. Under the auspices of eradicating disease, tenements were torn down and narrow alleyways opened into wide boulevards. Displaced residents moved up to the vertical favelas that were increasingly dotting the city's surrounding hills or out to the expanding industrial suburbs.[18]

Social, cultural, and religious practices associated with the Black population were also seen as a menacing blemish on the modern city. Drawing on the public health rhetoric of the time, one journalist described capoeira as a blight "like yellow fever," and a police chief called it the "strangest moral disease of this great and civilized city."[19] Articles 402–4 of the new 1890 penal code outlawed *capoeiragem,* defined as "doing exercises of physical agility and dexterity. . . . running amok with weapons . . . provoking tumult or disorder . . . or instilling fear of some evil."[20] Individuals thus engaged were subject to six months in jail; malta chiefs, double that penalty. By the turn of the century, the maltas had been disbanded and members killed, jailed, or exiled.

Despite persecution, Afro-Brazilian expressive practices continued to flourish in pockets of Rio at the beginning of the twentieth century. In the borderland neighborhood of Lapa, nestled below the famous whitewashed aqueduct that marks the transition from Rio's downtown to wealthier residential areas, a vibrant nightlife generated a new mixed-demographic sociality: fancy cabarets rubbed shoulders with dilapidated brothels; tuxedo-clad white cariocas solicited scantily clad Afro-Brazilian prostitutes; and European visitors drawn to Rio by the Brazilian musical revues were hustled by malandros.[21]

The malandro, during his heyday in belle epoque Rio, was the poor cousin to the Parisian flaneur, or dandy. Always dapper in a linen suit and straw hat, charming in speech and manners, and as comfortable in a Lapa cabaret as a favela samba party, the malandro cultivated an air of leisure. But unlike the flaneur, with no cash to bankroll his chosen lifestyle, the malandro was a rogue and hustler who used the art of malandragem to live off the fortunes of others. Rio's most famous malandro was João Francisco dos Santos (1900–1976) known by his stage name, Madame Satã (Madam Satan). A cross-dressing, homosexual cabaret performer who lived, worked, and hustled in Lapa, Madame Satã was also a fierce capoeirista arrested many times for assault and robbery.[22] The figure of the malandro kept capoeira alive on Rio's streets and in the social imagination until it would reemerge in the Zona Norte in the mid-twentieth century.

The 1950s and 1960s in Brazil saw massive construction and migration. The new Bahia-Rio highway brought migrants, among them capoeiristas, from the poorer northeastern states to the wealthier south. Rio's peripheral neighborhoods swelled with these migrants, entrenching what today looks like a geographic apartheid: the wealthy live in maximum security high rises and gated condominiums and drive armored cars, while the poor live in informal neighborhoods and are subjected to the criminalization of poverty enforced by a corrupt and brutal policing system. "The marvelous city," another of Rio's many nicknames, is increasingly the "divided city."[23] Yet, it continues to be a "porous city," reminding us that segregation and mobility are not necessarily mutually exclusive.[24]

Black and brown cariocas cross borders every day as they commute from favelas and subúrbios to Zona Sul jobs in boutiques, condominiums, and restaurants. Besides labor, popular culture flows across socio-spatial borders. Music, dance, fashion, theater, and art flow down from the favelas and in from the periphery; and increasingly, middle-class youth and tourists venture into marginal areas to socialize. Now, Rio's high cost of living has shifted the line between "the asphalt" (*o asfalto*) and "the hill" (*o morro*) as cariocas call the formal/informal city divide. Middle-class residents and entrepreneurs move into favelas to live and open hostels, tour businesses, and cafés. Gentrification and urban renewal have pushed low-income residents from Rio's center out to the Baixada Fluminense.

When I first began traveling to Rio de Janeiro in the 1990s, the city was still a decade away from some of these more radical changes. The country was emerging from a repressive military dictatorship (1964–1985) and a period of hyperinflation. Brazilians still joked about the sacks of *cruzeiros,* the old currency, they'd had to haul to the store to buy bread and soap. The economy was beginning to stabilize, with the new *real* currency, but the gap between rich and poor was increasing. Violence was on the rise in Rio with its escalating drug wars, police retaliation, and vigilante groups. Along with recounting the days of hyperinflation and bank account freezes, Brazilians bitterly reminisced about the relative security of the dictatorship when the government had a monopoly on violence and there were fewer weapons in circulation; some even hinted that the country would do better with a return to military rule as it seemed to be failing at democracy.[25] Young Black men were and continue to be disproportionately affected by the increased violence; the elevated number of their murders by police suggests a "state-sponsored genocide."[26]

I stepped into this complicated city through the portal of capoeira. My guide, Mestre Beiçola, with whom I had been training for several years in California, was intimate with Rio's social and racial segregation. He had grown up in a low-income housing complex in the Zona Norte, but by his thirties, his talent for capoeira had taken him to the United States. Like many Brazilians who traveled abroad during the economic crisis of the 1980s, Beiçola never returned to live permanently in his homeland. Instead, he became part of a new class of transnationally mobile, cosmopolitan capoeiristas. In his new identity as a cultural broker, Mestre Beiçola discovered his hometown anew and in the process introduced his students to Rio.

Capoeira/Carnival Tour

In 1995, Mestre Beiçola refashioned himself as a tour guide. A charismatic and talented capoeirista, musician, and dancer, Mestre Beiçola came to the United States as a performer with a Vegas-style Brazilian stage show. When his two-year contract expired, Beiçola stayed in California and established himself as a capoeira and samba instructor and performer. He supplemented his income over the years through various entrepreneurial identities, including masseuse, silk screener, and computer technician. In the 1990s he became a one-man carnival/capoeira tour company.

Capoeira tourism was not yet booming, and carnival tours, while abundant, were arranged and led by professional companies. Beiçola convinced a small group of his students—ranging in age (from twenty to sixty) and ethnicity (Anglo, African American, Chinese American, Latino, Afro-Caribbean) and none having traveled to Brazil before—to inaugurate his first carnival-capoeira tour. He arranged everything on his own, relying on his improvisational skills and large roster of local childhood and ad hoc friends.

Our base was a hotel in Leme, a small, beachside neighborhood in the Zona Sul. I wondered what the hotel staff thought of Beiçola with his oddly shaved head, charm, teasing humor, and multicultural line of tourists following him around like ducklings in a row. He was from the Zona Norte, like most of the staff, and yet was staying in a hotel with room rates that exceeded their monthly salaries.

We were rarely in the hotel or vicinity, however. Beiçola had no interest in giving us a bikini and *caipirinha* cocktail vacation that never ventured past Copacabana's famous black-and-white mosaic beachfront sidewalks. I recall going only once to the beach when Beiçola dragged us out of bed at 6:00 a.m. for an impromptu training with a capoeira friend who had come looking for us at the hotel.

Beiçola wanted us to see, feel, and experience *his* city. He took us out to the Zona Norte and Baixada Fluminense on public transportation, teaching us to negotiate crowded buses and to "surf" empty ones (keeping our balance in the middle of the isle, without holding on, as the driver raced around corners). He bought us fresh coconut water, *picolé* (popsicles), and *pipoca* (popcorn) on the street, sometimes our only food for the day. After snacking on street food, he would pass me his garbage, teasing: "You are not going to find a trash can. Just throw it on the ground like everyone else in this city!" I would arrive late at the hotel sweat-drenched and dirty from samba rehearsals and capoeira classes, my pockets filled with greasy crumpled paper bags and sticky popsicle sticks.

Ever the capoeirista, Beiçola moved with ease and confidence through the city, relying on improvisation and, at times, dissimulation. He had, I learned, quite a reputation as a capoeira mestre. One evening, during a street party, I scrambled to keep up with him as he charged through the shoulder-to-shoulder wall of sweaty people in carnival costumes. Berimbaus bobbing up and down over the crowd indicated a roda under way. Beiçola jumped in to play and transformed from the teasing Hare Krishna with japa prayer beads in his pocket to a serious player. He played rather roughly with a teenager whom he had spoken to before their game, heads held close as they crouched at the foot of the berimbau. Beiçola knocked him around the roda like a rag doll with well-timed sweeps and precisely placed kicks, which, while not intended to injure, certainly bruised the ego. At the game's end, Beiçola gave his partner the ritualized hand shake and said something, a big smile on his face, his playfulness back. The youth ducked his head and slunk away.

I peppered Beiçola with questions.

He chuckled and said, "Before we played, the kid asked who I was. I told him 'nobody' and then I asked who *he* was. He told me he was Mestre Beiço-la's student!"

Beiçola played along, out-deceiving the deceiver, only at the end of the game telling the boy his name. It was my first lesson in malandragem, the power of reputations, and the importance of group affiliation in capoeira.

Sometimes my assumptions that Beiçola's reputation preceded him were wrong. One night he took us to a samba school rehearsal. The samba school parades are the heart of Rio's carnival celebration, which has become a global, multimillion mega event in the past thirty-five years. Until the 1980s, the carnival parades, consisting of marching band, singers, floats, and hundreds of costumed dancers, took over the streets of downtown Rio. In 1984 the Sambódromo, a special bleacher-lined avenue that holds 75,000, was built to showcase the competition parades on the nights before Shrove Tuesday.[27] Box seats cost thousands of dollars. To parade rather than just spectate, tourists and middle- and upper-class Brazilians can purchase costumes and join a samba school *ala* (wing) to sing and dance down the avenue for eighty minutes along with hundreds of other paraders in identical costumes. Throughout the year, and more intensely in the weeks leading up to carnival, the samba schools hold parties.[28] The *quadras,* large open-air squares, located in favelas and poor suburbs, fill with locals (and tourists) eager to dance, drink, and rally around their school in hopes of a championship that year.

The Beija Flor (Hummingbird) school is located in Nilópolis, a city in the Baixada Fluminense. Riding a bus for what seemed hours through a string of poorly lit neighborhoods, we arrived at an open-air quadra with an elevated corrugated metal roof. We entered through turnstiles into the crush of sweaty bodies clad in as little as possible to combat the heat (intensified under a metal roof) to a deafening blast of the *bateria,* dozens of men on all kinds of percussive instruments. Beiçola had brought along his newly acquired semiprofessional video camera (another nascent hobby). The monstrous machine was perched on his shoulder, and I could sense eyes on it— and us. I figured Beiçola knew what he was doing, until he caught my eye.

"I think I may have made a mistake bringing this," he said under his breath.

"But don't people know you here?"

"I've never been here in my life!" Beiçola said before plunging into the crowd, his tail of tourists scrambling behind.

That night was fine. More than fine as I caught the infectious rhythm of samba. Remarkably, the whole trip went off without a glitch. Beiçola's personality, capoeira skills, and developing cosmopolitanism allowed him to engage his city in new ways. I would learn what extreme borders Beiçola had crossed—from subsidized housing in the Zona Norte to a bedroom community in California's Silicon Valley—when he took us to his childhood home. That day, I would also meet my capoeira *avô* (grandfather).

Our destination in Vila da Penha, a suburb in the Zona Norte, was the Conjunto de Quitungo, Beiçola's childhood home. Quitungo, and the adjacent Guaporé, are clusters of concrete apartment buildings quickly erected in 1970 to initiate a government program to remove favelas from the Zona Sul. Ten thousand residents from Catacumba, a hillside favela in Lagoa, a desirable neighborhood across a lake from the beach neighborhood of Leblon, were forcibly removed overnight, some to subsidized housing in the Zona Norte, others to favelas in Rio's farther, rural West Zone. Displaced Catacumba residents recall the shock of forced removal. Ripped from the homes and community they had built on the hill in Lagoa, they found themselves in apartments with concrete floors, no internal doors or running water, and far from shops, services, and work.[29]

Beiçola grew up in a small apartment with his parents and brother in one of Quitungo's five-story buildings clustered around a dirt courtyard. After his father died and his mother moved to a rural community in the West Zone, one of Beiçola's students, now a mestre himself with a wife and two small children, moved in. Mestre Kinha and his wife, Salmair, ushered us into a living room and adjoining closet-sized kitchen with a shower curtain for a door. Salmair served us hot, sweet coffee, and Kinha showed me old photographs of teenaged Beiçola teaching capoeira.

"I started capoeira when I was seven, and by the time I was eight I knew I wanted to dedicate my life to it," Kinha said in his soft, serious voice.

Most of Beiçola's students, including Kinha, grew up in or around Quitungo. Kinha and Salmair had just returned to Rio from several years in southern Bahia. Kinha had liked the slower pace of life there but could not find work, and so they had moved back. He was now a lifeguard in the Zona Sul and trying to establish himself as a capoeira instructor. He took me on a tour of the neighborhood ending at a dirt soccer field.

"Beiçola and I used to train capoeira here when we were kids," Kinha said. "Romário grew up in a favela nearby and used to play soccer here. He still comes around sometimes."

Soccer players, known by their first names, are beloved in Rio, especially those like Romário who played for the local Flamengo team and then the national team, winning best player in the 1994 World Cup. Post-soccer Romário would go into politics, getting elected to city council, championing youth sports programs, and seeing that the soccer field of his youth was astroturfed.

For Beiçola, it was not soccer, but capoeira that grabbed him. He learned his first moves from his father, a migrant from Bahia who, while not a capoeirista, "loved a good street fight." Beiçola's mother was not happy when Beiçola took to capoeira.

"Capoeira was an excuse for my son to go out in the street and fight," Dona Celina would tell me years later as she served me coconut cake in her small house in Manguariba, where I mistook her parrot calling out "Dona Celina! Dona Celina! Dona Celina!" on the back porch for a busybody neighbor.

I would hear this sentiment repeated by other mothers of capoeiristas of Beiçola's generation. In the 1990s, capoeira's past as an aggressive male activity was still too-recent history. Some mothers would only be mollified when their sons become internationally successful mestres.

In his teens, Beiçola sought out a well-known mestre in the nearby neighborhood of Penha. When I met Mestre Touro on that first trip to Brazil, he was forty-five years old, but still the "bull" of his nickname with a powerful torso swelling over short, strong legs. Despite a waist expanding by what he called his *remédio* (medicine), or beer, he seemed poised to charge. When at rest, this charge was hidden by a slow, stiff-legged gait and loose arm swing. His round face had a star-shaped scar, shallow and wide like a delta valley, on the right side of his forehead, and his eyes glinted with intelligence. In the roda, the glint turned menacing as he let out a roar and launched his signature attack: a cartwheel to his opponent's back, slapping his feet—heavy as tree logs—down onto shoulders.

On that first trip, trudging through the summer heat from the bus stop to Touro's house, I had no idea how familiar this street and Penha would become, and how well I would come to know my capoeira avô. Though too young to be my biological grandfather, in capoeira lineage Touro is my avô, mestre of my mestre. And on that day Touro gave me my *apelido,* my capoeira nickname.

Pink as Shrimp

On the bus ride from Quitungo, I caught my first street view of Nossa Senhora da Penha. The church suddenly loomed above us, its cool presence belying the hot congestion below. We descended at Rua Dionísio, a street of broken asphalt, on the less affluent side of Penha. One of the many favelas that cling to the hills that ring the suburb stretched up and away to the right of the street in a bright, chaotic jumble of reds and browns. We arrived at a low wall with an iron gate that hid a concrete patio and bungalow. Mestre Touro and his three young children lived in the one-room house crowded with capoeira paraphernalia, and the patio was his capoeira "academy."

In a heat still near 100 degrees at 5:00 p.m., we moved across the patio, avoiding the areas of broken concrete, executing kicks, defense moves, and acrobatics as Mestre Touro barked out corrections. I thought I would explode from the heat and pounding of joints on the hard ground. A crowd of spectators gathered, as word must have gotten around that Mestre Touro was hosting a group of Americans. Shirtless young men and boys in bermuda shorts and flip-flops sat along the top of the walls and perched in the guava tree; young mothers with babies and elderly neighbors slipped in through the gate to sit on the benches lining the walls.

After training, Touro pointed at me and shouted, "*Camarão!*" Touro's young students giggled.

"You have a nickname now," Beiçola told me, "Shrimp!"

My fair skin turns pink with heat and exertion, and with extremes of both that day, "beet" may have been more appropriate. My nickname, like many capoeira nicknames, pokes fun. In a particular brand of Brazilian humor, no physical characteristic—skin color, facial feature, ethnicity, height, weight, and even disability—is off limits. A fat capoeirista is nicknamed Pesado (Heavy); a deaf capoeirista, Mudinho (Little Mute); and a capoeirista with an atrophied arm, Bracinho (Little Arm). Afro-Brazilian capoeiristas might be Chocolate, Urubu (Vulture), Chá Preto (Black Tea), Café, King Kong, Pretão (Big Black Guy), or Pretinho (Little Black Guy); white capoeiristas are often Russo (Russian), Galego (someone from Galícia), or some variation on Neve (snow); and capoeiristas with Asian or Amerindian features are Sushi, Saki, Peixe Cru (Raw Fish), Eskimo, Índio, Tupi, or Pocahontas. Other nicknames may arise from arbitrary, first impressions: one capoeirista I met was saddled with the nickname, Cara Suja (Dirty Face), which he'd received on his first day of training as a grubby six-year-old. In any case, a nickname is bestowed, not chosen.[30]

Nicknames date back to the nineteenth century when they provided aliases and promoted street reputations among the members of the maltas. But nicknames are a widespread practice in Brazil. As in other places where first names are reused, often within the same family, children will receive and be known into adulthood by a diminutive nickname, such that Ronaldo becomes Ronaldinho or Naldo.[31] But in Brazil, even the famous have nicknames. Former President Luiz Inácio da Silva, is only ever known by his nickname, Lula, and Brazil's most famous soccer player is simply Pelé. Calling politicians, athletes, and soap opera stars by nicknames indicates Brazilians'

self-styled informality and intimacy. Much like Brazilian overuse of diminu-
tives noted by historian Sérgio Buarque de Holanda, nicknaming "serves to
bring us closer to people or objects and to simultaneously pay more attention
to them. It is a way of making them more accessible to our feelings and closer
to our hearts."[32] Nicknames can also play with Brazil's strict social hierarchy:
through nicknaming people claim intimacy with, or perhaps diminish, those
who rank above them in economic or social prestige.

In capoeira, nicknames bestow affection, individuality, and sometimes
humility. Mestres avoid recycling popular nicknames within their group so
that each student's individuality is preserved. Yet, in a highly performative
sport full of large egos, nicknames can also be a reminder of imperfections
and vulnerabilities: one can't help but chuckle at an impressively macho
capoeirista called Popcorn or Tangerine. Mestre Touro's nickname I first assumed came from his bullish physique and personality. But it, too, was the
result of teasing:

"My friend Babá gave it to me when we were kids because I was an awful
soccer player." Touro told me. "I would get in the game and charge at the ball
like a crazy cow and Babá would scream '*olé touro!*' like a matador, and the
name stuck."

Not all mestres embrace the nicknaming practice. Some who work with
youth in neighborhoods with heavy drug trafficking avoid the practice because nicknames are also popular among drug dealers. And today, with a
growing Black consciousness movement in Brazil, nicknames that draw
on racial epithets or cruel humor are recognized as offensive. Several well-
known Brazilian mestres have modified or stopped using their nicknames
because of racist overtones.

Among female capoeiristas, nicknaming was not common at first. Many
of the 1980s pioneering generation of Brazilian female capoeiristas are known
only by their first names. Today female capoeiristas often receive stereotypi-
cally "feminine" nicknames like Little Strawberry or Mermaid. Capoeiristas
in Brazil are often surprised by my unfeminine nickname. But I like it. I like
that it pokes fun and makes people chuckle. I like that shrimp are popular
in Brazil, skewered, grilled, and sold on the beach by ambulatory vendors
whose cries of "Camarão, Camarão!" never fail to make me look up to see
who's calling me. I like that other capoeiristas tease me by singing out a line
from a samba—"the shrimp who sleeps is taken away by the wave"—when
they see me. I liked that the nickname sealed my identity as a capoeirista:
from then on, I was known in the capoeira world of Rio and beyond as
Camarão.

I enjoyed my "capoeira/carnival tour" but it left me thirsty for more.

Mestre Beiçola had given us anything but a sheltered, sanitized experience, but we were still tourists. In a moment of stubbornness that led to one of my not infrequent fights with Beiçola, I refused to join the group on the second night of carnival when they paraded with Beija Flor in the Sambódromo. I disapproved of swooping in and paying several hundred dollars for a costume. I wanted a more "authentic" experience—to live in the favela for the year, to get to know the community, and help to make the costumes—much as journalist Alma Guillermoprieto had done in the 1980s and whose book, *Samba*, I was devouring on the trip.

Years later when I finally did parade with a friend of mine, a carioca and die-hard Portalense who lived a stone's throw from the Portela Samba School in the suburb of Madureira, we also simply bought our costumes and joined a wing of strangers, as do the vast majority of parading Brazilians. I realized then, as I stepped onto the avenue at 5:00 a.m., the sun rising over the hill at the far end, the last lingering fans in the stands, and the deafening bateria propelling me forward among hundreds of joyful dancers costumed like me, that the particular convivência of carnival is just this: an intoxicating mix of sound, glitter, movement, and emotion—the conjoining of fantasy and human—in an ephemeral moment of ecstasy and camaraderie among strangers.

While I had lofty reasons for refusing to join the parade, Beiçola simply read it as my tendency to resist being part of the group, which repeatedly caused friction in our mestre-student relationship. That night, in frustration, Beiçola told me to skip the parade and wait with his friend Brito on the outside. "But you are going to regret your decision," he warned me. He was right. As soon as we arrived in the Concentração, the massive line-up of that night's parading schools along the Avenida Presidente Vargas, I felt the excitement and energy and regretted not being part of it.

The night became more miserable when I lost Brito. I wandered alone for an hour, panicked by the hordes of people, overpowering smell of grilled meat and beer, and drunk revelers stumbling into me. Later, after my several years living in Rio and three carnivals, I would come to love the claustrophobic chaos and crushing humanity of street parties, at least for short stints. But on that first trip, I was not yet equipped to navigate the sensorial tumult of Brazilian public celebration on my own. Miraculously, Brito found me. I felt guilty about my prideful decision when I registered his panic and then relief as he grabbed and hugged me. Brito was from the Zona Norte and not as comfortable as Beiçola navigating other areas of the city. He told me as we walked back to the hotel that he'd once been robbed by a kid with a gun on Copacabana beach.

Then he chuckled and said, "I was standing there with nothing, not even my shoes, wondering how the hell I'd get home when the kid stopped and came back to me. He asked if I had bus money. And when I said no, he gave me some from my own wallet!"

I was troubled and touched by Brito's story. The poverty that would drive a kid to mug an adult not much better off—and then his acknowledgment of their shared suffering. My abbreviated experiences in Rio told me I had to return to understand this complex city with its complicated convivência.

Return to the "Land of Honey"

In 1996 I returned to Brazil for three months of solo travel. Post college, I'd been working at a children's art studio in Berkeley, training capoeira, and beginning to think about graduate school. But I had an itch to get back to Brazil to deepen my connections to capoeira and to explore some of the vast country. Still relatively unknown abroad, capoeira, I discovered, was all over Brazil, from the Germanic cowboy state of Rio Grande do Sul in the south to the indigenous, folksy state of Pernambuco in the northeast. Everywhere I went, I sought out capoeira and was welcomed into rodas, trainings, and homes with enthusiasm and hospitality.

Sometimes I caught the darker side of capoeira. A few days before carnival in Olinda, a lovely northeastern colonial town famous for its large puppet parades, I stumbled across a rough-and-tumble street roda. One poorly strung berimbau and an old pandeiro suggested that music and artistry would take a backseat. The commanding capoeirista wore a grubby pair of white nylon shorts that rode high on his bulging thighs and a bandage or brace, hard to tell beneath the grime, wrapped around a bare foot. His torso was thick with muscles and slick with sweat. The games were fast and ugly, players landing kicks and swinging punches. Someone's teeth were knocked out. I slid the little berimbau I wore on a leather string around my neck under my collar, thankful I was not wearing a capoeira shirt. I would not play in this roda.

Another foreign capoeirista, German perhaps, showed up wearing a white uniform. Boldly she wriggled her way up to the top of the roda and, when she got a chance, entered to play. An athletic looking capoeirista wearing long pants, tennis shoes, and a T-shirt with Mestre printed on the back jumped in to play with her. His game was aggressive. After receiving multiple kicks and sweeps, the young woman stopped the game, and, refusing to shake her opponent's hand, backed out of the roda and disappeared into the crowd.

I looked for her, unsuccessfully, in the streets before I left Olinda. I had so many questions: Was this a typical roda? Was she known to these capoeiristas? Or was she a stranger, like me, who had jumped too eagerly into an unfamiliar roda and been taught a lesson?

I had much yet to learn about capoeira's rules of engagement. I enjoyed this unknown and exciting capoeira convivência as I traveled around Brazil, but eventually returned to Rio. I felt most at home in the Zona Norte, where, as I would later write in Mestre Beiçola's newsletter, "I was among generations of my mestre's students who played my capoeira and sang songs about my mestre." I settled in Irajá, a suburb near Penha, whose name means "where honey flows," in the indigenous Tupi language. The only resemblance to honey of the subsidized housing complex where I stayed was the sticky heat day and night. I trained with Sardinha, a student of Mestre Beiçola's who in his thirties was now a mestre with his own group.

My time in Irajá marked a milestone in my development and dedication as a capoeirista. In California, capoeira was a circumscribed part of my life, occurring two evenings a week and sometimes on weekends (even that was too much for my sister, who asked if I had joined a cult when she saw me coming and going in my all-white uniform). In Rio, capoeira defined life itself. I had, of course, come with the explicit purpose of reaching capoeira saturation. But the capoeiristas around me also lived for capoeira. It gave their lives—poor in opportunities but rich in convivência—meaning and purpose.

I stayed with Glayd, Mestre Sardinha's student and girlfriend, and her family. They received me with an offhand hospitality, never questioning the duration of my visit, which stretched from weeks into months. Their two-bedroom apartment was in a six-story gray building surrounded by other identical housing. The monotonous, nondescript architecture was reflected in everyday life, where not much seemed to happen. The adults and youth hanging out on the streets at all hours evinced the high unemployment rate and poor education system. Public elementary and high schools in Brazil (for only those who cannot afford the private ones) are so poorly funded that they operate in two shifts: students attend for four hours in the morning *or* the afternoon. Beyond capoeira, youth had little to occupy their free time.

I became like the fourth child in Glayd's family, sleeping on a bottom bunk with twelve-year-old Heverton above me, and Glayd, in her early twenties like me, on a mattress on the floor. It took me several weeks to realize there was another older son, whose bunk I had taken, who was sleeping on the couch and slipping out in the morning before I got up. When I realized this and protested, saying I could find somewhere else to stay, they shrugged it off. Housing another person was no big deal.

Vilma, Glayd's mother, had long brown hair, large glasses, and looked perpetually tired. Like her daughter, she rarely smiled. She was a seamstress, stacks of partially finished clothes piled around the sewing machine in her bedroom. She made *abadá* (stretchy white capoeira pants) for Mestre Sardinha's students. After scrubbing my fingers raw every night trying to get the dirt and sweat out of the abadá I had brought from the United States, which were made of the thick, tough cotton of karate gis, I paid Vilma to make me a new pair. The light polyester was easy to wash in the laundry sink and line-dried quickly. Mestre Sardinha silk-screened the name and logo of his group down one leg of the abadá and gave me a T-shirt, pleased that I now looked like his student.

Vilma's husband was a retired Navy officer and from the state of Bahia. Short, compact, and deeply tanned, Luarindo wore only shorts and flip-flops, thick silver necklaces nestled in his chest hair, as if he had just stepped off a boat. I was never sure where he spent his days. He would gesture to the streets when I asked. He came in just for meals, encouraging me to add spice to my food from a big bottle of Bahian peppered oil that he kept by his plate.

Mestre Sardinha did not have an easy relationship with his girlfriend's father. He never entered the apartment, instead sitting in the stairwell where Glayd would bring him a plate of food. When I asked why, Glayd said her father was upset that his only daughter trained capoeira and was romantically involved with a capoeirista. He held the popular view then that capoeira was a *coisa de homem* (a guy's thing), inappropriate for young women.

Ironically, it had been on a trip to visit her father's relatives in Bahia that Glayd had first seen capoeira and thought it beautiful. She had secretly wished to learn and jumped at the chance when her younger brother Heverton began training with Sardinha. Before long, Glayd was also dating Sardinha. Living with an aunt in a nearby favela and surviving on meager earnings from capoeira and occasional security jobs, Sardinha, Glayd's father worried, could not provide a secure future for his daughter. In fact, it was not financial but emotional stability that Sardinha would fail to provide. After moving in together and having a child, Sardinha began having affairs. While the affairs "stayed in the street," Glayd, as she would later tell me, ignored them. But when he started messing around with new students in the group, the gossip drove her to leave him.

I may have felt "in place," but life in the subúrbios—a sensory and social overload—was not easy for me. A lack of privacy and constant barrage of noise in the apartment often sent me into the bedroom for some solitude and quiet. But someone would inevitably find me and quickly turn on the smaller television, alarmed that I was sitting in silence. Visitors stopped by to meet the *gringa*—a term for foreigner that can communicate either affection or disdain—ask questions about the United States, and tease me about my capoeira obsession. Nights were little relief. The adhesive heat stayed trapped between the apartment buildings, and the noise wars intensified: televisions and radios competing with the street music from outdoor bars, punctuated by the frightening clatter of fireworks that my friends taught me to distinguish from the dry pop of gunfire.

What were at times sensory challenges for me were also the routine pleasures of keeping company with each other: learning to samba to that year's winning carnival song turned up to ear-splitting volume; sipping beer and watching the *balões* (hot-air balloons) light up the night sky in the square; and kite battles with the neighborhood kids on Sunday afternoons. I began to recognize my expected participation in everything, along with the teasing humor, as signs of affection, acceptance, and convivência.

Capoeira Convivência in the Zona Norte

In the late afternoons, Glayd, Heverton, and I snacked on bread rolls with butter and sweet black coffee watching the popular 6:00 p.m. *novela* (soap opera), *Malhação*. Novelas are as essential to Brazilian nourishment as rice and beans. Millions of Brazilians follow and gossip about the shows that run back-to-back in the evenings. *Malhação* (*Workout*), in its second season in 1996, follows the lives of a group of well-manicured youth who spend their lives working out, drinking fresh juice, and falling in and out of love in a chic health club in Rio. Glayd, Heverton, and I eagerly looked for the silhouette of capoeiristas, along with other athletes, that passed quickly in the opening credits. For forty-five minutes, we immersed ourselves in a world of landscaped lawns, perfectly tanned and fit bodies (always white by the racist beauty standards), and social worries revolving around who was flirting with whom. Then we headed out to a very different world. We trained in a concrete public schoolyard and usually drew a small crowd of spectators with nothing else to do on a week night, the presence of an American additional entertainment.

Sardinha was his mestre's opposite in appearance and personality, but his double in movement. His olive skin, narrow face, and close-set eyes, inherited from his Spanish father, were often set in a frown. He had little of Beiçola's charisma and humor, and even his playfulness had an aggressive edge. But if I squinted my eyes and watched Sardinha's fluid kicks, ginga, and movement on the ground, it was like watching Beiçola. Mestre Sardinha took pride in this similarity, boasting that of all Beiçola's students, he was the only one who had not changed his style.

In the late 1990s, all of Beiçola's students in Rio and the United States were part of a same group, Capoeira Besouro. Beiçola created the group in 1979, taking the name from a legendary early twentieth-century capoeirista from the northeastern state of Bahia known as Besouro (Beetle), whose magical powers transformed him into the flying insect when pursued. Beiçola designed a pen-drawn logo of a beetle overlaid with a drum and two crossed berimbaus, surrounded by a cord. The cord resembled the braided cord that students received when they officially join the group and continued to receive in different colors as they rose through the ranks. It also resembled the small woven cord that Beiçola and some of his students wore high on their arm that Beiçola called the *nimomolo*. As explained in the group's founding documents, the nimomolo was a reminder of the oppression of capoeira's ancestors and a symbol of Black peoples' many contributions to Brazilian culture and of their "enduring valor even when in chains."

Sardinha's classes were tough, emphasizing the fight. The nights we trained in a gym we took advantage of the padded floor of the jiu-jitsu ring, punching bags, and mitts. Other nights we used our hands as targets. When we worked in pairs or had a roda at the end of class, Sardinha would encourage us to spar—landing our kicks. My shins and thighs were perpetually bruised from kicks that met their mark and sweeps that landed me heavily on the ground. At first the other students were hesitant to play roughly with me. But as our intimacy grew and I became a temporary member of the group, they engaged me in this more aggressive training. I felt slightly absurd. What was a women in her midtwenties doing exchanging blows with boys five or ten years younger than her? Sardinha's students, however, were simply delighted (if slightly mystified) by my interest in them, as I was in their interest in me.

This more aggressive, or "objective" training, as capoeiristas say, is known as *jogo duro* (rough play), which is distinct from a *briga* (fight). Sardinha explained the difference to me through the example of seventeen-year-old Fernandinho. With a body as thin and tight as slate, and an opinion about everything, Fernandinho talked a mile a minute, often while draping himself on me in a kind of hyperactive flirtation. He was a strong capoeirista but inconsistent in his training, and at one point disappeared for longer than usual.

"I banned him from training for a while," Sardinha told me. "He was going to too many *bailes funk* on the weekends and getting into fights."

The bailes funk, increasingly popular in the 1990s, were dance parties held in Rio's favelas and sponsored by drug traffickers. Two-story stacked speakers or "walls of sound" blasted loud *funk carioca*. The name came from Rio's 1970s Black Power movement, when DJs began spinning American funk in Zona Sul nightclubs. When the dances eventually moved out to the suburbs and favelas, the soft R and B melodies and "Black is Beautiful" lyrics were replaced by the hard-edged sound and messages of Miami Bass hip-hop. The all-night parties, accompanied by hypersexualized dancing and ostentatious displays of guns, drugs, and bling were vilified by Rio's middle class and hated by many residents of the favelas because of the all-night noise and connection to drug trafficking.

Fernandinho frequented the underground *bailes de corredor*. These parties were called "corridor dances" because at certain points in the evening the MC would call out "5 minutes of happiness," and the crowd would part down the middle leaving a vacant corridor of about ten feet. In a perverse game of "Red Rover," individuals entered the corridor to attack each other and avoid being dragged to the opposite side, where the mob would eagerly clobber them. Whether banning Fernandinho from training was the appropriate consequence or not, Sardinha wanted to channel his student's aggression away from the dangerous free-for-alls of the funk parties to the disciplined combat of the capoeira roda.

Aggressive sociality of activities like jogo duro and corridor parties was mostly male, but not exclusively. Sardinha also encouraged Glayd and me to train jogo duro. While I liked the added intensity, pushing my body harder, especially on the punching bags, I had no desire or motivation to hurt or be hurt. It felt disingenuous for me to embody jogo duro.

It was different for Glayd.

"I like exchanging blows. I don't feel scared. I like it because . . . how can I put this?"

Glayd thought for a minute. Then pushing up her cat-eye glasses, continued in her soft, serious voice, "I feel equal to men. I like to get beaten up (*gosto de apanhar*). I feel better, more secure. I say to myself, 'Glayd, today you got beat up and cried. But tomorrow you will be here again and you will try again and you will succeed.'"

With a feminist twist—feeling equal to the boys—Glayd expressed a sentiment I would hear frequently: jogo duro prepares you for the hard knocks of life. I would also come to understand that jogo duro reflects the violence of poverty and discrimination that so many capoeiristas in Brazil live with daily.

Sixteen-year-old Bocoió, Sardinha's most talented student, loved jogo duro. Rather incongruously, he was shy, rarely spoke, and had large brown eyes framed by thick lashes. He lived in Amarelinho, a large favela home to northeastern immigrants and notorious for drug trafficking and police violence. To get to Amarelinho meant crossing the Avenida Brasil, a ferocious multilaned highway a stone's throw from Glayd's apartment. I was terrified of the Avenida after I learned that Bocoió had watched his sister get killed by a car when they attempted to cross it on foot as young children. I knew always to use the *passarelas* (pedestrian bridges) that passed above the racing traffic, when I went to help Bocoió with his kids' capoeira class. I would bring art supplies for the kids, thirsty for attention and entertainment, so they could draw after class. Their artwork reflected Amarelinho everyday life: unpaved roads with roaming chickens and goats that gave the favela a rural feel, police, guns, and capoeira.

Along with being a tough fighter in the roda, Bocoió was as graceful as a ballet dancer. With long arms and a flexible waist, he could contort his body into an upside-down U, hands and feet simultaneously on the ground, and then with the control of a tightrope walker, slowly lift his body into a one-armed handstand, legs split open, toes of one foot grazing the ground. Bocoió's skills eventually earned him a coveted scholarship at the National Circus School that led to a short international career in Cirque du Soleil. But when I knew him, he was a rough, scrappy kid who left bruises on my shins from kicks and sweeps.

Not all of Sardinha's students enjoyed jogo duro. Splynter, with thick dreadlocks and a pudgy body, was less interested in capoeira as a martial art then as a Black art. He proudly wore the nimomolo, not just to symbolize his membership in Grupo Besouro, but as a reminder to fight for Black liberation. The last time I saw Splynter, he had stopped training because of an injury; he had taken a bullet in his back while protecting a child during a shootout on a bus.

Jomar always seemed uncomfortable with jogo duro. Tall and lanky with an irrepressible smile, he was awkward in his movement like a colt finding its feet. Jomar seemed to be the only of Sardinha's students with a curfew and a mother who made him study. On Saturday afternoons, we would gather under his apartment window, Sardinha playing the berimbau and calling up for Jomar to come join us, who never could because of homework. What sorrow I felt years later to hear a rumor that Jomar, less fortunate than Splynter, had been killed by a stray bullet; and what relief to see Jomar on a subsequent trip, alive and well, and a mestre!

After training, we would stroll over to the dusty square to sit at a kiosk to share a plate of fried sausage and onions, a tall bottle of beer for Sardinha, Glayd, and me to share, and soda for the younger students. We would banter about capoeira and life as people stopped by to greet us. Sardinha would tease Jomar for his gullibility; scold Fernadinho, for being a "tourist" and not training regularly; and command Heverton, thin as a reed and as flexible as a contortionist, to do the splits. It was then that I realized what those evenings outside the Safeway in California were all about: Beiçola re-creating capoeira convivência as he knew it in Brazil.

Affects of Place

I began to crave relief from the heat and mundanity of the suburbs. I was restless, sensing a seductive, unexplored city on my doorstep.

After weeks of pestering, I persuaded Sardinha and Glayd to take me to one of the beaches that lay tantalizingly on the other side of the city. One Saturday afternoon with students and instruments in tow, we caught a bus to the train station that would take us to the downtown Central Station. The train was rickety, slow, and hellishly hot. We added to the general chaos of the commuter train—crowded even on a weekend with kids selling gum and cough drops squeezing by the standing passengers—by playing instruments and singing. Sardinha improvised new verses to capoeira songs—sometimes poking fun at the people sitting around us—encouraged by smiles and chuckles.

With Central Station in sight, the train came to a halt and the electrical system shut down. We sat in the stifling heat. Sardinha tried to keep the mood light with a new round of singing that riffed on the theme, "Brazil is shit." Eventually he got bored and gesturing to the windows indicated for us to climb out. Other passengers followed our lead, children and the elderly assisted down, large packages passed from hand to hand. We trudged in silence along the tracks in the hot sun, our mood dampened. Sardinha led us through the crowded station out onto the wide Avenida Getúlio Vargas, where we caught another bus.

We got off the bus at the Praia de Botafogo, a dirty beach along the inner Guanabara Bay, far from the creamy white sands of Ipanema. I protested. Sardinha insisted this was a good beach—calm waves and no pickpockets or *arrastões* (big sweeps).

News stories abounded that summer about favela youth sweeping down the beaches robbing everyone in their wake. A 1992 arrastão on Copacabana beach by alleged *funkeiros* (frequenters of bailes funk) had created a moral panic among Zona Sul residents. Calls were made for absurd policing strategies, such as closing the tunnels to the beach neighborhoods to anyone who did not have a resident's ID card.[33] In 2004, populist governor

Garotinho would create the infamous Piscinão (Large Swimming Pool) in the Ramos suburb. The artificial beach and swimming area were carved out of the most polluted stretch of Guanabara Bay. Supposedly a filtration system purified the water, but no one was fooled: the summer the Piscinão de Ramos opened, it became the butt of unending humor, one newspaper cartoon depicting Black people happily diving into a large toilet bowl. Couched as a public work for the *povo* (people), it was a thinly disguised attempt to keep the Zona Norte residents, and Black people, from enjoying the Zona Sul beaches.

Whether Sardinha was actually worried about being mugged or just uninterested in the additional bus ride and fare it would take to get to the Zona Sul beaches I don't know. I shrugged off thoughts of pollutants and played in the waves with the other students, happy as clams at this rare beach visit.

After that trip, I started going alone to the Centro and Zona Sul for solitude and autonomy. I never risked the train again, instead catching one of the many buses along the Avenida Brasil. At the bus stop on my first trip, the man selling snacks at a kiosk asked if I was "going down to the city," and then cautioned me about pickpockets. "Going down" captures the geographic and social dissonance between the Zona Norte and Zona Sul: the journey from Irajá to Ipanema that day was like traveling from one city—or country—to another. It imprinted in me a sensorial map of Rio's race and class segregation.

Leaving the congested Avenida Brasil, the bus traveled at high velocity through the downtown, port district, and inner bay. Then, plunging through one of several tunnels that cut through the mountains, it arrived in the sequestered beach neighborhoods that rim the Atlantic Ocean. Modern high-rise hotels and stately nineteenth-century apartment buildings replaced the cement housing complexes and graffitied bungalows of the Zona Norte; manicured parks with fountains, playgrounds, and kiosks serving cappuccino punctuated the landscape instead of the dusty squares with rusty calisthenic equipment and hotdog stands; elegant boutiques and air-conditioned shopping malls replaced outdoor markets selling cheap electronics and pirated CDs; and the famous beachfront black-and-white mosaic sidewalks replaced broken pavement and burning rubbish.

The human geography looked different too: thin, wiry Zona Norte bodies worn down by hard labor and scarred by poor medical care were replaced with toned, groomed, and well-dressed ones. Class lines were clearly demarcated by occupation: white adults and children sat at outdoor restaurants, played volleyball, or sunbathed on the beaches, while Black and brown adults and children walked the beaches selling cold drinks, guarded parked cars, or begged between cars at stop lights. Dogs were different too: no fierce guard dogs chained in front of houses, but lapdogs exiting grooming salons strapped to owners' chests in baby slings.

One afternoon I stayed longer than usual in "the city." I had stopped by the large open-air market downtown to see Sonia and her mother, who ran a stand selling capoeira paraphernalia. They kept a large visitor's book as proud evidence of the many capoeiristas and researchers who stopped by. They seemed to sell little, however. I always bought something—a CD or the latest capoeira magazine. That afternoon a mestre I knew from the Zona Norte stopped by after his job in the nearby public transportation office.

Suddenly I realized it had grown dark. I have never gotten used to the way night falls quickly in the tropics, moments after sundown. That evening was darker than usual as rain clouds gathered. The mestre walked me to the bus stop. He seemed concerned and offered to accompany me to Irajá. I knew that would mean another bus to his suburb so I said I would be fine even as my confidence ebbed with the coming rain and rush-hour crush.

"Do you know where to get off?" he asked.

"Passarela 26."

Satisfied, he disappeared into the crowd.

I found myself crushed in the center isle of the bus surrounded by tired commuter faces. The seated passenger below me gestured to his lap, and I thankfully put down my backpack. Twisting my body low and looking through hanging arms, I could just see out. Rain sliced the dark windows like thin daggers. I thought back to a conversation with Glayd several days before as we'd sat on the sofa watching rain come down. I'd said I loved rain.

"I hate the rain," Glayd said. "It means death. People die in the favelas every time it rains."

I felt the weight of my privilege and ignorance. I had not thought of Bocoió's family and the thousands of others across the Avenida Brasil who lived along unpaved alleys that turn into rivers of mud with rain. Or the residents of Zona Sul favelas who live in precarious shacks perched high up on hillsides that give way to landslides at the slightest provocation. Even for people who don't live in informal housing, rains are a dangerous nuisance as Rio's streets become impassable and whole neighborhoods flood due to poor drainage. Cariocas stay home, if possible, when it rains.

But there I was riding a bus at rush hour, in the dark and rain. I tried to gauge where we were through the windows. The bus terminal slid by, and then the concrete overpass with hand-painted advertisements for "healers of the heart" and fortune-telling services, and then we were on the Avenida Brasil. And I then realized that I would not be able to see the numbered oval plaques on the pedestrian footbridges. I watched stretches of favelas and tire repair shops flash by, grasping for landmarks. Then I saw lights rising up and away to the right of the highway. Amarelinho! I had missed my stop.

"Driver! Driver! Please stop! I want to get out!"

Thankfully in Rio you can call out a request to get off, even between stops. Tired faces perked up around me.

"Stop driver, the girl needs to get off!" voices called out.

I pushed my way forward, and as the bus slowed, I saw through the windshield Passarela 27 not far ahead. An elderly gentleman looked at me with concern.

"Miss, use the passarela!"

With a carioca's intimate knowledge of Rio's geography, he intuited that I needed to be on the other side of Avenida Brasil. As I descended the steps of the bus, someone murmured "Go with god, daughter," a standard leave-taking in Brazil, but ominous in the moment.

I stepped into the gutter and cold water and garbage swirled around my ankles. I felt vulnerable in my light summer dress and flip-flops, standard year-round clothing in Rio, but not much of a barrier against the grime that washes off the city in a heavy rain. I ran toward the passarela. In a city that moves at a leisurely pace, rain breeds speed. Women scurried home from work holding large purses over their heads, in an attempt to preserve straightened hair. I slowed only when I reached the familiar buildings where I would cut in. I glanced back. It wasn't so far, why had I been so nervous?

If my first trip to Brazil had awakened me to new sensations of place, this second, longer trip had imprinted on me the affects of place. Urban environments can elicit an array of emotions, from nostalgia to hope to fear, which in turn influence how people live and move through the space.[34] While such place-affects are often tied to personal or collective memories, they can also be generated through media representations and political discourses for regulatory and policing purposes.

In a city such as Rio, where urban "renewal" has been an ongoing project since the eighteenth century, the built environment creates a spatial segregation that enforces social and racial stratification and breeds fear of the unknown. In Rio's cityscape citizens know their place, whether a housing complex in the Zona Norte or securitized condominiums in the Zona Sul. To venture out from where one belongs to where one does not belong is, in the words of anthropologist Mary Douglas, to be categorically "out of place."

Mestre Sardinha and Glayd had resisted taking me to the Zona Sul not out of laziness or unfamiliarity, but because they felt uncomfortable, maybe even fearful, in a place they did not belong. Sardinha and his students were not, at least not yet, cosmopolitan capoeiristas like Beiçola, who had learned to move around the city. They stayed within the comfort zone of the familiar Zona Norte.

On my return to Rio, I would no longer be just a capoeirista but also a nascent anthropologist. My research and practice would take me beyond the confines of a local neighborhood. I would begin to understand capoeira as, at least for some, a vehicle to move through, and even beyond, Rio's spatial segregation.

Before my return to Rio, however, I would travel to Salvador, Bahia, the "cradle" of capoeira; a city with deep ties to Africa, entangled in contested notions of authenticity, haunted by the traumas of a brutal slavocracy, and plagued by ongoing racial violence. I would feel these hauntings in the streets, rodas, and religious houses in Salvador; and I would also grapple with my own losses that had recently shaped my life.

2

AUTHENTICITY AND LOSS

BAHIA, 1996

Smells ignited my senses first upon my arrival in Salvador. Closer to the equator, with a much more humid, tropical heat than Rio de Janeiro, this sultry, two-tiered seaport capital of the northeast state of Bahia presented new sensations of place. A jungle breath of moss and mildew hung in the air, olfactory evidence of a perpetual, clammy dampness. Nothing—not my uniform and cord, towel and bikini, hair and skin—ever dried completely.

Mixing with the fecund aroma of earth and water was a pungent, unfamiliar smell that would also become my predominant taste memory of Salvador. The northeast is famous for its distinctive cuisine, abundant in the rich palm oil, dendê, introduced into Brazilian cuisine from West Africa. Its smell wafted out of restaurants serving *muqueca* (fish stew) and rose from street food stalls where *acarajé*, originally a West African dish, sizzled in big bubbling pots of the thick, deep red-orange oil; for only a few *reais,* these black-eyed pea fritters filled with dried shrimp, okra, and hot pepper became my daily meal. Years later in Ghana, I took my first bite of a fish dish steeped in palm oil and a Proustian rush transported me back to the streets of Bahia.

Dendê is just one of many threads tying Brazil to West Africa. Strikingly, in renditions of Pangea, the pretectonic drift supercontinent, the whole coast of Brazil nestles into the crook of West Africa from present-day Nigeria to South Africa. The two land masses share geographic and vegetational similarities. But it was, of course, the people forcibly brought to Brazil from Africa who wove this transatlantic web. Starting in the sixteenth century and continuing for almost four hundred years, an estimated twelve and a half million Africans were ripped from their homes and, if they endured the Middle Passage, faced lives of forced labor in the Americas. Almost half of those enslaved ended up in Brazil, where slavery persisted until almost the twentieth century, Brazil being the last nation in the Americas to abolish the brutal practice in 1888.[1]

When Portuguese explorer Pedro Cabral landed on the southern coast of Bahia in 1500, he planted a cross and called the new colony Terra de Vera Cruz (Land of the True Cross). Later the colony took the name Brasil from the Pau Brasil (Brazilwood) tree, the rich red bark of which glows like a burning coal (*brasa*) and produces a dye, similar in color to dendê, that fetched a fine price in Europe. But it was sugar and tobacco, produced with slave labor on plantations in the fertile lands of the Recôncavo around the Bay of All Saints, that created wealth for the colony. Salvador, perched on the bay, became Brazil's first capital and South America's first slave market.

In the eighteenth century, when the wealth of the colony drifted south to the gold mines and new capital, Rio de Janeiro, Salvador's economic power quickly declined. If not for the shift in national discourse around race, a burgeoning interest in Afro-Brazilian culture, and nascent tourism that began in the twentieth century, Salvador may have remained a slow, provincial town. Instead, it is now celebrated as the nation's "African heartland." Tourists flock to Salvador (synonymously known as City of Bahia or simply Bahia) to visit its colonial old town and beaches, pray in its houses of Candomblé, dance alongside carnival groups, and play capoeira.

Bahia's image as the little Africa of Brazil—80 percent of its population is of African descent, and Afro-Brazilian culture is on display on every street corner—drew me there. When I told Brazilians and Brazilophiles what I was studying, they told me I had to go to Salvador to find "authentic" capoeira. A slippery term indeed, authenticity in this context implied that Bahian capoeira was more bona fide because closer to its origin. In fact, where and when capoeira emerged is uncertain, as evidence suggests its presence in both Salvador and Rio since at least the late eighteenth century.

An 1835 engraving by Bavarian artist Johann Moritz Rugendas could be an early depiction of capoeira. Entitled *São Salvador,* the engraving shows a gathering of people in a forest clearing against a sliver of bay and a distant town. While the gathering could be any form of *batuque,* as African dance and music practices were collectively known, the movement of two men facing off are suggestive of the ginga, and the deep knee-bend lunge, similar to what we today call *negativa.* The rural setting, presumably on the outskirts of Salvador, might support the etymological theory that the name comes from the Tupi (native Brazilian) word *ca-puera,* meaning clearing or second growth forest. But other nineteenth-century paintings that specifically name or describe capoeira depict urban settings, many in Rio de Janeiro.

The prominence of Bahia's African roots often overshadows Afro-Brazilian histories and lifeways in other parts of the country.[2] The commodification of Afro-Brazilian cultural practices has kept the Bahian economy afloat and has generated disputes over authenticity by those who live from its expression. Surrounded by celebratory Afro-Brazilian culture, in Salvador I was also acutely reminded that Brazil was built and continues to operate on laboring Black bodies and violence. While certainly also on display in Rio, in Salvador the historic and continued exploitation of Black labor felt more proximate: the ornate baroque churches and massive colonial buildings crowded together in the small historic center were a constant reminder of the forced labor that lifted every stone to build Brazil. Outside the churches, *baianas*— Afro-Brazilian women dressed in the voluminous white skirts of devotees of Candomblé—sold acarajé, and six-year-old Black boys crouched on their rough-hewn wooden shoe shine boxes while souvenir shops at their backs sold postcards with their smiling images. Black pain and suffering jostling up against performances of exuberant Black joy has made Bahia, in the words of anthropologist Christen Smith, a place of simultaneous Black fantasy and Black death.[3]

The tragic story of a young capoeirista captures this paradox. Joel, the son of a local capoeira mestre, was featured in a 2010 Bahiatursa promotional travel video, playing capoeira and talking about his aspirations for the future. The video dubbed him, and other radiant, smiling, young Afro-Brazilians in the video, "the new face of Bahia, the land of happiness." Shortly after the commercial aired, military police invaded the peripheral neighborhood where Joel lived with his family. A stray bullet entered Joel's home and struck him in the face. The police refused to help Joel's father as he ran into the street holding his dying son.[4]

In Search of Authenticity

Recovered from my twenty-seven-hour bus ride from Rio de Janeiro, I set out on foot to explore the city. Despite signs of a tourist face-lift—public telephones shaped and painted like berimbaus and palm trees—Salvador in the mid-1990s was still a rather seedy, run-down town. The major renovations that would turn the historical center with Latin America's largest and oldest concentration of Baroque buildings into an Easter egg basket of pastel colors—and displace thousands of poor residents in the process—was in its early phase. Only the heart of the historic neighborhood, or Pelourinho as it is known, had been restored, pushing residents out to adjacent streets of decaying buildings.

I was staying with an old college friend in a neighborhood that was in walking distance from the Atlantic beaches to the east and to Pelourinho that perches on the high bluffs of the Cidade Alta (High City) above the western bay ports of the Cidade Baixa (Low City). Though a smaller and more navigable city with a languid pace compared to Rio, Salvador sparked wariness in me. I felt like a tourist and walking target for pickpockets and scammers.

These vulnerable feelings arose largely because I had left behind the con-vivência of my capoeira family in Rio and become an anonymous traveler. Yet, even years later when I had lived long enough in Rio and had a good enough command of Portuguese, local bus routes, and dress style to be mis-taken for a transplanted *gaúcha* (a fair-skinned resident of the southern state, Rio Grande do Sul with its large Germanic-descent population), in Salvador I still always felt like a gringa. A global city like Rio, Salvador offers a generic backpacker's travel experience found worldwide from Goa to Zanzibar or anywhere that offers decent beaches, cheap digs, strong cocktails, and good-looking, available locals. Pelourinho of the 1990s was thick with reggae bars frequented by rastas and their temporary gringa girlfriends, and hippie Ar-gentines making and selling wire jewelry and Middle Earth–inspired clay pipes in doorway-urinals.

Along with cheap consumption of a generic exotic other, however, Salva-dor also offers "authentic" experiences of Afro-Brazilian cultural practices. In particular, the African-Brazilian religion, Candomblé, draws practitio-ners, researchers, and tourists from around the world. One of the first in a long genealogy of Candomblé anthropologists was Ruth Landes. A student of Franz Boas at Columbia University, Landes came to Salvador in the 1930s to conduct fieldwork on race relations. She came to the quick and errone-ous conclusion that there were no race problems in Brazil, a commonly held belief among academics studying race at the time who favorably compared Brazil with its color spectrum rather than "one-drop" racial system and ab-sence of segregationist laws to Jim Crow United States. So, Landes turned her attention to religion.

In her ethnographic memoir, *City of Women*, Landes tells the story of the powerful women who led Salvador's Candomblé *terreiros* (houses of worship). Tucked into Landes's observations of sacred and secular life are glimpses of capoeira. Observing a roda at a religious festival, she describes the "mocking verses" that initiated the game as "a song of challenge and hope and resignation, containing fragments of rebellious thoughts [that] summa-rized a type of life and of protest" and the game as "a slow-motion, dream-like sequence that was more a dancing than a wrestling," apparently robbed of its "original sting."[5]

Influenced by her companion, folklorist Edison Carneiro, a professed capoeira aficionado and defender of Afro-Brazilian culture, Landes seems to suggest that under police oppression capoeira had transformed from a dangerous art of rebellion to a staged performance.

In Salvador, capoeira street gangs had not existed as they had in Rio, and so capoeira was not persecuted by law in the same way. Nonetheless, with abolition, Bahian elites became increasingly anxious to control the city's large, free African population. No longer able to justify banning gatherings of Blacks as a preventive measure against slave rebellions—one of which had rocked the city in 1835—the authorities rebranded their repression of Afro-Brazilian practices as "a campaign of civilization against barbarism."[6] Police raided Candomblé terreiros, samba parties, and capoeira rodas.

In protest against this repression, a group of Bahian intellectuals and artists rallied around Afro-Brazilian expressive and religious practices. Academics such as folklorist Edison Carneiro and anthropologists Artur Ramos and Roger Bastide, and artists and writers like Carybé and Jorge Amado began documenting and calling for the preservation of African-derived culture in Salvador. Also popular at this time was the revisionist history of sociologist Gilberto Freyre. After studying with Franz Boas at Columbia University, Freyre proposed a Brazilian exceptionalism of mixed Indigenous, African, and European miscegenation that resulted in Brazil's harmonious "racial democracy." The African elements so prevalent in Bahia were exalted as an important component of Bahian, and Brazilian, identity. The interest of elite Bahians, often with political and financial connections, intensified internal politics among Candomblé terreiros. Bolstered in part by academic interest in old world "retentions," claiming greater "African-ness" and purity became a mark of authenticity and thus prestige for houses of worship.[7]

Over the course of the twentieth century, as capoeira in Bahia attracted more Brazilian and international practitioners and researchers, similar debates around authenticity, purity, and tradition would build. By the twenty-first century a full-blown capoeira tourist industry to rival that of Candomblé's, would intensify these politics. In the 1990s, Salvador was not yet inundated with foreign capoeiristas. There were, however, a few of us roaming the city in search of "authentic" capoeira, though I was not sure what that would look like.

All I knew was that I had to find the Mercado Modelo, and Mestre DiMola.

"You need to be careful." Mestre Beiçola had said when I told him I was traveling alone to Salvador.

"Find Mestre DiMola. He will take care of you."

Street Capoeira at the Mercado Modelo

The Mercado Modelo, Salvador's former customhouse-turned-tourist bazaar, is as iconic as the Lacerda Elevator that connects the Cidade Alta and Cidade Baixa and delivers you to the market's doorstep. Wary of the hidden bends in the steep, crooked alleyways that also connect the upper and lower parts of the city, I opted for the elevator. Inspired by Lisbon's smaller-scale wrought iron and glass Santa Justa Elevator, Salvador's commuter shuttle drops a dramatic 250 feet from the high to low city.

Across from the elevator a musty yellow building stands against the blue bay. Built in the nineteenth century as a customhouse, the Mercado Modelo was renovated into a souvenir market in 1986. The ground floor stalls sell everything from handwoven hammocks to refrigerator magnets, and the second-floor restaurant offers typical Bahian dishes and folkloric night shows. Though catering to tourists, the Mercado still held pockets of local activity that were a step back in time to the 1940s of a Jorge Amado novel: vendors selling the lacy, full, white skirts and petticoats worn by devotees of Candomblé; bars selling two dollar plates of food and shots of cheap, rot-gut *cachaça* (sugarcane rum); and fish mongers in front of wooden carts slicing up fresh catch from the bay.

Walking through the indoor market and out to the other side, I reached a circular wooden platform, the "official" capoeira roda.

Capoeira at the Mercado Modelo tends to be written off today as "inauthentic," a mere tourist spectacle at best, and a scam at worst. Ethnographic studies of capoeira in Salvador mention it only in passing, if at all. Travel guides encourage visiting the academies for "authentic" capoeira and to negotiate a price with the Mercado performers beforehand or "run the risk of being suckered for an absurd fee."[8] Yet the Mercado Modelo is one of Salvador's historic capoeira sites. Pierre Verger, a French photographer who lived in Salvador and documented Afro-Brazilian practices, took hundreds of photographs of capoeiristas playing near the fish market that once stood next to the customhouse. And a short 1954 documentary film about capoeira was shot on a set that evoked the nearby docks with players and musicians in the rolled pants and wide-brimmed straw hats of fishermen.[9]

It's not just location that marks a historical continuity with capoeira in the Mercado Modelo. In one of the first comprehensive studies of capoeira from the 1960s, ethnographer Waldeloir Rego writes that it was common for *capoeiras* to play in front of bars to entertain and receive money or beer from the spectators or bar proprietor.[10] *Vadiação,* an alternate name for early twentieth-century capoeira, connoted loitering, bumming around, or idleness verging on vagrancy. By the 1990s, street performances at the Mercado Modelo had been somewhat formalized and sanctioned by Bahiatursa, the city's tourist organ, with the addition of the raised platform. But the capoeira retained an air of vadiação. Like the Bahaian *capoeiras* of the 1930s Edison Carneiro describes to Ruth Landes as "tough customers," the Mercado Modelo capoeiristas seemed a rough bunch; the scent of malandragem wafted off them along with the acrid-sweet smell of cheap cachaça and sweat.

I had seen street capoeira performances in downtown Rio. Young, scruffy, male performers who would draw a crowd with their set repertoire of kicks and acrobatics and circus stunts like diving through a flaming ring. They often lacked instruments—at most a pandeiro or poorly strung berimbau—and if they did play games, they were brief and showy, encouraging audience participation like counting off the number of repeating circular kicks.

In the Mercado Modelo capoeira was for show, but games were real, not staged, and could turn from playful to threatening; at times I had trouble distinguishing between feigned and sincere aggression. Though the "performances" seemed rather haphazard and informal, there were in fact two crews allowed to work the crowd on alternating days. While local and visiting capoeiristas sometimes stopped by—a guarantee to elevate the unpredictability and excitement of games—only those who were part of the crew could cash in on that day's earnings. The performances were ostensibly free, but as soon as a tourist took out a camera, one of the capoeiristas would descend from the stage to badger them, sometimes unpleasantly, to put money in a cap.

Mestre DiMola, wiry and fit in his forties, dreadlocks and beard inflected with gray, headed one of the crews. Aptly nicknamed "of springs," he was fast, bouncy, and flexible in his capoeira game and street malandragem. Born in the interior of Bahia, he'd fled rural poverty for the streets of Salvador where he eked out a living with other kids in street performances. These performances, in Mestre DiMola's historical telling, were the origins of the Mercado Modelo roda.

Despite his humble beginnings and what seemed to be a perennial lack of money, Mestre DiMola had for a while been an international capoeirista. Like Mestre Beiçola, he had traveled abroad with folkloric shows and had even married an American and lived in California for a time. When I met him, however, his main source of money seemed to be what he could make on the streets and occasional tourists gigs at hotels and restaurants for which he would scramble to put together a group of performers. Mestre DiMola's biography illustrates the inextricability of show or staged capoeira in the development of the practice and lives of Bahian capoeiristas. Though many practitioners critique show capoeira for being inauthentic, the capoeira played today was greatly influenced by its inclusion in folkloric presentations beginning in the 1950s. Dance scholar Ana Paula Höfling argues that rather than representing a "loss" of tradition, these performances in fact offered capoeiristas "a space for invention and creativity in a setting that allowed for the recontextualization of aspects of capoeira that were otherwise being phased out offstage."[11] Today, some practitioners are scornful, accusing capoeiristas who perform too many acrobatic moves during a game as "playing alone" or "doing a solo." Yet it cannot be forgotten that capoeira has always also been, and continues to be, a performative crowd-pleaser.

Mestre DiMola welcomed me as one of Beiçola's students, and I took to hanging around the Mercado Modelo. His crew seemed to enjoy having me there and occasionally pushed me onto the platform stage to play; the novelty (at that time) of a gringa capoeirista sometimes landed more money in the cap. One of the first times I played, a youth about my age jumped in the roda with me. With a bushy afro tinted orange from the sun, dramatic facial expression, and energetic game, he was a compelling performer. He didn't hold back with his kicks, and I was kept busy dodging. Yet, at some point, somehow, I managed to land a hammer kick (*martelo*) to his ribs. He scowled, stopped the game, and stalked off the platform. I worried that I had somehow breeched the etiquette of a performance roda and had made an enemy who would exact revenge.

Later that week, walking on the beach I heard a friendly "Iê capoeirista!" and turned to see the youth ambling over to me with a big smile, his hair sparkling with water and sun. We became friends. He laughed when I called him Maluco (crazy), a corruption of his nickname. Maluco made money shuttling foreigners from their yachts anchored in the harbor to the Low City in his row boat. He often befriended these wealthy tourists over the course of days or weeks they were moored, and one afternoon he borrowed a motor boat from one of them and took me around the bay. On the Ilha de Itaparica he shimmied barefoot up a twenty-foot *mangueira* and threw down mangoes, so heavy with ripe, sweet flesh that they fell through my hands and burst on the ground when I tried to catch them.

Many of the Mercado Modelo capoeiristas, like Maluco, were untitled and unaffiliated—they had no group, lineage, or rank. Some, like DiMola, were mestres, but had no active group. Others were mestres with regular students and classes. Intrigued to know what these mestres' capoeira looked like outside of the tourist roda, I accepted the offer to train with one of them from the alternate crew. It took a couple of weeks of his repeated offers, as I found this mestre rather intimidating in his game and intense stare. He drew a map and told me what bus to take.

The training space—a dim, concrete basement room in a housing complex—was not unlike places I had trained in Rio, but felt rather unwelcoming, as did the eight male students, when I arrived one evening. I felt out of place, my cord and bright white uniform garish against the others who blended into the surroundings with their dark training pants and bare chests. The mestre, looking somewhat surprised I'd actually shown up, gestured for me to join in without any introduction. The training was relentless and militaristic with jumping jacks and pushups followed by partner work of straight kicks, using our hands as targets. We ended with a roda without music and lots of standing kicks. I was used to this kind of training with Mestre Sardinha in Rio, but with smaller, younger capoeiristas who laughed a lot. These were strong men who took their training seriously.

I was exhausted, dripping sweat and filthy from the floor (I understood then why the other students wore dark clothing) by the end of training. I was proud that I had kept up, but also worried that my ego had gotten the better of me in a situation where I may have gotten hurt. I left with as little ceremony as I had come, finding my way alone to the bus stop. What a different experience from Rio, where I always felt like an honored family guest! Were this mestre and his students not used to hosting foreigners, or were they *too* used to hosting foreigners? Or was I just not welcome in that space, despite the mestre's invitation?

As I looked out the bus window at the dark streets rolling by at 11:00 p.m., I wondered who I was trying to impress. What did I find so exciting about training capoeira with people so different from me, some of whom might accidentally, or intentionally, injure me, and most of whom I would never see again? Was I just another tourist in search of authentic experience and an escape from my privileged background?

I have always been something of an "experience junkie." Squatting in a vacant house in San Francisco during my punk rock phase in high school; dropping LSD in my hippie phase in college; and traveling alone through Morocco when I was nineteen. I enjoy experiences that fire my senses, challenge me to step into another world and temporarily wear a different skin. This attraction had first led me to theater. But my desire for backstage immersion, rather than staged artifice, eventually brought me to anthropology and the possibilities of ethnography.

With capoeira, however, I wasn't just in search of new experience. I was obsessed. Now when I witness this obsession in other new capoeiristas, I tease that they have "caught the bug" and are *viciado* (addicted). For many, this addiction is temporary, and they move on to new interests after weeks, months, or years. For others the obsession engulfs and consumes. Sometimes capoeiristas even refer to capoeira as their lover. In my early stages of infatuation, I, too, acted as if with a new lover: wanting to spend all my time with capoeira, to completely absorb and be absorbed; to see capoeira in every possible light and discover its every secret; to be around and learn from those intimate with capoeira.

Referring to capoeira as a "lover" raises the specter of the eroticization of Black culture. In her ethnography of sex tourism in Bahia, Erica Williams argues that the city's touristscape is an entanglement of racism, eroticism, and commodification of Black bodies and culture. Moving beyond a simple economic analysis of sex tourism, Williams offers insight into the "ambiguous entanglements" across age, race, gender, class, and nationality in which "sexual relationships move beyond commercial exchanges to encompass intimate and emotional exchanges as well." The lure of Bahia, Williams argues, is the conjoining of "exotic culture" with hypersexualized Black bodies that responds to tourists' "desire for intimacy and alterity."[12] Dominated as it was in the 1990s by fit, shirtless Afro-Brazilian men, the Mercado Modelo capoeira was a perfect arena to fulfill this desire.

My staunch commitment to capoeira as my lover protected me from other messy entanglements: I was determined not to jeopardize what I hoped would be a lifelong relationship with capoeira through any precarious and possibly emotionally damaging romances with capoeiristas. The macho culture of capoeira and the relationships I had so far witnessed among capoeiristas and their girlfriends or wives, Brazilian or gringa, convinced me further not to get romantically involved. I stuck to going only to DiMola's rodas and hanging around his crew. I felt welcomed and safe, but I was not naive. They invited me onto the stage to play because it was an amusing diversion. And I knew when to keep my mouth shut.

One afternoon a group of tourists stopped to watch. Mestre DiMola was on fire playing his *gunga* (a large berimbau) and singing:

Gunga é meu,	The gunga is mine
Foi me mestre que me deu	My mestre gave it to me
Gunga é meu, gunga é meu	The gunga is mine, the gunga is mine
Gunga é meu,	The gunga is mine,
Foi meu pai quem me deu	My father gave it to me
Gunga é meu, gunga é meu	The gunga is mine, the gunga is mine
Gunga é meu,	The gunga is mine,
Eu não dou para ninguém	I won't give it to anybody

After the games, a tourist approached Mestre DiMola.

"How much for your instrument?" he asked in English.

"One hundred dollars."

The tourist pulled out his wallet, handed DiMola the bills, and strode off with his new souvenir.

My jaw dropped. On the other side of the market much prettier painted berimbaus were for sale for ten dollars! The tourist berimbaus didn't sound any good, but that wouldn't matter to someone who didn't know the name of, let alone play, the instrument.

Mestre DiMola caught my eye and winked.

He knew I wanted a berimbau, and he knew I wouldn't pay one hundred dollars for it.

It wasn't about the money, even though I was on a limited budget. I wanted to *make* a berimbau. Like the tourist who hashed out one hundred for a berimbau out of the hands of a capoeirista, I, too, wanted an "authentic" berimbau; but for me that meant *making*, not buying it.

So I bugged Mestre DiMola until he caved.

"Okay, *tá bom*" he grumbled, "meet me here tomorrow morning."

First Berimbau

Capoeira's iconic instrument and its name, like the game itself, are of uncertain origin. Musical bows, the family of instruments to which the berimbau belongs, are found around the world and throughout history (possible musical bows accompany hunting bows in some cave drawings). We can assume that the berimbau was introduced in Brazil by Africans as there are no known examples of musical bows among Indigenous Brazilians. In West Central Africa these one-string instruments of simple construction are known by different names (for example, *hungo, urucungo, mbulumbumba*) and can be played vertically or horizontally, and with mouth, ground, or gourd resonation.

The berimbau is a vertically played gourd-resonating bow that appeared some time in colonial Brazil. Nineteenth-century paintings suggest the berimbau was used by Africans to solicit alms or trade in the streets. Artistic and written representations of capoeira from the same time make no mention of the berimbau; capoeira, prior to the twentieth century, appears to have been accompanied only by drums and tambourines.[13] Today, the berimbau has become such a synecdoche for capoeira, that its absence in early representations is troubling to some practitioners who might stencil it in on reproductions of historical paintings or LP cover art.[14]

While certainly present at least in Bahia in the 1930s—Ruth Landes mentions three berimbaus in the roda she witnessed—the instrument would not take on its physical, symbolic, and spiritual importance until later in the twentieth century. Today, while other instruments may be absent from a roda, the berimbau commands the beginning and end of games, establishes the rhythm and speed, and dictates the feel of play. In this role, the lead berimbau, or gunga, is given an almost animate authority. Though it is the capoeirista playing the gunga (usually the most experienced mestre or the host of the roda) who decides on the duration and type of games, the berimbau is often referred to in this role. Capoeiristas will call out "pay attention to the gunga!" if players are off rhythm, and they will be "called back to the berimbau" if there is reason to restart a game. The berimbau is a transmitter of knowledge and an extension of the mestre, who will often teach with the instrument in hand, gesturing with it and instructing students to listen and respond to its rhythm.[15]

Berimbaus are also imbued with a spiritual or magical power. It is considered bad luck if the wire of a berimbau breaks during a roda—especially during a tense moment in a game—capoeiristas often making the sign of the cross or another protective gesture should this happen. I have heard tales from earlier times that capoeiristas would not let a menstruating woman touch or pass under a berimbau lest she rob its power. And some mestres have a special berimbau that others are not allowed to play. The berimbau, like the ginga, becomes an extension of the self through which, in the words of Mestre Acordeon, one learns "to imprint in its body traces of one's personality."[16]

Whether magical or not, the berimbau certainly does seem to exert a powerful pull over people. Many capoeiristas claim it was the music, and particularly the berimbau, that first attracted them. Sentiments such as "*o berimbau me chamou*" (the berimbau called me) appear frequently in song. Now with my years of teaching and doing lecture demonstrations, I can attest to its immediate attraction: audiences quiet at the first sound of my berimbau, and it is always the instrument children want to pick up first to play. Partly it is its singularity, as the berimbau is fairly unknown outside of Brazil and capoeira circles. Perhaps, its simple, elegant stature and resemblance to a weapon attracts. But mostly, the berimbau's resonating tone seems to tap into something deep within us. I used to wonder what my son in utero felt when he heard the call coming through the gourd pressed against my belly.

The berimbau's call has attracted musicians beyond the capoeira roda, most famously jazz musician Naná Vasconcelos and the funk band

Berimbrown, and has come to symbolize Afro-Brazilian, and by extension, Brazilian identity and creativity. And yet, in 2008 a professor at the Federal University of Bahia responded to critiques of low student test scores with a racist joke about how Bahians only know how to play one-stringed instruments.[17] Yet another illustration of the jarring ways in which Afro-Brazilian culture is appropriated and celebrated on the one hand and Afro-Brazilians denigrated on the other.

For me, and many capoeiristas, the berimbau is a symbol of identity; one cannot be a true capoeirista until one has, and plays, one's own berimbau.

As I got off the elevator on the morning designated for berimbau-making, I half expected Mestre DiMola not to show. I had learned that in Brazil, at least among capoeiristas, things often did not happen on the first try. One must have patience and let things occur at the "right moment," however mysteriously determined that might be. Apparently, that overcast, muggy morning was the right moment for making a berimbau.

"Did you cut the *verga* under the light of a full moon?" I teased DiMola as he sidled up to me with a five-foot stick in his hand. Legend has it that *biriba,* the wood from a tree indigenous to northeastern Brazil used for the *verga,* or bow part of the berimbau, must be cut "from a live tree in the forest on the right day under a proper moon" to ensure the requisite combination of strength and flexibility.[18]

"But of course, *madame,* only the best for you!" DiMola smiled and bowed with a flourish of his hand.

In fact, the wood looked not ideal, thick and stiff, which would make it difficult for me to *armar* (arm or string) my instrument. But, the stringy bark still clinging to it suggested it was freshly cut.

We headed along the bay, deeper into the Cidade Baixa to the Feira de São Joaquim to buy the remaining materials. I had gotten a glimpse of this working market from the water when Maluco pulled up to it during my harbor tour, and we watched men stripping huge stacks of sugar cane for the juice machines and boys diving off the docks into water thick with market refuse. Inside was a den of alleyways, bustle of activity, and assault on the senses: the pungent smell of raw meat mixing with the perfume of overripe pineapple; bright piles of hot red peppers and dried pink shrimp next to neat rows of plastic bottles filled with tricolored dendê—bright orange at the bottom, deep maroon at the top; the hum of conversation punctuated with the urgent shouts of men pushing carts loaded high above their heads to clear a path.

DiMola seemed to know everyone. As we wove through the aisles, he shouted out to porters, teased the vendors, and helped himself to handfuls of roasted peanuts and dried shrimp. We passed a young man carefully examining mangoes, and DiMola sang out a line from a samba song:

"Watch out boy that fruit has stones!"

The stall owner shooed us away with feigned annoyance.

We arrived at the section of the market selling everything Candomblé related. I was familiar with the *boticários* in San Francisco's Mission District that sell love potions, votive candles, and statues of Cuban and Puerto Rican versions of the African spirits and deities. But here I was awed by the overwhelming quantity of stuff. Towering stacks of different sized burnt umber clay dishes for food offerings; heaps of fragrant leaves for cleansing baths; hundreds of bead strings color-coded for different gods; giant statues of *preto velhos,* spirits of old Africans, and *pombagiras,* the voluptuous, Wonder Woman–esque female spirit, counterpoint to Exu, trickster, spirit of the crossroads and messenger to the gods. I was struck not by the exoticism of these religious objects, but by their everyday ordinariness: magic and spirituality for sale alongside recycled plastic liter bottles of neon-colored cleaning products.

We stopped at a stall selling *cabaças,* the round gourds used for the resonating mechanism of the berimbau, where for one *real* I bought a medium-sized one. At another stall selling woven goods we found bundles of *caxixi,* the small wicker shaker filled with seeds that accompanies the berimbau. I chose one that slipped easily over my two middle fingers and would nestle in the palm of my hand when I played.

Back at the Mercado Modelo, DiMola announced that it was time for lunch. His regular spot—a hole-in-the-wall bar with a rolling metal shutter for a door, the distinctive rattle-bang of which you hear all over Brazil morning and evening as businesses open and close—was tucked into the bottom right corner of the Mercado Modelo. It was a male space—manual workers having a quick midday meal and old men precariously perched at the bar palming shots of cachaça or hot coffee in kindergarten-sized juice glasses. Heaping plates of rice, beans, and fried fish sprinkled with manioc flour appeared before us. The tourist hustle of the Mercado Modelo melted away to the rumble of banter and clink of silverware. After we ate, I paid at the bar. The price suggested I had also picked up DiMola's monthly tab, a bit of his malandragem I was happy to absorb. As we headed out, DiMola gestured to a bottle on a shelf behind the bartender.

"Damn!" I thought. No more berimbau-making and capoeira that afternoon.

But outside, DiMola handed me the bottle, which I saw had only an inch of cachaça.

"Take a slug."

I took a small sip feeling the rough sugarcane liquor burn my throat. Cheap cachaça is only bearable with the muddled lime and sugar of a caipirinha.

DiMola tipped back his head, drained the bottle, and with a swift motion, smashed it against the wall. He picked out the biggest piece of broken glass and handed it to me along with the verga.

I got to work removing the bark and sanding the wood smooth with the glass, while DiMola wandered around the market gathering the rest of the tools and materials we needed: from a fishmonger a large knife, which he cleaned off in the bay; from a jewelry maker a hammer, three nails, a hand drill, and a scrap of leather; and from the hammock seller, some string.

DiMola cut a small circle from the leather scrap and with the hammer and nails secured it to the top of the verga.

"This holds the *arame*." Reaching into his pocket he pulled out a coiled wire.

The berimbau's wire, about the size and strength of piano wire, is cut from old tires. Arames are harvested by slicing into the rubber along the inner rim with a large knife and prying out the stiff coils, which then are sanded free of residue rubber. A dirty and hot job—a sanded wire can burn a hand.

DiMola cut a piece of the string and tied it through the small loop he made at one end of the arame, his strong thumbs twisting the wire as easily as a pipe cleaner. He fashioned the *pé*, or foot, at the opposite end of the verga by cutting a groove a half inch from the bottom and then peeling away the outer layer of wood with the tip of the knife to leave an indented inner circle of wood. Hooking a slightly larger loop around the foot, he stretched the wire over the top of the berimbau across the leather patch. Securing the berimbau's foot against the instep of his own foot, DiMola used the other knee to push against the verga while applying pressure in the opposite direction at the top of the verga with his left hand. The verga didn't budge. He released it and tried again, his bicep bulging. My heart sank. There was no way I would ever string this berimbau. DiMola called over one of the other capoeiristas, who were beginning to show up for the afternoon roda. Together they pulled, and the verga slowly arced into a bow. With his right hand DiMola grasped the string on the arame and wrapping it around his hand, pulled until the wire came taut. Keeping the tension, he wrapped the wire and string around the top of the verga and tied it off. He relaxed his grip and gently tapped the top of the berimbau on the ground. The wire made a popping sound as it settled into place—the verga was ready for its cabaça.

DiMola cut a circular opening at one end of the gourd and on the opposite end used the hand drill to puncture two holes. Through these holes he looped and tied a short length of string, the tuning mechanism. Grabbing the verga close to the foot, DiMola gently squeezed the wire toward the wood with one hand, and with the other hand slipped the string of the cabaça onto the berimbau and worked it up the wire.

"The cabaça should sit about a hand width from the bottom of the berimbau," DiMola said. He demonstrated by putting his pinkie at the foot of the berimbau and then stretching his hand up to show me that the cabaça rested just above his thumb.

"Now you need your *baqueta* and *dobrão*."

At a stall selling hair wraps and barrettes, I bought a wooden chopstick for securing a bun.

"It's a little short, but will do for now as your baqueta." DiMola drew a round, flat, smooth stone from his pocket.

"Some capoeiristas say you should only use an old coin. But a flat stone or a big washer work as well for a dobrão."

DiMola picked up the berimbau in his left hand: his pinkie under the string of the cabaça balanced the instrument (the trickiest part of learning to play a berimbau), while his thumb and first finger secured the dobrão, the three remaining fingers wrapping around the verga. The other hand held the caxixi and the baqueta. DiMola hit the arame with the baqueta, cocked his head, and listened. He gently worked the cabaça slightly up and down the verga, tuning the instrument until he found the pitch and tone he wanted. Then he began to play: pulling the berimbau slightly away and up from his body to produce a deep "open" note (dong) and then returned the cabaça quickly to his chest so the resonation made a warbling sound. He struck the baqueta again twice quickly against the arame, this time with the dobrão lightly held against the wire to produce a buzzing note or *repique* (tchi, tchi) and then hit the arame again with the dobrão pushed firmly into the wire to produce the higher-pitched, "closed" note (ding).

DiMola grinned. "Not bad seeing as we didn't 'marry' the cabaça and verga."

To "marry" the parts of the berimbau is to find the right combination of length and width of stick to size of the gourd. A *viola,* the highest pitch berimbau in the orchestra has a small gourd; the *gunga,* or deepest-toned berimbau, has the largest gourd; the *médio,* which we had made, has a medium-size gourd and a tone somewhere between the viola and gunga. DiMola was happy that the combination we had made a bright, loud sound. He was also pleased, I am sure, to have come through on his promise and to be done with my pestering.

I stopped hanging around the Mercado Modelo after that. I sensed that Mestre DiMola had grown weary of me. I suspected that with my youth, limited budget, and obsession with capoeira to the exclusion of other tourist plea-sures, I had proven less the benefactress than he had hoped. These suspicions were confirmed when another capoeirista told me he'd overheard DiMola referring to me as "the gringa who doesn't pay for anything." At the time I was offended, but now I cringe. I had side-stepped my uncomfortable feel-ings about the tourism economy in Bahia by imagining myself not as a tour-ist but as a capoeirista-traveler, a dedicated and passionate participant, not a mere spectator. But foreign capoeiristas are just as entangled in structures of inequality as other kinds of tourists when they come to learn from Brazilian mestres. I brushed away any discomfort by deciding Mestre DiMola and the Mercado Modelo capoeiristas had simply lost interest in me. Besides, there was a larger world of capoeira in Bahia to discover.

My explorations began in Pelourinho.

Capoeira Angola in Pelourinho

In an 1840 lithograph by Frederico Guilherme Briggs entitled *Negroes Going to be Whipped,* three enslaved men in ankle chains are led by two soldiers, one carrying a long thin whip. One of the prisoners carries an agogô under his arm and the other a sign that reads "capoeira." Until the development of the modern prison system, punishment was a public spectacle meant to both entertain and deter others from committing similar crimes.[19] Perhaps these prisoners were being paraded through the streets with a placard announcing their crime on their way to the pelourinho. The pillory. The whipping post.

Most tourists in Salvador are oblivious to the meaning of the name of the quaint, pastel-hued neighborhood they wander around clicking photos and buying berimbau keychains. The name is not mentioned on official tours.[20] In fact, at the beginning of its one-hundred-million-dollar renovation begun six years after its 1986 designation as a UNESCO world heritage site, the *cen-tro histórico,* or historic center, became the preferred name over Pelourinho. The pillory is gone. But the cobblestone streets, ornate churches, and colonial buildings are silent reminders that Pelourinho, Salvador, and all of Brazil was built on the backs of "black bodies in pain."[21]

In his ethnography *Revolt of the Saints,* John Collins tells the twenty-year story of Pelourinho's gentrification. An all too familiar narrative of historic Black neighborhoods from New York to New Orleans evacuated of Black people, Pelourinho's gentrification has had a particular trajectory. In Col-lins's telling, it has not been a simple story of sanitation, beautification, and elevated rents to deliver a desirable neighborhood to more "deserving" (white and wealthy) denizens of the city. Nor has its restoration just been a

"Disneyfication" of the colonial past vacant of social life. Rather, Pelourinho has become a "living museum" in which its Black inhabitants have themselves become national patrimony, the state co-opting their very bodies and lifeways as "intangible heritage" marketable to tourists.[22] This is but the latest iteration in a long history of exploitation of Afro-Brazilians in Pelourinho.

Starting in the 1920s, after Salvador's wealthy abandoned their homes in the center for more spacious and clean peripheral neighborhoods, Pelourinho became a quasi-autonomous area of the city. The area had always had a large Black presence, with wealthy African freedmen buying properties in the early nineteenth century. Now, lower-class Afro-Bahians took over the quickly deteriorating buildings in which they had once worked as servants. Pelourinho became a hub of informal economy, prostitution, gambling, and alcohol on offer. Similar to Lapa in belle epoque Rio, Pelourinho was demonized in public discourse as immoral and dirty, yet Salvador's (male) elite continued to visit the neighborhood to enjoy a particular sociality not allowed in the city's more "respectable" zones.

Along with the sensual pleasures Pelourinho's residents offered, they were also a source of fascination to artists and intellectuals for their folk lifeways—music, religion, and capoeira. Jorge Amado set many of his novels in Pelourinho, and the artist Carybé's engravings and drawings are populated by Afro-Brazilians and their practices. These romanticized and celebratory depictions contributed to the growing notion that Afro-Brazilian culture was an important component of *baianidade* (Bahianness) and by extension, *brasilidade* (Brazilianness).

Taking advantage of this new celebration of Afro-Brazilian culture, Mestre Pastinha and Mestre Bimba, capoeira's most famous mestres, opened the first official capoeira academies in Pelourinho. Recognized during their lifetimes as important cultural figures in capoeira's ascent from persecuted social threat to celebrated national sport, both mestres nevertheless died poor and disillusioned: Pastinha buried in an unmarked wooden box in a pauper's grave still waiting indemnification from the state for eviction from his Pelourinho academy when the building was designated for restoration; and Mestre Bimba in self-exile from Bahia, disgusted with the politicians who promised much but delivered nothing. In a clear denunciation of the way in which capoeira had been patrimonialized while capoeiristas were left in poverty, Mestre Pastinha told *A Tarde* newspaper shortly before he died in 1981, "Capoeira doesn't need anything, I do."[23]

Black residents of Pelourinho today, as documented by Collins, vie for state recognition as bearers of tradition in a desperate (and largely unsuccessful) attempt to stay in their homes. Capoeira has also become a locus of dispute around notions of tradition and authenticity. Stylistic debates reach back to Mestres Pastinha and Bimba and the two distinct styles—*capoeira angola* and *capoeira regional*—developed by them and their descendants.

Mestre Pastinha and Mestre Bimba

Vicente Ferreira Pastinha was born in Salvador on April 5, 1889, to a Spanish father and Bahian mother. Small, frail, and blind by the end of his life, Mestre Pastinha was contemplative by nature, more philosopher and artist than fighter. Though uneducated past primary school, he wrote extensively, leaving behind a published book, *Capoeira Angola,* and several unpublished manuscripts. In Pastinha's account, he was initiated into capoeira at age ten by an African named Benedito. Witnessing Pastinha being bullied by an older boy, Benedito offered to teach him capoeira, which according to Pastinha, allowed him to exact revenge on his bully within a few months. In his twenties, after serving in the Navy and holding various odd jobs including carpenter and casino bouncer, Mestre Pastinha began teaching capoeira in the back of a bicycle shop. His initial foray into teaching did not last long, and he withdrew from capoeira from 1912 to 1941. He was eventually drawn back to teaching at the behest of the older mestres in the city, who believed that the literate Mestre Pastinha was the best advocate and spokesperson for maintaining capoeira's tradition, which they felt was being diminished. Their accusations of the modernization and corruption of the practice were levied at Mestre Bimba.

At his birth on November 23, 1900, Manoel dos Reis Machado was given the nickname by which he would be known for the rest his life. The midwife, seeing he was a boy, called out "Bimba!" or "little penis." Despite growing to be a strong, skilled capoeirista and fierce fighter who cut an imposing figure at six feet (tall by Brazilian standards), the nickname stuck. In his youth, he was also known as Três Pancadas, or Three Blows, the alleged number of punches no opponent could withstand before falling. Unlike Mestre Pastinha, Bimba welcomed innovations, including movement from Asian martial arts, and introduced capoeira in the boxing ring, winning several famous matches.[24] He called his style Luta Regional da Bahia (Regional Fight of Bahia), later known as *capoeira regional.* Mestre Bimba maintained two academies—one in his home in a peripheral working-class neighborhood and the other in Pelourinho.

Given the marginalized and resource-poor status of most Afro-Brazilians in Salvador, the stylistic rivalry between the two mestres might not have gained legs if not for the intellectual elite that became attached to the two schools. Mestre Pastinha won the support of the same intellectuals concerned with issues of purity in the Candomblé terreiros. Edison Carneiro and Jorge Amado invited Mestre Pastinha to perform his *capoeira angola*—known by that name to emphasize its more "traditional" and "African" qualities—at the 2nd Afro-Brazilian Congress held in 1937, and they helped him open an academy in Pelourinho.

Mestre Bimba also won the support of the educated middle class, many of them his students who were also students at the School of Medicine located near his academy in Pelourinho. This new student demographic, along with his stylistic innovations, led to accusations that Mestre Bimba was diluting and "whitening" capoeira, despite his deep commitment to Afro-Brazilian culture, including as an active practitioner of Candomblé.

In truth, Mestres Pastinha and Bimba had much in common in terms of the capoeira they played and their hopes for it. They both, in their own ways, wanted to preserve capoeira as a living and dynamic practice, not just a folkloric show; to divorce capoeira from its reputation as a marginal, violent, and delinquent activity; and to promote capoeira as a legitimate sport. To this end, they both taught within academies with set rules, pedagogy, and uniforms and insisted that their students hold either student or worker documents. The seriousness with which they trained their students in the practice's rituals and fighting techniques exceeded the view of capoeira as just a tourist spectacle, yet they both participated in staged performances around the city.

Mestre Pastinha and Bimba's ambiguous and at times contradictory views on and relationship to capoeira reflect their deep commitment to seeing both the practice and themselves—as lower-class Black men in a racist, hierarchical Bahia—survive. Their contradictions are also testament to the adaptability of capoeira. Mestre Bimba went from championing capoeira in the boxing ring in the 1930s and 1940s to establishing a successful folkloric troupe in the 1950s and 1960s. In any event, it is largely due to the efforts of Mestres Pastinha and Bimba that the practice underwent an institutionalization that launched it onto its remarkable ascent through the twentieth century, proclaimed by President Vargas in 1953 as Brazil's "one true national sport."

As capoeira's popularity grew throughout Brazil and then the world, identity politics around authenticity and style intensified. The bifurcation between *capoeira angola* and *capoeira regional* that began in the 1940s has today rendered them distinctive practices from movement, ritual, and music to uniforms and trainings. Most groups that claim to practice either *capoeira angola* or *capoeira regional* today do not in fact stick to the rules and limited movement repertoire of Mestres Pastinha or Bimba. Other groups refuse to ascribe to one or the other style, claiming, to the ire of purists, that *"capoeira é uma só"* (there is only one capoeira). Sometimes, it seems, these disputes have made enemies of those who should be allies.

Music, Spirituality, and Theatrics

The Escola de Capoeira Angola Irmãos Gêmeos (Twins Capoeira Angola School) on Rua Gregório de Matos, stands not far from the location of Mestre Pastinha's former academy in Pelourinho. The second-floor studio with its checkered floor and incensed air was the domain of Mestre Curió, one of a small cadre of aging mestres in Salvador who claims direct descent from Mestre Pastinha. In the 1990s, Mestre Curió, short in stature but large in personality, was a daily presence on the cobblestone streets of Pelourinho. In his late fifties, he was both ancient and youthful. Walking with a cane, his barrel chest rolling atop a bow-legged gait and chiseled face dancing under a straw fedora, he was an aging elf. In the roda, years floated off him like the molting feathers of a songbird, the *curió,* for which he is nicknamed. He hopped, dipped, strutted, cackled, and made lewd gestures.

Mestre Curió welcomed me into his academy like a long-lost friend (perhaps he confused me with another gringa capoeira tourist). Adamant he was carrying on Mestre Pastinha's legacy, he maintained the former's schedule: trainings on Tuesday and Thursday and a roda on Friday evenings. On my first Friday, I climbed the stairs, dropped five *reais* in the donation jar and took my place among the other spectators on benches across from the semi-circular roda. The music began, and the power of a full orchestra broke over me: three berimbaus, one atabaque, two pandeiros, a reco-reco, and square wooden blocks in place of an agogô. The singing, strong and melodic, sent shivers down my spine.

The elaboration of music, like the berimbau, appears to have been a later addition, most likely after capoeira's mid-twentieth-century-folkloric staging. In 1964, Mestre Pastinha claimed that while "musical or rhythmic ensemble is not indispensable," the "melodies and improvisations" of musicians and singers furnish "grace, tenderness, charm and mysticism that stirs the souls of the capoeira players."[25] Dance scholar Ana Paula Höfling suggests that the addition of music "feminized" capoeira, further distancing it from its former masculine violence."[26] Nonetheless, perhaps unwilling to completely surrender capoeira's potential, on a voiceover track on his 1969 LP, Mestre Pastinha described weaponizing his berimbau by attaching a small "curved blade" to one end.[27] Similarly emphasizing capoeira as self-defense, Mestre Bimba claimed that "real capoeira is what we use to defend ourselves from an enemy. If I am somewhere and I am attacked, am I going to wait for the berimbau in order to react? Not the berimbau or the pandeiro!"[28]

When capoeira resurged in Rio in the 1950s, it remained more "masculine" and fight-oriented with little attention to music. I had inherited this history: training with Mestre Beiçola and his network in Rio, live music was often an afterthought. We trained to recorded music or no music at all, and our rodas at the end of class often lacked a full array of instruments. My berimbau playing was stumbling and my song repertoire limited.

Seated in a circle on the floor arching out from the orchestra, Mestre Curió's students, largely young men, with a sprinkling of women, wore black pants and belts, tucked-in yellow T-shirts with the group logo, and shoes. When I later asked Mestre Curió why he used black and yellow, and not all white as so many groups do, he told me they were the colors that Mestre Pastinha used in his school. And when I asked why Mestre Pastinha used these colors, he grinned and told me they were the colors of Mestre Pastinha's favorite soccer team, Ypiranga. I had thought the colors might have a religious or political significance, but then again, Brazilians' allegiances to their soccer teams are quasi-religious and political!

Despite the secular colors, Mestre Curió's academy and roda were imbued with spirituality. Posters and paintings of *orixás,* the Candomblé gods, adorned the walls, and he began by lighting a sage smudge stick and opening the four directions. Playing the gunga, Mestre Curió began the roda with one of Mestre Pastinha's short *ladainhas:*

Maior é deus!	God is great
Pequeno sou eu.	I am small
O que eu tenho,	All that I have
Foi deus que me deu.	God gave me
Na roda de capoeira, haha!	In the capoeira roda, haha!
Grande e pequeno sou eu.	Big and small am I

The ladainha (litany) is a solo sung before a game begins. Its lyrics often praise God, orixás, and capoeira ancestors. A call-and-response *louvação* (prayer) follows the ladainha. The chorus must stay attuned as the lead singer may vary and improvise the phrases.

Iê, viva meu deus	Iê, praise God
Iê, viva meu deus, camará	Iê, praise God, comrade[29]
Iê, viva meu mestre	Iê, praise my teacher
Iê, viva meu mestre, camará	Iê, praise my teacher, comrade

Iê, quem me ensinou	Iê, who taught me
Iê, quem me ensinou, camará	Iê, who taught me, comrade
Iê, a capoeiragem	Iê, capoeiragem
Iê, a capoeiragem, camará	Iê, capoeiragem, comrade
Iê, o galo cantou	Iê, the cock crowed
Iê, o galo cantou, camará	Iê, the cock crowed, comrade
Iê, vamos embora	Iê, let's go
Iê, vamos embora, camará	Iê, let's go, comrade
Iê, dá volta ao mundo	Iê, around the world
Iê, dá volta ao mundo, camarada	Iê, around the world, comrade

The mixing of Candomblé and Catholic spirituality in Mestre Curió's academy also imbued the personal rituals of individual players. The two capoeiristas called to play the first game crouched at the foot of Mestre Curió's gunga during the ladainha and lovação. Once the *corridos,* or songs that would accompany play began, they touched the ground in front of the instruments and raised their hands to the sky. One made invisible marks with his fingers on the floor as if tracing in dust, calling down the orixás for protection; the other made the sign of the cross. Then they shook hands and entered the roda with low slow cartwheels.

The relaxed, loose-armed ginga of Mestre Curió's style was not dissimilar to the ginga I had learned with Mestre Beiçola. But the rhythm was different: the angoleiros were off-kilter and full of breaks, occasionally tapping out rhythms with their feet or slipping in a quick samba step. And there were opportunities to touch: experienced players executed *balões,* or throws, in which one player grasped the other and launched him over his shoulder to land, with an acrobatic flourish, as softly as a cat. Games were punctuated with *chamadas,* one of the most dramatic and characteristic elements of *capoeira angola.* In a chamada, one player stops and "calls" the other to join him in a stylized waltz with parts of their bodies—hand to hand or head to belly—touching. Chamadas can be a way to acknowledge that a "point has been scored" and thus can be dangerous if the one scored against uses the proximity of his partner to launch a counterattack. According to Greg Downey, "the chamada helps to maintain this ambivalent even ironic form of play. The sequence allows players to manipulate the contradictory facets of the art: overt antagonism, exquisite artistry, personal expression, competitive interaction, solemnity, honor, and rough humor."[30]

Handing off the gunga, Mestre Curió indicated he was ready to play. He removed his hat, tightened his belt, and draped a hand towel around his neck like a prize fighter to wipe the rivulets of sweat from his face. He was a whirl of activity in the roda: his leather shoes scraping the ground, his short legs darting out attacks, his face an evolving landscape of expressions. His younger partner struggled to keep up and at one point broke off play and walked counterclockwise around the inside of the roda. *Volta ao mundo* (turn around the world), like other chamadas, can restart the game sometimes simply when one player needs to catch his breath. Mestre Curió stalked behind his opponent, his head thrust forward, his mouth in a pout, drawing laughter from the audience. When his partner turned back toward him to reinitiate play, Mestre Curió jumped in the air feigning surprise and fear. Then he leaped from the roda and ran to the desk by the door. Rummaging in a drawer he pulled out a small dagger and brandishing it above his head, charged back to the roda. At the edge he abruptly stopped, grabbed a tourist off a bench, and advanced slowly toward his adversary cowering behind his human shield.

Mestre Curió didn't just enjoy displays of feigned violence, recalling legendary *capoeiras* of yore who'd pull daggers on each other in the roda. He also indulged in lewd gestures. He'd glance down curiously as his body began to shake, and when the shaking burst into a vigorous pumping of his pelvis, he'd look up at his partner with a coquettishly cocked eyebrow. I had never seen anything like it in a roda. Perhaps it was a throwback to the raunchy, (homo)erotic tactics of the famous Mestre Canjiquinha, who in the 1960s delighted tourists with capoeira-variety shows.[31]

Whatever his performance may have signified, Mestre Curió was apparently a voracious lover of women in life. Rumor had it he had twenty-one children. Fact or fiction, I don't know. But when I said goodbye to Mestre Curió upon leaving Salvador, he opened the fanny pack he always wore to give me his card. As he rummaged through it, packets of condoms spilled out. He looked up with an impish grin and winked.

Radical Capoeira in the Forte de Santo Antônio

On the north side of Pelourinho, up a long cobblestone street of dilapidated buildings that ended in the decaying remains of a fort, I discovered an edgier, politicized *capoeira angola*. Forte de Santo Antônio, which stands on a high bluff, was built after the Dutch invasion in the seventeenth century to defend the city from future attacks. Later it became a prison and then in 1978 earmarked to become a Popular Culture Center. It would take another thirty years for that to happen.

In the 1990s the fort had a reputation for being dangerous, a drug users' haunt, and shelter for homeless families. But it also was the rehearsal space for the carnival group, Ilê Aiyê, the seat of Black radicalism in Salvador. Founded in 1974 during the re-Africanization of popular culture in Bahia, Ilê Aiyê had weathered accusations of reverse racism for allowing only Blacks to join and for promoting Afrocentric music, costumes, and themes. The percussive group that paraded in the streets during carnival was popular with Bahia's Black youth. Saturday evening rehearsals at the fort drew crowds from the surrounding neighborhoods, along with a handful of more adventurous tourists tired of the tamer rehearsals of Olodum, another Afrobloco with less radical politics and greater international fame.[32]

Three or four *capoeira angola* academies crouched in the remains of the fort's dimly lit former prison cells. There was no love lost between Mestre Curió and the mestres in the fort. He had made sure I'd seen the newspaper articles tacked to the wall in his academy, detailing the disputes over who was the legitimate heir to Mestre Pastinha's legacy and proper spokesperson for *capoeira angola*. At the fort, above the academy of Mestre João Pequeno who, in his eighties at the time, was the oldest living of Mestre Pastinha's students, was Mestre Moraes's school. It was this younger mestre, credited with re-Africanizing and revitalizing *capoeira angola,* who most ruffled Mestre Curió's feathers. By the 1990s Mestre Moraes was the leader of a large international group, Grupo de Capoeira Angola Pelourinho (GCAP) and a new generation of *angoleiros,* as practitioners of *capoeira angola* call themselves.

Born in Bahia, Moraes spent the 1970s in Rio de Janeiro while serving as a Navy marine. Playing in street rodas in a city that was embracing the U.S. Black Power movement through a music, fashion, and intellectual scene known as Black Rio, Moraes's capoeira politicized. Espousing Black liberation did not rest easily with his position in the armed forces of a dictatorship that practiced censorship, torture, and disappearances, and so he deserted.[33] Following fifteen months of military imprisonment, Mestre Moraes returned to Bahia with carioca capoeirista Cobra Mansa to develop his work with GCAP to "popularly preserve what remains of the authenticity of black arts and African culture in Brazil."[34] Not unlike Mestre Pastinha fifty years before, Mestres Moraes and Cobra Mansa found support among intellectuals, but this time ones who opposed assimilationist race politics for a more critical stance: Brazilian university students and professors, and U.S. scholars and capoeiristas who embraced capoeira as a pan-African manifestation.[35]

As important as their politics, Mestres Moraes and Cobra Mansa were charismatic young men with street credibility in Rio's tough rodas. By the

1980s, as Rio and São Paulo had become hotbeds of new developing contemporary styles that emphasized speed and fighting efficacy, *capoeira angola* had been relegated a folkloric *coisa de velhos* (old guys thing)—a view that must have irritated Mestre Curió. GCAP transformed this perception by developing a *capoeira angola* based in the teachings of Mestre Pastinha but which also incorporated new elements that were developing in capoeira in Rio and which could hold its own in the roda. Internal politics over style and authenticity between the old guard and new generation of angoleiros were further complicated by city and state politics: many of the old guard aligning with the powerful and conservative politician Antônio Carlos Magalhães—who as governor of Bahia had instituted the reforms of Pelourinho and worked through a system of patronage—and the young generation aligning with the socialist Workers' Party.[36]

I didn't spend much time at the GCAP academy, which by then was under the sole direction of Mestre Moraes, Mestre Cobra Mansa having moved to the United States and founded his own group. I never felt particularly welcomed there. Then again, I didn't make an effort to establish convivência. The first time I showed up for the Sunday roda, I arrived late and so according to the rules, could not sit in the roda or play. As I watched from the sidelines, my initial frustration was replaced by relief. The roda was large and intimidating. Several foreign students played, and the Brazilian students seemed to mock them and use every opportunity to knock them to the ground. The atmosphere felt heavy and not terribly playful or friendly, something I was unaccustomed to in capoeira. Perhaps what made me uncomfortable was that, unlike in the studios of Mestre Curió or Mestre João Pequeno—who with his group's rainbow logo welcomed everyone with open arms—here I was confronted with my whiteness.

Mestre Moraes's academy espoused a racial politics I was familiar with in the United States. My first exposure to Afrocentric capoeira had been in Oakland, California. An African American man who had trained with Mestre Acordeon—the first mestre to bring capoeira to the Bay Area in the late 1970s—had splintered off to form his own group. He became an angoleiro affiliated with GCAP and eventually was recognized as a mestre. I went once to his roda in Oakland and felt uncomfortable, as I was not used to being in predominantly Black spaces.

Despite its liberal politics, Berkeley is a segregated city. In 1968 the Berkeley Unified School District pioneered a two-way busing system to fully integrate public schools. Soon the city had elementary schools named after not only Martin Luther King but also Malcolm X. Yet, by high school, I was increasingly aware of racial tensions. Similar to what anthropologist Savannah

Shange describes in her 2019 ethnography as the "progressive dystopia" of a social justice–themed school in San Francisco, Berkeley High School in the 1980s was troubled: despite an African American Studies Department and Swahili classes, my high school was academically and socially segregated. In my tracked classes, my few Black friends were called "oreos" by less highly performing Black students, and the schoolyard was divided territory, Black and white students sticking to their areas to eat lunch and socialize. After my senior year I worked at a city recreational camp and was surprised to be placed not at the park near my house in the North Berkeley foothills, where I had gone to camp as a kid, but in the working-class flats of West Berkeley. Biking to work every day where I was the only white female counselor among an almost all Black staff and campers, felt like entering another city and a social world where I was tolerated but not particularly welcome.

Perhaps part of my attraction to capoeira and Brazil had been what I perceived as an easier way to navigate race relations. I had always been attracted to Black culture—the drumming on Sproul Plaza, *Soul Train,* jazz and tap dance—but as I got older, I began to feel it was not available to me because I was white. Capoeira, at least as I first experienced it with Mestre Beiçola and in Brazil, was a Black space that welcomed, or at least was open to, me. Early on, Mestre Beiçola had a student who left the group over race politics. He was an older African American man who was accomplished in other martial arts and ran a Black youth empowerment program. When Beiçola made it clear that he did not agree with this student's philosophy that African-derived fighting techniques should be exclusively for Black people, the student left the group to form his own. I felt comfortable with Beiçola's race politics and his inclusive capoeira.

What I experienced with these more Afrocentric capoeira groups was not the interpersonal racial hostility and anger I had sometimes encountered in my younger years that made my body constrict with shame and confusion. I was, instead, confronted with my whiteness as part of larger structures of exclusion, and erasure of Blackness; I was entering a Black space where whiteness was not needed or necessarily wanted, and which rejected the white appropriation of Black culture, reclaiming it for Black people. In the GCAP academy I entered a space that privileged and encouraged Black freedom of movement and expression in a city that placed restrictions on such mobility for anyone who did not carry white privilege.

Creating a predominantly Black space in Brazil in the 1990s was still a radical gesture, evident in the critiques leveled at Ilê Aiyê. In the United States, Black people had been fighting for political and civil rights since abolition and the institution of Jim Crow laws. In Brazil, though there have been individuals and groups fighting against anti-Black racism throughout the nation's history, the insidious ideology of "racial democracy," color spectrum over one-drop-rule, and absence of segregationist laws, made it difficult for large-scale mobilization around Blackness.[37] Speaking out against this ideology was an act of bravery, especially during the military dictatorship. Among those who took this risk were several Afro-Brazilian feminists, Beatriz Nascimento and Lélia Gonzalez, who despite all odds against them rose from impoverished backgrounds to academic positions. Lélia Gonzalez's powerful declaration: "We Blacks are in the garbage can of Brazilian society. . . . [and now] the garbage is going to talk," would pave the way for a more visible, vocal, and mobilizing Black movement in the twenty-first century.[38] Similarly, several pioneering Afro-Brazilian female capoeiristas—Rosângela C. Araújo and Paula Cristina da Silva Barreto, both students of Mestre Moraes and PhD students in the 1990s—would go on to become Mestra Janja and Mestra Paulinha, founders of Grupo Nzinga (and professors at the Federal University of Bahia), helping to pave the way for more Afro-Brazilian women to become leaders in capoeira.

With my visits to the rodas of Mestre DiMola, Mestre Curió, Mestre Moraes, and Mestre João Pequeno I had but nicked the surface of capoeira in Salvador. There were probably close to one hundred mestres in the city and its surroundings, with different lineages, philosophies, styles, and politics. Some I would visit: the barefooted, gray-bearded elfin Mestre Nô in Boca do Rio with his fast, bouncy game; Mestre Nenel, the son of Mestre Bimba, with tidy dreadlocks and striking blue-rimmed black eyes, who taught in his father's style in a bright, clean karate studio in the peripheral neighborhood where he had grown up in the famous mestre's house-academy; I visited Mestre Bimba's former academy in Pelourinho, my skin goose-bumping as I mounted the stairs to the second-floor studio, imagining all the capoeiristas who had tread those stairs for half a century before me; and Mestre Lua Rasta, with waist-length dreads, a former performer with Mestre Canjiquinha, who played what he called "street *capoeira angola*" and made beautiful burnt-designed berimbaus in his Pelourinho workshop.

But I was restless and tired of the urban environment. What, I wondered, did capoeira look like outside a city?

Capoeira Contemporânea in the Recôncavo

Mestre Medicina lived and taught in a small town in the Recôncavo, a two-hour bus ride from Salvador and another site of historical capoeira memory.

For centuries, Afro-Bahians labored on sugar and tobacco plantations in the Recôncavo, a lush area around the greater bay. In some origin narratives, capoeira developed in the *senzalas* (living quarters for the laborers) on these plantations alongside *maculelê*, a stick or machete fighting dance that mimics the cutting of sugarcane. Kept alive through oral history—capoeira's fight disguised as dance and maculelê's dance disguised as the fight—historical evidence of these practices in this area comes from the early twentieth century. Folkloric dancer Mestre Popo (re-)invented maculelê in the 1940s, and the only Recôncavo *capoeira* for whom we have a name and scant biographical information was born around the time of abolition.

Besouro Mangangá was born in the town of Santo Amaro da Purificação—famous today as the birthplace of musical superstar siblings, Caetano Veloso and Maria Bethânia. Almost nothing is known about Besouro, beyond his nickname, Beetle, but capoeira lore abounds with anecdotes and songs commemorating his rebelliousness and supernatural powers. Beyond an obituary (murdered by knife in his twenties), the only historical record of Besouro is a 1918 judicial account of his expulsion from the army after brawling in a police station when trying to retrieve a berimbau from a pile of confiscated arms.[39] Legend has it that Besouro was a skilled knife fighter and had the ultimate *corpo fechado,* or protected body, impervious to bullets, and with the power to metamorphose into a beetle when pursued.

Riding into the lush green inland from Salvador, I was reminded how big Brazil was and how little I had seen beyond the capoeira roda. The bus dropped me in Cachoeira, a colonial town that has become the crowning jewel of African American "roots tourism" in Bahia. If Santo Amaro is a memory site for capoeira, Cachoeira is one for Afro-Brazilian religion, annually celebrated with the Festa da Boa Morte (Good Death Festival). The three-day festival in honor of the Virgin Mary is presided over by the ancient Black women of the Good Death Sisterhood. Black sisterhoods (and more commonly brotherhoods) were Catholic mutual aid societies that helped their members in everything from buying freedom to paying for burials. One of the few still existing of these organizations, the Sisterhood of Good Death has become a mecca for African Americans interested in diasporic culture. Every August 13–15, Cachoeira swarms with kente-cloth-wearing middle-aged African Americans, on roots tours that largely keeps the sisterhood afloat.[40]

On a weekday afternoon there was not much to see in the sleepy town, and I wondered how I would pass the time before catching a bus to nearby Muritiba for Mestre Medicina's evening class. As I wandered the cobblestone streets, I caught the twang of a berimbau floating from the upper windows of a colonial building. An old man sitting in a doorway gestured to the building's entrance around the corner. A group of boys and young women in their early twenties—the most female capoeiristas I had yet seen in a class in Brazil—were training while a group of tourists, sent by the Cachoeira Visitor Center, snapped pictures. The capoeiristas were delighted when they discovered I could play and invited me to train. Afterward they paraded me around town, stopping occasionally to drink water at friends' houses as the day was hot, showing me off—to the old woman at the Sisterhood of Good Death Museum, to the director of the language school where one of the students taught, and to the butchers at the market stall where another student worked—as the "American who plays capoeira."

In the late afternoon, Rosa, a delightful twenty-four-year-old music student who lived in Muritiba took me by bus and foot to Mestre Medicina's doorstep. I decided, as we walked along the town's dirt roads, with my first glimpse of stars since arriving in Brazil and the smell of open country and the warm night air wrapping me like a freshly laundered blanket, that I would move to a small town in the Recôncavo and train capoeira.

Mestre Medicina had the aura of an aging (and fit) Berkeley hippie with long graying hair and beard, a soft voice, and gentle manner. Besides a mestre, he was a gynecologist and obstetrician and father of five children. The youngest were seated with him around a kitchen table ladened with a lavish afternoon snack: buttered bread rolls, black sweet coffee, a pitcher of warm milk, coconut cake, baked cinnamon bananas, and thick rice pudding. This capoeira-playing family was bathed, in uniform, and ready to train.

The three-hour evening class was friendly, relaxed, and a mix of thirty young men, women, and children. It was well structured, integrating stretching, strengthening, and movement combinations. Mestre Medicina's style was clean and elegant with elongated kicks and acrobatics. I was familiar with this style as it was similar to Mestre Acordeon's whose academy in Berkeley I had frequented (an infraction for which Mestre Beiçola would have kicked me out of his group if his wife, a former student of Acordeon's, hadn't intervened). The style traces back to Mestre Bimba's lineage and would later be popularly known as *capoeira contemporânea*. Mestre Medicina's style, pedagogy, and students were a refreshing change from the capoeira I had been around in Rio and Salvador.

I tore myself away from Mestre Medicina's ample breakfast table the next morning. On the bus ride back to Salvador, I anxiously mulled over the idea that I had chosen (or been chosen by) the "wrong" capoeira style. Perhaps, I thought, I should live in Muritiba for a year and become Mestre Medicina's student. Life would be easier in a small town. I would learn quickly with his pedagogy and identify more with members of his group, many of whom were university students.

There was another possibility. Maybe capoeira was not in the cards for me at all. While the high, spinning kicks came easily because of my dance background, I found everything else challenging: the acrobatics, the strategizing, the speed and quick changes of direction and level. My long legs slowed me down and high center of gravity threw me off balance. Though I loved to train, I often felt self-conscious in the roda. And my knees hurt constantly in Brazil. I had suffered chondromalacia, a grinding of the patella on cartilage that creates painful inflammation, since I had begun capoeira. Sometimes after training I could barely walk. Perhaps capoeira just wasn't for me.

Before I left Salvador, this possibility would be vocalized by a Candomblé priestess.

Candomblé Convivência

Craving a physical and emotional break from capoeira, I started tagging along with my college friend, Eric, as he visited Candomblé terreiros. At 6'7" with waist-length, black, curly hair, Eric cut a distinctive figure in Salvador. He was there for a year of fieldwork on Candomblé for his PhD in anthropology. When he wasn't visiting terreiros, Eric and his guitar were playing open mics in Pelourinho, where he delighted crowds with Crosby, Stills & Nash and Green Day covers.

Besides Reed College, anthropology, and a love of folk and indie-punk rock, Eric and I had something else in common. Eric had just returned from his father's funeral in the United States. And I was still reeling from the death of my father and my brother in the space of a year. We didn't talk much about our losses, but I sensed that Eric was comforted to have a friend close by who understood his pain, especially during what can be the loneliness of fieldwork. While still grieving, I was also thinking forward to graduate school in anthropology. Eric offered to show me the ropes of fieldwork, and I began accompanying him to Candomblé ceremonies.

The terreiros that Eric frequented were not powerful, well-known ones, such as Gantois, formerly led by the priestess Mãe Menininha, and Ilê Axé Opô Afonjá under Mãe Stella. Some of the wealthier terreiros commanded large terrains of land with individual orixá temples nestled in the trees and lavish ceremonies open to the public. The terreiros I visited with Eric were small, neighborhood affairs, often just single rooms attached to the house where the *mãe de santo* (priestess) lived. Eric and I would add our shoes to the pile of flip-flops before entering, and inevitably, by the end of the evening, a neighborhood kid would be clomping around with glee in Eric's size fourteen basketball shoes.

At these terreiros, as in the market with Mestre DiMola, I was struck not by the exotic but the mundane. Even the appearance of gods summoned by the drumming, singing, and dancing had a familiar everydayness to them. The "living gods" as the orixás are called, are not the distant, celestial gods of the monotheistic religions. Like Greek and Roman gods, the orixás, who make up the pantheon of West African Yoruba gods in Candomblé, are humanized: they have virtues and vices and complicated backstories often involving love triangles, jealousies, and vengeance. When they appear during ceremonies, incorporated by initiates of the terreiro, they mingle with their devotees in an earthly convivência—bestowing hugs and whispering advice, displaying anger and making demands, being humorous and playful.

I remember the evening I was introduced to *caboclos,* indigenous Brazilian spirits who, like orixás, come down to heal and offer advice. Some coboclos have boisterous personalities that add levity and comic relief. It was toward the end of what was supposed to be a short ceremony on a weekday night. There were worried glances at the clock when a coboclo showed up in a large man who had been dancing all evening, remarkably graceful on his thick legs under a big belly. He immediately demanded a cigar. And then in a drunken strut with loud guffawing, he made his way over to the musicians. He leaned against the tallest drum, smoking and staring down the lead drummer, eliciting snickers around the room. With what must have been a command for louder, faster drumming, the caboclo staggered backward and danced for another forty-five minutes before departing.

Some elements of the rituals felt familiar to me. Unlike the more "African" terreiros, the ones we visited were mixed with Catholic ritual and iconography. Mãe Jorgina insisted that anyone initiated into her terreiro be baptized in the Catholic church, and she opened her ceremonies with a series of Our Father and Hail Mary prayers. Her altar and walls were adorned with depictions of orixás and their corresponding Catholic saints: Xangô, deity of thunder and lightning with Santa Barbara; Iemanjá, goddess of the sea with the Virgin Mary; Obaluaiê, god of disease and healing with St. Lazarus.

I had resisted my Catholic upbringing. It angered me to be told what to believe, how to act, and who my friends were. I felt constrained by my parochial elementary school and the same thirty classmates with whom I spent eight long years. Once I left home for college, I stopped practicing Catholicism, attending mass only at Christmas to please my mother. Yet now, in Mãe Jorgina's terreiro I was moved, sometimes to tears, by the rituals, the murmuring of prayers, the singing and palpable convivência of the attendees.

I was in a vulnerable place. Catholicism had reentered my life unexpectedly and unbidden two years before. On February 14, 1993, my brother, twenty-five and two years older than me, hung himself in the subbasement of my childhood home. Mark had been diagnosed with manic depression as a junior at Yale University, estranging first his roommates with his metaphysical rantings and all-night bike rides and later me, who could no longer recognize in the things Mark did and said and felt the brother who had been my best friend for twenty years.

During Mark's funeral arrangements, my anguished mother asked the priest if her oldest son would be denied heaven because of his suicide. Out of my own fog of grief, rage, and guilt, I yelled that no god would deny comfort in death to someone so racked by pain in life. Whatever God's decision, our fellow parishioners brought us comfort and support without judgment: for days they showed up on our doorstep with offerings of prayer and food until our kitchen table overflowed with casseroles, coffee, cakes, and cards.

One month shy of the one-year anniversary of Mark's suicide, my father died. On the evening of January 1, 1994, my mother called the parish priest. Father Patrick walked up to our house, sat with my father, then gently told us how to say goodbye and left. We each spent time alone with my father and then gathered around his bed. My younger brother, whose childhood bedroom my father occupied during his short battle with cancer, was only nineteen years old, yet had already experienced a lifetime of loss: as an adoptee he never knew his birth mother and culture; in high school his best friend died suddenly from heart failure; and he had helped carry his older brother's casket. Now he held my father's hand, and seeing him struggle to keep his eyes open, said, "It's okay Daddy. You can go."

The next morning, for a second time in less than a year, parishioners arrived with food and prayers. At the funeral mass I stood before them and told them how angry I was at God, whose existence I doubted, for taking both my brother and father. But I was also thankful, I said, to Father Patrick, the ritual of the mass, and all of them, for helping me let go. At the funeral a man we didn't know came to shake our hands. Awkward and tearful, he told us he was the parking garage attendant at the Department of Public Health where my father had been chief of an indoor air pollution lab, and where, he said, every day my father brightened his day by stopping by on his bicycle to say good morning.

Shattered by tragedy, it was no surprise I found comfort in the Candomblé ceremonies. Practitioners of Candomblé, likewise, turn to religion at times of individual difficulty. But they also come together to pray, sing, drum, and make offerings to the gods in an ongoing, everyday practice that recognizes not only individual but also social suffering. Though Candomblé, like capoeira, draws people across race and class, it is deeply rooted in the Black experience. The quiet greetings and hugs, prayers and songs, and whispered supplications to the gods bring solace in the aftermath of tragedy and fortitude in the face of the everyday social, medical, economic, and emotional hardships for so many in Brazil.

I was also drawn to Candomblé because of its tangible similarities to capoeira. The three sacred Candomblé drums mirror the three berimbaus in size and tone; the agogô that marks time in a capoeira roda calls down the gods; and verses about orixás, Catholic saints, and the sea appear in both Candomblé and capoeira songs. Capoeiristas and devotees of Candomblé show respect to the musicians by crouching before them and touching their head to the ground—and employ gestures and amulets to "close" or protect the body. And like rodas, candomblé ceremonies are gatherings to share sociality and food, offered first to the gods and then to the congregants. These ritual gatherings establish affinities and mutual obligations and distribute axé, the life force of Candomblé and capoeira.[41]

Perhaps I found in capoeira what I had not in the Catholic religion.

Obaluaiê and Xangô

I went one afternoon to Mãe Jorgina's consulting hours to have my *búzios* read. Búzios, or cowrie shells, are used in Candomblé divination. Determining the orixá who "owns one's head" through the shells is the first step in initiation, and also popular among laypeople. For initiates who are destined for incorporation, these are the orixás (usually a primary and secondary) who will manifest during ceremonies. Once the orixá descends, she or he is whisked away by attendants and adorned with the colors and trappings of the god: the metalworking tools for Ogum, god of war and iron; the whisk broom for Obaluaiê to spread or sweep away disease; or a mirror for vain Oxum, goddess of beauty and fresh water. Once adorned, the orixá dances, counsels, and heals the congregants. These are the gods initiates tend to for the remainder of their lives: avoiding foods the gods do not like, dressing in all white on certain days, wearing saint's protective beads tucked under everyday clothes, and making offerings. For a layperson, knowing one's orixás might help explain personality quirks and offer guidance in life.

I harbored a secret desire for Xangô, god of thunder, lightning, and justice, as my orixá. I assumed my spirit would be male because of my tomboyishness and passion for capoeira. And I had settled on Xangô after seeing the 1984 Brazilian film, *Quilombo,* that tells the story of Zumbi the warrior king of the independent African maroon society, the Palmares Quilombo, that resisted subjugation for most of the seventeenth century. In the film— a utopian and liberatory reimagining of Blacks in a Brazil that was at the time of its making emerging from a military dictatorship—Xangô appears in gleaming white feathers and shells. Incorporated by King Zumbi, Xangô does ginga and with a circling kick knocks out a quilombo invader.[42] How could I, or any capoeirista, resist Xangô? When I learned that some devotees consider Xangô to be a Sagittarius (like me) and that in Brazil his day of worship is Wednesday (the day of the week on which I was born), I thought these auspicious.

I waited in the large room with others also there for consultations. When Mãe Jorgina came out to receive me, she was walking slightly off-balance and her tone was deep and gravelly, her Portuguese inflected: she, now he, was a caboclo. In the consulting room we sat across from each other at a table holding a glass of water and sixteen búzios inside a bead necklace. He threw the búzios, contemplated their pattern and whether they lay "mouth" up or down, before informing me that he could only divine one of my orixás. The other would come from another land. At the next throw, he uttered,

"Obaluaiê."

My heart sank. Obaluaiê is a male god, but not one I had ever identified with. Oldest son of Nanã, mother of all orixás, Obaluaiê contracted a dis-figuring pestilence as a child. Unable to cure her son, Nanã left him by the sea where Iemanjá, goddess of saltwater and fertility, found him and nursed him back to health. So scarred in face and body was Obaluaiê (also known as Omolu), that Iemanjá wove him a raffia and shell covering. He would become the terrifying orixá of disease who always dances covered.

What an unsexy and scary god to have as mine!

But Obaluaiê is also orixá of the earth and all its healing properties. His name contains the honorific title Obá (king) and he is feared, respected, and loved. Perhaps he was sent to help heal my pain; Obaluaiê is not just a deity of physical affliction, but emotional suffering as well.[43] Worshippers turn to Obaluaiê for healing and understanding: "to worship Omolu, or to dance and pray for him, is not to pray for illness but to pray for an indication of the *meaning* of illness. . . . why those we love fall ill and die."[44] Perhaps Obaluaiê had come to me as a spiritual father on the death of my biological father, to lessen my pain and guilt and to assure me that he would guide my brother to a happier afterlife.

My grief and guilt could not reach those of my mother and father. No parent should have to survive the death, especially the suicide, of a child. I would not hear my mother laugh or sing for many years. It was a miracle when she began to laugh again: rusty and timid at first, and then building back to its wide-mouthed, full throttle pitch. Several years later she returned to singing in her church choir. But still to this day, my mother cannot bear to see a photo of Mark or utter his name aloud.

My father's grief consumed him entirely. His cancer was first detected in his lungs, in Chinese medicine the site of unresolved grief. Diagnosed nine months (the gestation of a baby) after my brother's suicide, he was gone six weeks later. He held out for the new year, telling us in his morphine delusions that there could not be "two plane crashes in one year." Perhaps he died for my mother. To comfort her in death in a way he never could in life. She believes her husband and son are together now in the afterlife. Or perhaps the burden of being the one to have found his oldest son hanging from the rafters was too much for a father to bear.

My guilt is more circumscribed than my parents', who must have agonized over every possible thing done wrong since his birth. For me, memories of my childhood and teenage years with Mark are, for the most part, happy; I find some comfort knowing I meant as much to him as he meant to me. My guilt pools around the last few years of his life when he descended into bouts of mania, paranoia, and depression. I was experiencing my own anxiety and insomnia as I struggled to write my senior thesis. Mark wrote me encouraging letters to which I didn't respond; I was too scared that I had what he had. My guilt lies here: Had I asked him for help, would he have felt less alone in his pain? Would helping me have helped him? Perhaps Obaluaiê brought my own mental anguish—a bit of Mark in me—to help me accept his suicide; to experience a fraction of the immense suffering it alleviated. But forgive me Obaluaiê, I struggle to find meaning in my brother's death.

The only sense I can find in Mark's suicide is realizing and fighting against the ways in which we as individuals and a society fail each other. In some genealogies, Xangô is brother to Obaluaiê. There is logic to this order: thunderous and fiery strength is needed for individual healing. But it is justice—also Xangô's dominion—that is needed for social ills to heal.

Twenty years after Mãe Jorgina's prediction, I would discover my secondary orixá in another land. On a trip to Cuba I had Ifâ divination read. The opélé seeds revealed Xangô.

The caboclo was restless, ready to be done. Before we ended, he asked if I had any questions for the búzios. I've always been fearful of what fortune-telling might reveal. But the question occupying my thoughts those days burst out:

"What is my future in capoeira?"

Suddenly the caboclo was gone, and Mãe Jorgina snapped back. In a clear, disapproving voice without consulting the shells, she said, "There shouldn't be a future for you. Capoeira's no good!"

I remembered that Edison Carneiro had told Ruth Landes that Candomblé priestesses did not like capoeiristas because they drank a lot of rum, didn't believe in God, were sometimes lawbreakers, and, most importantly, because there was "no place for women among them."[45]

I qualified my question.

"But I don't mean to make a living with capoeira. . . . or marry a capoeirista," I added quickly. "I want to study it as an anthropologist, like Eric."

Mãe Jorgina snorted and seemed somewhat appeased.

But I left the terreiro unnerved. Her response added to my growing confusion over my path in capoeira. Should I be training at all? If so, what style and with whom? And what was authentic capoeira? If authenticity was tied to the past, would the vadiação at the Mercado Modelo trump all as it was closest to the preinstitutionalized capoeira? Was it more authentic to play with malandragem or direct force, barefoot or with shoes? To play in Salvador's colonial center near Mestres Bimba and Pastinha's former schools, in a quiet Rocôncavo town haunted by the ghost of Besouro, or on the streets of Rio where maltas once rumbled?

Xangô and Obaluaiê, guide me!

Leaving Bahia

Despite, or maybe because of, conflicted feelings over style and authenticity that Bahia stirred in me, I knew that Rio was my city. Rio, with its variable and cosmopolitan cityscape thrilled me in a way Salvador did not, and it was where I felt connected to a capoeira family.

I would return briefly over the years to Salvador and its transformations. Pelourinho's renovation was completed by 2012, with all but six hundred of its original four thousand residents evicted.[46] In the once seedy Praça da Sé at the entrance to Pelourinho, tourists could step behind life-size cutouts to be photographed as a baiana in a full skirt and headwrap or a capoeirista with dreadlocks and berimbau. Venture further into Pelourinho and in the Terreiro de Jesus square, real baianas selling acarajé and capoeiristas in a roda will snap a selfie with you for a charge.

Move to the heart of Pelourinho and the simulacra unravels: in 1998 the grungy reggae bars were relocated to the Reggae Plaza, a sleek, whitewashed outdoor venue that charged an entrance fee. In similar digs at Garotinho's Piscinão and its poorly veiled urban planning strategies of racial segregation, the locals took to calling the Reggae Plaza "Bob Marley's Jail" and the "Black

People's Cage."[47] Since 2011, the Reggae Plaza has been shuttered and used as an informal garbage dump, promises of renovations abandoned.

Forte Santo Antônio had a similar face-lift. In 2007 it was inaugurated as the Capoeira Fort, complete with museum, parking lot, bathrooms, electricity, and security. At one point the fort housed seven different capoeira groups all vying, alongside several new schools in Pelourinho, for recognition and patronage from the tourists and capoeira pilgrims who visit for a day, a week, a month, or a year.

On one of my returns a Bahian capoeirista complained to me:

"Everyone in Salvador is *sugando* someone."

The foreign capoeiristas "sucking" experience and knowledge from the local capoeiristas and the local capoeiristas sucking money and the possibility of travel or life abroad from the foreign capoeiristas; and both sucking sex and romance from one another. A cynical view, for sure, and representative of just one of the many capoeira experiences one can have in Salvador. Nor is "sucking" experience or resources limited to Bahian capoeira. But Salvador does put under the spotlight the tensions of capoeira as a global commodity.

As for the capoeiristas I knew in the 1990s: Mestre Curió eventually moved his academy to the Capoeira Fort and joined the great international capoeira network with affiliated groups in Mexico. Mestre DiMola I would never see again. In 2002, he died from knife wounds inflicted by a pregnant woman in the street while he was out walking with his wife on the evening of his forty-ninth birthday. A jilted lover? Mother of his baby?

In my memory Mestres DiMola and Curió, so different in personality and play, are equally "authentic" and "traditional" capoeirista. Perhaps, as Alma Guillermoprieto suggests in her book, *Samba*, "tradition is often simply the training provided by years of endurance."[48] These mestres, like Mestres Pastinha and Bimba and many others over the years, endured despite all odds as Black men in Salvador, in dedicating their lives to capoeira. Mestre Curió in the music and high theatrics of a folkloric capoeira in his academy; Mestre DiMola in playing a rough capoeira in the streets, hustling tourists, drinking cachaça, and dying at the point of a knife.

Authenticity is not about style, location, or historical continuity. For me, at least, it is about convivência and the connection that comes from being-in-something with others. In her discussion of the dynamic inheritance of West African dance from one generation to the next, anthropologist Adrienne Cohen argues that "what remained constant was not the form of the dance or the particular identity it signaled but rather the relationship by which dance emblematizes and authenticates persons. . . . the affective relationship between people and cultural products that makes all inheritance meaningful."[49] Similarly, in his discussion of racial identity, anthropologist John L. Jackson Jr. offers the concept of *sincerity* over authenticity. Authenticity, on the one hand, presumes a subject-object relationship, the subject wielding authenticity as a measuring stick to distinguish real from fake and perpetuating stereotypes that rob the "object," or other individual, of agency. *Sincerity,* on the other hand, encourages subject-subject interaction between "social interlocuters who presume another's humanity, interiority, and subjectivity."[50]

My berimbau was "authentic" not for what it was; I never could string or play it, and I eventually cut it up into sticks for maculelê. But I kept the end of the no-longer-a-berimbau that has burned into it my name and the date Mestre DiMola and I made it, because it marks my brief convivência with Mercado Modelo capoeiristas. Similarly, I had an "authentic" Candomblé experience not because of the particular terreiro I attended; Mãe Jorgina's terreiro with its mixing in of Catholic rituals would score low on the authenticity scale in terms of purity. My experience was real—sincere and heartfelt—because it evoked emotions that connected my own experience of loss to the personal and collective losses of others in the terreiro.

Returning to Rio the next year, I would deepen my convivência to carioca capoeira and capoeiristas. And I would continue to grapple with tensions around style and technique, this time played out, quite literally, on my body.

3

AN ANTHROPOLOGIST IN THE RODA

RIO DE JANEIRO, 1997

"Alôôô!"

Mestre Touro's rich, melodic voice through the telephone transported me from my fifteenth floor apartment in New York City to the streets of Rio de Janeiro.

In 1996 I moved to New York City to begin a doctoral program in Anthropology and Education at Columbia University. As an undergraduate, I had eagerly taken my first anthropology classes. I enjoyed writing essays on stone axes and Marxist theory and listening to tales of fieldwork in faraway places, but, ironically, had trouble seeing the social relevance of the discipline. I had become involved in education and social justice, spending my summers working at inner-city youth programs. I loved to read and write and was fired up by my literature classes that moved from John Milton to George Eliot, Mariama Bâ to Chicano comics. I became an English major and unwittingly wrote a partially ethnographic senior thesis that analyzed novels by Toni Morrison and Sandra Cisneros alongside stories I had gathered from the children I worked with in the summers.

After several post-college years of teaching and international travel, I settled on a graduate program that would combine my interests. I decided to return to Brazil for my first summer of fieldwork to explore capoeira as a possible dissertation topic. At Mestre Beiçola's suggestion, I decided to stay with Mestre Touro who had moved to a larger house, liked hosting American capoeiristas, and was well connected in the Zona Norte.

Fieldwork and capoeira would be complicated for me that summer. I was in a double transition: I was undertaking my first fieldwork—a rite of passage for novice anthropologists—and feeling woefully underprepared; and I had joined a new capoeira group in New York City, which was reshaping my capoeira style and identity. I had seen a grainy video of Mestra Edna Lima, the only female capoeira master in the United States at the time, playing in

Brazil and was impressed with her high, fast kicks and ability to hold her own in an all-male roda. A pretty woman in her thirties with dreadlocks and warm smile, she had been given the title of mestra by her teacher, Mestre Tabosa in her hometown of Brasília. By the time I began training with Edna, she had affiliated with ABADÁ-Capoeira, one of the fastest growing international capoeira networks under the direction of Mestre Camisa in Rio de Janeiro.

Edna was tough, having risen through the male-dominated capoeira ranks in Brazil. She was a fierce fighter and demanding teacher. Also a black belt in karate, she had come to the United States in the 1980s to participate in martial art tournaments and eventually inserted herself into fast-paced New York City: she played a part in the 1989 B-rate film *Rooftops,* which told a story of cross-fertilization between capoeira and breakdancing; and her teaching took her all over the city, from Harlem public schools to the Alvin Ailey Dance Studios to the posh Chelsea Piers Health Club, where she once introduced me to Brazilian actress Sônia Braga.

Capoeira popularity was reaching its height in the late 1990s, and I trained alongside upward of forty students, men and women in their twenties and thirties, and as ethnically diverse as the city: Dominican, Puerto Rican, Brazilian, Haitian, Japanese, Chinese, Israeli, Italian, Russian, French. After a three-hour training on Friday nights, we'd eat pierogi at a Polish diner, stop in Times Square to play capoeira with a group of b-boys drumming on buckets, and then dance salsa to a cigar-smoking Cuban band in a cramped East Village bar. I would collapse on the subway at 3:00 a.m., wearing my second sweat of the night after seven hours of moving to the thrum of percussive music.

Edna taught very differently from Beiçola. Trainings began with high intensity combinations performed in lines facing the mirrors, more advanced students in the front and beginners in back. I was sweating and breathing hard within the first ten minutes. Partner work was a rapid-fire exchange of attacks and counterattacks followed by an energetic roda: the syncopated clapclap-clap, the same as used in samba, that Beiçola had taught us was replaced with a driving, evenly paced 1-2-3 clapping. Edna rarely played with us, instead keeping a strong rhythm going on the gunga and leading us through a repertoire of recent songs composed by ABADÁ capoeiristas.

I enjoyed the challenge of this new style and pedagogy that was familiar to my dancer's body. The elongated lines and sharper movement were easier to incorporate than the slow rootedness of Beiçola's style. The theatrics and trickery of malandragem, so elusive to me, was replaced by the aesthetics of gymnastics and the straightforward competitiveness of sport. This was a precision technique—shaped, corrected, and imprinted through the mirror rather than felt in the body and reflected in one's partner. Progress was linear, uniform, and direct. I gauged where I would be in a few years by looking at the more advanced students in the group. Edna was getting a degree in physical education and would throw out words like "technique" and "efficiency" and sometimes had us check our pulses. She manipulated our bodies with her hands to create the angles and lines that defined "proper" style. My ginga eventually shifted from a relaxed, upright swing, arms loose at my sides, to a low, grounded stance, muscles tensed, shoulders hunched forward, arms up protecting my face.

Edna encouraged me to break the "bad habits" of my previous style, a formidable task akin to transforming one's posture or walk. I had to regain awareness of movement that had become automatic, break it, and then rebuild it in a similar but different form. I still felt loyal to Mestre Beiçola and Grupo Besouro and told Edna that I wasn't ready to change affiliations. She told me to take my time, train with her group, and see how I felt. This left me in an awkward place between style and group loyalty, which would cause problems for me that first summer of fieldwork.

Back to Our Lady of Penha

Arriving at the airport with a backpack stuffed with clothes, capoeira uniform, notebooks, tape recorder, and camera, I was nervous that Mestre Touro wouldn't be there to meet me. Pre-social media and cell phones, I had spoken only once more with him to give him my flight information. I cleared immigration, stepped through the frosted sliding doors, and there he was standing next to Mestre André, younger and with a car.

On the twenty-minute ride to his house, Touro remarked that one of the advantages of living in Penha was its proximity to the international airport. Not, I thought, that working-class cariocas had many chances to go to the airport—domestic and international airfare still prohibitively high. But in the next moment Mestre Touro told me he was leaving in two days for the United States for a month to visit a student who had split off from Mestre Beiçola and formed his own group. I was dismayed. My first unexpected fieldwork roadblock—my chief research subject gone! Ironic but not surprising. Capoeira and capoeiristas were rapidly becoming transnationally mobile. My own research would also eventually seep beyond the borders of the Zona Norte, Rio de Janeiro, and Brazil, becoming the "multisited" work of many anthropologists today.

Mestre Touro chuckled at my dismay and said that his girlfriend Bete and his kids would take care of me. We arrived at the new house, in spitting distance to Our Lady of Penha Church. An imposing three levels behind a high wall, the house stood on a hill at the back edge of Penha with a western view of the suburb, which sits in a bowl surrounded by favela-dotted hills. Across the street, nicely maintained houses and cars suggested a more affluent neighborhood than that of Touro's last house, now exclusively his capoeira academy. The new house, however, had several bullet holes in the walls, evidence that it abutted a favela.

The nicest feature of the house was a veranda and large window with wooden shutters that when thrown open allowed conversation to flow between the front room and porch. Beyond this the house was rather dingy and sparsely furnished. A narrow hallway, flanked by two bedrooms and a bathroom, led to the kitchen with an orange rust–streaked refrigerator rumbling like a tiger. A cement staircase, so steep and narrow I had to go up on tiptoe, led to an unfinished second floor with bunk beds, capoeira trophies, and weight lifting equipment. Bete later confided to me that the house's shabby sparseness was not due to lack of money—Touro made a decent salary as a maintenance man in the city council building downtown. Rather, she said, it was because the children were rambunctious, and Touro preferred to spend money on beer and meat for his monthly rodas.

The kids—Janaína 15, Aline 13, and Jorginho 10—were gathered in the living room watching me intently when Touro asked me where I would like to sleep. Caught off guard, I suggested the spare bed in Janaína's room rather than the one upstairs so as not to break my neck coming down in the night to use the bathroom. Janaína leaped off the couch looking pleased and led me into her room to show me where to put my clothes and which short, narrow, hard bed would be mine for three months of tossing and turning, my feet dangling off the end.

The Baptism

"Are you ready to go?"

Bete was serving me a plate of beans, rice, and chicken from pots on the stove.

"Touro, she just arrived! She doesn't want to go to capoeira!" Bete turned to me. "Aren't you tired from your trip? You know Touro only leaves an event when the trash is taken out!"

"Not true!" Touro said. "I leave when the beer is finished!"

I was tired but eager to start fieldwork, even though I had no idea what that meant. How, exactly, was this summer supposed to be different from my last summer in Rio? In my methods course we had talked about participant-observation, snowball sampling, interviews, and field notes. But it all felt rather abstract now that I was sitting in the kitchen with Touro and his family. I decided to follow the practical and attainable advice of famous anthropologist Clifford Geertz, that fieldwork is "deep hanging out." Training capoeira, going to rodas, and copious beer and conversation would be my research.

The event, a *batizado* (baptism) and *troca de cordas* (change of cords) was in Nova Iguaçu. Driving through the concrete warren of suburbs, some with an abandoned or bombed-out feel, that make up the Baixada Fluminense, I realized the relative wealth and infrastructure of the Zona Norte. The large sports complex where the event was being held, however, was breezy and well-maintained. On an enormous outdoor court seventy-five capoeiristas crowded around a roda vying to play, easily outnumbering the small audience in the bleachers. Taking a quick tally of cord colors, I realized there were more mestres and instructors there to help "baptize" than students.

Baptizing a student symbolizes their rebirth as a capoeirista. The ritual is performed by a mestre or instructor who, while playing with the novice, uses a move that will bring them to the ground. The mestre—or designated godmother or godfather, perhaps a relative—then knots the student's first cord around their waist, symbolizing their new identity and affiliation with the group. At batizados other students receive their next level cord. Many of the Zona Norte groups follow a graduation system created in 1972 with the first Capoeira Federation. The braided cords mimic the colors of the Brazilian flag: combinations of green, yellow, and blue for students, and a four level mestre cord, braided white with green, yellow, blue, ending in pure white, once a mestre has reached a certain number of years of mastery. In truth, this system, and others that have since developed, are subjective and flexible and often a source of dispute.

While ostensibly for the students, batizados also showcase the hosting mestre. Every detail—the number of participating students and guests, venue, T-shirt design, punctuality, after party, and quality of games—will be scrutinized and evaluated by those attending. An important and stressful moment for the hosting mestre is to make sure everyone of rank is properly introduced. Those introduced will often take the opportunity to thank and praise the host and announce their own upcoming events.

Among the more than twenty capoeiristas called to the microphone that day was a thin, middle-aged mestre with a reddish-brown beard and hair balding into a monk's ring. Dressed in a plaid shirt, jeans, and flip-flops he looked more like an archaeologist than a capoeirista. This, to my surprise, was the legendary Mestre Camisa I had heard so much about. He spoke at length about the rising popularity of capoeira and invited everyone to the second iteration of the ABADÁ World Games (Jogos Mundiais), a biennial event that brings together international capoeiristas for a week of workshops and competitions. This year's theme, Camisa said, would be women in capoeira. I looked around at the majority male capoeiristas and wondered how ABADÁ's gender makeup differed from that of groups in the Zona Norte.

At the barbecue afterward, Touro kept my glass filled with beer and paraded me around to meet the mestres. I received more invitations to trainings, rodas, and batizados than I could possibly attend in three months. I introduced myself to Mestre Camisa.

"You've got to come to the World Games!" he told me. "You will see capoeira as it is supposed to be played: effective and controlled. No fights! And you are going to see some good female players."

Looking around, I saw the number of women had shrunk to just a few young female students and the mestres' wives or girlfriends, of whom only a few had on uniforms. I introduced myself to Monica, an advanced student in her husband's group, who had a four-year-old on her lap. I asked if she came to a lot of events.

She laughed, and replied: "This is our fourth this weekend—two batizados, a roda, and a school presentation. On weekends I pack a bag with everything we might need because I don't know when we'll get home."

Monica raised the piece of grilled meat that she had just taken from a circulating platter. "At least we fill up on meat! I save money on food during the week because I know we will get our fill on the weekend."

I asked Monica about Mestre Camisa's announcement.

"There are a lot more women in ABADÁ and other Zona Sul groups. Life is easier there. Women have more time and money for capoeira and working out in gyms. And lots of them have dance or gymnastics backgrounds. Poor girls here in the Zona Norte don't have those opportunities. It's harder for us to get to an advanced level. You might see a lot of girls in class, but by the time they become teenagers they drop out. They get jobs or start having kids. Or their boyfriends get jealous!"

At a circle of mestres, André was showing off the shirt I had given him as a thank you for picking me up at the airport. "Look! There's even printing on the sleeves—little capoeiristas!"

Everyone admired the vibrant colors and computer-generated designs both front and back. Mestre Beiçola's new hobby was silk-screening, and his shirts looked professional compared to others on display that day, many with simple hand-drawn group logos and names.

Mestre Nacional, with a belly to rival Touro's, and a bulbous W. C. Fields nose, snatched the shirt away from André and stuffed it down his stretchy capoeira pants. Catching my eye, he said in a loud voice, "Rio de Janeiro is full of thieves. You have to be careful here."

Mestre André turned to me. "Camarão, promise him a shirt so he'll give mine back!"

I hesitated, worried I would run out of shirts.

"I don't make promises," I said.

The mestres laughed, nodding their heads in approval.

"Malandra! She will do well in Brazil!" Mestre Nacional said.

I accompanied Mestre Touro in beer and conversation until my eyelids drooped. Mestre André took me back to the car where I slept in the backseat, waking in the dark to Mestre Touro swaying back to the car. I was relieved to see that Mestre André had not been drinking—Brazilian drunk driving laws are strict, and police road checks in Rio frequent—and again in possession of his T-shirt gift.

Everyday Life and Violence in the Zona Norte

Mestre Touro left two days later for California with (in contrast to my over-stuffed backpack) a half empty athletic bag containing a few capoeira uniforms and changes of clothes. It wasn't until he was back that I realized how relatively quiet the house was without him. Touro was a loud disciplinarian with the kids he had been raising solo since his wife left when Jorginho was two years old. Touro's dictatorial stubbornness extended beyond his family. Over the years, I would witness Touro's fights and split-ups with students, colleagues, and friends for months, or even years. People complained that Touro was "brutish," "ignorant," and "uneducated." Though he certainly could be harsh, Touro's dedication as a single father in successfully usher-ing his children into adulthood—by no means a given for poor families in Brazil—attests to his true character.

Janaína, Touro's oldest child, was high strung and prone to dramatic out-bursts. She often butted heads with her father, would fly off the handle, and then mope sullenly. Despite her initial pleasure to have me as a roommate (Touro had given me the choice as the kids had been fighting over where I'd sleep), I never knew whether she liked me. Tall and angular with a large smile and big front teeth, she looked more like her uncle than her father.

Her capoeira nickname, Dentinha (Little Tooth) was both an ironic reference and an homage to Touro's brother, Mestre Dentinho, a legendary and singular capoeirista. Aline and Jorginho were their father's spitting image in appearance, if not personality. Stocky, strong bodies and round faces, they were perpetually cheerful and giggly. Jorginho had also inherited his father's keen intelligence and took me up on my offer of English lessons while working to improve my still stumbling Portuguese.

On Tuesday and Thursday evenings, we headed over to the old house, now capoeira academy. The kids trained like their personalities: Janaína prone to injury and dramatics; Aline *levava jeito* (had a knack), but giggled too much; and Jorge with cheerful gusto, his nimble and strategic game graced with a smile. Class was rather haphazard: we'd practice a sequence of moves and then another, sometimes forgetting to do both sides. The other students were a ragtag bunch: Tiririca, a northeastern immigrant in his thirties, who I suspected did not read and write, worked in a bakery and brought fresh bread to Touro's house; Pudgy thirteen-year-old Bruna trained half-heartedly, finally admitting she only came because her father made her; small, speedy Simone who looked thirteen but was eighteen; seventeen-year-old Tartaruga, whose parents didn't support his practice after witnessing a student get his teeth knocked out during a batizado; and a former student whose flamboyant gayness provoked constant teasing, but who nonetheless found some kind of shelter and convivência in Touro's group.

Twenty-two-year-old Fatal was the most advanced student and taught classes while Touro was away. He was doing his obligatory two years of military service and so rose at 4:00 a.m. every day to ride his motorcycle to the barracks in São Cristóvão near downtown Rio. Thoughtful and considerate, Fatal hated both military service and his nickname. Touro had given him the name the very first day Claudio had shown up in the academy, an awkward twelve years old. Touro taught him the upside-down spinning "half-moon" kick, capoeira's most distinctive and potentially dangerous attack. If the heel of the kicking foot makes contact, it can break a rib or knock someone out. Remarkably, and unexpectedly, Claudio achieved this outcome on his first try, sending another student to the hospital. Though the student was fine, Claudio's new nickname stuck because of his "fatal" kick.

As with training with Mestre Sardinha and his students the year before, I witnessed again the "everyday violence" of poverty, illness, poor healthcare, crime, and policing for so many in Rio.[1] Fatal lived in Chatuba, a favela visible from Mestre Touro's academy and part of the Complexo do Alemão, an enormous conglomeration of favelas that straddles the hills connecting a number of suburbs. In the 1990s and early 2000s the area was notorious for its drug traffickers, and in 2011 Chatuba would become one of Rio's first favelas to be occupied and "pacified" by the military in a failed attempt to "clean up" the city before the Olympic Games.

In the few months I was there, three of Fatal's friends died in Chatuba. I visited the favela only a few times, when Fatal deemed it safe enough. The house where he lived with his mother, sister, and nine-year-old brother, like the surrounding houses, was made out of hollow, orange-red bricks; when there is a little extra cash flow, families buy more bricks and mortar to add on another room or floor. "*Está em obra,*" or "it's under construction," is a common excuse for appearances. The room Fatal shared with his brother Dudu was on the top floor. And though incomplete, the space provided greater air flow than the dark rooms below and stunning views of the favela. Fatal pointed to the top of the hill, where the houses thinned and thick vegetation took over.

"That's where the *donos do morro* live. They build big houses up there to hide out from the police. Some of them haven't been down to the asfalto in years."

In these mountain strongholds, difficult to access, drug traffickers, or "owners of the hill," hid out and assassinated enemies. In 2002 a well-known reporter, Tim Lopez, was murdered on one of those hills while investigating allegations of child prostitution at a baile funk party, like the ones held in the open-air recreation space just below Fatal's house. Like many favela residents, Fatal hated the drug-trafficker-sponsored parties that went on at ear-splitting decibels all night while drugs and firearms freely circulated. Years later I would go to a baile funk in Chatuba: the assault of the music from the towering wall of speakers rattled my body for days afterward alongside memories of teenage girls gyrating in skintight shorts and bikini tops and adolescent boys raising automatic weapons over their heads when 2:00 a.m. fireworks and gunshots reverberated from the hills to celebrate a drug trafficker's birthday.

When she wasn't staying with Touro, Bete returned to her house, also in the Complexo do Alemão in Bonsucesso, a suburb adjacent to Penha. Short, with tan skin and eyes the color of Caribbean seawater, Bete suffered terrible asthma, which she blamed on the high levels of pollution in Bonsucesso. Once a sugarcane producing area, the suburb was Rio's industrial center until the 1980s. Bete lived near the old Coca-Cola factory down a narrow alleyway, where smoke rising from the stalls serving grilled meat mixed with pollution in a yellow haze like Dickensian London. The night I spent there sleeping in a low-ceiling windowless bedroom next to

Bete's teenage daughter, Deborah, and twenty-two-year-old son, Emerson, I woke up drenched in sweat, gasping for air, with a panicked sensation that the house was about to collapse, bringing the favela above crashing down on us.

Shortly before Touro came home, Emerson brought his eight-month-pregnant girlfriend to live with us. Nineteen-year-old Michelle had dated a drug trafficker before Emerson and had fled the favela for her grandparents' village when her jealous former boyfriend cut off her long hair. Now she had come back to Rio to give birth. Fearing for Michelle's life if she returned to the favela, Bete brought her to Touro's house.

Anxiety and stress, along with fog or smog, worsened Bete's asthma. I came home one foggy, damp night to find Bete sitting outside a neighbor's house struggling to breathe. Touro's fierce watchdog, Jubi, who terrified Bete, had not let her in the gate, and she needed her nebulizer. I managed to grab and chain Jubi and get Bete inside, only to find that her nebulizer wasn't working. With the help of Janaína and a neighbor, we got Bete to the over-crowded public hospital, where she spent the night with little more attention than a saline drip.

No-Holds-Barred Capoeira

The violence with which people lived daily in the Zona Norte seeped into capoeira. A fatality in a roda eight months before had led to increased debates and accusations. In October 1996, in the mountainous town of Petrópolis near Rio de Janeiro, a roda heated up with games fast and furious. A capoeirista received a kick to his side that knocked him out of the roda. Winded, but able to walk, he didn't realize the kick had broken a rib and punctured his lung. A few hours later he died. A recording of the game looped for days behind television newscasters, and headlines read "capoeira roda murders."[2]

The kick that killed the young man, a *ponteira*, is a forward thrust like the *benção*. But unlike the benção, which is delivered with a flat foot in a pushing movement, the ponteira strikes with the ball of the foot in an upward motion. If directed at a sensitive part of the body it can do fatal damage.

The incident, though ruled an accident, fueled an already heated debate over appropriate movement in capoeira. In 1995, a Zona Norte capoeirista, Mestre Hulk, was victorious in a Vale Tudo (no-holds-barred) competition in Brazil. As muscle-bound as his cartoon namesake, Mestre Hulk had created a major upset when, twenty-three seconds into the match, he knocked out the favored fighter, a Gracie trained jiu-jitsu champion. The victory made

Mestre Hulk a local hero among Zona Norte capoeiristas but was also polarizing. Integrating kicks and grappling techniques from other fighting forms became popular in trainings and rodas, especially among the younger generation. Older mestres disapproved of this "corruption" of style, which they claimed was creating a more aggressive capoeira.

Looking to direct blame, some capoeiristas called for a "boycott" of ABADÁ.[3] Though the victim (and not the aggressor) at the event in Petrópolis had been an ABADÁ student, many blamed the group anyway, claiming their presence had intensified the aggressivity of the roda. ABADÁ students had a reputation in Rio for being dangerously competitive with their technically effective high-speed kicks and takedowns.

The 1990s also marked the growing professionalization of capoeira.[4] As the practice's popularity increased abroad, there was a blowback effect in Brazil where it became more mainstream. No longer only offered in working-class neighborhoods and favelas, capoeira was now in health clubs, private nursery schools, and universities throughout Rio de Janeiro. Vying for jobs, especially in the lucrative Zona Sul, capoeiristas were preoccupied with keeping capoeira's reputation clean and not scaring off the new clientele, middle- and upper-class women and children. Capoeira groups designed T-shirts with slogans such as "Practice capoeira, not violence" and organized discussions and workshops around pedagogy and professional comportment.

While there was consensus among many carioca capoeiristas that violence needed to be addressed, there was little agreement as to what this violence looked like and whether the practice was more or less dangerous than earlier capoeira. For some, capoeira of the 1970s and 1980s was a hypermasculine space of aggression. Stories circulated about Rio's infamously rough street rodas, where capoeiristas showed up to fight or steal instruments. The most notorious was the Central Station roda where someone once died of a gunshot wound.[5] More common were knife wounds—several of which older mestres proudly showed me. For this older generation, such extreme injury was uncommon back then as capoeiristas generally played roughly but without intention to do real damage. Today, they complained, capoeiristas trained to do harm.

Capoeira *Bambas*

"My capoeira is folkloric."

Touro was home and I was playing the anthropologist, jotting down his words in my notebook:

"In my time, that is, when I was first recognized as a mestre, there were fifty mestres in Rio. And I knew them all. Now there are five hundred or more, and most of them are shit." Touro waved his hand in the space between us with an irritated dismissiveness.

"These young mestres don't know anything about capoeira. They don't know how to play with a straight razor between their toes like the old *capoeiras* did. They play with aggression, not elegance."

I had seen Touro demonstrate a game with razors at one of his rodas, Jorginho nimbly evading his sweeps with the blade.

"Used to be I could recognize a capoeirista from a distance just by his swagger," Touro said, sounding like French sociologist Marcel Mauss who, in theorizing what he called "techniques of the body," claimed to tell a Frenchman by the way he walked.[6]

"Now they just look like athletes pumped up on steroids."

Muscle-building supplements had become popular among some capoeiristas.

I asked Touro who gave him the title of mestre.

"*O povo.* The people. Back then, if you were good at capoeira, had disciples and fans who liked to see you play, then people started calling you mestre in the street. I got that title when I was fourteen years old!"

Like many of the older mestres I spoke with, I never knew how much of Touro's narratives were embellished—years shaved off or added on, reputations padded, events hyperbolized.

I asked, "But didn't you have a teacher?"

"Of course! But only until I was fourteen. I learned from my friend Celso Pepe, who was Mestre Leopoldina's student. But then Celso moved to Copacabana, and I took over the classes and people started calling me mestre."

Touro had been five when he first saw capoeira at the roda da Penha. The roda, one of the oldest in Rio, is held at the foot of the church during the Festa da Penha, a religious festival held every October since the 1800s. Touro had moved to Penha with his parents and sixteen siblings from the neighboring state of Espírito Santo. Poverty and crowded conditions at home drove him to the streets. He referred to himself as an "illiterate street kid," even though a dock worker and his wife who already had four children eventually adopted him informally. Touro referred to the elderly couple, who still lived in Penha, as his parents and his kids' grandparents.

"Celso and I started messing around with capoeira in this empty lot where all the market trucks parked. I helped Seu Rafael at his stall, and he let me sleep in his truck at night. Then we moved to a gym on the Rua Nicarágua. That was better, because the place was owned by a policeman. Capoeira back then was still considered something for *vadios* (delinquents). I was arrested a number of times. Even though I was a minor, they'd lock me up for the night in the Invernada de Olaria. Just for playing capoeira, or sometimes just for carrying a berimbau in the street!"

The Invernada de Olaria, today the sixteenth precinct of the Military Police, was a notorious place of torture and disappearance when it was opened in the 1960s at the beginning of the military dictatorship. Later, the infamous death squads—violent vigilante groups of off-duty policemen—came out of the Invernada.

"And then in 1964 I formed my own group, Corda Bamba. A *bamba* is an expert in capoeira or samba, or whatever they do. And we come from the best. Mestre Leopoldina was the last of the original bambas of carioca capoeira. Mestre Leopoldina learned from Quinzinho, and Quinzinho learned from the Guaiamus!"

Touro raised his index finger skyward as if God were his witness.

Mestre Leopoldina, who died in 2007 at age seventy-four, was indeed recognized by many as Rio's last living tie to early twentieth-century capoeira. Little is known about Quinzinho, Mestre Leopoldina's alleged teacher. Touro's claim that Quinzinho learned from Guaiamus, one of the largest and most famous capoeira maltas eradicated in 1889, is highly unlikely, as Quinzinho was only in his twenties when Leopoldina met him in the 1950s. Nevertheless, Mestre Leopoldina, often dressed in an all-white suit, tie, dress shoes, and straw fedora, did channel the malandros of Rio's belle epoque. He even used the erudite Portuguese word, *flanar,* to describe his first encounter with capoeira when he was "bumming around" (*flanando*) the Central Brazil train station. As a kid he sold candy in the station and acquired his nickname after the locomotive whose sound he used to imitate.[7]

One day, as Mestre Leopoldina narrates it, he was watching two kids brawl in the train station, when an older youth jumped between them. Rising up and spinning on one arm and executing other "strange movements in the air," the youth said, "You two want to fight, then fight like this!"[8] When Leopoldina learned that this "fight" was capoeira and that the youth taught it in a nearby favela, he sidled up to him, buying him a beer one day, a shot of cachaça the next, until Quinzinho invited him to train. The apprenticeship was short, as a year later Quinzinho was arrested and died in prison.

After Quinzinho's death, Mestre Leopoldina trained with Artur Emídio, a recent arrival from Itabuna, a city in southern Bahia. Mestre Touro laid claim to a pure carioca capoeira lineage dating back to the nineteenth century, but it was probably Artur Emídio, and thus a Bahian style of capoeira, that most influenced Mestre Leopoldina—and subsequently Touro's and most capoeira in the Zona Norte.

Whatever the truth of his lineage, Touro was proud to be a "folkloric" capoeirista. He used the adjective to distinguish his capoeira from that of the new international megagroups, disapproving of their more mechanical and uniform style. He particularly enjoyed critiquing ABADÁ, knowing I was training with the group in New York. He called Mestre Camisa "Camisinha," or "Little Shirt," his former nickname until the word became popular slang for condom. As Camisa's international success grew, making him a capoeira celebrity, Touro and other Zona Norte capoeiristas critiqued, but often also admired and claimed intimacy with him. Touro boasted that Camisinha, five years younger than him, used to crash in his *barraca* (hut, or slang for home) when he first moved to Rio as a teenager.

Touro complained that these international groups churned out identical capoeiristas with a robotic ginga. He compared this ginga—raising his arms in front of his face and stiffly shifting them back and forth—to his own and his brother's. Dentinho and Touro had grown up playing together, but their capoeira was radically different. Though younger than Touro, Dentinho looked older with a rail-thin body, Fidel Castro beard, and a condition that left his face increasingly covered in bumps. He had never held down a full-time job, scraping together a living working "security" at a local bar, which seemed to entail sitting at a table drinking beer all day. Dentinho was legendary in Penha for running in the heat of summer from the suburbs to Copacabana beach, barefoot, in a speedo swim suit, and his T-shirt wrapped around his head like a keffiyeh (a headwrap he also donned in the roda). His capoeira, which like Touro he called "folkloric," was unlike anything I had ever seen. He leaped, strutted, pounced, contorted, and threw his body around the roda like a rag doll or canon-breaking postmodern dancer. He grinned, cackled, and yelled, mocking his opponent and defying all conventions. Unpredictable and dramatic, he could also be as fierce and rough as Touro.

Besides the mechanization of capoeira, Touro resisted its commercialization. He complained that mestres were giving away titles and cords in order to build bigger groups faster. He had stopped wearing his own mestre cord, saying it had been devalued. He mimed throwing a handful of cords in the air, releasing his closed fist and watching the cords fall to the ground; or he would mimic tying a cord around his own waist in reference to self-appointed mestres. "Varig Mestre" had become a derogatory title for Brazilians who traveled abroad on the Varig national airline hoping to make a living with capoeira without proper credentials.

"Back in my day you couldn't just hang a berimbau or physical education certificate on the wall and call yourself a mestre! You had to prove yourself in the roda."

Touro also complained that capoeira's commercialization was making it more competitive and violent. As more instructors attempted to make a living just with capoeira, they honed their bodies and skills to attract more students. Touro complained that these capoeiristas had more time to work out in gyms and didn't have to worry about going to work early the next morning. He explained that when he played roughly it was violent but without hate, and that he beat people up but with elegance and respect.

"I am not going to really hurt you because tomorrow you have to work. Besides, if I hurt you, who will I play with? In my day capoeiristas liked to be beaten up by me. It was an honor they would thank me for afterward!"

Even as he aged, Touro still commanded fear and awe—younger capoeiristas attending his rodas with trepidation. When Fatal started teaching his own classes in Chatuba, he brought his students to Touro's rodas as a rite of passage to get roughed up by the sibling mestres.

While some capoeiristas enjoyed the rough games of mestres like Touro and Dentinho, a new generation of instructors disdained their "sloppy," aggressive capoeira. They preferred a more athletic and technically effective game. In either case, many capoeiristas expressed the opinion that aggression in capoeira emerged because of the everyday violence of life in Brazil.

As Glayd had told me the summer before, "Our practice is different from other martial arts, which are trained in academies behind closed doors. Capoeira spills out into the streets and into our everyday lives. Capoeira is part of our culture and society, and Brazilian society is a big mess right now."

Hard Play, Fights, and *Brasilidade*

In a Brazilian cartoon two dogs watch a street roda. One dog says to the other "I have always considered capoeira to be a manifestation of brasilidade (Brazilianness)." And the other says "Oh yeah? Why?" In the next panel the roda deteriorates into a brawl with ugly name-calling and shouts of encouragement. In the final panel the cops arrive and the one dog says to the other, "Ah, now I get what you mean!"

The cartoon uses irony, a "hallmark of Brazilian self-portraits,"[9] to poke fun at brasilidade or that elusive "Brazilianness." The search for a national identity took off in the early twentieth century when the new Brazilian Republic was struggling to consolidate and define itself as a nation.[10] Proud to

have transitioned to independence without civil war, and to distinguish itself
from Jim Crow United States and Apartheid South Africa, Brazil adopted a
foundational myth as a harmonious and peaceful nation.

Bolstering this myth was the revisionist history of Gilberto Freyre, which
claimed that because of the long history of miscegenation—Portuguese colo-
nists having sexual relationships with African and Indigenous women—the
white, Black, and Indigenous populations lived harmoniously in Brazil. Another source of this myth, and largely misunderstood, was the 1936 treatise
on Brazil's "roots" by Sérgio Buarque de Holanda. The historian suggested
that "the Brazilian contribution to civilization will be cordiality—we will give
to the world the 'cordial man.'" But he continued that the "familiarity, hospitality, generosity" lauded by foreigner visitors and defining the "Brazilian
character" were not simply "signs of 'good manners' or civility." Rather they
came "from an incredibly rich and overflowing emotional background." Holanda reminded his readers that "cor-diality" means "from the heart," where
both amity and enmity dwell in the "sphere of the intimate, the familiar, the
private."[11]

Holanda's invocation of the "cordial man" is, in fact, an indictment of the
Brazilian state. An overabundance of emotion and insistence on family ties
has made it difficult for Brazil to free itself from a colonial past that, contrary
to Freyre's rosy portrayal of it, operated through rape and a "culture of terror and space of death."[12] Despite political consolidation as a democracy in
1985, Brazil persists as a personalistic state in which there is deep distrust of
the rule of law, and many citizens condone the justified use of violence. This
has produced a "disjunctive democracy" in which universal citizenship is
recognized, yet individual civil rights disregarded.[13]

In his ethnography of carnival in the Brazilian city of Recife, Daniel Linger argues that brasilidade is less about shared identity as it is about shared
predicament. Using the example of "dangerous encounters" between strangers during street parties, Linger suggests that a flirtation with violence, often
leading to physical altercation, enhances the carnival experience for some.
These encounters, scripted and policed by bystanders so that they do not
become too violent, provide a pleasurable "controlled release" (desabafo) of
pent-up emotions and frustrations.[14]

Capoeira is also an arena in which bodies clash in ways that can push the
boundary between play and aggression. As I had learned the summer before,
there is a distinction between what capoeiristas call jogo duro (rough play)
and a briga (fight). While certainly not attractive to all, or even most capoeiristas, in Rio many do seek out jogo duro. They describe the pleasure of
rough play in similar ways to some carnival revelers, as a venting of pent-up

emotions. They also describe it as a way to test the efficacy of their training and to feel prepared for *a luta que é a vida* (the struggle of everyday life). Jogo duro must stay within the unspoken rules of capoeira—no punches for instance—so that it does not slip into a briga. If the play-frame breaks, others in the roda may have to step in to separate the players.

Jogo duro is similar to the "controlled violence" described by sociologist Loïc Wacquant in his ethnography of a South Side Chicago boxing gym. He argues that the gym is a "sanctuary" in which problems are left at the door, and everything—from sparring in the ring to conversations—is ritualized and regulated. This ordered violence, Wacquant argues, stands in "symbiosis and opposition" to the arbitrary violence of the ghetto.[15] The highly monitored environment gives fighters a sense of control in juxtaposition to the outside world that is shaped by forces—bosses, policemen, poverty, and racism—beyond their control.

Jogo duro similarly stands in juxtaposition to the everyday violence of Rio de Janeiro. However, rather than a symbiotic relationship to the outside world, the capoeira roda is in one of osmosis. As Glayd had reminded me, capoeira happens not in closed-door gyms but in open, public spaces: capoeiristas often train in outdoor areas, and they test their skills in street rodas. Mestres will often invite students to talk about issues in their lives and allow the roda to be a space to blow off steam—and even at times to work out interpersonal conflict.

Capoeiristas' responses to my questions about aggression in the roda often resonated with wider social acceptance of justified violence: "no one likes violence, but it is necessary for survival" and "anyone who says capoeira is not violent is a liar. It has always been violent. But you need to know how to use violence for a just cause."[16] For many, what happens in the roda is a reflection of life outside the roda, which in Brazil is unfortunately too often shaped by violence.

Who Was Rio's First Mestra?

An 1878 Rio newspaper article entitled "Even the Beautiful Sex," reports that three women—Isabel (known as Baby), Ana, and Deolinda (an enslaved)—were arrested in Riachuelo Street near Lapa for fiercely fighting "to the point of exhaustion." The article concludes that "Isabel and Ana spend their lives fighting; hence they challenge whoever directs toward them a disagreeable word, and in any fight prove themselves experts in capoeiragem."[17] This rare reference to women and capoeira in nineteenth-century Rio, along with a smattering of ambiguously nicknamed possibly female Bahian capoeiristas—most famously Maria Doze Homens (Mary Twelve Men)—are exceptions that prove the rule that capoeira was a male space well into the twentieth century.

The increasing involvement of women in capoeira in the 1990s—due to its popularity among women abroad as well as a growing feminist movement across Brazil and Latin America—generated a healthy debate over who could lay claim to being, or having taught, Rio's first mestra. Artur Emídio claimed to have taught tennis champion Lucy Maia in his academy in Bonsucesso in the 1950s. There were also rumors of a Mestra Sandrinha whom I heard about for the first time at Mestre Nacional's monthly roda.

A "folkloric" capoeirista like Mestre Touro, but with a more easygoing personality and game, Mestre Nacional was well-liked. He lived and taught in a suburb bordering the Baixada Fluminense and spent his weekends traveling from one event to another—always with a black bag containing toilet paper, deodorant, towel, swimsuit, beer glass, linen suit, and straw hat. "I am prepared for anything!" he once told me as he revealed the contents over a post-roda beer. Nacional's monthly rodas were well attended and slightly chaotic. Without Touro's dictatorial personality and strict rules, he had a tendency to let his rodas run out of control, and fights were not uncommon (perhaps adding to their popularity). The roda in which I heard about Sandrinha for the first time began with verbal sparring. During introductions one elderly mestre in street clothes stepped to the microphone. He told us that he had graduated Rio's first female mestre, Sandra, twenty years earlier. A uniformed woman in her thirties with black bobbed hair became visibly irritated and began speaking over the mestre.

"I'm Mestra Sueli Cota. I've been a mestra since 1989. And when I started training capoeira, I heard about *this* Mestra Sandrinha. I looked for her at rodas and never saw her. I searched for her classes and never found them. What kind of mestra doesn't play or teach?"

The older mestre took offense, and there was a loud back and forth, until Mestre Nacional cut them off. During the roda, Mestra Sueli Cota played frequently and fiercely as if to prove her point. Whatever the truth of the mysterious Lucy Maia and Sandrinha, the first pioneering wave of female capoeiristas, of which they were at least several dozen, entered the scene in the 1980s.[18]

Intrigued by Mestra Sueli Cota, I asked my friend Célia to take me to her class. Spunky and independent, twenty-one-year-old Célia was more obsessed with capoeira than me. Originally from São Paulo, she lived in a suburb near Penha, where she trained capoeira with a mestre who was also her fiancé and eighteen years her senior. Célia had a grueling schedule, getting up at 6:00 a.m. to take the metro and bus to Ipanema where she was a home caretaker for an elderly person, and then in the afternoon taking two buses to her job as a telephone operator near the airport. Despite her long days, Célia trained most evenings, taught a kids class in a favela near her house on Saturdays, and attended rodas and batizados on Sundays. Though still only on her first level cord, Célia hoped to become a mestra the same year that her fiancé received his highest level mestre cord. I didn't doubt her ambition, watching the intention with which she trained and networked: at every event she scanned the room for mestres she didn't yet have a photo with to add to her album.

When I asked if she would take me to Mestra Sueli Cota's class Célia readily agreed, replying: "She's a good teacher and capoeirista even though you wouldn't know it from seeing her in the street, she is so petite! When she was coming up in capoeira she was a real firecracker, always getting into fights in the roda."

Sueli Cota taught in a health club in Madureira, a densely populated suburb famous for the Portela Samba School and its enormous cut-rate market. Her large class of thirty students was nearly half women. Afterward I chatted with Sueli and a student who had been training with her for ten years. He showed me a scar on his forehead.

"This is why I started training with Mestra. I was walking past the gym one night, and I heard the berimbau and came in to investigate. When I saw it was a woman in charge of the group I didn't want to join because I was really macho back then and I thought a woman couldn't teach me anything. But I decided to try a few classes. And during a roda at the end of one class, I tried to get her with a kick and she came in under my leg and knocked me to the ground. That's how I got this scar and I haven't thought about changing groups since!"

"Not all male students would stay after that," Sueli Cota said. "It's a real problem for female instructors. A lot of Brazilian men won't tolerate a woman showing them up in the roda or getting rough in trainings. When I started capoeira twenty-two years ago, there were hardly any women. There weren't any classes like mine with all these female students."

"Why are there so many more women today?" I asked.

"It's fashionable. When Mestre Boneco appeared on *Faustão,* that really did it."

Sueli was referring to the mestre of a large Zona Sul group. Nicknamed "Doll" for his purported good looks (white, tan, and muscular), Boneco had a parallel career as a model and actor. In 1996, he appeared on a popular Sunday afternoon talk show with some of his female model students. They promoted his classes at a chic health club in a wealthy southern suburb, Barra da Tijuca, as an expression of "our culture" and a "great way to tone the abs and buttocks." By the new millennium, most of the health clubs in the Zona Sul would offer capoeira classes and capoeira-inspired workouts, including a short-lived "capoeira water aerobics."

Not uncommon when women first enter a male sport, female capoeiristas were hyper-feminized and sexualized. A capoeira magazine launched its first issue with a cover picture of a blonde-haired model in uniform executing a high kick that revealed more crotch than skill. The two-page spread in the "social" section entitled "women in the roda" was a photo collage of female capoeiristas in uniform, but none playing capoeira.[19] The next issue, dedicated to "sexy [sic] machine" Tiazinha, featured the actress Suzana Alves playing berimbau with head thrown back, long loose hair cascading over her bare shoulders, wearing her signature black carnival mask. The centerfold displayed Tiazinha modeling lingerie and "playing" capoeira in uniform but still wearing her mask, not only eroticizing her but putting her at risk in the roda where peripheral vision is essential.[20]

Such media images of female athletes, according to feminist scholars Leslie Heywood and Shari Dworkin, can do both "progressive and regressive cultural work, sometimes simultaneously."[21] While the magazine images certainly made women into sexualized ornaments in capoeira (outraging many serious female capoeiristas), they also opened up space for women in Brazil to train.

I asked Sueli Cota what she thought of the future for women in capoeira.

"I worry about that all the time! People like to see old mestres, like Mestre Leopoldina, playing. But no one wants to see an old woman in the roda! It is going to be ugly."

Yet another double standard: men get to age gracefully into dapper malandros, women become unattractive hags.

"But in general," Sueli continued, "I think women are here to stay. It's not just a fad. We are conquering our space."

On the bus ride home Célia and I continued the conversation.

"It's really going to change things when there are more advanced female players," Célia said. "Right now, I prefer to train with men because they push me harder and they don't hold grudges. Women are jealous and catty and vie for the guys' attention. For instance, if a woman learns a difficult acrobatic move, she's not going to teach any of the other women in the group, because she wants to be the only one to do it and impress the guys. Guys aren't like that. They show each other stuff. But as more women get better that culture will change. Women just need to claim space in the roda."

Mestra Sueli Cota and Célia's words would prove true. Women would indeed claim their place in the roda and rise through the ranks. By the second decade of the 2000s, more and more female capoeiristas would challenge the masculinist, and heteronormative, capoeira culture.

A Capoeirista on the Page

Janaína, hands on her hips, was standing in the living room glaring at me.

I had just arrived home and was exhausted. Every weekday, I joined the hordes of Zona Norte commuters, getting up at 6:00 a.m. to arrive at the language school in Copacabana where I was taking classes. Unlike the "outside" buses I had taken the summer before that traveled along the multilaned Avenida Brasil, bus 350 took the "inside" route traversing the suburbs. Despite the circuitous route, the bus still raced at alarming speeds, and I learned to sit like other passengers: one hand clutching my bookbag on my lap and the other braced against the back of the seat in front of me to keep from keening over into my neighbor when the driver took bumps or corners too quickly. On my early afternoon returns with a lighter bus, less traffic, and fewer stops, the driver would race even more maniacally, simultaneously carrying on a shouted conversation with the conductor hanging on to her tall seat by the turnstile at the back. I enjoyed the speed but would stare anxiously out the window at the suburbs blurring into each other—Bonsucesso giving way to Ramos, passing into Olaria—until I saw Nossa Senhora da Penha rising above me and knew the next stop was mine.

That afternoon I had stayed late downtown and had stood up for the two-hour bus ride through rush-hour traffic. I was still unclenching my body from the ride, and now Janaína was mad at me. She turned abruptly and stalked over to the dining room table where my field notebook lay open. She lowered her head over a page and then jabbed her finger down. My chest tightened as I knew what was coming.

"You are writing about us! I see my name, and Aline's, and Fatal's!"

"Yes, Janaína I am writing about you. That is my field notebook."

"Why? I thought you were studying capoeira, not us!"

"But you are capoeira, aren't you?"

I had not brought my computer—a used laptop and an extravagance on my graduate student budget—as I had worried something would happen to it, and I thought a notebook would be more discreet. But now I'd messed up. We are taught as anthropologists to protect the anonymity of our "informants" by using pseudonyms. This practice, however, has been called into question, especially as we increasingly work with people who very well might read and have opinions about our work. Sometimes anonymity seems to do more to protect the ethnographer from the critiques and possible anger of her interlocutors.[22]

I explained to Janaína that I was interested in the social world of capoeira—how and why people practice it. I translated and read out the passage she had pointed to, a description of training the night before. She seemed mollified that it wasn't *fofoca* (gossip), but it caused another rift in our already uneasy relationship.

The incident drove home for me that despite this summer's similarities to my previous visits to Brazil, something had shifted permanently in my relationship to capoeira; I was now also a researcher. In some ways, this new identity alleviated the doubts and difficulties I was increasingly experiencing as a practitioner. I was bothered by the sexist and homophobic attitudes expressed by some Brazilian capoeiristas. I was also wary of the unquestioning dedication and loyalty expected of students to their mestres and upset by the methods some instructors used to discipline students. I had witnessed mestres humiliating students in class for transgressions or unruly behavior within or beyond the roda. Some of the students thus reprimanded told me later that they needed this kind of "tough love"—that such punishment was the only way to get through to them and to keep them on a straight track.[23]

Slipping into my anthropologist skin, I could distance myself from these practices and maintain a neutral position as a marginal, rather than fully, integrated member in any one group. But this detachment bothered me corporeally, emotionally, and politically. Physically my body was caught between styles, and emotionally I was spread thin among groups that wanted my attention and loyalty. Politically, I began to question the goals of ethnography and the power dynamics that shape anthropological inquiry: For whom do we write and to what ends? Is it enough to observe and write about others simply to increase the ethnographic record of the world? Should the language we write in be accessible to the people we write about as well as to academics? Should maintaining a culturally relativistic view—a driving tenet of anthropology that asks us to suspend judgment in order to understand practices and beliefs within the logic of a culture—justify a lack of action? These questions, that underly all ethnographic projects, are not easily answered. We should always consider what work our research and writing will do in the world.[24] One thing I did know then and now is that I want those I write about to recognize themselves in my words and to feel the respect, interest, and affection I hold for them.[25] I hope they see themselves not as static names on the page of a detached observer but as complex individuals who matter to, and move (with), me.

An Anthropologist in the Roda

Games were under way when the metal gate clanged open. Dressed in his white uniform, Mestre Sardinha marched in followed single-file-soldier-style by Glayd and seven students, all in black training pants and shirts. Everyone knows Mestre Touro insists on white uniforms at his monthly roda.

My stomach lurched, and I regretted wearing my abadá with Mestre Sardinha's group logo running down one leg. Mestre Touro had let it be known that Mestre Sardinha and his students were not invited to his roda that month. Touro and Sardinha had a volatile relationship that stretched back to when Sardinha was just a teenager training with Touro before Beiçola began his own group. Stories circulated about how Mestre Touro had roughed him up at one batizado, and Sardinha's mother leaped from the audience into the roda to smash a chair across Touro's shoulders. In some versions of the story, it was the only time Mestre Touro was nearly knocked out in a roda.

This time it was an incident at the recent batizado of Mestre Biquinho, a student of Mestre Touro's, that ignited Touro's anger. Mestre Sardinha and his students had apparently shown up looking for a fight and had gotten it—the roda dissolved into a brawl.

At Mestre Sardinha's entrance, Mestre Touro broke off his game and returned to the top of the roda. Squatting at the foot of the gunga, he indicated for the music to continue and then watched as Mestre Sardinha approached, bent down, and said something to him. Mestre Touro's response was inaudible over the music. Mestre Sardinha gestured to his students to join the roda.

Games recommenced, and I jumped in to play with Mestre Touro. His eyes and body blazed with anger. He broke off our game before I'd barely begun to ginga and stalked counterclockwise around the roda in a *volta ao mundo.* I followed him "around the world," keeping my distance. He took his time, removing his shirt and rolling it into a fat sausage and tying it around his forehead. Done to keep the sweat out of his eyes, this performance is also a warning to play with caution. He charged at me. I dodged several kicks and launched a straight benção kick at his chest. Mestre Touro screamed something and delivered a *rasteira* (sweep) to my standing leg, which landed me heavily on the ground.

One of Mestre Sardinha's students leaped in to "buy" the game and take my place. Mestre Touro backed his young opponent to the edge of the roda and raised his leg in a *queixada,* or cross-body kick. With nowhere to escape, the student grabbed onto the leg hoping to stop the attack—an inelegant and disapproved of tactic. Mestre Touro slammed down his leg, seized the student around the waist, and swung him back and forth like an angry bear before tossing him across the roda. Mestre Touro raised his arm to stop the music. The boy clambered out of the roda, his shirt torn, coming to rest next to me. I gave him a sympathetic look. Mestre Touro yelled.

"People! You need to respect the house of others!"

He glared around the roda, then returned to the foot of the berimbau. The music began again and Sardinha joined Touro in a squat. They entered cautiously with guarded ginga. In quick succession Touro cracked a benção into Sardinha's ribs and, when he retaliated, delivered a rasteira. Sardinha caught himself on his arms low to the ground and jumped up positioned to deliver a "scissors" takedown, but Touro launched an *aú batido* over Sardinha's leg, his broad feet smacking down on his opponent's back as he cartwheeled to safety. Mestre Zé, came in to buy the game, but Mestre Sardinha put his arm out to stop him. As Mestre Zé retreated, Sardinha entered a powerful *pisão rodado,* the spinning kick knocking Touro into a line of students. Regaining his balance, Touro charged toward Sardinha and then abruptly stopped. He raised his arm above his head and yelled:

"Get out! Grupo Besouro get out!"

A moment of suspended stillness ran through the roda and audience as the music stopped. Then Mestre Sardinha started yelling from his position in the middle of the roda:

"Mestre Touro, your capoeira is shit! You are shit! There are lots of younger mestres who are better than you! And you're taking advantage of *my* mestre! You only went to the United States because of *my* mestre!"

Sardinha turned, searching for me, and then pointing his finger continued:

"Katya, write this all down! Write down everything I say! Tell your mestre how his mestre is treating me!"

Mestre Touro had calmly returned to the foot of the berimbau and now raised his voice over Sardinha's.

"That's right! That was my *third* trip to the United States, paid for by Mestre Beiçola and his students! And next month I am hosting Mestre Acordeon and *fifty* American capoeiristas here at my roda!"

Mestre Sardinha indicated for his students to follow him out. At the gate he blew kisses to the audience and then turning back to the roda shouted, "I will be back to next month's roda with 170 Besouro students!"

Then they were gone.

Mestre Biquinho, on the gunga, commanded the music to begin again and launched into a short ladainha of his own authorship:

Capoeira tem perversidade	Capoeira has perversity/wickedness
Tem maldade	It has bad intentions
Capoeira tem fundamentos	Capoeira has fundamentals
É verdade	It is true
Capoeiristas sempre dizem	Capoeiristas always say
Que eles são irmãos	That they are brothers
Vão ao pé do berimbau	They go to the foot of the berimbau
E dão aperto de mão	And shake hands
E na roda, e na roda	And in the roda, in the roda
Eles disseram irmão	They say brother
Mas um tenta pôr	But one tries to knock
O outro no chão	The other to the ground
Iê viva meu mestre	Long live my mestre

The chorus rose up in response:

Iê viva meu mestre, camarada	Long live my mestre, comrade

And the games began again.

In Search of Interpretation

A throbbing pain in my leg woke me early the next morning. Still groggy from the after-roda beer, I threw back my sheet and examined my left thigh. A large bruise was visible where I'd landed hard on the ground from Touro's sweep. I lay back in bed with a groan. Why had he done that? And what had he screamed at me? As I began to replay the events of the night before, I heard three sharp claps from outside. A visitor at the gate. Janaína lay motionless under her sheet on the bed across from me. I put my feet gingerly on the ground testing my leg. In shorts and a tank top, my pajamas in Brazil, I decided I was dressed enough, and limped out into the living room. I moved through the dark to the front door and unlocked it, taking the keys with me. Thankfully Jobi didn't appear.

"Good morning," the man at the gate said. "Is the mestre home?"

I nodded and unlocked the gate. He introduced himself and told me he was a former student of Touro's but lived out in Campo Grande now, too far to train. He'd wanted to come to the roda last night, he said, but couldn't because he was working.

"But I heard about the *bagunça* (mess)."

"Already?"

He responded: "Last night after work I ran into someone who'd heard about it from someone who was there. I had to make an early delivery this morning so I thought I would stop by to find out what happened."

I did the calculations: Campo Grande was an hour to the west. He must have been up late to have heard the roda gossip and up early to be here now. Coffee was in order. As I headed to the kitchen, Touro emerged. And when I returned with the coffee carafe and glasses, he was rehashing the roda blow-by-blow.

"I told him when he asked to play that he and his students weren't welcome. But they stayed anyway. And dressed in black! What disrespect!"

The family woke up one by one and gathered on the porch. Everyone spoke over each other in their eagerness to re-create the roda, the kids still giddy with excitement.

"Did you see him blow kisses to the audience when he left?" Janaína said.

"Like a soap opera star!" Aline giggled.

"And what about his threat to come to next month's roda with 170 students!" Jorginho chuckled.

"Sardinha doesn't even have fifteen students!" Touro said, waving his hand dismissively. "He's just jealous because I'm hosting the Americans next month."

"Did you see Tiririca run into the academy to get the maculelê machetes?" Bete said.

"Or what about when Sardinha told you to 'write everything down' Camarão!" Aline said.

"Oh, Katya, you were trying to hide behind the students next to you in the roda. You were getting smaller and smaller!" Bete teased.

It was true. I'd been mortified to be called out. To divert the conversation, I showed Mestre Touro the big bruise on my thigh.

Touro grunted.

"Why did you give me that big sweep to my *benção?*"

"Your *golpes* (kicks) are wrong."

"What did you yell at me?"

"Your kicks are wrong," Touro repeated.

"That's what you yelled?"

He grunted again.

"What do you mean my kicks are wrong?"

"You're confused. That was not a benção you gave me, it was a ponteira."

Seeing the uncertainty on my face—I was wishing I'd filmed the roda— Touro continued.

"See! You don't even know! What is the difference between a ponteira and a benção?"

"The benção strikes with a flexed foot. A ponteira strikes with the ball of the foot."

"Exactly. I don't teach ponteiras. They're not capoeira. Whoever taught you that kick in capoeira was wrong! They're dangerous. Kicking with the flat of the foot might leave a bruise, but it is not going to kill you."

Jorginho chuckled and started to sing a popular new capoeira song by Mestre Burguês in homage of Mestre Hulk's victory in the MMA ring:

Foi no clarão da lua	In the light of the moon
Eu vi acontecer	I saw it happen
Num Vale Tudo com o jiu-jitsu	A no-holds-barred fight
A capoeira venceu!	And capoeira won!

"Shut your mouth, Jorginho! Capoeira has no place in those competitions!" Touro yelled.

Not satisfied with Mestre Touro's description of my game and explanation of his scream, I decided to ask others. As Bete had told me, it is important to discuss rodas afterward because "everyone sees something different and has something new to add." I had become impressed with how closely capoeiristas attended to games, photographically capturing them in their memory, and often pointing things out to me about my own game I didn't remember. If I had video-recorded that evening, we would have parsed every moment of the roda. Even then, "truths" would have been partial, subjective, and hotly debated. In anthropological parlance, I was "triangulating" data: observing behavior, asking individuals about that behavior, and asking others about those people's behavior. I started with Fatal.

"Ah, Katya. You want to know what Mestre Touro screamed at you? He said, 'We don't break bones here! Only ABADÁ does that!'"

Essentially telling me the same thing as Mestre Touro—that my kicks were wrong and dangerous—Fatal put a label on the blame. He took a dim view of my growing involvement with ABADÁ, warning me that my capoeira would lose its raça (grit or character) and become mechanical and violent.

I showed up at Mestre Sardinha's class one evening to get his reading of the roda. I was nervous, as I hadn't spent much time with his group that summer, but he wasn't angry, just complained loudly that I had "abandoned my old capoeira family." I asked him what Mestre Touro yelled at me in the roda.

"Here we don't dance ballet! Go back to the United States!"

Mestre Sardinha was not referring to my dance background or the fact that I was a live-in dorm adviser at the School of American Ballet in New York City. In opposition to Mestre Touro and Fatal, Sardinha was letting me know that he thought my capoeira was weak and soft: that I had lost the tough edge that I had developed with him the summer before.

In the end, what upset me most was not what people thought of my capoeira or group affiliation. Fights and rifts happened all the time: Mestre Touro and Sardinha would patch things up and then fight again. What had made me uncomfortable was being called out as an anthropologist and foreigner. When Mestre Sardinha told me to write everything down, he was not just using me as a messenger, or directing me to tell his story. He was also implicating me in a power play. Mestre Sardinha, as many would tell me after the roda, was jealous of Mestre Touro's international trips. He had never traveled abroad. An accomplished capoeirista, percussionist, and sambista like Beiçola, Sardinha had tried out for the same touring folkloric group. He had not been selected, according to some, because he is not Afro-Brazilian, the desired look for those shows. Mestre Sardinha hoped to travel to the United States as an invited guest mestre. He saw me as a possible conduit and perhaps was upset that I had, in his eyes, shifted allegiances to Mestre Touro. This last roda of my fieldwork colored my remaining weeks with anxiety and doubt.

Leaving Penha and Rio, I was sad and exhausted. I was ready to go home but also wished I could do the three months over again. I felt I had done everything wrong. I had not gotten enough good "data," I had not improved my capoeira, I had not given enough back to my capoeira family, or as it were, families.

We stood around awkwardly on the porch the morning of my departure. There were no displays of emotion, reminiscence over made memories, or affirmation of me being part of the family now. The best anyone could do was Michelle, with her newborn in arms, telling me she'd miss me and that this "*não é falsidade, não*" (wasn't a lie). In my already low frame of mind, I interpreted Michelle's statement as an indictment of my own "falseness" or insincerity. Did they think I had used them for my research? Did they think I had been deceptive about my group affiliation? Did they interpret my leaving as a betrayal? Worry filled me as I left in the taxi with little ceremony, the day behind me continuing like any other day on Rua Paul Müller.

In retrospect, I realized that the lack of overt emotion was just the Bem-vindo family way, mixed perhaps with the precarity of life for many in Brazil:

Oi Sim, Sim, Sim,	Oh, Yes, Yes, Yes
Oi, Não, Não ,Não,	Oh, no, no, no,
Mas hoje tem, amanha não	Today there is some, tomorrow there is none
Oi olha pisada de Lampião	Look at Lampião's footstep

As this capoeira song suggests: people, things, and opportunities are present one day and gone the next. Perhaps this can lead to a certain emotionless resignation, a passive acceptance of the inevitable.[26] Perhaps my new capoeira family was ready to admit before I was that the convivência we cultivated that summer was fleeting; our worlds too different to permanently meld.

But the Bemvindos didn't know something that I did: I don't give up on people or friendships easily. I would keep stubbornly coming back—albeit never for such a long stay—showing up for rodas, a Sunday lunch, on Christmas Day. I would keep my bond to Zona Norte capoeira alive. It would never again be a day-to-day convivência, but it was still, at least on my part, deeply felt.

Making Sense of It All

I was lost and confused when I got back to New York City and my graduate studies. I had to write up my "findings" to present to my department. As I struggled at my desk, I was tormented by the sight of a broken berimbau, beautifully painted with the Brazilian flag, standing in the corner of my room. A mestre had shown up with it at Touro's roda, and when I admired it, Touro had insisted he give it to me. The mestre was reluctant, but when I tried to give it back when Touro wasn't looking he refused. The first time I tried to string the berimbau, the bow had broken with a loud crack. My clumsiness and the broken wood became a symbol of all I thought I had done wrong—and gotten wrong—on my first summer of fieldwork.

As I read snippets of my field notes, they appeared to be nothing more than a jumbled mess of gossip. Bete had told me that capoeira is just "*fofoca e briga*" (gossip and fights). But maybe that is what anthropologists trade in after all; the "poetics and politics of ethnography," as one ground-shifting text put it, just the gossip and fights of everyday life.[27]

After weeks of stalled productivity, my adviser suggested I transcribe my handwritten field notes into the computer so I could more easily "code" for emerging themes. At first it felt like a colossal waste of time. But then, as the hours and days of reading and typing plunged me back into the field, I started to gain both distance and insight into my experience. As an analysis of power emerged, I worried about representing capoeiristas and capoeira in a negative light. Nevertheless, I knew I wanted to move beyond earlier scholarship that beautifully, and rather romantically, read capoeira as a "technique of resistance" and the roda as a "ring of liberation" and "world upside."[28]

Resistance was a hot topic in the 1980s and 1990s. Focus had shifted away from large-scale social movements and revolutions of the 1960s and

1970s to subaltern everyday acts of resistance and "weapons of the weak." But others, such as anthropologist Sherry Ortner, critiqued resistance studies for refusing to "know, speak or write of the lived world inhabited by those who resist (or do not, as the case may be)." In hesitating to expose internal rifts and disagreements, studies that focused on struggles against oppression tended to disappear the very individuals in the struggle.[29] These studies also were hampered by the increasingly fraught terrain of ethnography that questioned scientific objectivity and empirical truth-telling.[30] Perhaps, as Ortner argued, we needed to strengthen our commitment to looking for places in our research and texts where ethnographic subjects push back. Mestre Sardinha's performance at the roda was in part an attempt to direct my attention to what he considered important (and, thus, what I should consider as well).

In contemporary capoeira, who was resisting whom and what? When I asked capoeiristas to define their practice, resistance was often the first thing they mentioned—yet with varying meanings. Historical interpretations offer capoeira as an example of cultural resistance, an African expressive practice that survived the Middle Passage; and as physical resistance, enslaved on plantations developing a fight disguised by dance, and on the quilombos as a form of guerrilla warfare. Contemporary interpretations continue to view capoeira as physical resistance—keeping bodies and minds healthy and strong in the struggle of everyday life in Brazil; or as cultural resistance against the encroachment of global, and particularly U.S., culture. For some, malandragem is a form of resistance, a way to game the system or live in the interstices of mainstream society; for others capoeira resistance is pushing back against marginalization through professionalization and teaching jobs in the formal economy.

In the end, as anthropologist Lila Abu-Lughod reminds us, resistance as a category of social analysis may be most helpful as a diagnostic for the many ways in which people are ensnared in webs of power.[31] What then did my experience that summer tell me about the politics of capoeira and perhaps its future? My implication by Sardinha in a power play that stretched from Rio to the United States illuminated a growing global capoeira and global Brazil. Still within the first decade of democratization after a repressive military dictatorship and a neoliberal opening of the economy, nonelite Brazilians were increasingly imagining themselves, and their futures, beyond Brazil.

Capoeiristas, like other Brazilians, were turning to global opportunities to better their local lives. By the new millennium there would be increased effort to insert capoeira into international markets. Differing factions, older and younger mestres, Zona Norte and Zona Sul instructors, and now also female capoeiristas, were vying for a stake in capoeira's future. The playing field would only get more crowded as the practice continued to expand.

With more questions than answers, I knew I needed to return to Brazil for a much longer stint of fieldwork and life as a capoeirista.

Perhaps Michelle's parting words were after all, whether intended or not, an indictment. Because when I returned several years later, I lived in a different part of Rio, established convivência with a different group, and played a very different capoeira.

4

"ONLY INTELLECTUALS LIKE MISERY"

RIO DE JANEIRO, 2001–2004

My body is an archive of memories. I close my eyes and will myself back into their embodied presence. . . .

Ash Wednesday dawning. I have done it. I samba-ed as if my life depended on it for eighty minutes down the Sambódromo avenue, the percussive bateria driving me forward, and the waving arms and singing voices lifting me up. My sweat dries into the salty, afterlife traces of the labor and pleasure of a dancing body. I am walking home now through deserted streets of carnival detritus; my enormous feathered leopard droops from my shoulders, weary like me. Sequins wink from between crushed cans and meat-greased paper; the gunpowder smell of fireworks drifts above the tang of beer and piss. Almost-slumbering fantastical beasts creep by, pushers' muscles straining to return the allegorical floats to their hangars where they will sleep until resurrection next year. I reach my hill. The moto taxis slumber too. I take a deep breath, my hamstrings flex and I start up, the final push. As I rise, a new sun pinks the sky.

Some of my carioca memories, like carnival's end one year, are singular and ephemeral. Others are deep-rooted states of being. I came alive in my body during my three years of fieldwork and convivência with Rio in new ways. What had been flirtations with new corporeal habits in my earlier visits became transformative once I lived there for an extended time. I incorporated new ways of being and moving through the world as I came of age as a capoeirista and woman. As my body became leaner, stronger, and more alert from playing capoeira every day, I shed the punk and hippie of my younger years but retained the feminist. I learned in Brazil that to be a fierce, dancing warrior did not mean I couldn't also take pleasure and pride in my body and embrace things coded "feminine." I experimented and discovered I enjoyed dressing in bright colors and patterns (if Rio's garbage men could wear hot pink and pastel purple, why couldn't I?) rather than the de rigueur blacks and grays of New York City graduate students. I got my first pedicures and replaced baggy androgynous T-shirts and shorts for tight tank tops and miniskirts. I was awed by the parade of female bodies of all shapes and sizes on the beach: pregnant bellies swelling between tiny strips of bikini and middle-aged cellulite-pocked fat tumbling out of thongs. I shed my self-consciousness about my height, wearing platform sandals for the first time. Amused and appreciative whispers of "*gigante*" (giant) did not shame me the way "daddy longlegs" and "stilts" had growing up. I learned how to flirt without the promise of more.

As I opened my body to new sensations and pleasures, I also learned (less successfully), to close it. My carioca friends reprimanded me for being too "transparent" with my emotions and too direct in my speech. Life in Brazil, they warned, was like a "bucket of crabs" clawing and climbing on each other to get to the top. I had to protect myself with the armor of distrust and dissimulation from the *olho grande* (big eye) of other people's jealousy. In the land of "cor-diality" where emotions from the heart run high, direct confrontation, they warned me, is unwise. Like safe flirting, I needed to convey messages beneath surface appearances, using body rather than verbal language.

The open and closed body are tropes in sacred and secular domains in Brazil. In Candomblé, the body is literally and symbolically opened, and then closed, during initiation. Small knife incisions to the scalp, upper arms, chest, or feet prepare the initiate for receiving the orixás. Scarification from the incisions then marks the initiate's body as "closed"—protected by the gods and Candomblé community.[1]

In capoeira, the open and closed body are strategically deployed. An open body is an offensive body: an "open" cartwheel or telegraphed kick "calls" (*chamar*) one's opponent into an attack. The *corpo fechado* (closed body) is a defensive body: legs close to the torso when upside down or arms shielding the head protect. Closing the body is a physical skill and also an attitude: the ultimate protection, and weapon, in capoeira is malandragem or malícia. A *malicioso* capoeirista is strategic and opportunistic: he hides his intentions while getting what he wants by manipulating the situation—a skill good to have in Brazil beyond the roda. If "closing" my body physically was challenging (it was hard to make myself small with my long legs and high center of gravity), closing it through malandragem was even more difficult. I was not used to moving in an environment that demanded dissimulation and deception.

As I struggled to manipulate and use my body in new ways, I also became increasingly cognizant of the privileged and problematic place of the body in Brazil. The body is overwhelmingly visible in Rio where almost-naked bodies parade on the beach year-round, dance on enormous floats in front of television cameras during carnival, and grace advertisements for plastic surgery clinics. Rio's body cult was even celebrated one carnival season with a parade dedicated to Doctor Pitanguy, Brazil's most famous plastic surgeon. Pitanguy helped normalize body modification: not only for the rich but also for the poor. Plastic surgery in Brazil is now considered a human right to boost self-esteem.[2] As an integral part of carioca social life, the body can be a site of liberating pleasure but also of domination, policing, and pain; it can be an avenue for cultivating virtuosic physical skills and creativity but also a site of disciplining self-governance.

The "open" and "closed" body resonates with anthropologist Teresa Caldeira's conceptualization of the body as "unbounded" in Brazil and therefore vulnerable to intervention and violation in medical, political, and social arenas. Acceptance of infringements on the body in Brazil is reflected in the popularity of cosmetic surgery and cesarean births; the majority support of legalizing the death penalty; the normalization of domestic violence; and the enjoyment of the messy collision of bodies during carnival street celebrations. Yet Caldeira also wonders if there is a way to close the body without losing its openness to interpersonal relations that contribute to the sensuality, pleasure, and beauty of much of Brazilian social life.[3] Perhaps capoeira, which deploys a body that is both closed and protected yet open to corporeal convivência, and at times unruly collision, is a site for just such a possibility.

Catete: Flower of My People

I moved back to Rio in 2001 to begin what was to be one year of dissertation fieldwork but which would extend into three. I settled into my new Rio life in Catete, a small, historic, residential neighborhood between the city center and Zona Sul. I had discovered Catete when I had lived with Glayd's family in Irajá in 1995, on one of my solitary rambles. Walking south from downtown, I had passed under the arches of Lapa and into the dilapidated and slightly seedy Glória neighborhood. The split avenue (the lower level a popular haunt for sex workers) that runs along the Guanabara Bay ends at a hill topped with a jewel of a church, one of Rio's oldest. The Carioca River once ran out to the bay here, and it is this name (also in some accounts the name of a Tupinambá village once located where the church now stands) by which Rio's inhabitants are known.

Glória bleeds into Catete. The small neighborhood is easily mistaken for a continuation of Glória as it doesn't yet have the majestic palm trees, art nouveau apartment buildings, and old-money elegance of Flamengo, the next neighborhood in the promenade toward the Zona Sul. Dotted with the same deteriorating colonial buildings as Glória, Catete also has more strollers, shopping carts, boutiques, and bookstores. On that early evening, I wandered into the deep green oasis of a park. Dusk brought stillness to the lush canopy, vine-cooled air, and earth smells. The soft, nostalgic twang of a *cavaquinho* enhanced the soothing enchantment. A seated circle of elderly cariocas gestured for me to join them as they sang *choro*, a musical genre older than samba that highlights a flute alongside the *cavaquinho*, a small guitar similar to the ukulele. I lingered longer than I should have, and as I turned to leave, a young man was setting up for a book launch at the edge of the park. I stayed to meet Augusto Boal, the famed political activist and founder of Theatre of the Oppressed. On the bus ride home, heady with the aesthetic and intellectual pleasures of the evening, I promised myself that if I ever lived again in Rio it would be in Catete.

I later learned that this nook of Rio was a most appropriate place to launch my research. The streets of Catete and Glória run deep with capoeira memories. In the final decade before the fall of the monarchy and rise of the First Brazilian Republic, one of the last and most powerful maltas claimed Glória as its territory. Maltas had swelled in numbers with the return of discontented soldiers from the largely failed war against Paraguay (1864–1870), many of whom were *capoeiras* enlisted with the later reneged promise of freedom. Newly politicized and connected after their time in the army, the *capoeiras* became involved in the struggle between the Republicans and Conservatives, working as bodyguards and hired thugs at political rallies. The most famous of these politicized maltas was aligned with the conservative politician Luís Joaquim Duque-Estrada Teixeira. The malta came to be known by the name Flor da Gente when Teixeira used the expression "flower of my people" at a victory speech to refer to his capoeira strongmen whose intimidating and knife-slashing tactics outside the voting polls in Glória had secured his election.[4]

Cascão, a capoeirista born and raised in Glória, told me he thought that the Flor da Gente malta had left an ancestral haunting that continued to draw capoeiristas to the neighborhood. On the street of his childhood home, Rua Santo Amaro, some of Rio's most well-known capoeiristas had once lived, and a new generation continued to live. The Glória Sunday market, where Cascão had seen capoeira for the first time as a kid, continues to host a weekly roda. During my fieldwork, in Catete and Glória capoeira classes were offered in three schools, one dance studio, two health clubs, and two favelas; there was also a *capoeira angola* center that housed four different groups (one called Flor da Gente); and the neighborhoods hosted three

monthly street rodas. Though perhaps slightly overrepresented, the proliferation of groups in Catete and Glória was indicative of the capoeira boom
in Rio, and worldwide, at the turn of the millennium.

I lived on Rua Tavares Bastos, a steep, cobblestone street that snakes up
the hill that marks the back boundary of Catete. Like the rest of the neighborhood, the street was built in the nineteenth century as commerce was
growing and Rio was expanding away from the ports and inner bay toward
the sea. Rua Tavares Bastos gave access to—and housed the owners and
workers of—a quarry, stones from which built Rio's churches. The street is an
architectural pastiche: *sobrados,* or multilevel houses decorated with Portuguese blue-and-white tiles where nineteenth-century merchants lived, bump
shoulders with workers' bungalow row houses; unattractive mid-twentieth-
century apartment buildings punctuate the line of colonial facades. The
eclectic housing reflects the mixed income of the mile-long street, at the
top of which perches a small favela. Once a *chácara,* or small rural property
where food was grown, after World War II the top of the hill became an informal settlement. Today, the small favela of just a few thousand families is
relatively crime-free due to the instillation of a BOPE headquarters, the special police force for fighting drug trafficking. In the last decade the Tavares
Bastos community has become a favorite for "favela tourism" and film sets
for Brazilian soap operas and Hollywood films.

I lived just below the entrance to the favela. My apartment was in a renovated sobrado divided into four split-level pastel-painted attached houses
that were visible from Catete's "formal" neighborhood below. My lower-level
studio apartment in the "blue house" opened onto a tiered backyard with
stunning views of Guanabara Bay and Pão de Açúcar. When I was home,
I left the front and back doors open so that through-breezes worked as a
natural air conditioner. The residents of Tavares Bastos were as eclectic as
the architecture. Above me: Dalva, at whose outdoor bar I enjoyed many a
beer; David, the Argentine baker who sold me fresh baked bread from his
kitchen window in the mornings; Bob, the English expat whose home and
jazz club at the heart of the favela I frequented before it become a Lonely
Planet entry; and Vilma's house *em obra,* where I hung out with her two
teenage daughters. Below me: the moto-taxi boys who whisked me up and
down the hill when I was too tired to walk and brought me newspapers and
an occasional roasted chicken from below; several bohemian artists who
lived in bungalow row houses; and most importantly, Tourinho, Erik, and
Debora, three youths who lived in a dilapidated, crowded boardinghouse at
the last bend before Rua Tavares Bastos meets the asfalto and who became
my capoeira companions.

I never stopped marveling at the luck of finding such a magical home in Rio. The decision to live in Catete, however, was also strategic. There were direct buses to Penha, so I could easily visit Mestre Touro and my friends in the Zona Norte; and in the opposite direction, buses would take me to Humaitá where I would train in a public schoolyard with Mestre Camisa three nights a week. I had made the full transition to ABADÁ, and it was this group that would shape my life and research for three years.

Training at the CIEP

Rio's CIEPs—Integrated Centers of Public Education—are identical, drab concrete schools spread throughout the city and state. Popularly referred to as Brizolões after Governor Brizola, whose 1980s project they were, the gray rectangles on pillars look more like parking decks than schools. Accenting splashes of primary colors do little to soften their brutalist architecture, or to distinguish one from another. The CIEP in Humaitá—a neighborhood that sits across a lagoon from the beachside neighborhoods of Leblon and Ipanema—is named Agostinho Neto. Mestre Camisa likes the symbolism of teaching capoeira in a CIEP named after Angola's first postindependence communist president. Angola is capoeira's ancestral home, and capoeira, like public education, is "for the people," as Camisa liked to say.

Following explicit directions from someone at a bus stop near my house—once again impressing me with cariocas' knowledge of urban landscape and public transportation—I boarded a bus that left Catete and flew along the avenue that curves around the bay before plunging into the dense Botafogo neighborhood. Traffic slowed to a rush-hour crawl on the Rua São Clemente, and I arrived in Humaitá after dark. The CIEP sat above a foreboding slab of wall at the base of a hill with an unlit driveway behind a partially open gate. I paused, hesitant to enter, until I heard the twang of a berimbau.

The school "playground," a long concrete patio under the CIEP's pillars with dirty, dysfunctional bathrooms at one end and a water fountain I would be warned against drinking from, was lit by hanging kerosene lanterns. The smoking, golden light gave the training space a clandestine feel; several months later when the electricity came back on (an energy crisis had temporarily cut after-hours lighting in public buildings), I was sorry to transition to the harsh illumination of naked ceiling lightbulbs. A student was stringing berimbaus—and another sweeping the concrete floor. Welcomed with little fanfare, I grabbed another broom to help sweep as students trickled in. When Mestre Camisa arrived, he looked as I remembered from four years before but with a bit more gray in his hair and beard and a few more wrinkles around his deep-set, intelligent eyes. He listened intently, tilting his head slightly toward me as I reintroduced myself. When I said I would be in Rio for at least a year to research and train, he nodded in approval.

When class began, Mestre Camisa playing his gunga and directing us, I was surprised that there were fewer than a dozen students. ABADÁ was the fastest growing group in the world, drawing hundreds of practitioners to the World Games in Rio every two years. But over the next two hours, students kept arriving until there were sixty moving, sweating capoeiristas stretched down the length of the yard. There was a handful of women, yet few wore cords that ranked them as advanced students or instructors. The racially mixed bodies looked different from capoeira bodies in the Zona Norte. Many of the men removed their shirts to display well-sculpted torsos and tattoos; women wore small tank tops and snug, low-cut abadá with tattoos peeking out from the gap between the two.

Despite a rough floor that tore at my bare feet, class was more similar to Edna's in New York City than ones I knew in the Zona Norte. We trained in lines with the more advanced in the front. Training progressed—warm-up, combinations, strengthening, stretching, partner work—at an intense and exhausting pace. Students were serious and focused, hoping to catch Mestre Camisa's eye and approval.

Class culminated in a roda like none I'd ever seen. Students eagerly pushed at the edges to get in to play. I hung back. With a full orchestra of three berimbaus, two pandeiros, atabaque, and agogô, and a chorus sure to be heard in the street below, the roda felt like a performance in which only the best should play. Games were stunning: kicks, dodges, cartwheels, flips, and takedowns at incredible speed. A short, bouncy capoeirista coiled like a spring executed a standing back flip when his partner came in with a sweep. How was that even possible?! A cheer went up when he landed the flip and retaliated with a circular back kick that launched his partner into a cartwheel that melted into a crouching arm balance.

As the roda went on and on, I wondered if and when I would ever get up the nerve to play among this crowd of elite athletes. Then I felt hands pushing me forward. Mestre Camisa had silenced the orchestra and was asking if anyone had not yet played. I moved to the top of the roda. The rhythm began again, bright and quick. I squatted at the foot of the gunga, excited and worried when the back-flipping capoeirista jumped down next to me. With a grin and quick hand shake, he led us into the roda and transformed into a whirl of movement around me. Mercifully he slowed his kicks so I could dodge. I played too quickly and heard shouts of *"calma!"* When someone bought in to take my place, I thankfully backed out to the anonymity of the roda's edge.

Tired, dirty, and chilled by a night breeze that had kicked up, I was relieved when the roda ended at 9:00 p.m. and then astonished when a second, advanced training began: some students left, others arrived, and many stayed. At one point, while we worked kicks with rasteiras in partners, Mestre Camisa became frustrated.

"Why isn't anyone landing on their butts! Don't mark a sweep, do it for real! Do it so your partner learns how to fall!"

Camisa grabbed an advanced student whose pants and sweaty, bare torso were streaked with grime after three hours of training. Still in his flip-flops and berimbau held away from his body with one hand, Camisa demonstrated a perfectly timed rasteira when the youth threw a kick. Camisa's sweeping foot caught and pulled the student's standing leg when his kick was at its apex, landing him heavily on the ground. The student bounced back up.

"Again! Another, a different kick!" Camisa roared as he handed off his berimbau to someone.

Again and again the student launched full-force attacks, knowing each time he'd be knocked down.

"See! That's what I am looking for!" Camisa said.

I was stunned by Camisa's casual elegance and powerful skill—and by the willing submission of the student.

My training partner murmured, "Now that's why I came to Rio!"

We had chatted between trainings. He told me he had just arrived in Rio from the Amazonian state of Rondônia that borders Bolivia, an exhausting multiday bus journey. Now he was sleeping on the beach where he planned to sell jewelry he made during the day. He was seventeen years old and had come alone to Rio with the sole purpose of training with Mestre Camisa.

At 11:00 p.m. we were finally done and students streamed out of the CIEP to a few parked cars and motorcycles or to bus stops. I was surprised by the quick dispersal, no one inviting me to share a beer and snack as I had become accustomed to in the Zona Norte. I settled for a juice and ham-and-cheese roll at the gas station.

My life in the Zona Sul had begun.

Capoeira Convivência in the Zona Sul

The capoeira convivência I settled into in the Zona Sul was different from the one I had lived in the Zona Norte. Many of Mestre Camisa's students came from peripheral neighborhoods and had lives similar to the Zona Norte capoeiristas I knew. Yet, due to the location of our trainings, and the fact that ABADÁ was rapidly growing internationally, there was a cosmopolitan feeling to the group. And a number of students were close to me in age, class, and education. Mestre Camisa was passionate about the rising popularity and growth of capoeira, while also dedicated to ensuring that it stay deeply rooted in the popular classes.

He told me: "People complain these days that capoeira, especially in the Zona Sul, has changed too much. That today there are too many middle-class practitioners. But capoeira has always attracted participants from all segments of society. It has also always been most popular among the lower classes and that's still true today. Look at my students! They come from all over the city, but the majority of them are poor. Capoeira is for them; they are the ones that can have better lives because of capoeira."

Criticism of Zona Sul capoeira stretches back to the 1970s when Mestre Camisa had just arrived in Rio de Janeiro. Though he has the accent, comportment, and attitude of a carioca, Mestre Camisa is Bahian. His early years were spent on a farm where he learned his first capoeira moves from his five brothers. When the family moved to Salvador, Camisa frequented street rodas and Mestre Bimba's academy with his older brother, Camisa Roxa. When Camisa Roxa started performing and traveling around Brazil with the folkloric troupe Vem Camará, Camisa tagged along. His brother left for Europe in 1972, and Camisa, just a teenager, stayed behind in Rio. At the time, capoeira was still reemerging in Rio. Capoeiristas like Artur Emídio had migrated from Bahia in the 1950s, along with thousands of other northeasterners looking for work and better lives, and had begun teaching capoeira in the Zona Norte where it quickly became popular.

There was also, by the 1960s, a group of middle-class male youth from the Zona Sul equally impassioned by capoeira. Two brothers, Paulo and Rafa Flores, had trained for several months in Mestre Bimba's academy on a trip to Bahia and then returned to teach friends what they knew on the rooftop terrace of their building in Laranjeiras, a middle-class neighborhood near Catete. They were joined by two other brothers, Gato and Gil Velho, from Ipanema and a couple of kids, Sorriso and Garrincha, from the Dona Marta favela. Without a mestre and lineage, they began innovating and incorporating elements from other martial arts. They focused on technique and fighting efficacy. By the early 1970s, when Camisa joined forces with what was then known as the Grupo Senzala, various members had become mestres with distinct styles and students. Camisa quickly gained a reputation for being a fierce and technical player, and by the 1980s he'd attracted a large group of disciples. In 1988 Camisa split from Senzala to form ABADÁ-Capoeira.

The group's name comes from an Arabic word for the long white frocks worn by Muslims from Yorubaland. The frocks were dubbed "war garments" by police in Bahia in 1835 when hundreds of these Malê Africans staged a nearly successful revolt.[5] Today the word abadá refers to the white pants that capoeiristas wear, and perhaps the choice of group name was also a humorous gesture to the founding mestre's nickname, Camisa, or "shirt." But the name, emblazoned across a globe in the logo, is primarily an acronym: Associação Brasileira de Apoio e Desenvolvimento da Arte-Capoeira (Brazilian Association for the Support and Development of the Art of Capoeira). This bureaucratic name, diverging from the more poetic names of many groups, signals ABADÁ's mission to professionalize and diffuse capoeira around the world.

Mestre Camisa's claim that capoeira was for everyone was evident in the diversity of the students who trained at the CIEP: there were *camelôs* (street vendors) and seamstresses from the Zona Norte and Baixada Fluminense; factory workers from the rural West Zone who traveled two hours to arrive in Humaitá for the second training; doormen and car washers who walked from their homes in the nearby Dona Marta favela; private high school students who lived in apartment buildings in Copacabana, Humaitá, and Leblon; university students from the bohemian hilltop neighborhood of Santa Teresa. There were students who had come from much farther away too: the youth I'd met the first day who had traveled from the Amazon and the Haitian adoptee whose parents had moved from Belgium so their adolescent son could fulfill his dream of training with Mestre Camisa. Social workers, teachers, unemployed single moms, lawyers, dentists, civil engineers, a former professional female soccer player, and a near-to-retirement sergeant in the army were regulars at the CIEP.

Foreign capoeiristas from Europe, Japan, and the United States also frequented the CIEP. Most stayed a few weeks or months at most. Perhaps the lack of enthusiasm I perceived when I first arrived was because everyone assumed I wouldn't stick around long. But as my convivência transitioned from weeks to months to years, I became an integrated member of the group, especially after Mestre Camisa gave me my *corda azul* (blue cord) that indicated my status as a "graduated" or advanced student. In the Zona Norte, I had always felt a bit like an anomaly, the "American capoeirista." In my new carioca life, I felt like an ABADÁ capoeirista. I also developed a new relationship to capoeira as an athlete. I came to not only embrace but also crave the intensity of Mestre Camisa's trainings and the challenge of playing in the roda. When I finally mastered a difficult move or when a more advanced student nodded and shook my hand with appreciation after a good game in the roda, I felt immense joy and pride. When I stuck through a particularly difficult second training, shaking with exhaustion by 11:00 p.m., and then got up at 6:00 a.m. the next morning for a two-hour bus ride to help with a batizado in a favela in the Baixada Fluminense, I experienced a new sense of camaraderie with my fellow capoeiristas. A camaraderie built on exhausting physical training, a commitment to bringing capoeira to underserved populations, and the difficult work of creating a career in capoeira.

Being so immersed in the lives and work of my fellow capoeiristas was not only productive for my fieldwork but also helped me feel I was giving back in small ways. The conflicted feelings I had during my first summer of fieldwork were somewhat assuaged by knowing that I was not just extracting knowledge and experience but contributing to the group. I was called on to film events with my video recorder, and I joined a photography lab so that I could gift large prints of the photographs I took, sometimes one of few pictures capoeiristas had (before the proliferation of phone cameras) of themselves playing. Most rewarding was working alongside various instructors in their youth classes in peripheral neighborhoods.

On the last Friday of the month, Mestre Camisa hosted an *aulão,* or "big class" that often gathered close to two hundred ABADÁ capoeiristas from all over the city, state, and beyond. Some months rented minivans or buses pulled up to the CIEP carrying students from São Paulo, Minas Gerais or even further states. Sometimes an instructor would bring a special group of students—senior citizens (or "third age" as they are poetically called in Brazil) or students with physical disabilities. Similar to monthly rodas in the Zona Norte—a time for mestres and their students to fraternize and show off in the roda—Mestre Camisa's aulão was a chance for instructors to socialize and show off not only their game skills but also their work.

The core group of about forty instructors and advanced students with whom I trained and became friendly were all attempting to make a living through capoeira. They scrambled to find jobs in the expanding capoeira market, primarily in schools and health clubs, while keeping up their free community classes, often in the favelas where they had grown up and continued to live. Besides teaching duties, these instructors were kept busy attending other instructors' events and performances: they shuttled between presentations in private elementary schools and favela community centers, floor shows in nightclubs, and once a performance at the foot of the Cristo Redentor for an international delegation touring cities bidding to host the Pan American Games. I spent my days and evenings moving with them between these incommensurable city spaces.

One afternoon I found myself on the set of a soap opera in the Barra da Tijuca suburb that sits beyond Leblon in the West Zone of the city. *Malhação,* the soap opera Glayd, Heverton, and I had eagerly watched before training in Irajá, was in its ninth season and still following the lives and loves of rich youth in a fancy health club. In 1996 capoeira had made a cameo appearance in the opening credits, and now it was a plot line: one of the main characters, MauMau (BadBad), starts training capoeira at school, much to his friends' ridicule and parents' bemusement. MauMau has a problem with aggression and breaks a friend's arm with a capoeira kick when his friend calls his mestre an idiot (*burrão*) and teases MauMau and the other capoeiristas for dressing in white pants and "clapping hands and singing like little kids." The mestre, described as a "nice caveman" on the *Malhação* website is reprimanded by another teacher (who also corrects his grammar) for "teaching violence." Mestre Leão repents and begins to focus on the "philosophy, sport, history, and culture" of capoeira rather than the fight. Later on, MauMau is redeemed in the eyes of everyone when he uses capoeira to defend an elderly woman in the street who is assaulted by a group of young thugs.

Though trading in stereotypes, the *Malhação* storyline mirrored the transformations and polemics of carioca capoeira: the increasing association of capoeira with kids and schools; the desire to divorce capoeira from its aggressive reputation; and the push to use it as a vehicle for building character and professionalism. The *Malhação* actors needed training, and a high-ranking ABADÁ instructor had landed the gig. He invited me to tag along and be an extra for the day.

I stopped on my way to pick up Hamster who lived in Dona Marta in Botafogo. Nestled in the hill below the Cristo Redentor statue, Dona Marta is one of Rio's most picturesque favelas, and also a hotspot of drug wars in the early 2000s. I came frequently to the Dona Marta *quadra,* an open-air space that hosted samba school rehearsals, baile funk parties, and capoeira classes taught by two instructors, Bacurau, who had grown up in Dona Marta, and his best friend, Chá Preto. Seventeen-year-old Hamster was one of their most gifted students. As tall as me, lanky, and with orange-tinged blond hair and pale skin with a penchant for turning red, Hamster, Bacurau liked to tease, could be my son.

I spent a lot of time with quiet, easygoing Hamster. He had dropped out of high school and was unemployed, so had a lot of time on his hands. One afternoon we'd hiked to the top of Dona Marta, up though steep, narrow alleyways that pressed the air out of my lungs. We passed the Michael Jackson statue that honored the 1996 filming of his "They Don't Care About Us" music video in the favela, and emerged onto the small hilltop soccer field that required skillful ball-handling so as not to lose the ball over the edge. Hamster pointed to our destination, another hill favela near my house in Catete, an hour's walk away.

"Most people don't know that you can traverse the city without ever touching asphalt!" Hamster told me.

He also warned me never to attempt this on my own as we passed encampments of people living like fugitives in the jungle. Hamster had started training capoeira a few years before because classes were free and near the one-room house in Dona Marta where he lived with his father and brother. He told me he started because he had "nothing better to do." Hamster had a knack for capoeira, and his game developed quickly, full of long-legged acrobatics. He occupied his time training and tagging along to events and performances.

The day of the filming we caught a bus that took us from Botafogo, through the beach neighborhoods, and along the narrow road that skirts the dramatic cliffs that lead to the city's West Zone. Had we taken the interior route, we would have cut under the mountains, Rocinha, the largest favela in Brazil with over 100,000 inhabitants, looming above us. Either route spits out onto the multilaned Avenue of the Americas in Barra da Tijuca. The most recently developed part of Rio de Janeiro, Barra was growing exponentially as cariocas with means migrated from other parts of the city to what they considered the more modern, clean, safe, and spacious suburb. An unbroken stretch of white beaches runs along one side of the Avenue of the Americas and along the other side a monotonous string of shopping malls, high-rise apartments, and securitized condominium complexes. I found it a depressing simulacrum of the worst of the United States. One mall even had a replica of the Statue of Liberty in front of it—Las Vegas kitsch without the irony.

The private club where O Globo was filming *Malhação* was an expanse of green lawn, tennis courts, soccer fields, swimming pools, and thatch-roof cabanas. As we waited outside the gates, I realized we were all white and largely inexperienced students.

"They want capoeiristas of *boa aparência*," the instructor told me when I asked. "And they don't want the extras playing better capoeira than the actors."

Boa aparência or "good appearance" in Brazil is code for white. Though the phrase is now prohibited on job announcements, it is still used informally. Boa aparência is not just about skin tone, but about "white" behavior, including speaking standard Portuguese, using polite manners, and dressing properly. In other words, whiteness is read on the body through much more than skin color.[6] Thus, though we were all white-presenting phenotypically (and this too is complicated in Brazil) that day, we were a diverse group on the spectrum of boa aparência. Hamster's favela slang, bermuda shorts, and flip-flops, however, would be erased by his capoeira uniform and silence as an extra on set, and would blend in nicely with seventeen-year-old Graviola's manicured nails and sleek brown hair that fell in a curtain past her shoulders. Graviola lived with her family in Leblon and was studying fashion. Not only the same age as Hamster, Graviola had a surprisingly similar capoeira story. She had started training on a whim because classes were offered at the gym down the street from her apartment, and she fell in love with capoeira (and eventually the instructor). Despite their similarities, Graviola and Hamster's futures would diverge radically: by their midtwenties Graviola would be married and pursuing a career in fashion, and Hamster would be dead from his involvement in drug trafficking.

If I was surprised all the capoeiristas that day were light-skinned, I certainly was not to find the same of the actors. Brazilian television has been, until recently, notoriously racist: dark-skinned actors only appearing as maids, enslaved, or criminals. The two lead characters, Pedro and MauMau, chatted with me about my research. When I asked about capoeira, Pedro, tall with an American movie star look and the main love interest on and off screen that season, became uncomfortable and defensive.

"I don't like having to pretend I play. I have never been interested in capoeira, and I am no good at it. I don't like seeing myself doing it on tape," Pedro said.

MauMau was more enthusiastic. He admitted that he also was no good, but liked capoeira. His father had trained at one point and had some old capoeira LPs.

"And besides," he added, "I'm better for the role because I look more Brazilian."

With his dark curly hair, olive skin, and full lips, though still coded white, MauMau had a more mixed look than Pedro.

Our involvement in the filming that day included a lot of waiting around and repetitive shooting of short scenes in which we were a backdrop. After eight hours with only coffee and water to sustain us, my secret fantasy to star in an action movie was somewhat dampened.

My experience on the *Malhação* set emblematized the complicated everyday experience of space, class, and race in Rio. Anthropologist Leticia Veloso uses the term "compulsory closeness" to describe the way in which the constrained geography of Rio, hemmed in by mountains and sea, has created a city in which the rich and poor live cheek by jowl.[7] In the United States, whole city neighborhoods—Manhattan's Upper East Side or the Berkeley Hills—are sequestered upper-class enclaves devoid of any signs of poverty, or Blackness. This is impossible in Rio's Zona Sul, where the entrances to favelas are often squeezed between luxury apartment buildings with penthouse views onto the informal settlement below. One of the attractions of the more spacious Barra da Tijuca is that it mimics U.S. bedroom suburbs far removed from urban blight; but even in Barra, informal communities exist, one of which was completely razed during the construction of the 2016 Summer Olympic Village.

Even if one lives in a gated community in Barra da Tijuca cut off from visible signs of poverty, there is a good chance that one's daily commute will traverse one of the city's poor areas. One day I visited a wealthy family in Barra, friends of friends in the United States. On hearing about my research they looked concerned, until they lit on the solution that I could work with the capoeira instructor who taught in a gym near their house. While driving me home at the end of the day (also concerned that I lived in Catete), the father apologized that our route took us under Rocinha. His wife complained that "they lived like animals" there and that the favela should be pulled down and everyone moved to housing in the suburbs. When I suggested that Rocinha's residents might prefer to stay local, close to their jobs, the father snapped back "but I too have a long commute from the suburbs!" He was referring to his air-conditioned drive from a 4,000 square foot luxury home in Barra to a downtown office, rather than a hot bus commute from a cramped apartment in the Zona Norte to an underpaid job selling drinks on the beach or minding cars in the Zona Sul.

Compulsory closeness moves far beyond geographic proximity that demands at least an awareness of the other. Rio's economy also depends on cross-class and cross-race interactions. Every day wealthy white carioca women are in close physical (and often emotional) proximity to the Black women who clean their houses, watch their children, and wax their bikini lines. Expectations of patronage in the hierarchical Brazilian society means that these relationships often stretch beyond the transactional; maids may spend an entire lifetime working for a family, come to expect extra financial or emotional support in times of crises, and even have patrons who visit their homes or god-parent their children.[8]

Problematic indeed, these entangled economic relationships mirror similarly complicated cross-class, interracial social relationships. Anthropologist Livio Sansone argues that there exist in Brazil two social arenas of racial interaction: the "hard" domains of employment, policing, and marriage and the "soft" domains of leisure activities and socializing.[9] We can add sex to the soft domain if we consider the "old saying" quoted in sociologist Gilberto Freyre's revisionist history, "white women for marriage, mulatto woman for fucking and Negro women for work."[10] The ways in which cariocas live with these opposing domains produces what anthropologist Jennifer Roth-Gordon calls a normalized racial contradiction that simultaneously maintains racial hierarchy and downplays racial difference. This contradiction, along with the absence of segregationist laws, has allowed the myth of racial democracy to endure in Brazil. And it is the reason why two seventeen-year-olds like Graviola and Hamster, with such extremely different lives and destinies, could move, sweat, play, and spend a day together on the set of Brazil's most popular soap opera.

An unproblematized racial cordiality was in full swing in the capoeira arena in the early 2000s when the practice was at its height of popularity as a fitness fad. Every toney health club in Copacabana, Ipanema, Leblon, and Barra da Tijuca offered classes. The majority of instructors were fit, good-looking, Afro-Brazilian males. This reflected the male-dominated hierarchy of capoeira, and also the health clubs' expectations (women took fitness classes and men worked out in the weight room). For their part, many of the instructors liked having predominantly female students, some of whom looked like, or were, models. And they enjoyed—with occasional invitations to Ipanema penthouse parties—access to exclusive spaces and people in the city otherwise denied them. This was a two-way street. Some of the middle-class, white students I got to know in the health club classes also found it thrilling to have access, through capoeira, to areas of the city previously off limits to them. They took to training and socializing in the favelas where their instructors taught and/or lived, partying on rooftop lajes and at bailes funk.

The instructors I knew who taught in Zona Sul health clubs were well aware that their new employment and sociality were precarious. They described themselves as not really belonging in those spaces and carefully guarded their jobs, knowing that if they made a slip in boa aparência—being tardy or speaking poorly in the work place—they could easily be replaced by one of the many other instructors in the city. They also described their best work as happening in the communities, "where real capoeiristas are made," as they told me; not in health clubs and private schools, but in the favelas where so many of them had also first found capoeira.

I witnessed the "making" of a capoeirista through my convivência with Tourinho, Erik, and Debora.

Birth of a Capoeirista

"Manda salta aí, rapaz!"

Obligingly, Tourinho launched his short, muscular body forward on the steep, cobblestoned slope of Pedro América. A round-off cartwheel into a back handspring, flip-flops somehow staying on his feet. My heart skipped a beat, worried this time his arms would fail and land him on his head. The men seated on plastic stools outside the corner bar who had called out "show us a flip!" cheered and raised their beer glasses. Tourinho grinned at me, demanding praise. At the bottom of Pedro América we cut through the alleyway that connected to Rua Tavares Bastos and there, parted ways: Tourinho turning left for a short downhill walk home, and I turning right for a longer walk home uphill.

Tourinho lived, along with his friend Erik and Erik's seventeen-year-old cousin Debora, at the first curve after cobblestoned Tavares Bastos leaves the asphalt of Rua Bento Lisboa. They lived in one of Rio's still-standing cortiços. The narrow facade of the two-story building—flush against the cliff—is deceptively small. Pass through the dilapidated doors and you will discover a third, subterranean level and a long walkway flanked by one-room apartments leading to an outdoor courtyard and communal toilet. The single toilet served dozens of families.

At eight, Tourinho, or Matheus as I first knew him, was physically small yet mature for his age: the lingering baby fat of his cheeks and belly at odds with his strength and independence. Erik was Matheus's best friend. A year older, he was tall and lean, his skin deeply tanned and his long blond hair bleached from hours spent with Debora and Matheus at the Flamengo beach. While Matheus was a bundle of energy, unruly and disdainful of adult authority or affection, Erik was quiet and contemplative, ready to tuck his hand into mine as we walked down the street. Debora was Erik's seventeen-year-old cousin and despite a sometimes-sour expression possessed a lanky beauty. She had dropped out of high school and, not working, spent her time looking after her younger siblings, nieces, and nephews. She had also adopted the care of Erik, whose mother was sick, and Matheus, whose single mother had six children under the age of ten.

On Tuesday and Thursday evenings, Matheus, Debora, Erik, and I trudged up Pedro América, the hill next to Tavares Bastos to the *casarão* (big house) community center, at the entrance to the Santo Amaro favela. Slightly larger than the Tavares Bastos favela, Santo Amaro maintained a drug traffic. I could see the fireworks from my house, warning signals set off by young boys hired by the traffickers to alert them to deliveries or police activity.

Some evenings when we arrived in Santo Amaro, the casarão was dark, class canceled as mothers were too scared to send their children through the favela past traffickers with semiautomatic guns, waiting a delivery and alert to trouble.

But most capoeira nights the casarão, a one-room building despite its name, was aglow with activity. Debora, Erik, Matheus, and I would add our flip-flops to the growing pile outside the door next to the mothers peeking in to watch class. The young mothers were there as much to watch the teacher, Naldo, as their children. Twenty-six-year-old Naldo, with a well-sculpted, tattooed body, warm smile, intelligence, and talent, was well known and admired in the favela.

I had met Naldo and his vivacious wife Ana at the CIEP, and when we discovered we lived near each other, we often rode the bus home together. Naldo and Ana, who had met as students in Mestre Camisa's class, had just returned to capoeira after a seven-year hiatus following the birth of their daughter Nathalia. Naldo had been born and raised in Santo Amaro, his grandmother one of the first settlers on the hill. As a teenager, she had come to Rio from Minas Gerais to work as a nanny in the Rua Paissandu in Flamengo, when "the water still met the street." Her poetic description places her arrival in Rio prior to the 1965 completion of the Aterro do Flamengo—a large park that was created by filling in a portion of the bay with earth from a razed hill in Rio's center. Naldo's grandmother remembers it was difficult to climb up through the forest to get to the small community that was developing on the hill; but she enjoyed living in her own rather than an employer's house with a view of the Guanabara Bay. This house, which Naldo lived in with his grandmother, mother, brother, Ana, and Nathalia, still had the bay view as the community had grown above it.

Ana was proud of her pale skin and strawberry blonde hair that gave her the capoeira nickname "Snow White," and enjoyed fooling cariocas into thinking she was a gringa when out with me. But Ana was as much a *carioca da gema* (from the yolk) as Naldo. She had grown up with a single working mom in downtown Rio but moved to Santo Amaro once she became involved with Naldo. Every morning, she donned a smart business suit, smoothed her hair, left her daughter in the care of her great-grandmother, and headed down to her bank job in the city center.

During his time away from capoeira, Naldo had served several years in the military and held various jobs, including as a computer graphic designer. But he missed capoeira and its lifestyle. Like Cascão and other capoeiristas who had grown up in Glória-Catete, he had first seen capoeira as a kid in the street roda at the Glória Market. He discovered that a capoeirista who lived in Rua Santo Amaro was teaching in a small boxing gym at the top of the hill, and he started training. By the time Naldo returned to capoeira, classes had stopped in Santo Amaro, the teacher having moved away. With the help of his buddy Farofa, Naldo took up the mantel. Their class in the casarão was instantly popular and soon had morphed into three consecutive classes serving close to one hundred children, adolescents, teens, and adults.

The community classes paid very little, if at all, and so Farofa and Naldo found part-time work teaching capoeira in private schools, which kept them ping-ponging around the city, Naldo on his motorcycle until it was stolen. That, along with falling back into the capoeira lifestyle—training and doing performances at night, traveling on weekends to out-of-state capoeira events, partying with other capoeiristas, and being surrounded by female students— would eventually contribute to the demise of both their marriages.

Matheus was Naldo's most talented student. With his strength and fear-lessness (which earned him the nickname Little Bull), Tourinho easily mas-tered even the most difficult floreios. Naldo would demonstrate an acrobatic move and after a few attempts, tip of his tongue poking through his lips in concentration, Tourinho got it—shouting out "Look, I'm Naldo!" It was not just Naldo's game that Tourinho imitated but also the posture and attitude of an older capoeirista. He swaggered to class, shirt tucked into the top of his abadá, wearing the beaded necklace I had given him from my trip to Angola. He boasted of his exploits in the street, and (with Debora's encouragement) of his many little girlfriends.

When Naldo started taking Tourinho to Mestre Camisa's monthly aulão he was a hit and soon accepting invitations to batizados and performances around town; a pint-sized capoeirista with such skill was an ensured crowd-pleaser. Tourinho would show off the T-shirts he was given at these events, provide blow-by-blow accounts of the games, and, like a baseball card col-lector reciting the stats of famous players, teach the other kids the names and characteristics of his favorite capoeiristas.

Not all of Naldo's students were as physically talented as Tourinho. Less daring Erik struggled with the acrobatic moves. I worried about him al-ways in Tourinho's shadow and not gaining the same recognition or sense of achievement. But there are many avenues to success in capoeira. One day coming down Tavares Bastos, I heard a high-pitched twang. Rounding the curve, I saw Erik standing in front of his house with a small berimbau. Dente, a friend of Naldo's and a skilled capoeirista and instrument maker, had seen that Erik took an interest in the music—hanging around after class to learn drum rhythms—and made him a child-sized berimbau. Erik be-came as skilled in music as Tourinho was in movement.

Debora also developed as a capoeirista. She was reluctant at first as she was older and taller than the other students at the casarão. But I convinced her to try, and over time she shifted from caretaker of Tourinho and Erik to capoeirista in her own right. Debora's mother, a tired woman with five children, had worried: "My daughter is already such a tomboy and a *brigona!*" she told me. It was true that Debora was a "fighter," bruises and scratches on display from her tussles with her brothers and kids on the street. But capoeira in the casarão did not incite aggression. Rather, it gave the youth an alternative way to express with their bodies. Sweeps and kicks that met their mark—something that in the street would have sparked a fight—were amicably accepted in the kids' rodas. When Naldo started giving Debora more responsibility in his classes and suggested that eventually she might become his teaching assistant at one of the private schools, her mother admitted that there might be a future for Debora in capoeira.

For months before their first batizado, Naldo's students speculated which instructors would "baptize" them. On the morning of the event, Erik and Tourinho waited for me outside their house, bathed, abadá rolled and bound with their raw cords soon to be replaced with colored cords. They ran ahead to the CIEP in Glória where dozens of instructors, students, family members, and friends were gathering. The several-hour ceremony included presentations of maculelê and samba, which Naldo's students had been practicing for weeks. For Tourinho and Erik, the batizado was the most important event of their lives so far.

Tourinho's "I am Naldo!" verbalized a desire to become someone with skill and recognition. A "somebody in an environment of nobodies," as another capoeirista who also grew up in Glória put it. Like Tourinho, he had spent his childhood hanging out in the streets, and when he saw kids playing in a roda was impressed:

"Someone arrives and you don't know who he is, he's nobody from the street. But then he jumps in and starts playing and you see him in a totally different light—he's got respect. I wanted that for myself. For a lot of kids in my neighborhood the only way to get respect was through drug trafficking. Capoeira gave me another way."

As Tourinho's self-confidence and recognition as a capoeirista grew, so did his swagger and rebellion. He started acting out in school, saying all he cared about was capoeira. After he broke a window in the street, his mother forbade him from going to train and ripped up his uniform.

Naldo felt responsible. "He wants to be just like me, so I have to be a role model," he told me. "Sometimes he tells people I'm his dad, and I go along with it because I want to be involved in his life, not just in capoeira."

So Naldo went to Tourinho's school to talk to his teachers and bought his protégé new school supplies when his behavior improved.

Naldo also told me, not without some pride, that Tourinho, with all his brashness, was an innate capoeirista: "Tourinho is the essence of capoeira. Capoeira is in his blood. Even if he stops training tomorrow, he will always be a capoeirista."

While seeming to naturalize Tourinho's knack for capoeira, Naldo also recognized that it was the environment that children like Tourinho grow up in that make them capoeiristas: "Kids in the favelas have no limits. They are always overcoming barriers and adapting to new circumstances. So, if you give them a little reassurance and affirmation they learn quickly."

Ironically, having "no limits" comes from growing up with limited resources. When the only playgrounds are the streets, soccer is played barefoot, and homemade paper kites are flown from rooftops, kids develop daring and physical dexterity. When resources are scarce—sometimes only a spinning top or a sense of self-worth—kids develop strategy and creativity (and at times malandragem and aggression) to hold on to what is theirs. These activities foster resourcefulness and self-reliance, survival skills in precarious life conditions. Capoeira also cultivates these attributes, but with a sense of grace, beauty, and camaraderie.

It was not just physical skills, however, that Mestre Camisa and instructors like Naldo worked to cultivate through capoeira.

Intelligent Bodies, Inspired Minds

"Have any of you heard of multiple intelligences?"

It was 10:00 p.m. on a Monday night in the CIEP. Training had ended, and Mestre Camisa was settling in for one of his *bate papos* (chats). I was swapping out of my sweaty T-shirt for a dry one to stave off the chill and stiffness that set in during these hour-or-more discussions. I paused at the mention of educator Howard Gardner's theory.

Mestre Camisa was holding up an article.

"Here, someone else read this out loud, I'm too slow."

Camisa nodded along at the description of Gardner's eight intelligences— visual, logical, linguistic, intrapersonal, interpersonal, naturalistic, kinesthetic, and musical.

"There are probably more than eight," Camisa interjected. "But you see, this is what I mean when I say that capoeira develops intelligence. A stupid guy (*burro*) comes to train with me, and after a year he's only half-stupid!"

Camisa's chuckle invited laughter from around the roda.

"What intelligences do capoeiristas have?"

Students shouted out "musical, kinesthetic, spatial, artistic."

"That's right! I think we have a lot already. I think you can teach everything—math, history, sociology—through capoeira. We should make a school that teaches all subjects through capoeira," Camisa said, unwittingly evoking the early twentieth-century experiential education of John Dewey.

"Look at me," he continued. "I only have an elementary school education, but I've learned a lot through capoeira. I learn from my students, and the people around me. A student gave me this article, see? You need to associate with people better educated than you, who talk better than you, so that you can improve yourself. And capoeira can do that for you. It's done that for me. Capoeira has given me everything."

Camisa closed his bate papo that night with a phrase he often repeated: "Capoeira is not just about pretty moves and cultivating a nice body. It is about knowing your place in society."

Camisa's phrase, "knowing your place in society," troubled me. On the one hand this, and many of the things Camisa said, are suggestive of *conscientização,* the cornerstone of Brazilian educator Paulo Freire's "pedagogy of the oppressed." Drawing on Karl Marx, Frantz Fanon, and John Dewey, Freire's theoretical and activist work posited popular education as a mechanism of social change if it engages critical pedagogy that works to expose oppressive conditions. Conscientização, or "critical consciousness" is a dialogic tool that allows the disenfranchised to dismantle internalized negative images of themselves that oppressors maintain through a "culture of silence." By becoming aware of their own oppression through the process of literacy (or theater as Augusto Boal elaborated) the dominated can liberate themselves and in turn, their oppressors and the world.[11]

Though only vaguely aware of Paulo Freire, Mestre Camisa nonetheless seemed to regard capoeira as a vehicle for conscientização. However, rather than the first step in a revolution for radical social change, as Freire saw it, conscientização in Mestre Camisa's usage was about *resgate de cidadania,* or "rescuing citizenship," a phrase popular among capoeira groups and NGOs at the time. He often used one of his former students as an example:

"Before capoeira he couldn't read, write, or speak properly. He had no teeth, no documents, no citizenship."

What is troubling about this citizenship discourse is its failure to question a social hierarchy that values some lives over others. "Knowing one's place in society" seems to uphold rather than dismantle race, class, and gender categories that express and maintain power relations. The onus then falls on the *individual* to move up the hierarchy from noncitizen to citizen in the classic neoliberal mold of personal achievement. Even while recognizing structural racism and classism, many Brazilians seem to endorse the idea that the *consequences* of poverty and racism—failure to get ahead—are a result of individual flaws rather than an unjust system that disproportionally allocates resources to some communities at the expense of others.

As an example, Mestre Touro was outspoken about racism in Brazil; yet when I asked him why he had a steady job and nice home while his brother Dentinho still lived in the favela and was chronically unemployed, he told me that this was because his brother had a "*cabeça fraca.*" A "weak head" suggests laziness, ignorance, or weak-will. In fact, Mestre Dentinho's personal flaw may have been his inability (or refusal) to use personal connections and *jeitinhos* (little ways) to land a government job as Touro had.

Claiming citizenship in Brazil is sometimes, unfortunately, nothing more than distancing oneself from racialized criminality in a system in which the rule of law is neither guaranteed or trusted. In Brazil, to be a citizen is to be subjected to, but not always protected by, impersonal laws, which the privileged get around through personal connections and/or bribery. As the Brazilian saying puts it: "To our enemies the law; to our friends, everything!"[12]

Mestre Camisa is an example of a system that works in favor of whiteness. While he often cites his own lack of formal education, it cannot be overlooked that his skin color has helped facilitate his success as it protects him from the racism, police harassment, and criminalization that many of his Afro-Brazilian students and other accomplished mestres experience day-to-day.

Parafuso fell in step with me as we were leaving the CIEP several hours later.

"Mestre certainly has the gift of the gab!" he chuckled.

"Are you heading back to your mom's?" I asked him.

"Yeah, but not for long, Camarão. I swear I am going to get out again!"

The first capoeirista I had played with in the CIEP whose game had awed me, Parafuso had become a friend. He taught in the neighborhood of Laranjeiras near my house, and so on Tuesdays and Thursdays I would race down from Naldo's classes in Santo Amaro to catch Parafuso's training, and I often hung out with him and his students on weekends. Parafuso was a dedicated capoeirista and instructor. He didn't socialize much with the students at the CIEP, preferring to hang out with his own students. He told me he liked to "*ficar na minha*" (keep to myself) to avoid gossip and competition.

Parafuso had grown up in a favela in the center of Rio where he still taught community classes. Several months earlier he had managed to save enough money to move into a room in a single occupancy hotel in Laranjeiras. And then the hotel burned down. In that particular dark humor I often witnessed in Brazil, Parafuso's misfortune became a source of teasing and jokes among his students:

"Kid finally get out of the favela and what happens! Fire! Back to mama's!"

This kind of teasing and laughter is a way to "acknowledge the utter absurdity of misfortune," but also a way to share, or carry part of the burden of the pain caused by that misfortune.[13] Dark humor in Brazil can be a way of witnessing and even speaking out against social suffering.[14] While going along with the humor, twenty-seven-year-old Parfuso, one of seven children of a domestic worker and alcoholic father, also confided to me how upset he was.

"I was so relieved to get out. I hated growing up there. I was hungry a lot and there was violence. Once when I was about twelve years old, I was hanging out on the street with a friend, and these cops were coming up the hill with their guns out. They told us to go home, but we were stupid kids and didn't listen. A little while later, we hear gunshots and then here come the cops back down the hill with a dead body in a sheet. They got pissed when they saw us, and you know what they made us do? They made us carry the body down the hill. I'll never forget it. The heavy feet kept slipping out of my hands, and blood was getting all over me. I started crying."

In the early 2000s, homicide was the leading cause of death for Black males between the ages of fifteen and twenty-four in Rio de Janeiro. So, it was no exaggeration when Parafuso and many other capoeiristas from the favelas told me they would probably be dead if not for capoeira. They often began interviews by thanking God, capoeira, and Mestre Camisa for being alive. It was the music and movement that first attracted Parafuso, but he soon realized that capoeira could also be an escape from his marginal status as a Black man from a favela. He took to wearing his uniform home after class so if there was a police check at the entrance to his favela, he would get through hassle-free.

"The cops would see me in uniform and know I wasn't a *vagabundo* (bum) or *marginal* (criminal). Some of them liked capoeira, or had even done it themselves."

In lieu of work documents (*carteira assinada*), a capoeira uniform, like the lunchbox or callused hands of a manual laborer, or the Bible of an evangelical, is proof that someone is an "honest citizen."[15] In fact, capoeira uniforms carry a variety of symbolic values deployed in different ways. Every capoeirista seems to have a story to tell about the protective power of their uniform: one Zona Norte mestre swears that one late night when his car broke in a deserted part of town he was approached by two men he was sure intended to rob him until they saw his capoeira uniform and decided to help him instead; another student had a gun held to her head through her car window while at a red light until the youth saw her uniform and, remembering she had taught free capoeira classes to him and other street kids when he was younger, lowered it and said, "Sorry, auntie." A middle-class capoeirista told me that she, like Parafuso, wore her uniform home after training but for a different reason: "I figure I won't get robbed or worse, because I am all dirty and sweaty. I'm unattractive and it's obvious I'm not carrying anything besides my bus fare."

The uniform is also a source of pride and respectability for young capoeiristas. In his classes in Santo Amaro, Naldo reminded his students to come to class freshly bathed in clean uniforms. One of his students, the six-year-old son of an alcoholic mother who had trouble maintaining her household, regularly came to class in a soiled uniform. A neighbor noticed and instructed the young capoeirista to drop his uniform off at her house after each training and she would have it washed, ironed, and folded for him before the next class.

Beyond the "magical" powers of its uniform to bestow respectability, self-esteem, and protection, capoeira can also lead to modest social mobility through professionalization. Parafuso realized this soon after he started training with Camisa:

"I saw other Black guys (negões) like me from favelas making a living teaching in schools and health clubs. And I thought I can do that! Now when I think back on the first classes I gave, I'm embarrassed. I didn't know how to speak! I made all these grammatical errors and said stupid shit. But like Mestre said tonight, even though I never finished school I can improve myself through capoeira. I hang out with more cultured people now—like you and some of my students. My kid's mother taught me a lot about speaking better. I still make mistakes, so I don't talk much at work. I don't want to say any stupid things (besteiras)."

Culture, in the way Parafuso used it here, means acting middle class and white, or in other words maintaining boa aparência. As the primary indicator of class and education (and therefore whiteness), language becomes a source of shaming. Uneducated Brazilians, like Parafuso, will often choose silence over losing face in certain situations.[16] Culture also means having the financial and social capital to adopt "non-Brazilian" qualities. In the early 2000s there were billboards all over Rio advertising an English language school with the ironic slogan, "Get some Culture!" In a country that purportedly prides itself on brasilidade, its African-European-Indigenous mixed national culture, the hierarchy is clear: "real" culture belongs to those with the means, and looks, to assimilate foreign, non-Black influences.

Mestre Camisa was outspoken about resisting encroachment of foreign culture in Brazil.

"If you want to talk about capoeira as resistance," he told me during an interview, "then think of it as a resistance against deculturation. Brazilians don't know their own culture anymore. And it's so rich—every region of Brazil has its own dance and music traditions! And since capoeira was and is all over Brazil, it teaches all that. Brazilians come to know their own culture through capoeira—they're brasilified!"

Camisa would remind his students that capoeiristas needed not just to play capoeira but also to dance samba and jongo, a regional dance from the state of Rio. Sometimes he played the samba rhythm on his berimbau at the end of class and urged us all to dance, some students quick to show off their adept footwork, and others shuffling awkwardly to hoots of laughter.

Mestre Camisa insisted on a personal refusal of foreign cultural influences. He never drank Coke (or national sodas, for that matter), and despite his robust international travel to capoeira events, he refused to learn English, stating, "Foreign capoeiristas need to learn Portuguese! You can't have convivência with capoeira if you don't speak the language."

At the same time that Camisa felt strongly about maintaining Brazilian traditions and resisting especially U.S. cultural imperialism, he was adamant that culture, and capoeira, are not something folkloric to preserve in a museum: to the contrary, he claimed that capoeira was "living and dynamic." He thus saw no contradiction with professionalizing capoeira—what some practitioners equate with modernizing, and commercializing the art.

"This idea that to be a capoeirista you have to be poor and uneducated, and only teach capoeira to people like you or worse, is ridiculous! It's like that famous line by Joãosinho Trinta: 'only intellectuals like misery.'"

Trinta, the famous Beija Flor set and costume designer, transformed Rio's carnival parades in the 1980s into over-the-top glitter fests. When asked about his ostentatious floats and costumes he responded that "those who like poverty are intellectuals, the poor like luxury."

Camisa's statement also reminded me of the uniform aesthetic I'd seen in a *capoeira angola* group I had started visiting near my house in Catete. The students were predominantly middle-class university students who lived in the Zona Sul. Many of them were politicized around issues of race and were drawn to *capoeira angola* for this reason. Their uniforms were often ripped, faded T-shirts, cheap, worn-out tennis shoes, and old pants held up by bits of string. The aesthetic replaces a politics of respectability with a bohemian, countercultural one; only intellectuals—and those with social and racial privilege that allow them to move around the streets free of police harassment—like torn, dirty clothes.

Intimate relationships were also a site of cross-racial, cross-class mixing that could lead to increased social status. Parafuso, and other male instructors who taught in Zona Sul venues, often dated, and sometimes had children, with students of a higher social and economic class. These male instructors used their body capital as strong, good-looking, talented capoeiristas to move up the social ladder through their romantic or marital relationships. For the fortunate few, romantic relationships with foreign capoeiristas could sometimes lead to immigration abroad, where with the help of their student-wife they would eventually achieve residency and legitimate work in their new home. More often than not, these relationships ended due to infidelity or the pressures of cross-cultural communication and expectations.

In Rio, many instructors maintained ties to the favelas where they grew up. Capoeira had given them an alternative lifestyle to the drug trafficking that many male favela youth turned to in order to escape the drudgery of low-paying jobs in the informal economy.[17] Capoeira also provided them with the income, respect, and access to Zona Sul material and affective relationships valued in favela youth culture. Some of them would teasingly refer to each other as "playboys," a carioca label for white, middle-class males who wear expensive name-brand clothes. They knew however that any rise in status was temporary and would dissipate as soon as they lost their teaching jobs in the wealthy health clubs.

While being Black could increase male capoeiristas' cultural capital, the same could not be said for female capoeiristas.

Women Warriors

"I didn't talk to anyone when I first started training at the CIEP. I was from a Zona Norte group so my abadá and cord were ugly. And I had bad hair (*cabelo ruim*)," Cafeína told me when we finally sat down for an interview.

It had taken me several months to approach Cafeína, one of only two female instructors who trained regularly at the CIEP, and who, like Parafuso, kept to herself. When other students began to greet me with big smiles and handshakes, Cafeína continued to nod curtly—and only after I greeted her first. At thirty-seven, she was one of the older students at the CIEP. She was short and strong and tough in the roda. She intimidated me. When I asked others about her they said, "Cafeína is a warrior: Black, poor, from a favela in the suburbs, old, a single mother, but she fights."[18] In other words, despite a nexus of identities that put her on the bottom rung of the social hierarchy, Cafeína was a fighter. I needed to get to know her.

When I finally screwed up the courage to ask if I could visit her at her home to chat about her experience in capoeira, Cafeína's guarded face opened up in pleasure and with an almost girlish giggle she said, "You are going to come all the way to the Baixada to visit *me?*" On the appointed day, I took three buses to make the two-and-a-half-hour journey that Cafeína made three evenings a week to get to the CIEP, often with her six-year-old son in tow. At her family's favela compound—a cluster of buildings in various states of construction around an outdoor kitchen—Cafeína apologized for the unfinished cinder block structure where she lived with her mother, her son, and the teenage son of her ex-husband. She ushered me into her sister's more complete house, with tiled floors and doors. Her brother-in-law kept us supplied with snacks and soda as we talked.

Cafeína, like so many of Camisa's students from favelas, started training capoeira when she was an adolescent because it was one of the few activities available for free at an open-air samba rehearsal space near her house. She admitted sheepishly that she first went to watch the "*gatinhos*" or "cute guys." The mestre noticed her hanging around and invited her to train. She discovered she "identified" with it, a term capoeiristas use when capoeira grabs and holds on to someone.

Cafeína explained: "Here in the Baixada we poor people don't have a lot of options. I didn't have a father, my mother worked all the time, and we often didn't have food on the table. So, capoeira became something for me. I liked to train hard and engage in jogo duro, it was a way to release the tensions of the day. We suffer a lot in the suburbs. We don't have jobs, we sleep badly, eat badly—I would come to train after not eating all day—and playing hard made me feel better."

Despite lack of support from home—her mother didn't like her daughter doing a "man's thing," especially when it took away from her duties taking care of the house and her younger siblings—Cafeína stuck with capoeira and rose through the ranks of her group. When she split up with the father of her son, a capoeirista in the same group, Cafeína looked for a change.

"It wasn't viable in the group anymore with him still training."

A pattern I would hear repeatedly: when couples from the same group break up, the woman is expected to leave, no matter her rank. One advanced capoeirista I knew told me she left her group after splitting up with her boyfriend of the same rank when the teacher started singing songs about snakes (code word for a duplicitous woman) in the roda as she played.

Cafeína continued: "It wasn't a bad thing as I'd gotten to the end of the road with that group and style. I wasn't going to develop anymore."

Like other capoeiristas who had switched to ABADÁ, Cafeína was attracted to Mestre Camisa's innovations. She and others described their previous styles as constrained to just one type of game "played fast or slow." Mestre Camisa had developed, with the input of his students, five distinct games. *Angola, São Bento Grande, Benguela, Iúna,* and *Amazonas* are played to similarly named berimbau rhythms developed by Mestre Bimba and vary not only in speed but also in characteristics: Iúna is an acrobatic game; São Bento Grande a faster or more "objective" game with high kicks and takedowns; Angola is slow and cunning; Benguela, low and fluid; and Amazonas mimics animal movements.

The ABADÁ style offered new avenues for creative self-expression, and the ABADÁ organization provided possibilities for professionalization. Mestre Camisa regularly held workshops on pedagogy and encouraged his students to think about other ways—such as going back to school—to enhance their CVs and gain regular employment. Inspired, Cafeína went back to night school, first getting her high school diploma and eventually starting a college degree in physical education. Like others with her class and educational background, she enrolled in one of the many private "universities" that had sprung up in Brazil in the 1990s as a neoliberal push to "democratize" education. These profit-driven institutions were expensive and often unaccredited. Despite the payments and grueling schedule, Cafeína persisted and eventually got her degree.

Along with teaching capoeira and physical education at a Catholic elementary school, Cafeína taught free classes near her house. Though she had a number of adolescent and young adults, it was difficult, as a woman, to build a strong group.

"One time I was teaching a takedown and I demonstrated on a male student. He said, 'What is this! Are you crazy! You can't do that to a man!' I told him, look, this is not about being a man or woman. I am your teacher and I am showing you something. Better you learn it from me then out on the street! He stopped training with me after that. Now if I had been a male instructor, he would have accepted it. They *want* a male teacher who will rough them up."

Compiling Cafeína's challenges as a woman was her race:

"If you're a big Black guy you're going to get respect and do well in capoeira. Even if that might be the only place in your life that you're successful! Because of its history, people associate capoeira with Black men. They want to see a strong Black man playing. They don't want to see a Black woman! It's ugly to them, unfeminine. I used to get called a lesbian because I played capoeira. That's why I felt so uncomfortable when I first started going to the CIEP—all those white girls in their tight-fitting abadá."

Cafeína was particularly sensitive to the fact that, as her capoeira had improved and she rose through the ranks, she had never been abroad.

"All these ABADÁ groups abroad, they don't want a short, Black female capoeirista. They want a big Black guy or a pretty female capoeirista with her long straight hair!"

Capoeira's racial fault lines were driven home to me again several years later when Cafeína finally got an invitation and secured a visa to an event in California. She came with Maestrinha, the other female instructor I was close to in Rio. A few years younger than Cafeína, Maestrinha was a hard-working, middle-class white woman who had made her way up the ABADÁ hierarchy. She had a fast, explosive game, pretty floreios, and a quick temper. On more than one occasion I had to diffuse volatile social situations (once physically removing her from the bleachers in the Sambódromo one carnival night when she got in a fight). Maestrinha was not scared to hold her own in the roda and was laid up for a while from a knee injury a male player had intentionally given her because he didn't like the way she was playing (tough and competent) with him.

Despite training hard, playing well, and receiving the title of instructor, Maestrinha did not have any adult students. For a number of years, she had dated another instructor and together they had built up a small satellite group. But when the relationship crumbled, the students stuck with her former boyfriend. Maestrinha taught youth all over Rio—in nursery schools, condominiums, favelas, a home for children with AIDS, and a school for the deaf. At one point she even counted the daughter of television star Xuxa among her students at the American School. She went back to school to get her masters in physical education. She wrote and self-published several short books on her work with capoeira. Still, jobs were precarious and underpaid. She toyed with going abroad, remarking that it was no coincidence that the only two ABADÁ female instructors, Edna Lima and Márcia Treidler, had built successful groups only once they had migrated to the United States.

By the time Maestrinha and Cafeína traveled together to California, Maestrinha had already visited the United States several times. Even though Cafeína had work documents through the school where she taught capoeira, she had been denied a visa on multiple occasions because of her race and class. Thrilled that Cafeína had finally fulfilled her dream, I introduced her, explaining to the audience the hardships she had endured, as a Black single mom from a favela, to get where she was in capoeira today. Maestrinha didn't talk to me for the rest of the evening.

It was not the first time my friend had given me the cold shoulder. In fact, our friendship solidified after another time Maestrinha put me "in the freezer" as they say in Brazil. I had accidently unbalanced her motorcycle while she was maneuvering us onto a sidewalk to park before training, toppling it onto a birdcage and liberating the bird to the irate yells of the owner. Maestrinha refused to talk to me through class. Finally she sidled up to me during the roda and sung under her breath a capoeira song with the chorus "*pomba voou, pomba voou*" (the dove flew, the dove flew), an indirect message that we were okay again.

In California, I had to break the silence and ask Maestrinha why she was mad. She was offended that I had made a big deal over Cafeína. She, too, had struggled to make her way up through the sexist world of capoeira and what was more, she told me, it was harder for her: she was not Black, not from a favela, not a single mom (yet)—just another aging white woman overlooked in capoeira.

Saudades

I got the news via Facebook in 2015. Debora, who by her early twenties had abandoned capoeira, married, had a daughter, and moved to Brasília, had a new post: a video of eight-year-old Tourinho playing capoeira, RIP scrawled beneath. My heart stopped for a little bit. Then I searched through my photo archive, pulled up a couple of black-and-white close-ups of Tourinho playing in the roda and posted them. There was a flurry of online commentary and emotions for a week or two and then Tourinho's death slipped quietly into the internet netherworld. He was one of the luckier ones: so many young, Black, male deaths in Brazil go unaccounted for—undocumented and un-commemorated.

I found out the circumstances of Tourinho's death, but never the full story, when I returned to Brazil in 2016. Naldo told me what little he knew as we sat at a juice stand after training one night.

"Oh Katya. I couldn't stop it. He started messing around with the drug trafficking in Santo Amaro."

Like ten years before, when Tourinho misbehaved in school and Naldo went to his teachers, Naldo paid a visit to the traffickers on the hill.

"I asked them not to let Tourinho get involved. I told them he had potential as a capoeirista."

Out of respect for Naldo and capoeira, they agreed. But it didn't matter in the end. Tourinho's mother moved her family to another favela higher up in the hills beyond Santa Teresa.

"Way up there, God knows where," Naldo gestured upward. Favelas are islands unto themselves, little communication between them unless there is a hostile drug-trafficking takeover. In his new home no one knew Tourinho or cared about his talent for capoeira. There he slipped into trafficking and eventually landed in jail.

"How did he die, Naldo?"

"I can't really tell you. All I heard was that he'd been locked up for a couple months and his mom went to visit him. He looked bad, and he told her he thought he was going to die. And then a few days later he was dead."

What was it about Tourinho that prevented him from committing to capoeira? Why didn't he pursue his childhood dream, as he often told me, of one day becoming an instructor "just like Naldo"? Did other life forces just prove too strong? Perhaps in the end Tourinho's talent was a disservice. Perhaps capoeira came too easily and so he grew bored and restless with nothing to work toward. Perhaps he learned to fly too high, too young. I will never know as we never had that conversation.

I am so sorry, my little friend. Saudades.

Figure 1. Roda in a Favela. Rio de Janeiro, 2003.

Figure 2. Mestre Beiçola.
2009. Photographer
unknown. Photograph
courtesy of Mestre Beiçola.

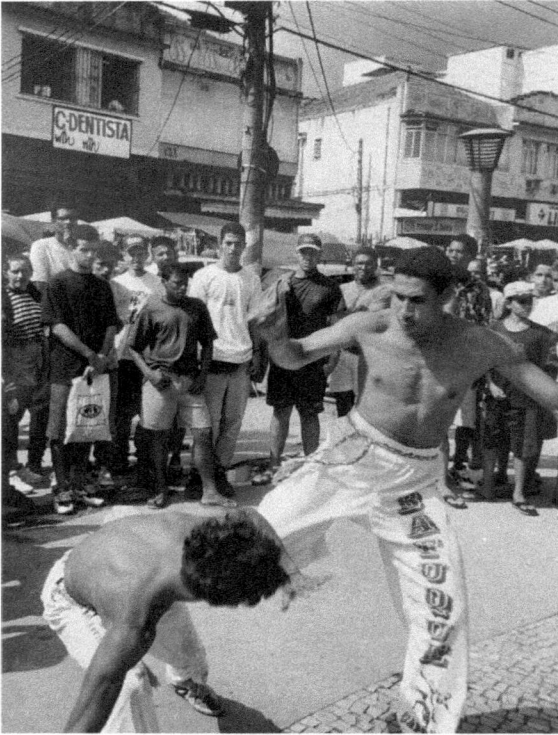

Figure 3. Street roda. Mestre Sardinha (*facing camera*) and Fernandinho. Zona Norte, Rio de Janeiro, 1996.

Figure 4. Mestre Touro playing with a *navalho* (straight razor) in a demonstration of how nineteenth-century *capoeiras* used weapons. Penha, Rio de Janeiro, 2002.

Figure 5. Mestre Dentinho at Mestre Touro's monthly roda. Penha, Rio de Janeiro, 2002.

Figure 6. Jorginho (age 15). Penha, Rio de Janeiro, 2002.

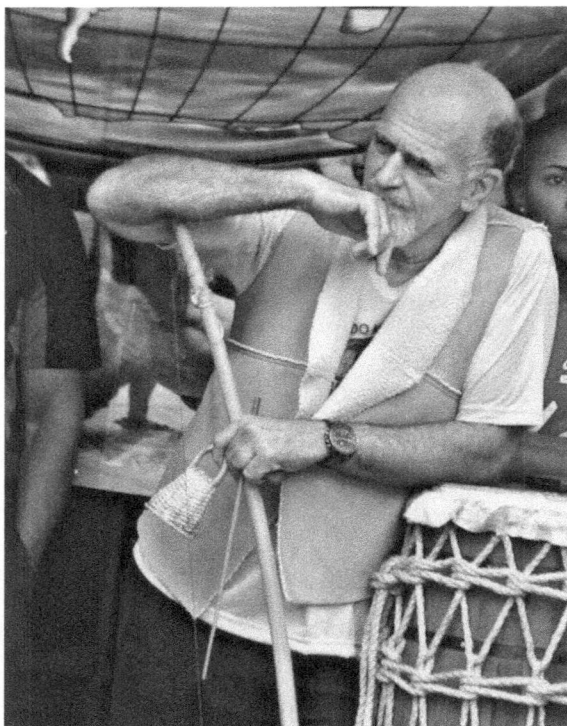

Figure 7. Mestre Camisa. 2018. Photograph by Raquel "Gasparzinha" Costa.

Figure 8. Parafuso. Street roda at the Mercadinho São José, Rio de Janeiro, 2003.

Figure 9. Tourinho. Street roda at the Mercadinho São José, Rio de Janeiro, 2003.

Figure 10. Cascão at the Cristo Redentor during a performance for the delegation from the Pan American Games. Rio de Janeiro, 2002.

Figure 11. Bacurau (*facing camera*) and Chá Preto in a chamada at the foot of the Cristo Redentor. Rio de Janeiro, 2002.

Figure 12. Kids class in Dona Marta. Rio de Janeiro, 2003.

Figure 13. Hamster at the top of Santa Marta Hill with Pão de Açúcar in the background. Rio de Janeiro, 2003.

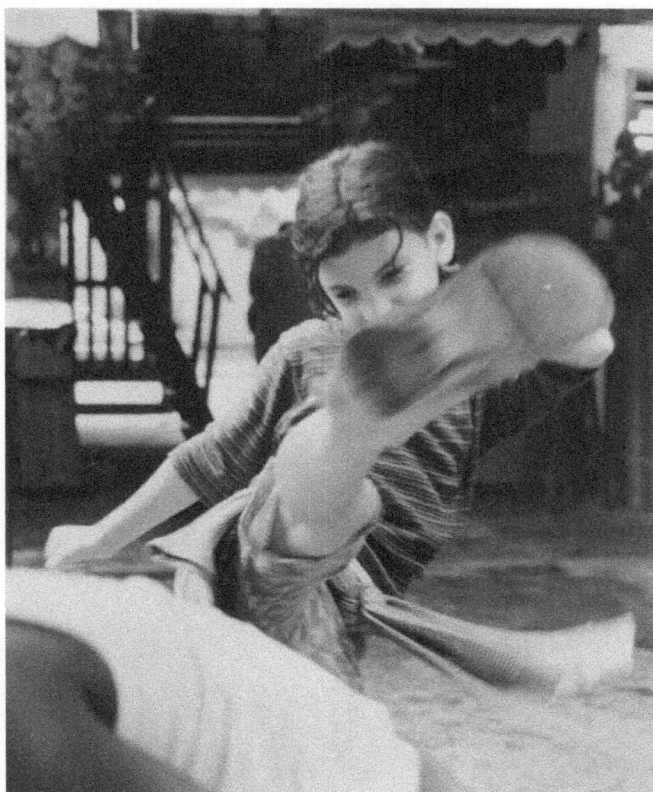

Figure 14. Pirulito (Lollipop), Debora's sister, playing capoeira in the street. Rio de Janeiro, 2003.

Figure 15, (*above*). Naldo. Street roda, Mercadinho São José, Rio de Janeiro, 2014.

Figure 16, (*left*). Maria Preta, ABADÁ capoeirista, dancing jongo. Mercadinho São José, Rio de Janeiro, 2018.

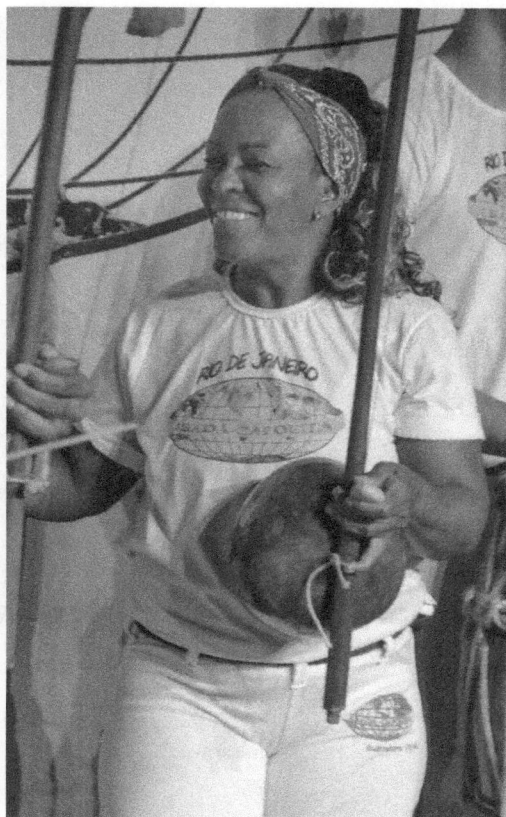

Figure 17, (*left*). Cafeína at her students' batizado. Rio de Janeiro, 2019. Photograph by Raquel "Gasparzinha" Costa.

Figure 18, (*below*). Maestrinha, 2003. Photographer unknown. Photograph courtesy of Maestrinha.

Figure 19, (*above*). Camarão (the author). Street roda in Ipanema. Rio de Janeiro, 2003. Photographer unknown.

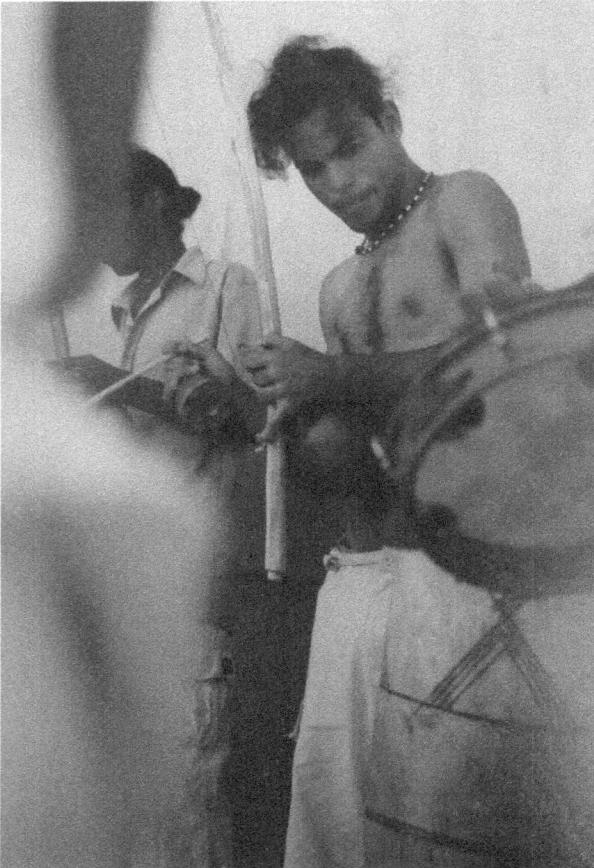

Figure 20, (*left*). Playing locally made instruments in Benguela, Angola, 2002. Crash on the berimbau.

Figure 21. Cabuenha. Still image taken from the video *Planeta Africa Cabuenha Poesia no Imbondeiro,* produced and directed by Cabuenha and Yewa; used with the permission of Cabuenha.

Figure 22. Camarão (author) playing with son Lucien in a roda. Mestre Cabello on the left berimbau, Santos Flores on the right berimbau. The Ark, Durham, NC, 2015. Photographer unknown.

5

IMAGINING BRAZIL IN AFRICA

ANGOLA, 2002

Mestre Camisa was urging me to drink more tonic water.

"Camarão, you know I don't drink soda, but I'm making an exception because the quinine in tonic is antimalarial."

I didn't tell Camisa, also a teetotaler, that I would have preferred my tonic mixed with gin to settle my nerves before our flight to Angola. I wasn't nervous about going to a country just months out from a brutal twenty-seven-year civil war. I was nervous about traveling as the only student, and female, along with Mestre Camisa and two high-ranking instructors, or *mestrandos*.[1]

In September of 2002, a year into my fieldwork, Mestre Camisa had announced in the CIEP after class one evening that he would be returning to Luanda. The Angolan rebel leader, Jonas Savimbi, had been killed, ending the civil war that had devastated Angola since its independence from Portugal in 1975. Mestre Camisa dubbed the trip "In Search of Roots."

"Just ask him! I'm sure he'll take you," Maestrinha encouraged me after class when I told her I wanted to go.

"But I'm barely a graduada, I just got my blue cord!"

Maestrinha rolled her eyes. "Camarão, you're a researcher. He'll understand. He will *want* to take you."

So, on a balmy late October evening I found myself stepping off a TAAG flight onto the warm tarmac of Luanda's small airport. Mestrando Duende, from Bahia, dropped to his knees and with tears in his eyes, kissed his fingers, touched them to ground, and said, "I have come home."

Angola plays a large, and largely romanticized, role in the capoeira imaginary. Often evoked in song and touted as capoeira's ancestral home, Angola can appear frozen in time. Joining other Afro-Brazilians in search of what Patricia de Santana Pinho calls the "imaginary community" of Africa, and African Americans who visit West African slave forts to reckon with their own pasts, Brazilian capoeiristas journey to Angola with the hope of uncovering capoeira's past and creating a deeper spiritual connection to their art form.[2] What we in fact encountered on our roots trip to Angola was a modern, chaotic city emerging from a near half century of war in search of its own sense of self.

I also experienced in Luanda a capoeira convivência with a particular postcolonial-postwar African flare. "Conviviality and improvisation," historian Achille Mbembe tells us, "are inherent in the postcolonial form of authority."[3] Used here to understand the singular mix of intimacy and parody, often dark, that Mbembe argues is endemic to the relationship between postcolonial African authorities and their subjects, conviviality and improvisation also speaks to the ways Africans negotiate and move through their built environments and social worlds. In his architectural ethnography of Monrovia, Liberia, Daniel Hoffman argues that modern African cities generate a "proliferation of identities and performances" that lead to new forms of connectivity, collective belonging, and mobilization.[4]

In an ironic twist, while Brazilian capoeiristas imagine Africa in Brazil, Angolan capoeiristas now imagine Brazil in Africa as a means for shaping their identities and futures. Brazilian culture—from soap operas to music and fashion—are popular in Angola; and capoeira is particularly attractive because it is from Brazil yet originally Angolan! Claiming capoeira as something that is "in our blood" gives young Angolans pride in their homeland, an identity and community, and a direct connection to Brazil and the wider world. As a form of "associational life" that springs up in urban environments with uncertain futures, capoeira provides aspirational opportunities within, and perhaps beyond, African cities and states.[5]

For both Angolan and Brazilian capoeiristas, their practice becomes a way to simultaneously *root* themselves in a local (if imagined) past and *route* themselves to a global future (perhaps equally imagined) of transnational mobility and cosmopolitanism. While some of the Angolan capoeiristas I met in Luanda were already transnational, most were not, and probably never would be. Nonetheless, being part of an imagined community that stretched from Africa to Europe to the Americas allowed them to connect their own experiences and lives to a larger world and possible future that exceeded their postwar present.

For me, the trip to Angola would be another sensorial introduction to an enchanting and troubling city—and to the capoeiristas who skillfully move through it.

Nostalgia in a City of Concrete Skeletons

In the novel, *Os Transparentes* (*The Transparent City*), Odonato becomes increasingly translucent and weightless as he searches Luanda for his missing son. In a poetic narrative that mixes Afro-pessimism and magical realism, Angolan author Ondjaki captures a shattered Luanda in the year 2002. The war has ended, and yet the city seems at the edge of an abyss. Buildings crumble and burn; orphaned refugees from the war-torn provinces wash cars, sell seashells, and make public announcements on the National Radio about their missing mothers; American business men and Angolan politicians gather over imported whiskey in boardrooms to discuss plans to privatize water and drill for oil under the city; and foreign scientists and tourists arrive at the airport to witness what the government first touts as the "most Angolan of solar eclipses" and then miraculously cancels when it no longer proves politically profitable.[6]

The novel's action revolves around a group of people—a war widow, an orphan, a former army general, a postman, a journalist, and a man with an enormously swollen testicle—thrown into circumstantial convivência by a deteriorating and mystical apartment building. A looming co-presence among the novel's characters, the building is ephemeral, fluid, and shifting. Water flowing from burst pipes reshapes the contours of the first floor and materializes new dangers in the hallways and stairwells. Living in uneasy convivência with the building, the residents are wary but also find an unexpected, restorative comfort when they bathe their weary feet in the waters. The building captures the "liquidity" of modern African cities.[7] Nothing can be taken for granted when the built environment shifts underfoot.

Not just liquid, African cities—or at least certain ruinous neighborhoods—are also invisible. And those who live in the ruins, or interstitial gaps of the "legible" city, also become illegible and invisible.[8] The novel's main character is struck by a rare malaise that erases him bit by bit. By the end, Odonato has become as insubstantial and translucent as the balloons that decorate Luanda to celebrate the first oil excavations. Devastated by the news that his son, arrested for a petty crime, has died in police custody, Odonato begs his wife to tether him to the roof terrace so that he can float and contemplate his beloved, ravaged city below. His wife worries that he will drift away but he assures her that "nostalgia ties me to this city."[9]

Reading *Os Transparentes* twenty years after my first trip to Angola reignited my sensorial memories of Luanda: a bombed-out city with interiors of buildings exposed to the sky in a penumbral glow. It was not warfare that wreaked this destruction. Waged predominantly in the interior provinces, the civil war had only reached Luanda briefly in 1992. Luanda was not a destroyed city, but an incomplete city of concrete skeletons.

The nostalgia that ties Odonato to his city is a longing for a past, "the time before" ambiguously evoked by different characters throughout the novel.

But it is also a "nostalgia for the future": a particular postcolonial African affect, this longing is not for what *was* but for what *has not yet come*—for the unfulfilled promises of modernity and progress first augured by independence from colonialism and then by neoliberal development.[10] Luanda in 2002 was a city-in-waiting.

Unlike Brazil with its relatively early and bloodless transition to independence, Angola separated late and violently from Portugal. Four years after the first Sub-Saharan African country won independence (Ghana, 1957), Angola began its freedom struggle. Ten years later the Portuguese were close to defeating the Angolan guerrilla fighters, but then on April 25, 1974, the Carnation Revolution in Lisbon ushered in a new regime that promised independence to all of Portugal's African colonies—Cabo Verde, Guinea-Bissau, São Tomé and Príncipe, Moçambique, and Angola. By November 11, 1975, the official start of Angola's independence, close to half a million people of the six million population had fled the country, many leaving behind fully furnished apartments. Independence marked not the end, but the beginning of the war, and years of violence and suffering. From 1975 to 2002, 1.5 million Angolans would die in one of the worst African conflicts of the twentieth century.

The civil war was a power struggle between two former liberation movements, the MPLA (The People's Movement for the Liberation of Angola), which declared itself the governing party from its seat in Luanda, and UNITA (National Union for the Total Independence of Angola) that ruled from the interior provinces. While the MPLA was mainly comprised of Mbundu people in the coastal urban areas and UNITA by Ovimbundu people in the interior rural areas, the war was always more of an ideological than ethnic struggle. It rapidly became a theater for Cold War politics, with some ironic twists. MPLA president Agostinho Neto, and later José Eduardo Dos Santos who succeeded Neto after his death in 1979, was backed by a largely creole, Portuguese-speaking, wealthy, cosmopolitan population; yet because they espoused a socialist agenda, they gained the support of the Soviet Union and Cuba. Rebel leader Jonas Savimbi, whose UNITA supporters were largely Indigenous, rural, poor, and native-speaking, promoted Black nationalism; yet, because they were resisting communists, they garnered the support of the United States and apartheid-ruled South Africa. This international backing, as well as "blood diamonds" that allowed Savimbi to finance his struggle (and run up $500,000 tabs on his visits to a lobbying firm in Washington, DC) enabled the war to last twenty-seven years.

While Luanda may not have felt the direct horrors of war, it certainly experienced the collateral damage. The civil war displaced over four million people, many of whom fled to Luanda. The small colonial city could not handle the influx, and informal neighborhoods (*musseques*) sprang up in the city center and bled its edges. My first impressions of a battle-weary Luanda were actually those of an overpopulated city with an overtaxed infrastructure that had not been updated since 1975. Sparse street lamps along the wide, lane-less avenues from the airport cast an eerie glow as if portending the coming solar eclipse, announced on billboards: "The eclipse is marvelous, your eyes are precious!"[11] Traffic, not yet the gridlock it would become in the next decade as petro-dollars poured into the city, edged cautiously across intersections past dark traffic lights, useless as ornamental sentries.

The apartment building where I stayed with Brenda, one of the young Angolan capoeiristas, was in the heart of the city on the Praça Kinaxixi. The six-story building where Brenda had grown up with her single mother and younger brother—raised on pillars to create an open-air lobby—had once been a stylish example of midcentury tropical modernist architecture. But by 2002, like so many of the buildings in Luanda, it had slid into disrepair. The lobby, corridors, stairwells, and stalled elevators were filled with trash and rusty generators. Water was erratic, residents leaving bathtub taps open to catch water when it did suddenly start to flow to create reservoirs for bathing and cooking.

Cordoned off from the external decay, the inside of Brenda's apartment was a time capsule. Once a comfortable middle-class, three-bedroom home with a sunken living room, dining room, and enclosed terrace, the apartment had not seen any improvements in thirty years, with the exception of the room where I slept—to which Sylvia, Brenda's affable, talkative, and anxious mother, had given a fresh coat of paint.

Sylvia's apartment building was luxurious compared to others nearby. The Prédio da Lagoa (named after the filled-in lagoon on which Kinaxixi was constructed), was a high-rise hull of gray concrete, incomplete since 1975, hovering above the other buildings. Despite precarious conditions, the building was home to over a hundred families. Laundry hung on narrow, railing-less balconies, where you could also see cooking fires and toddlers playing, nothing between them and the eighteen-floor drop to the street below.

With its crumbling buildings and congested traffic, it was hard to believe that Praça Kinaxixi had once been Luanda's architectural and cultural hub. Built in the 1950s when the city was urbanizing and expanding, the large square has four main avenues radiating out in the cardinal directions. The Praça's main attraction had been an upscale shopping center, which after independence operated as an open-air market before closing for yet-to-begin renovations in 2002. The building stood abandoned and the vendors displaced to markets in the city's outskirts or left to sell what they could from plastic tubs on their heads as they walked the downtown streets.

With its skyscrapers, dominant Portuguese language, creolized population, and absence of the colorful wax-dyed clothing ubiquitous in other West African countries (only the *zungueiras,* or female street vendors, wore faded cloth tied around their waists), Luanda felt closer to Lisbon or Rio de Janeiro then Accra or Lomé. Even what the zungueiras carried on their heads—a running list of which I kept in my journal—were randomly cosmopolitan:

> One large roller-board suitcase
> Colorful zippers sticking up like a mohawk from a piece of styrofoam
> A stack of china plates
> A single purple platform shoe
> Neon-colored socks dangling in front of the face of the vendor like a
> psychedelic Obaluaiê

Despite their eclectic modern wares, these vendors seemed out of place in downtown Luanda rather than its peripheries. Much like Rio's asfalto-morro distinction that keeps certain bodies in certain places, Luanda's "concrete-musseque"—referring to the skyscrapers and shantytowns—distinction also organizes bodies in space.[12] Yet the formal and informal cities bleed into each other; tarmac roads suddenly turn to dirt in the city center and end abruptly in the dust and potholes of the suburbs. Unlike the SUVs and occasional Humvees driving around U.S. cities and suburbs, four-wheel vehicles are a real (if unattainable for most) asset in Luanda.

Queen Nzinga in a Four-Wheel Drive

It was from the window of one such vehicle, a small Cherokee jeep, that I experienced Luanda. The jeep belonged to Brenda who along with her partner Gindungo (a short and fast capoeirista nicknamed after the hot, red peppers that spice Angolan food) had organized the event. Brenda and Gindungo were among a small number of advanced students in Luanda responsible for the group. But it was Brenda, despite being one of the few women in a group of mainly young men and boys, who was the real powerhouse keeping things together. She deserved her regal capoeira nickname, Nzinga, after the fierce seventeenth-century warrior-queen of Ndongo who defended her kingdom against the Portuguese. Like Zumbi, the warrior king of the maroon society of Palmares and born in Brazil just two years after Nzinga's death, little is known about the queen. Yet, like Zumbi, Nzinga (also spelled Njinga and

Ginga) has become a symbol of national pride in Angola, and also a popular branding emblem, most prominently on the national coffee, Ginga Café.

Nzinga was the sister of Ngola Mbandi, ruler of the interior Ndongo kingdom that lay south of the Kongo Kingdom and east of Luanda. Adapting the Bantu word Ngola, similar in meaning to "king," the Portuguese called this area Reino D'Angola, which would eventually become the name of their colony and a cognate for West Central Africans sent to Brazil. When the Portuguese turned their greedy eyes from the arid coast around their ports in Luanda and Benguela to the fertile interior lands and slave markets, they were met by a formidable army. Ndongo male and female warriors were highly skilled in archery and hand-to-hand combat. According to one Jesuit chronicler, "all their defense consists of *sanguar,* which is to leap from one side to another with a thousand twists and such agility that they can dodge arrows and spears."[13] This agility—apparently cultivated since childhood through a rhythmic dance practice—was displayed in large military parades and mock battles.[14] Nzinga, herself a skilled soldier, performed in these military reviews into her eighties and bragged that in her youth she was not scared to "face twenty-five armed men."[15]

Eventually the Portuguese wore down Ndongo resistance and Ngola Mbandi turned to diplomacy, sending his then forty-year-old sister to Luanda. When instructed at court to sit on the floor before the Portuguese governor on his throne, Nzinga allegedly ordered a member of her entourage to crouch, and sat upon her as if she were a stool. Impressed by Nzinga's display of power (or persuaded by her consent to a Catholic baptism) the governor recognized Ndongo's independence. Peace was short-lived, and when the Portuguese renewed aggressions, Nzinga's hopeless brother killed himself. Nzinga became ruler of Ndongo, declared herself a man (insisting that one of her several husbands dress and act as a woman), and marched into battle with her soldiers. Despite her many tactics, including aligning with the Imbangalas (mercenary groups of roving male warriors feared for their violence), Nzinga was eventually defeated by the Portuguese, becoming a slave trade intermediary and converting her now vassal kingdom to Christianity.

After her death and well into the nineteenth century, Queen Nzinga became a source of fascination for European writers and a stand-in for the vilified, savage, and erotic African (she appears in a Marquis de Sade novel, forcing her soldiers to fight gladiator-style to the death for the prize of having sex with her).[16] By the mid-twentieth century, Queen Nzinga had become within Angola a symbol of the nation's struggle for independence, and outside of Angola a symbol of Black feminism (the first Afro-Brazilian female-led *capoeira angola* group in Salvador took her name for their group).

Fittingly, an enormous statue of Queen Nzinga stood outside Brenda's apartment building, recently erected in Kinaxixi Square to commemorate the twenty-seventh anniversary of Angola's independence.

Staying with the group's female leader named after a fierce warrior-queen relieved my anxiety over being the only woman, and student, on the trip. In fact, the trip was relaxed. Removed from the stress of life in Rio de Janeiro and his mobile phone from which he managed a multinational capoeira group, Mestre Camisa was more easygoing. He took turns sharing a bed or sleeping on the floor in the vacant apartment in an almost abandoned building that he and the other instructors were put up in; and when we discovered *gamba,* the jumbo shrimp popular in Angolan cuisine, he temporarily changed my nickname:

"You shouldn't be Camarão, they're too small. We'll call you Gamba!"

While the city may have had a stalled feeling with its decaying buildings and broken roads, it was alive with movement. People shuttling from one place to another, improvising life. In an exhausting two weeks, Nzinga and Gindungo carted us around the city in a whirlwind of activities. Along with rotating daily trainings in a health club, a boxing gym, a "nightclub," and an outdoor courtyard in a gated condominium, we visited politicians in impressive public buildings; were interviewed on National Radio; gave panels at private universities; and had an enormous street roda in Independence Square. These activities were all designed to publicize and gain political and financial support for the work of ABADÁ in Luanda.

Most of our days, however, began on the Ilha. Racing in Brenda's jeep to the end of the Marginal—the three-mile, multilane avenue lined with crumbling colonial buildings that curves around the shell-shaped Bay of Luanda—we would cross over the bridge to the Ilha de Luanda. The Ilha, as locals call it, is not actually an island but a narrow spit that juts out from the mainland, the bay on one side and the Atlantic on the other.

It was on the Ilha that the city of Luanda, and ABADÁ-Capoeira in Angola, had begun.

A *Ilha:* Ground Zero

The T-shirt boys were pissed. It was our last lunch on the Ilha, and Mestrando Charm had made good on his promise and brought T-shirts. But there weren't enough to go around. With his Ken-doll muscles, tattoos, and well-groomed shoulder-length skinny dreadlocks, Charm drew a crowd of people wherever we went in Luanda, the bolder reaching out to stroke a bicep. Every day we ate lunch at the same open-air, bamboo-walled restaurant on the Ilha.

Our visit was the day's highlight for the car-washing, trinket-selling youth who hung around in the street hoping to scrape together enough *kwanzas* to have a meal that day. Several of the older, more pugnacious youth, whom I took to calling the T-shirt boys, had been demanding shirts, and now they had arrived late and missed the handout. They charged into the restaurant to confront Charm. Along with the list of unexpected items women carried on their heads, I kept tabs on the out-of-place slogans adorning T-shirts Angolans acquire from piles of charity clothes on sale in the markets. Today, the T-shirt boys' slogans were sadly ironic: "You don't know who my lawyer is!" was shaking his fist in Charm's face while "I only sleep with the rich and famous" hovered behind him. The youth wearing a T-shirt with the fast-food slogan, "Hungry? We're on it!" had given up and retreated to sit out in the alleyway where women from a nearby compound of huts were cooking mid-day meals over open fires, watching children, and braiding hair.

Charm was no stranger to hardship. Like many of the high-ranking ABADÁ instructors, he grew up poor in Brazil before discovering capoeira. Yet, the difference now between him and the T-shirt boys was stark: Charm's body, sculpted from hours of weight lifting and dietary supplements, was always clean, perfumed, and clad in brand-name athletic wear. Whenever he traveled abroad to teach workshops, frequently now, he carried T-shirts with the ABADÁ logo, his name and image on them, as well as CDs. Along with his macho attitude and tough game, Charm had a lovely singing voice and composed melodic songs about birds and love, which added to his fame and popularity. ("Camarão, I am a sensitive guy!" he said when I kidded him about his romantic lyrics and sweet singing.) The T-shirt boys, who probably rarely left the Ilha, were rail-thin and wore the same torn clothes every day that emitted a smell of unwashed bodies.

It was not just our relative wealth as foreigners that contrasted with the T-shirt boys. The Ilha itself encapsulates the intense economic disparities of Angola's capital. On the Atlantic side, wealthy Luandans and European tourists enjoyed expensive beachside restaurants and nightclubs, while on the eastern bayside, youth like the T-shirt boys frequented trash-strewn beaches.

But the Ilha also retains a slower, calmer pace to the mainland. It is home to two thousand residents, many of whom have lived there for generations, scattered in small fishing villages and musseques. In a city of millions of refugees from the war, the Ilha has a revered and mystical aura as Luanda's Indigenous ground zero. The Portuguese navigator Paulo Dias de Novais landed on the Ilha in 1575, where he encountered the Axiluanda people who were a tributary of the Kongo Empire in the north. The Portuguese settlers stayed on the Ilha just long enough to gain control of the *zimbo,* or shells that the Kongo king used as currency, before moving to the mainland. They called their settlement Loanda (later Luanda) after the Axiluanda.

The Ilha is also ground zero for ABADÁ in Angola. The Centro Cultural e Recreativo Marítimo da Ilha, founded in 1945, boasts of being the country's first cultural and recreational center, hosting the who's who of Angolan music over the years. It was at the Marítimo, as the center is called, that Mestre Camisa first introduced his capoeira to Angola. In 1992, João Belisário, a Brazilian journalist who had been living in Angola since 1975, invited Mestre Camisa to Luanda. The visit was truncated when violence erupted in the city between MPLA and UNITA supporters, and Mestre Camisa and other foreign visitors were hurried out of the country. Camisa returned to Luanda in 1996, during another period of fragile peace accords, with a group of his students. They performed nightly shows in the Marítimo.

"I wanted to help rebuild the cultural life of the city. Things were so grim during the war," Belisário told me over a grilled fish dinner on my first night in Luanda. "And I knew capoeira would appeal to Angolans because they are warriors!"

He was right. The Marítimo was packed every night. Those who couldn't pay the small ticket price crowded outside the doors or stood on overturned plastic tubs to see through the gaps between the walls and tin roof. So enthusiastic was the response, Mestre Camisa persuaded one of his advanced students, Cascão, to stay behind and teach.

In his late twenties at the time, Cascão was the obvious choice as he had relatives in Luanda. His grandfather had been the national boxing champion in Angola before immigrating to Portugal and then Brazil.

"I was nervous at first," Cascão told me later. "But then Mestre Camisa explained to me that it would be important, pioneering work. I would be replanting capoeira in Angola, its birthplace. I was in Luanda for almost two years and I won't lie—it was rough. I had a place to live, but I didn't make any money, and life was hard. But the work was gratifying. The Angolans picked up capoeira so quickly. I think it is because music and dance are so much a part of life there."

Using the same problematic language that foreigners often use to describe Brazilians, Cascão continued: "I don't know how to explain it. Angolans are suffering people (*povo sofrido*), but they are so happy. I used to do street rodas and anyone walking by would stop, not just to watch but to clap and sing. There would be thirty capoeiristas and one hundred spectators clapping and singing! Sometimes women coming from the market would put down their bags and jump in the roda and start dancing. They'd never seen capoeira before but they didn't care—they would try to do it anyway."

With his street rodas, Cascão quickly made himself and his work visible.

"I sort of became a public figure. Especially after *Only the Strong* became popular, people would stop me in the street and sing the capoeira song, Paranauê."

Only the Strong was a 1993 Hollywood film about high school students, gang warfare, and capoeira in Miami. Most Angolans, however, had been introduced to capoeira through *Sinhá Moça,* a popular Brazilian soap opera that told a story of brutality, vengeance, and liberation on a plantation in nineteenth-century Brazil. Thus, as unselfconsciously equipped as they might have been to learn new rhythm and dance steps, Luandans were also already primed to adopt Brazilian cultural practices. Within a year, Cascão had close to two hundred students.

"My classes were popular. The Angolans liked what ABADÁ had to offer—the uniforms, the pedagogy, a way to a strong, fit body. It was something new and modern. But it was also familiar, theirs, even though they didn't know much about their own indigenous culture. For instance, a lot of Luandan youth only speak Portuguese. So, I would tell them I wanted to write a capoeira song in Kimbundu or another language, and I would get them to learn some words from their grandparents. My classes just kept growing, especially at the Marítimo. They were the poorest of my students, but that place is special, full of ancestry. The Marítimo is located exactly where there was a meeting place for the *sobas,* the chiefs, to gather and make decisions for the community."

Brenda also talked about the Ilha with a certain reverence. She recalled Mestre Camisa and his students going early mornings to the beach to watch fishermen pull in enormous nets. *Puxada de rede* is a Brazilian folkloric dance that often accompanies capoeira and maculelê and imitates the collective, rhythmic hauling of heavy fishing nets.

The Ilha, and Marítimo, were also my favorite spots. Every morning in the low bungalow with a cement floor and raised platform "stage," a ragtag group of adolescents and teens gathered. They wore an assortment of homemade abadá held up by a bit of string; a very few had threadbare capoeira T-shirts and faded cords. As we trained, young children, often with toddlers and babies and sometimes parents in tow, would pour in and gather along the walls. Shy at first, they would eventually start mimicking our movement and giggling until one of us went over and played with them, teaching them simple moves.

Training at the Marítimo felt like training in Rio's favelas, where I'd been repeatedly told that *real* capoeiristas were made. Classes were free at the Marítimo, and the mainly male students were intense and fearless in their training. They were also deeply emotional, many of them crying when they met Mestre Camisa for the first time and calling him *pai* (father). They sang their hearts out during the roda. Nineteen-year-old Balú, who proudly claimed Ilha heritage, wrote a ladainha he called *Terra Mãe* (Mother Land):

A ilha da Luanda	The island of Luanda
Terra da bassula e	Land of bassula and
Terra de Mãe Kianda	Land of Mother Kianda [a water deity]
E também seu Balú	And also of Balú
Também tem capoeira pura	It also has pure capoeira
no pé do berimbau	At the foot of the berimbau
Para voce lá jogar	For you to play there
Tem que ser bom jogador	You must be a good player
Eu não sei como falar	I don't know how to speak
Não sei como dizer	I don't know how to say it
Na roda de capoeira	In the capoeira roda
Quem fala alto sou eu	The one who speaks loudly is me

In the song Balú claims that along with "pure" capoeira the Ilha is home to bassula, a fighting technique practiced by fishermen. And it was bassula that presented itself as a compelling, distinctive, and convenient origin myth in our "search for roots."

In Search of Roots

"Why is it called 'chicken coop?'"

Afonso Quintas, the hipster host of *Viva Noite* on Radio Luanda, was not the first Angolan to ask us this. Many people we met were confused by capoeira's connection to Angola, and by its name. In Angola, the word "capoeira" is still associated with its original Portuguese meaning as a place to keep chickens. In fact, chicken coop is a possible etymology of the name: perhaps early capoeiristas sold chickens in the market and played capoeira to attract customers or pass the time. An eighteenth-century watercolor by German painter Johann Moritz Rugendas depicts a chicken vendor with a large basket on his head. (I have seen identical chicken baskets in village markets in Togo, another reminder of the deep connections between Brazil and West Africa).

Angolan Portuguese, much closer to the Portuguese spoken in Portugal in both vocabulary and accent, is a reminder that, while both countries were Lusophone colonies, Angola remained under colonial rule a century and a half longer than Brazil. Yet similarities in food, architecture, and daily life are a reminder of this common history. One older man remarked to me, "Brazilians who come to Luanda and say they feel a connection, well really what they are feeling is the colonizer's culture."

True though that may be, Brazil and Angola have also had a five-hundred-year connection that often bypassed Portugal. With the ignoble fame of being the earliest European slave traders in Africa, the Portuguese, by the fifteenth century, had established trade routes in West Central Africa that connected directly to Brazil without going through Europe. Over the next four hundred years approximately 5.6 million, or close to half of the total of enslaved Africans taken to the Americas, would originate from the ports in present-day Angola. Despite being the "common glue" in African American populations and cultures, these "forgotten ancestors" are often overlooked in popular and scholarly discourse on the Atlantic Slave Trade.[17]

This amnesia might be due in part to the fact that the West Central Africans who arrived in Brazil and other parts of the Americas were already accustomed to living among Portuguese in Africa. Many were Catholic and spoke Portuguese and so adjusted more quickly to life in their new home than the later wave of West Africans from the Nigeria-Benin area. But the amnesia also points to the invisibility, and at times erasure, of the history of slavery in Angola. Ghana and Senegal had far fewer enslaved leave their shores and yet have built memorials, largely in response to African American interest in roots tourism, around their coastal slave forts. Every year, thousands of African Americans visit the forts at Elmina, Cape Coast, and Gorée Island to light candles at ancestral shrines and walk through the "door of no return."[18]

The São Miguel Fortress in Luanda, built by the Portuguese in 1576 to protect its territories and export human cargo, makes no reference to slavery. Instead, it houses a military museum with a collection of old rifles. And the National Museum of Slavery located on the outskirts of Luanda emphasizes, through its reproductions of eighteenth-century paintings of slave life in Brazil and quotes from Martin Luther King, slavery and freedom struggles as existing in lands far from Angola.[19]

Yet, not only was Luanda the largest slave port in Africa but also the city, like Rio de Janeiro, depended entirely on slave labor. Wealthy merchants built social and economic capital on the number of enslaved, sometimes in the hundreds, who worked for them inside and outside the home.[20] Traces of this labor have been all but erased from public history, most dramatically in the demolition of the former eighteenth-century home and business of one of Angola's richest and most powerful slave traders, Dona Ana Joaquina dos Santos e Silva, daughter of an Angolan mother and Portuguese father. In 2000 the baroque building was torn down to build a new courthouse. While justice is perhaps served with a tribunal replacing a site of history's most egregious human rights violation, and while the government apologized for its oversight and rebuilt the courthouse as an exact replica of Dona Ana's house, that the demolition occurred in the first place indicates the lack of public memorialization of slavery in Angola.

The erasure of Angola's part in the Transatlantic Slave Trade may be also due to the nation's recent history of a protracted, violent civil war. Perhaps personal memories of a war that produced similar horrors to the slave trade—kidnappings, displacement, and death—are too recent and raw to dig deeper in history. Perhaps the urgency of unifying and rebuilding the nation makes officials reluctant to introduce memorials that remind Angolans of the political and social divisions that have long existed in the country.[21]

Along with Luanda's enslaved population, the city had a substantial Brazilian population: free Brazilians who worked in commerce as well as the formerly enslaved who'd been returned to Angola from Brazil for disorderly behavior. With a rigorous movement between the two countries, could there not possibly be mention of capoeira in the Luanda archives?

Diligent in my role as official trip researcher, I visited the Angolan National Archive one afternoon. I didn't find much beyond a copy of *Da Minha África E Do Brasil Que Eu Vi* (Of my Africa and of the Brazil that I saw) by Albano Neves e Sousa. Published in 1974, the slim book of drawings and text chronicles Portuguese artist Albano Neves e Sousa's travels through his homeland of Angola and in Brazil. In one section Neves e Sousa juxtaposed sketches of Mestre Pastinha's students playing capoeira in Salvador with drawings of n'golo, a Southern Angolan acrobatic puberty dance accompanied by rhythmic hand clapping. The objective of n'golo, which means zebra, is to "hit your opponent's face with your foot" with leaps and blows "similar to a zebra's kick."[22]

Neves e Sousa suggested n'golo as capoeira's possible origin. This idea was endorsed by Brazilian folklorist Câmara Cascudo in his 1967 book, *Folclore do Brasil,* and embraced in the 1980s by capoeiristas reanimating the nearly defunct *capoeira angola* style. Wanting to re-Africanize capoeira, these practitioners drew direct links between capoeira and n'golo, one group taking as its logo a capoeirista and a zebra playing together.

Less widely circulated or cited is another of Neves e Sousa's sketches that he identifies as bassula, "a style of fighting among the fishermen of Luanda Island, where the blows used are similar to some of the blows used in the Capoeira."[23] Unlike n'golo, practiced in an interior province where much of the war was waged and thus still difficult to get to in the early 2000s, bassula's home is right on the Ilha de Luanda. Be that as it may, it was still rather elusive.

I asked Balú and Muxi, natives of the Ilha, what they knew about bassula.

"I have vague memories of it from when I was a kid," Muxi told me. "My grandfather and uncles were fishermen. They would go out fishing at six or seven in the evening and come back in the mornings. Women waited on the beach with baskets to sell the fish. After work, fishermen would sometimes set up tents on the beach and relax. That's when I saw bassula."

I asked Muxi what it looked like.

"It's basically grappling—throws and takedowns—and also tripping. It's a bit like judo. Bassula in Kimbundu means *queda* (fall). It was just for fun, but sometimes there would be a real conflict and one of the fighters would get seriously hurt, but I never heard of any deaths."

Balú put me in touch with a sixty-year-old "bassuleiro" who promised me a demonstration on the beach with his friends but never showed up.

"You should have offered them palm wine, Camarão!" Balú said when I told him.

The most information on bassula I could find was from an article, rather ironically, in a recent TAAG magazine, a copy of which I got from the airline's office in the city center. The short article was accompanied by pictures of the septuagenarian Mestre Kabetula, apparently the last remaining teacher of bassula, demonstrating moves with a partner on the beach. Beginning with "the origins of this sport are lost in the mists of time" and ending with Mestre Kabetula's appeal for money to open a school so that the "game will not die" but be passed down "like the Brazilians do with capoeira," the author's descriptions of historical bassula are strikingly similar to Rio's nineteenth-century capoeira gangs.[24]

According to the author, Axiluanda fisherman used bassula's blows and counterblows, and sometimes knives and truncheons, to ensure fair pricing from the Portuguese fish traders. It was also a pastime to challenge and defend male honor: running a rope from one's shack to the sea in order to force another fisherman walking on the beach to enter the surf or step over the rope and thus accept the challenge to fight, and holding and crushing sand in a rival's direction were both rituals of provocation. Rival "dance teams," like the carioca maltas, staged running street battles during Luanda's carnival.

The article even mentions a feared police chief, Poeira, who persecuted the bassuleiras just as Rio's João Sampaio Ferraz had hunted down members of the maltas.

There is a possible explanation for the similarities between nineteenth-century bassula and capoeira beyond over-enthusiastic contemporary imaginings. Historian Matthias Röhrig Assunção points out that bassula, and the Axiluanda people, are of recent, creolized origin. The Axiluanda, who came to inhabit the Ilha, were not only ethnically mixed (Mbundu and Bakongo) but as fishermen were in close contact with outsiders who crossed the seas from all over the world. Given the back and forth between the ports of Angola and Brazil, is it not possible that capoeira influenced bassula?[25] What we might take from all this is that any attempt to find a single origin—whether n'golo or bassula—diminishes capoeira's complex history of movement and cross-fertilization.

In any case, it was less its origins that attracted Angolans to capoeira so much as, in Cascão's words, its modernity. Capoeira was similar to rural Angolan music and dance, but with the trappings—uniforms, fit bodies, pedagogy, and transnational mobility—of the world beyond Angola. This combination of being both *of* and *beyond* was a powerful draw. The young Angolans were proud to claim capoeira as theirs; and by becoming members of an international group, they could place themselves and their peripheral, war-torn nation in the larger world.

Brenda explained this one evening in the quiet of her apartment: "You've got to understand, our country experienced a huge identity crisis because of the war. Youth were lost. They didn't have anything to identify with, so they turned to North American rap and reggae and rock. Then capoeira's rhythm called them. They saw the movement, and they heard, 'this is yours, it was born here like you. This is your history.' And so, they find themselves in capoeira and discover they have a place in the world."

This social emplacement in the present could perhaps also bring future returns. Along with their pride in being from the Ilha and their interest in learning words in the Bantu languages of their grandparents, Balú, Muxi, and other students were concerned with creating a contemporary convivência with capoeira that moved beyond the ancestral past. Like other "urban associations forged by imaginative social bonds" in African cities, the capoeira group in Luanda was a place to create horizontal relationships of fictive kinship and affective bonds.[26] It was also a place to create vertical relationships for "articulating modest expectations from the state."[27]

This (largely failed) attempt to create political ties that might bring returns beyond the immediacy of the capoeira family was driven home to me at the culminating event of our Roots Tour trip.

Empty Thrones and the World's Largest Roda

Six red velvet thrones stood mid-court in the enormous gymnasium. As I set up my video camera, I wondered who had been tasked with finding and transporting the ridiculously heavy, ostentatiously high-backed chairs.

The thrones were for the VIPs. Every minister, university administrator, and radio personality we'd met over the last two weeks had received an official invitation to the culminating event of our trip. Not one of the dignitaries showed up, and like roped off museum pieces, the chairs stood empty throughout the three-hour batizado.

What audience did show up, family and friends, sat in the bleachers a good distance from the roda that we formed in front of the thrones. The event the night before, in a small, windowless boxing gym, had been close, intimate, and full of energy. This one, everyone agreed afterward, lacked axé.

"It was for show."

"The space was too big. The roda was too big. The audience was too far away."

"It was hard to play. I couldn't feel the energy. I got lost in the space."

The batizado began with a play about capoeira's origins written by Nzinga. The students reenacted scenes of slave catchers in Angola, plantation life in Brazil, and Africans coming together to share their different dances and create capoeira. In the final scene, Mestre Camisa and Duende joined the actors in a roda and played a game accompanied by Nzinga's beautiful and sorrowful rendition of Mestre Toni Vargas's song:

Quando eu venho de Luanda	When I come from Luanda
Eu não venho só	I do not come alone
Quando eu venho de Luanda	When I come from Luanda
Eu não venho só	I do not come alone
Quando eu venho de Luanda	When I come from Luanda
Eu não venho só	I do not come alone
Trago meu corpo cansado	I bring my tired body
Coração amargurado	My embittered heart
Saudade de fazer dó	Longing that hurts
Eu fui preso a traição	I was imprisoned by betrayal
Trazido na covardia	Brought by cowards

Que se fosse luta honesta	If it had been an honest fight
De lá ninguem me trazia	From there, no one would have brought me
Na pele eu trouxe a noite	In my skin I brought the night
Na boca brilha o luar	In my mouth moonlight shines
Trago a força e a magia	I bring strength and magic
Presente dos orixás	Gift of the orixás
Eu trago ardendo nas costas	I bring burning on my back
O peso dessa maldade	The weight of this evil
Trago ecoando no peito	I bring echoing in my chest
Um grito de liberdade	A shout of liberty
Um grito de raça nobre	A shout of a noble race
Grito de raça guerreira	Shout of a warrior race
É grito da raça negra	It's the shout of a Black race
É grito de capoeira	Shout of capoeira

The students poured their hearts into the performance with an emotion that matched that of the song lyrics and Nzinga's voice. Yet there were sprinklings of laughter and clapping from the audience during the depicted acts of brutality: the flogging of a runaway and a female plantation owner slapping her housemaid. When I asked Nzinga and her mother about this later, they shrugged and sighed.

"Sometimes laughter is the only way to deal with pain," Sylvia said.

Laughter and joking, as I had seen in Brazil, can be a form of witnessing and sharing pain in the face of tragedy and violence. In the postcolonial setting it can also be a type of agency: with inappropriate laughter, people "kidnap power and force it, as if by accident, to contemplate its own vulgarity" and demonstrate their "preference for conviviality."[28] Perhaps laughter during the batizado was an attempt to override the silence of the empty thrones as a mockery of the attempt to officialize capoeira as a symbol of the modern state.[29] And perhaps shared laughter was also a moment of convivência in which to witness the horrors of human abuses.

The day after the lackluster batizado, we had another closing ceremony: a street roda in Independence Square in the gathering dusk of later afternoon. Like an expanding puddle of water, the roda grew: over one hundred men, women, and children inscribing with their bodies the biggest, roundest circle I had ever seen.

Camisa called out to them: "What you are about to see belongs to you, to your land."

Collectively bemused and uncertain, no one pressed forward to see, and the circle kept its perfect shape. Realizing that the size of the roda would dwarf any single game, Camisa indicated for all the capoeiristas to find someone from the audience to play with. I grabbed one of the grubby kids who had been snickering at me as I stretched. Surprise turned to pleasure as I led him to a free spot in the roda and began moving around him in cartwheels. He spun on his feet trying to keep me in sight and then laughed, put his hands on the ground, and joined me in his own crooked cartwheels.

After the roda, the spectators crowded around Camisa, Charm, Duende, and me as if we were celebrities, asking for autographs on scraps of cloth or the palm of their hands, and pulling bits of colored thread from our cords to keep as souvenirs.

It was here in the energy of the streets and embodied convivência between everyday people, not in the empty thrones and aspirational connections to political elite, that the future of capoeira, and possibly Angola, seemed to lie.

Benguela: City of Dust and Acacias

"Mines! Don't leave the road!"

The signs, hand-painted in red and propped up by the side of the road, zoomed by.

"*Putain!*"

Philippe had barely missed another pothole big enough to swallow our jeep.

I don't know what freaked me out more: Philippe's crazy-angry, French expletive–inflected driving (he was so cheery and positive when not behind the wheel) or the signs.

The war left millions of landmines in Angola, many of them, apparently, along the highway from Luanda to Benguela.

I had met Philippe and his Angolan fiancée Patrícia in a capoeira class in the ELF condominium complex. I immediately liked Philippe, a smart, enthusiastic, and generous Parisian about my age. He worked for the French oil company and, while Patrícia appreciated the comforts and security of the gated community, Philippe hated living there.

"It's awful how all the foreigners working here are sequestered from the city—living behind closed gates. My colleagues only leave the complex to go to work. They don't speak Portuguese, and they certainly don't date local women!"

I had told Philippe a few days before our scheduled departure that I was reluctant to leave Angola after such a short time. With the batizados and other obligations done, Camisa was eager to get back to Rio in time to cast his vote for Lula in his fourth, and what would finally be successful, run for president. But I felt I had just scratched the surface of this, the geographically seventh largest country in Africa.

"I really want to see something beyond Luanda, maybe Benguela," I told Philippe.

His face lit up. "Patrícia and I were there for a wedding last year and loved it. We've been wanting to go back. Maybe we could go together!"

Road travel was still not safe. During the war car hijacks were frequent, so civilians gave up on travel. Now, with the war over, there was still the danger of running out of gas or breaking down on roads that hadn't been maintained in thirty years. But Philippe knew some "crazy ex-pats" who often did weekend road trips. A few days later, we joined a caravan of fifteen four-wheel vehicles traveling at an alarming speed, swerving to avoid potholes, and kicking up enormous clouds of beige dust that covered everything like a blanket along the highway from Luanda to Benguela. Twelve hours later, shaken and grimy, we arrived to more dust and beige punctuated by pink colonial buildings and red acacia trees. We parted ways with the caravan and drove around town until miraculously Philippe found the house of the family he knew. It was a holiday weekend and all the hotels booked, so the family insisted we stay with relatives in a nearby apartment.

The next morning, we awoke to visitors. I looked at Philippe in confusion. Who knew we were here? At the door a group of teenage boys politely waited. I took in the faded capoeira T-shirts and sweatpants.

"Capoeiristas! How did you find us!"

Mário, glasses, serious, hair frizzing out of corn-rows, and a cast on his arm, said, "Muxi called from Luanda yesterday to say you were coming down! We spent last night going to every hotel in town. We got really worried when we couldn't find you. Traveling the roads is dangerous."

He lifted his broken arm.

"Last time I came back from Luanda, the bus had an accident. I was unconscious for three days in a hospital."

"That's when we started calling him Crash!" A bubbly young man, Diabo Branco, said.

Shibango, rail-thin with a sweet demeanor, continued: "But then we ran into a friend in the street, and he mentioned that his friend's friend had some foreigners crashed in his living room, and we figured that must be you."

I grinned. The great, pre-social-media human news chain.

"We are excited and honored that you have come to Benguela," Mário said.

Then turning to Philippe, he said, "Muxi told us there was an advanced student coming. We would like you to teach us while you are here."

Philippe laughed, "I'm not the advanced student, Camarão is!"

Mário looked at me, quickly covering his surprise.

"We are very isolated here. We learn what we can from a few books and videos, and from any capoeiristas who come through town. And I go to Luanda once in a while to train. We would be grateful for you to teach some classes."

Though I was not yet at the same level in my game and music as many other advanced students, I was fairly confident after training with Mestre Camisa for over a year that I could mimic his class. That night, in a school-yard, I led a handful of male and female students through a series of warm-ups and combinations. When they began dropping out with exhaustion, Mário suggested a roda. Their instruments were rough-made and beautiful. I asked where they had come from, and Mário told me they had made them with local materials.

Diabo Branco told me, "We have found the perfect wood for berimbaus: *pau elefante* (elephant wood). It grows only in the village of Dumbe, not far from here. We will take you there."

On our last day in Benguela, Diabo Branco and another student accompanied us on the hour drive to Dumbe. Had we continued on the road 200 kilometers east we would have arrived in Huambo, the third largest city in Angola, which had been the headquarters of UNITA and suffered the worst fighting during the war. The road was even worse than the one from Luanda, and Diabo Branco gripped the door handle and kept asking Philippe to slow down. To distract him I asked about his nickname, White Devil.

No, it was not a reference to the white man.

"I got it from my father. It was his nickname because he always dressed in white and was good at discovering witches."

I dared not ask further. Savimbi, the erratic and unpredictable leader of UNITA, had become increasingly unhinged and paranoid toward the end of the war, flinging witchcraft accusations and ordering suspected traitors burned to death. And since war's end, there had been an increase in child witch accusations in war-ravaged, impoverished rural areas. It was hard to imagine Diabo Branco or any of the youth I'd met with their bright, enthusiastic dispositions living through the brutality of war and its aftermath.

After an hour of flat desert, a mountain range appeared on the horizon, and before long we had arrived at a striking mesa with an expanse of green laid out beside it—the municipality of Dumbe. The vista portended the lush valleys and central highlands of Angola's interior, so different from the barren coast. It was a tantalizing and teasing view, travel to these scenic parts of the country still difficult and dangerous.

We parked by the side of the road just past a bridge over an almost-dry river. Philippe had barely cut the engine when a group of curious boys materialized around our car. Diabo Branco asked who could take us to the soba, and a boy stepped forward saying he was the chief's youngest son. He led us down an embankment and past several small, cultivated fields, to the soba's compound of two stick-and-woven-palm-frond huts and a beaten-dirt yard. The soba, in his sixties and wearing a faded cloth around his waist, a button-down plaid shirt, and tire sandals, greeted us warmly. He remembered Diabo Branco from the last time he had come to cut wood and was pleased with the cartons of cigarettes we had brought him. His wife, in a dusty skirt, Flamengo soccer shirt, and black head wrap, led us to her son's hut through a forest of banana and dendê palm trees.

The soba's son, a younger version of his father, also welcomed us warmly, telling Diabo Branco he had been waiting his return and, donning a multi-pocketed workman's vest, grabbed a machete and took us to cut wood.

Pau elefante, with its multiple thin, silvery trunks and light green leaves, reminded me of birch. Diabo Branco had told me that the wood was sacred and that we had to ask permission from the soba and the ancestors before cutting any. So, I was rather disappointed when the soba's son made no ceremony, simply explaining that the trees were protected by law so that only certain people from the community had permission to harvest them to build huts. We cut down several trunks, straight and not too thick. In front of the soba's hut we stripped them of bark and wrapped them into a bundle with a piece of twine made from vine. Then we did a capoeira and maculelê demonstration to the delight and amusement of the soba and his family. We negotiated a price for the wood and headed out, with promises to return.

On the way home, in a market on the outskirts of Benguela, we were thrown back into the urban chaos of honking horns and throngs of vendors thrusting plastic bags of vegetables into the car windows. We stopped to buy gourds to make the berimbaus' cabaças. I would take one stick and a small gourd back to Rio where Dente would help me make it into a berimbau, complaining just slightly that the wood was too thick and heavy. It is a beautiful berimbau, nonetheless, with a tiny elephant burned into its foot. I still teach with it.

The boys had insisted on throwing us a going-away party when we returned that night. One of the students hosted it at his family's compound, and his sister served us red bean *feijoada* with Angolan spice at a table set up near the outdoor kitchen. Mário had let out his hair and everyone had on party clothes. We were awkward at first to socialize without capoeira. The boys were shy, reminding me how young they were. Sunburned, dirty, and tired from our trip, I was uncomfortable with being a guest of honor. Then someone put on music and we danced the popular "new" *dança da familia* (family dance), which looked suspiciously like the electric slide, and played capoeira. I was touched and honored when Shibango presented me with a pair of handcrafted leather sandals that fit perfectly. The new raw leather cut into my skin, but I wouldn't take them off. I danced and played capoeira with all the boys, and the red Benguela dust rubbed into the fresh cuts between my toes.

I didn't realize the extent of the sandals' damage until I got back to Rio a few days later, a message on my answering machine from Mestre Camisa who had expected me back earlier. I thought it was just exhaustion when I couldn't get out of bed the next day, or the next. When I realized I was running a fever and that the lymph glands in my groin were swollen, I went to the doctor. She saw my still raw feet and said I had an infection. I recovered, but for several years I could feel a pea-sized lump inside the top of my thigh: another memory worn on my body; a reminder of capoeira's "diasporic skin" and convivência that stretches across the Atlantic.

6

GLOBAL CONVIVÊNCIA

BRUSSELS, VENICE, ACCRA, HAVANA, 2008–2018

"Camarão! Where is your winter coat!"

My bare hands were shoved into my jean pockets, my thin jacket and the cap I had just bought turning white with snowflakes. Brussels in March. Coming from a Californian spring in bloom, I hadn't thought to pack warm clothes.

Bacurau, bundled in a thick coat, hat, scarf, and gloves looked at me reproachfully. "How could you come to Europe without warm clothes?"

I had last seen Bacurau four years before in 2004, at his going-away party on the laje of his mother's house in Dona Marta. He had been wearing shorts and flip-flops and drinking a *gelada* (frosty beer).

That had been an almost-going-away party for me as well. A few months later, I was on a plane heading back to the United States, leaving behind my life of three years in Rio. I wept as we took off. The woman in the seat next to me patted my hand and offered me a tissue.

"*Deixando um amor?*"

I nodded weakly and she looked satisfied, my tears justified. But it wasn't leaving a romantic lover, as my seatmate assumed, that made me weep. It was abandoning the love that had blossomed from my convivência with capoeira and carioca life. I knew I would be back; Brazil was too entwined now with my professional and personal life. But I would never re-create the intimacy I had reached through a daily convivência; my life would never again be so shaped by capoeira.

I had toyed with "going native," abandoning my academic trajectory and remaining in Rio. But a life dedicated only to capoeira was not in the cards for me, as the Candomblé priestess in Bahia had predicted those many years ago. I had other interests, and my commitment to capoeira lay not just in its practice but also in research and writing, as Mestre Camisa liked to remind me. Though my heart was breaking, I knew that a life of capoeira would have felt constrained after a while. And while my friends were sad and continued to joke that I was more carioca than many cariocas, they also always knew I would leave.

When I moved back to California in 2004 to write my dissertation, capoeira's visibility and popularity abroad was reaching its peak. In Berkeley, I saw a bumper sticker that simply read LEARN CAPOEIRA. No explanation needed. I had come full circle in my capoeira journey. But rather than return to Beiçola's group, I affiliated with the local ABADÁ group in San Francisco led by Mestra Márcia. A student of Mestre Camisa's and a pioneering woman in carioca capoeira in the 1980s, Márcia had immigrated to the United States in the 1990s, working in construction and teaching at dance studios in the evenings until she secured a permanent capoeira studio in the San Francisco Mission District. By the 2000s she had a large group of diverse students reflecting the Bay Area: gay, straight, and trans; tattoos, piercings, and rainbow hair; school teachers, artists, doctors, and bartenders; English, Portuguese, Chinese, Japanese, Korean, Tagalog, and Spanish speakers. We were solicited for performances at schools, nightclubs, the Gay Pride and Carnival Parades, Ethnic Dance Festival, and the halftime show at a Roller Derby. In popular media, capoeira was appearing in everything from family comedies (*Meet the Fockers*, 2004) to fashion spreads (*Vogue*, 2006), reality shows (*America's Next Top Model*, 2009), cartoons (*Bob's Burgers*, 2011), and *Tekken*, the popular video game, whose capoeira character, Eddie Gordo, had a name that suggested he should be eating burritos in Los Angeles rather than fighting in the streets of Rio. Like belly dance, bhangra, and Zumba, capoeira had become an "exotic" dance-fitness fad stripped of contextual signifiers and packaged for global consumption.

Taking advantage of this new popularity, many of the ABADÁ instructors I'd known in Rio left for Europe around the same time that I'd returned to the States. Now, in 2008, they had all gathered in Brussels for the European Games, a week of workshops and competitions modeled on the ABADÁ World Games in Rio. Having finished my PhD and with enough frequent flier miles and a bit of time before my first full-time academic job began, I had come to Europe to attend the games and to visit and follow up with my friends. I'd had trouble recognizing them at first all bundled in their winter gear. Now we'd settled around a long table in a restaurant. As coats, scarves, and hats came off, the capoeiristas also shed the weight of months of isolation in unfamiliar lands. Their drawn faces, guarded against the cold and unknown, softened as they soaked up the convivência along with the hot food and cold beer.

"Europe's turning into a favela!" someone joked, looking around the table. Everyone cackled, happy for the reference to home.

Europe was a popular destination for Brazilian capoeiristas. Unlike the United States, no visa was required for initial entry, and the growing network of colleagues and friends helped with the transition. But the adjustment was still brutal. The cold weather, unfamiliar food, more overt racism some of them experienced, the loneliness and isolation. The European Games were a first reunion for those who had not been able to travel because of a lack of proper documents or sufficient money.

"It's not easy, Camarão," Chá Preto had told me a few days earlier in Lisbon. He had been there a year, living on the outskirts of the city with one of his students, also a Brazilian immigrant. He couldn't travel to Brussels as he was still waiting for his work papers. He had looked devastated when he sent me off with greetings and hugs for everyone. He especially missed Bacurau, with whom he had spent every day of his life since boyhood. He also missed living in a city where he was recognized and greeted in the streets.

"I'm nobody here, Camarão. No one knows me or cares about me. And it is hard getting your work started. People in Brazil think you arrive and immediately start teaching and have a group. I've had to do a lot of other things to make money."

Capoeiristas abroad will pick up any kind of work—construction, security, janitorial services—to make ends meet. When I visited Chá Preto, he was working as a security guard at a fado night show. He liked and felt comfortable in this job from his own years as a capoeira performer. Show business had first brought Chá Preto and ten other ABADÁ capoeiristas to Europe in 2005.

Gavião, whom I had trained alongside in Rio when he was a recently minted twenty-three-year-old blue cord, had secured the European gig. Gavião lived in a favela in the Baixada Fluminense, a two-hour commute to the CIEP, so I didn't see much of him outside of class, but I had always admired and felt an affinity with him: we had both been introduced to capoeira by Mestre Beiçola in the late 1980s, albeit a continent and generation apart.

"I was seven years old and my mom took me to the Festa da Penha." Gavião told me. "We stopped at the street roda, and Mestre Beiçola was playing, and I was totally captivated. My mom had to drag me away, but I snuck away from her and ran back. I sat there so long watching that, finally, Mestre Beiçola grabbed me and threw me in to play. That day I knew I wanted capoeira for myself."

With his beautifully controlled acrobatic game, Gavião caught the eye of a recruiter who had come to Camisa's class at the CIEP to scout out performers. He contracted Gavião and a number of others to perform in a touring show that told the history of Brazil through music and dance. Gavião worked eight months with the show, traveling all over Brazil, and then moved to Germany when the company took up residency in an aquatic amusement park. Gavião and the other performers lived together in a hotel for five months, putting on two shows a day and earning 850 euros a month along with room and board. Gavião enjoyed the experience.

"Some of the capoeiristas complained. They felt like they were prisoners there. But that's just because they didn't take advantage of their days off. I saved up my money and traveled."

When his contract expired, Gavião decided to stay in Europe. With the help of Camisa Roxa, Mestre Camisa's older brother who had brought a folkloric show to Europe in the 1970s and still lived in Vienna, Gavião settled in a small Austrian city where he taught for two years. Eventually he moved to Italy, taking over the work of another instructor who had left for another European destination. I visited Gavião in a Milan suburb a few days before Christmas in 2018. Thirty men, women, and kids were gathered for the final class of the year and had organized a secret gift-exchange party. Gavião had not included himself in the exchange, and I sensed a wistful loneliness in him. He had just broken up with an Italian girlfriend, but I also couldn't help remembering the raucous gift-exchange parties we'd had at the last trainings of the year with Camisa's students in Rio. I was glad I had brought a blown-glass ornament from Venice to give him. Later over cappuccinos at a café, I asked him about his life and work in Europe.

"Austria was hard. It was cold. And there are so many rules—you can't even chew gum in the metro! I felt better once I moved to Italy. I like the Italians. They shout, they're noisy, like Brazilians! But I still miss home, the heat, the samba parties, the messiness. I miss teaching kids in the favelas who are willing to try anything. Kids here are more pampered. And schools here tend to prefer soccer, or judo—more familiar things."

"Why do you stay, Gavião?"

"Quality of life."

Like most of the capoeira instructors I knew in Europe who had come from favelas in Brazil, Gavião cited arbitrary violence and lack of opportunity as the main reasons for immigrating.

"Sure, there's violence in Italy. There's violence everywhere. But it's not like in Brazil where someone is going to kill you for a phone. Or you get hit by a stray bullet when you arrive at your front door after work. And there's more opportunity here and money to send home. I've moved my mother out of the favela and into an apartment in Copacabana, and I put my daughter through the best schools. She's at a federal university now. All thanks to capoeira."

Bacurau had come to Europe for similar reasons. In 2004, drug wars and police crackdowns intensified in Rio, making life difficult for Bacurau in Dona Marta where he had grown up and continued to teach capoeira. Three childhood friends—brothers who'd been living and teaching capoeira in and around Barcelona for a number of years—helped him immigrate. A masterful teacher and berimbau player, Bacurau never finished secondary school. When I visited him in Spain, he showed me the CV a student had designed for him. The watermark was a black-and-white photograph of him and Chá Preto playing capoeira that I had taken. A large print of this same photograph was displayed on top of the television in his mother's home in Dona Marta: the productive afterlife of fieldwork's materiality.

The classes I visited in Europe were in many ways identical to the ones in schools and health clubs in Rio. The students all dressed in uniforms and cords, the instructors teaching in Portuguese, the movement and rodas the same. Most of the advanced students spoke Portuguese, even those who had not yet been to Brazil.

"They learn with me so it's street dialect," Gavião told me.

I chuckled as I also learned Portuguese through my capoeira convivência, and I am still embarrassed to speak in academic settings with my strong carioca accent, grammatical errors, and generous use of slang—or what Gavião called "dialect."

Despite the popularity of capoeira in Europe and the apparent cookie-cutter continuity with their work in Rio, instructors had to work hard, and have a particular personality, to establish and maintain capoeira work abroad.

"You need to be adaptable, and you need to be a '*business man,*'" Gavião said, using the English term.

"All my Italian students smoked when they first started training and that bugged me. I'm a capoeirista, but I am also an athlete who promotes healthy living. But I couldn't just tell them to quit and be a disciplinarian about it as I would in Brazil. You need to be subtle here. And you have to sell your product and promote yourself on social media. That's how I got the opportunity to do a performance at a fashion show. A fashion show in Milan, Camarão!"

Gavião shook his head in disbelief.

"A poor kid from the Baixada working a Milan fashion show! The guy in charge saw my feeds on Instagram and thought my work looked professional."

I wasn't surprised at Gavião's success. Others weren't so successful. Perhaps they lacked Gavião's ambition and ability to promote their work. Or perhaps they just missed home. After thirteen years in Lisbon, with the urging of an aging mother and a former girlfriend, Chá Preto moved back to

Rio. Others I knew in Rio, excellent capoeiristas and instructors, never felt the desire, or courage, to leave. Perhaps they feared the intense saudades they'd have for the rhythms and convivência of carioca life.

By the close of the second decade of the new millennium, it was getting harder to obtain work in Europe. With the increasing number of European capoeiristas rising through the ranks and becoming instructors, there were fewer jobs to go around; getting work papers for being a capoeirista was harder when qualified national citizens could also do the job.

I had gotten an inkling of this displacement of Brazilians toward the end of my fieldwork in Rio.

Brazil to Europe and Back

By the early 2000s, there'd been a growing rotation of non-Brazilian capoeiristas training at the CIEP. They would often come for the World Games, arriving early or staying longer for additional training with Mestre Camisa and other popular instructors around Brazil. These foreign capoeiristas learned quickly, progressed rapidly up the cord hierarchy, and often won competition medals.

When Mestre Camisa was irritated with his students, perceiving a lack of motivation or sloppiness, he would chide: "Watch out! Foreigners are going to take capoeira away from us just like we took soccer from the English!"

His words were somewhat prophetic. In 2009 I ran into some European capoeiristas in the Rio airport after the World Games.

"Everything started late! And the location this year was so far from downtown Rio. There was nowhere to shower and to eat, and it took so long to get back to the hotel. We don't know if we're going to keep coming. It's far and expensive, and really we have everything we need in Europe now. Every month there are events in different countries, and some of the best Brazilian instructors live there now!"

Brazil was losing its status as the gold standard for capoeira.

The 2008 European Games in Brussels were a case in point. The event was punctual and well-run and brought together capoeiristas from all over Europe, Brazil, and the United States. The trainings, rodas, and participants were almost identical to the World Games in Rio. The tables had turned: high-ranking capoeiristas in Brazil who had not immigrated abroad were eager to secure invitations to come and teach workshops, some even paying their own airfare. Before long, foreign capoeiristas were receiving instructor titles, forming their own groups, and traveling to Brazil with their own students.

I first met instructor Polar from Sweden in 2003. He appeared one evening in the CIEP and began warming up before class. His technique was
textbook perfect, and he had mastered some difficult floreios. I approached
and greeted him in Portuguese, then switched to English. He had just arrived
from Umeå, a northern city in Sweden, and it was his first time in Brazil.

"There's capoeira in Umeå?"

"No, just me."

Polar explained he'd been training on his own for the past two years,
traveling occasionally to Stockholm where there was an ABADÁ group,
but largely learning from studying games online. Now he had finally saved
enough money at his construction job to come to Brazil.

Self-taught Polar was a novelty and big hit at the CIEP. He could easily
keep up with the more advanced students during training, but was less adept
in the roda, often out of sync with his partner. He had perfected the technique, but lacked the convivência.

When I visited Polar in Umeå in 2009, he had matured as a capoeirista
and ran a youthful group in the school gym of a working-class neighborhood. The class was strenuous, my entire body ached for days after. He softened the tough exercises by adding playful touches: lining up in *cadeira,* a
wide-legged stance, knees bent, thighs parallel to the ground, the first person
breaking rank and climbing down the line of bodies without touching the
ground. Contact improv dance meets CrossFit. There was a lot of sweaty
slipping, clinging, and laughter.

I would continue to visit ABADÁ and other groups whenever and wherever I traveled. But I would not experience capoeira convivência again until
I moved to Venice, Italy.

Venice, Italy: Watery Convivência

Burano was double parking. He cut the motor and tied his boat to the boat
parallel to his docked alongside the canal. Nimbly, he climbed across both
boats and hopped onto the *fondamenta* (pavement) to join me in front of the
school gym where we trained capoeira together twice a week.

"Can you do that? What if the owner of that boat needs to leave?" I asked
him.

"It's Venetian convivência," he said, using the Portuguese term.

I asked what he meant.

"Convivência is how we live here together. Venice is a difficult city. It's
crowded and space is limited. Sometimes you have to park your boat like
this. You just have to make sure that the other person can untie your boat

and move it out of the way if they need to leave. Then you hope they secure your boat!"

"I wish we could do that with cars!"

"But things are changing. We are losing convivência. The new Venice isn't like that anymore. People get angry and yell at you on the canals."

The "new" Venice is the Venice of a shrinking population of Venetians and ever-increasing tourists. Last count, Venice was down to fifty thousand residents and up to twenty-eight million tourists a year, the majority of whom arrive on cruise ships and stay for less than six hours. I had the pleasure of being a different type of visitor to Venice. In 2012, 2015, and 2018 I lived with my family in this stunning city on water for four-month stints.

Things had moved quickly once I started my academic life at Duke University in Durham, North Carolina. I had met my husband Orin, also an anthropologist, and within just a few years I was married, pregnant, and to my unexpected delight had an adolescent stepson and teenage stepdaughter. My life became shaped by a new convivência—of family and sharing my body for nine months with another human being. Through pregnancy I continued playing capoeira, exploring my body anew, adjusting daily to its changing capabilities as my belly swelled. The airborne lightness of floreios, always difficult for me, were even farther from my reach now. But I discovered a deeper attentiveness, rootedness, and precision in my movement as I could not afford to fall. When I played my berimbau and sang, I felt a deep connection not only to the other capoeiristas in the roda but also to the growing being within me. In my new shared body and my developing role as a capoeira teacher, I was beginning to see myself as not just a practitioner but a repository and transmitter of this art form.

Orin and I had jumped at the opportunity to live in Italy for a semester to teach at the Venice International University. Orin had spent time in Italy as a child while his Renaissance historian father did research. I also had spent a good part of my childhood in Europe visiting my mother's family in France, England, and Spain. After years of living and researching in South America (Orin in Peru), we were both ready for a return to our childhood memories of the beauty and pleasures of European life. But we were skeptical about living in Venice. Would the hordes of tourists and elevated prices keep us from knowing the "real" Venice? Was there even a "real" Venice left to know? How would we see beyond the Chinese-made masks and blown glass, overpriced "typical" Venetian dishes, and fluffy mounds of Oreo Cookie gelato?

Capoeira would be a key to unlocking local Venice, which, to my surprise, had quite a few similarities to Rio and Salvador. Barely three weeks after our move, I found myself drifting down the Grand Canal not on an eighty dollar, thirty-minute tourist gondola ride, or on a crowded, slow *vaporetto* (water bus), but in a polished-wood motorboat. My stepson Ray was splayed out next to me on the wide prow. Orin was in the back with our six-month-old baby, Lucien, while Pierangelo, a small, lithe Venetian capoeirista, skillfully steered around taxi boats filled with picture-snapping Japanese tourists. I looked up to the five-hundred-year-old *palazzi* (mansions) with their crumbling frescos and Moorish windows and was humbled and awed to be living in another of the world's most beautiful cities.

Venice—"a city of the eye"—visually captivates.[1]

On a late summer's day, the sunshine shimmering off the smoky green Adriatic canal water and casting sparkles on the white stone churches takes your breath away. Later, as the sun sets, the dusty-rose and ocher-orange facades lining narrow alleyways glow with a mystery that pulls you around another corner until you gasp at the sudden appearance of a tiny jewel box, the multicolored marble Miracoli (Miracles) Church. But as in Rio and Salvador, Venice engaged all my senses. Sounds, smells, and tastes are my place memories: differently toned church bells ringing out throughout the day in a cacophonic overlapping call-and-response, each eager to attract the faithful to its doors; the hollow echo of footsteps down an alleyway on a winter's night when the city has hushed; seagulls' cries, slap of water against stone and wood, grinding waterbus gears, and gondoliers' calls on the Grand Canal; sharp sewage smell rising from small canals; salt, sand, and fizz on the tongue from lagoon shellfish and prosecco at Bepi's Osteria.

Street life in Venice, that merges hard work and pleasure, is also reminiscent of Brazil. One of the world's most beautiful cities is dependent on manual labor. Everything from wine to household appliances are delivered by boat and then by porters pushing carts through alleys and over bridges. The porters' cries to clear a path are the calls of street vendors in Rio; the cafés where garbage collectors stop with their pushcarts for a shot of coffee are Salvador's bars; and the gondoliers—an unbreachable male guild operating on strict territorial boundaries—lounging canal-side and cajoling tourists to ride in their gondolas are the street capoeiristas in the Mercado Modelo. Above all else, in Venice, as in Rio and Salvador, there is a fierce loyalty to place: Venetians claim local over national identity, and many prefer speaking Venetian, or another of the many surrounding island dialects, over Italian.

Built on 117 islands in a crescent-shaped lagoon in the Adriatic Sea along the northeastern coast of Italy, Venice is shaped like a fish. The famous Grand Canal, the major transportation waterway that bisects the city, begins at the head, winds through the body, and empties out into the San Marco basin that wraps around the tail. Human habitation of the lagoon sedimented in waves starting in the fourth century. Early settlers were refugees fleeing armies of invaders who swept mainland Italy after the fall of the Roman Empire. Insular villages of reed-and-wattle houses, a church, *campanile* (bell tower), and *campo* (field) rose up on the islands, separated from each other by marshy waterways. By the ninth and tenth centuries, the majority of villages clustered around the Rivoalto, or "high bank" in the middle of the lagoon, became connected by bridges and canals. This area, known today as the Rialto, became the commercial center of the city with its famed fish market, operating six days a week for the last one thousand years.

Over six centuries in an awesome feat of engineering, Venice developed into an exquisite city of stone and water with an extraordinary mix of architectural style—Byzantine, Gothic, and Renaissance—and dripping with some of Europe's finest art. Designated a UNESCO world heritage site in 1987, Venice has in fact been a global city since antiquity. Detached from the mainland until the nineteenth century when a railroad bridge was built, Venice was isolated yet strategic, drawing seafaring merchants from around the world and producing the most famous explorer, Marco Polo. Its trade in silks, spices, wood, salt, and enslaved people made it an imperial power, and, by the sixteenth century, Venice had reached its height as a cosmopolitan commercial and artistic center with over 200,000 inhabitants.

Despite its worldliness, Venice was, and remains, a parochial city. For centuries, political life was dominated by a small number of noble families vying for power and to keep the ruling doge, elected for life, in check. Civil life was also rife with rivalry among residents of the six neighborhoods, or *sestieri*. Rivalries were enacted through mock warfare, a ludic form of civil disorder that resembled the street battles of Rio's nineteenth-century capoeira gangs. From the fourteenth to the seventeenth centuries, the *battagliole sui ponti*, or "bridge battles" raged between two neighborhood factions: the ship-building Castellani from the east side of the Grand Canal, and the fishermen Nicolotti from the west side. Bridge battles could draw hundreds of participants and thousands of spectators who crammed the canal below to watch from their gondolas as fighters stormed the bridge from the narrow alleys on either side and clashed with the intent to knock each other off into the stinking canals below.[2]

Today the bridge battles exist only in popular memory and in commemorative stone footprints on several bridges. Yet Venetians continue to identify with, and be fiercely loyal to, the sestiere—Castello, San Marco, Dorsoduro, San Polo, Santa Croce, and Cannaregio—in which they and their families have lived, often for generations. Though you can walk the length of Venice in forty-five minutes—from Piazza San Marco to Piazzale Roma—many Venetians shop and go to bars and cafés mostly in their own neighborhoods.

Our semester-long stays, network of Venetian parents through my son's school, and my capoeira practice gave us an inroad into local living. We learned to navigate the back routes to avoid the massive tourist blockages that could make us miss the ferry to get to work on time; where to buy locally grown produce and to eat fish caught from the lagoon or Adriatic; how to determine if gelato was made by hand or out of a machine; and how to navigate the canals in our bright orange, inflatable kayak, calling out "A-oi!" when we turned corners to warn oncoming gondolas and motorboats.

As usual before any travel, I had researched capoeira groups. There was more at stake this time, as we would be living in Venice for four months, and I wanted to train regularly. Gavião's group was too far away in Milan, and I was worried that given Venice's size and tourist profile, there would be no groups. There were in fact not one but two groups in Venice (and I had doubted capoeira's global spread)! I decided to try out the *capoeira angola* group. It seemed fitting to train an older more "traditional" style in a city that is a living museum of history. Little did I know that my time in Venice would start me on a new capoeira trajectory.

On a Thursday evening in September, I armed myself with a map, large water bottle (the lingering humid summer heat trapped in narrow stone alleys and wafting off canals still intense), and capoeira clothes. After countless bridges, wrong turns, and backtracking I found my way to the public-school gym where Contramestre Marquinho taught.[3] I had a moment of doubt outside the imposingly tall, heavy, wood doors. Was I still up for this? I'd given birth six months before, after a grueling eighty-hour labor and emergency C-section. My still-recovering, breast-feeding body did not yet feel my own again. Was I ready to prove myself in training and rodas? Was I ready to plunge back into the sociality of capoeira? It would depend, I decided, on the convivência of the group. I took a deep breath and stepped through.

Capoeira music was playing softly from a portable speaker and a group of four men dressed in white T-shirts, belted pants, and sneakers were stretching on the green, slightly squishy gym floor. Marquinho, his bald head wrapped in a red bandanna printed with the San Marco lion symbol of Venice, welcomed me with a warm smile and gestured to the floor. I found a spot and sank into a squat stretching my hamstrings. A few more students, about my age and including several women, slipped in and exchanged greetings in a mix of Italian and Portuguese. When ready, Marquinho began walking in a large circle. One by one, we fell in behind. When the circle was complete, Marquinho silently turned toward the center and began a slow, slightly hunched and shuffling ginga, his gaze down, focus inward. Class had begun.

With the same ease that I slipped into the training circle that first evening, I would fall back into comfortable convivência with the group every time I returned to Venice.

Training *Capoeira Angola*

In his early forties when I first met him, Marquinho lived with his Italian wife and young daughter in Sacile, an hour's train ride toward the mountains from Venice. His main academy was located in Sacile, but he taught in Venice twice a week to a group of six men and four women in 2012, and even fewer in 2016 and 2018 when I returned to teach and live. Reflecting the demographics of a shrinking Venice—only 14 percent of the population is under eighteen and the average age is forty-four—we were a dwindling group of gently aging capoeiristas.

Distinct from large, cosmopolitan ABADÁ, this group seemed a throwback to earlier times. In age and gender (predominantly male), if not in race (Marquinho and all his students were white), I imagined that we were much closer to capoeira schools of Salvador in the 1940s. Marquinho was affiliated with the *capoeira angola* school of the now eighty-nine-year-old Mestre João Grande, considered one of the last living "old guard" Bahian capoeiristas. Born in southern Bahia, Mestre João Grande came to Salvador as a young man where he pumped gas for a living, trained in Mestre Pastinha's academy, gained a reputation in street rodas, and performed in folkloric shows. In 1992, already in his fifties, he traveled for the first time to New York City to perform in a show and never returned to Brazil.[4] In New York he opened a school and started teaching for the first time. He drew a cadre of American and expat Brazilian devotees who helped the mestre, who could not read or write and never learned to speak English, adjust to life in the United States and build a reputation as one of the most "authentic" capoeira mestres.

Before its present location in Harlem, Mestre João Grande's academy was on 14th Street near Union Square. For a while when I lived in New York, I trained with Mestra Edna in a fitness gym in the same building as Mestre João Grande's school. Despite inhabiting opposite ends of the capoeira style spectrum, Mestra Edna and Mestre João Grande were fond of each other. We often stopped off to visit Mestre João Grande and his parrot after class, and on Sundays we frequented his long, afternoon rodas.

In size and pedagogy Marquinho's classes were a world away from the large, fast-paced ABADÁ classes. We began slowly, stretching individually or playing brief games to get blood flowing. Once we were in the circle, Marquinho began with a series of floor combinations that utilized arms, heads, and backs intensely. Demanding extraordinary upper body strength and back flexibility—no additional strengthening or stretching were incorporated in class as it all came through the movement—these combinations left me dripping with sweat. Heads, hands, and feet became transfer points of contact and shifting weight as we wove patterns on the floor. One of Marquinho's frequent moves, performed with a fluidity that at first evaded me, was the *rolê de cabeça*. Rolê, which translates as "roll," refers in capoeira to any of several ways of moving on the ground in order to shift the body to a new location. In this particular "head roll" the top of the head is the fulcrum around which the body rotates, legs moving from front to side, to back and front again. He also incorporated many more backbends, a post-cesarean challenge to be sure!

Just when I thought my knees, arms, and back would give out, Marquinho would shift to standing and lead us in ginga, kicks, feints, and footwork. Marquinho's ginga was the antithesis of my low, wide swinging ABADÁ ginga, torso tilted forward, arms up near my face. His ginga was understated, and if you didn't know better, seemed even hesitant. Upright, with a slight knee bend, shoulders hunched forward, arms held close to his torso, and gaze downward, Marquinho shuffled from left to right like an old man, the ginga of Mestre João Grande. Within this contained ginga however, Marquinho executed twirls, feints, and dodges, low kicks and standing headbutts, sweeps and leaps.

As challenging at first as the new-to-my-body movement was the spatial orientation of training: facing each other in a circle. Even with years of experience following new combinations, in the circular format I was easily disorientated. When Marquinho's movement took him out of the circle, I would move into the circle, following him; after long complicated sequences I often found myself facing the wrong way. Frustrating at first, I soon grew to appreciate this format. The circular training mirrored the game of capoeira itself and encouraged convivência rather than hierarchy. We were all, including Marquinho, training in the same space, rather than in ranked rows. The circle and quiet mimesis of instruction rather than verbalized commands and barked corrections, lulled me into a meditative state, giving me space to become more attuned to the music and to the internal rhythm of my body.

We trained exclusively to the music of old capoeira mestres. The rough edges of the early recordings, the mellow twang of the low-pitched berimbaus and gravelly voiced simple choral responses, were so different from the taut, bright, ring of modern berimbaus and the longer, melodically and lyrically complex contemporary songs. Sometimes the music would become just instrumental, and its percussive quality would amplify and intensify. Marquinho would become more playful and off-balance in his ginga then: tapping and shuffling feet, shaking and dipping shoulders reminiscent of someone dancing samba or for the orixás. These breakout sessions gave me license to move in more creative, fluid ways than ever before in capoeira.

In the second half of class, we worked in pairs, and Marquinho's pedagogy shifted. Now he talked, explaining and dissecting combinations. Every move had to be intentional. There was no reason, he would explain, to launch a kick or a headbutt, if it would not make our opponent move. Despite his shuffling ginga, Marquinho was highly attuned to the combative side of capoeira.

Simplicity and efficiency had attracted Marquinho to Mestre João Grande's style and pedagogy. Marquinho explained: "His movement is simple and objective. And he teaches by correcting errors. It's only when you make a mistake that the other player will get you. Mestre Pastinha wrote that in his book. And of course, you have to smile while playing."

He mentioned a game I had played recently with another student: "The game was good, only your smiles were missing. It was too tense, too heavy. Smiles bring levity and disguise your intentions. That's malandragem."

In the roda, Marquinho plays with intensity and a smile. He spares no sweep or headbutt, waiting for an opening or unguarded move to knock you down. Marquinho's tough play was in part shaped by his early development as a capoeirista in his hometown of Olinda in the northeast state of Pernambuco.

I told Marquinho about my experience with the rough street roda in Olinda on one of my first trips to Brazil and he chuckled.

"Yeah, that sounds like Olinda. The rodas were tough. One guy got all the bones in his face broken." Marquinho grimaced and passed his hand in front of his face. "He made a big deal out of landing a kick during a game, laughing at his opponent, to make sure everyone saw it. The guy got pissed and later in the game knocked him down and stomped on his face."

Marquinho continued with his capoeira history: "My first teacher was a street capoeirista, Telmo Anu. He didn't have a school or anything. It was like that film *The Karate Kid*. Me and a couple guys would hang out in his house all day, and he would teach us stuff, and we would do chores for him in exchange. He used to tell us that to test our capoeira we should go out looking for a fight but never alone, always with two or three friends. Crazy telling teenagers that, and we'd do it, especially during carnival. I liked fighting."

"But eventually I started training with Mestre Sapo, who had an academy. When I started, Sapo was in the process of switching from the *regional* to *angola* style. He made the change after he saw Mestre Cobra Mansa play in a really rough roda. Cobra Mansa was playing that beautiful game of his, elegantly knocking everyone to the ground, and no one could touch him. And the whole time that big grin on his face."

I smiled, conjuring Mestre Cobra Mansa's game. Cobrinha (as he was introduced to me) was the first capoeirista I met after Beiçola. They grew up together in Rio and came to the United States together as performers. With his humor, graceful agility, and unpredictable attacks, Cobrinha is a joy to watch.

"So Sapo became an angoleiro, and so did I. And then I came to Europe for an event in 1994. And I met all these guys who were living and teaching capoeira, and they were really professional and really good. They were living capoeira at a different level from the mess of the street in Olinda. I wanted that for myself, so I stayed. I spent five years in Germany before coming to Italy."

By 2018, only three of Marquinho's original students still trained: Mariano, a grumpy gondolier in his sixties with a rich baritone singing voice, lived alone in his childhood home—two rooms in a crumbling palazzo, a kitchen and cavernous workshop that housed his boat, bed, and stacks of comic books; Pierangelo, an intensely private man in his fifties who lived alone and worked himself to the bone at the bar he co-owned; and Marco, or Burano as we called him in capoeira, a forty-year-old, overgrown-teenage kite surfer and single child who still lived with his restaurant-owning parents on the nearby lace-making island that had given him his nickname.

Besides capoeira training trips to Brazil and vacations to Sicily, and other close destinations, Mariano, Pierangelo, and Burano have lived their entire lives in or around Venice. Mariano and Pierangelo grew up fishing in the canals, and Pierangelo attended the elementary school in Cannaregio where we trained. The women whom I had trained with on previous visits—Benedetta the large, jolly artist from Rome, Valentina from Milan, an activist who taught English to immigrants, and Lena the linguistics doctoral student from Florence—had all stopped capoeira or moved away.

"I am happy," Marquinho told me. "It is a small group now, but my students are good."

My capoeira convivência in Venice seemed appropriate to the setting: an ebbing group in a vanishing city. Just as Venice fights to remain a living city rather than a hollowed-out tourist attraction, Marquinho's group belies the homogenizing and soul-sucking forces of globalization and commercialization. Large international groups like ABADÁ offer the excitement of transnational mobility and cosmopolitan sensibilities; Marquinho's group offered a more intimate, local practice. Not that we didn't also do our part in spreading capoeira: one of my few excursions to the mainland was for a presentation at a travel agency promoting packaged tours to Brazil. We performed in front of a slide show of tropical birds and beaches and next to the Spritz truck supplying cocktails to the elegantly dressed guests who seemed rather mystified by capoeira and its connection to the Brazil images projected behind us. But for the most part, my capoeira convivência in Venice reminded me that the worldwide "does not abolish the local."[5]

Global South Convivência

In her ethnography of global tango, Kathy Davis suggests that the Argentinian dance has become so "de-territorialized" that it no longer fits easily into the Global North and Global South divide. Pushing back against earlier studies that argued that tango tourism always reenacts the gendered violence of the colonial encounter, Davis argues that while still entangled in complicated cultural imaginaries that can evoke (hyper)heterosexuality, dangerous exoticism, and cosmopolitan desires for authenticity, dancing tango today also promises "a togetherness that requires a bridging of difference."[6]

Further disrupting readings of global practices such as tango or capoeira as simply reproducing hierarchies of difference, is the fact that while these practices attract foreigners with the financial means for transnational travel, they also often attract foreign participants whose life conditions mean they only know their practice in small, local contexts. In the case of capoeira, it is often these capoeiristas—a construction worker in Sweden, an underemployed Dominican in New York City, a Haitian refugee in Paris, a Palestinian in the occupied West Bank—who find aspirational opportunities in capoeira, whether to fight oppressive social conditions or develop a profession.

Adding complexity, capoeira is increasingly popular in Global South locations beyond Brazil. Early capoeira migration from the 1970s to 1990s was predominantly to North America, Europe, Australia, and Japan—places where Brazilian instructors hoped to improve their quality of life. Starting in the early 2000s, capoeira groups were popping up in African, South American, and Caribbean locales.

In 2010 I directed a Duke summer abroad program in Ghana and heard rumor of a local group that trained Sunday afternoons on the university campus in Accra. What would capoeira look like in West Africa I wondered? What was the group's lineage and who was its leader? What kind of Ghanaians would be attracted to the practice? And would they feel connected to it as Angolans did?

I eventually found myself with a Sunday free, but worried that the soccer game that afternoon would take precedent. Ghanaians were euphoric to have qualified that year for the World Cup (and paraded in the streets shouting "Obama, we're so sorry!" when they beat the American team).

When I arrived within view of the designated campus field, I was relieved to hear the twang of a berimbau, and my heart beat a little stronger. At the edge of the field a young man with dreadlocks played a berimbau while a woman stretched.

"Ié capoeiristas!"

I called again louder surprised not to get a response. The man finally looked up when I reached them and introduced myself. In an American accent he told me the group was only for people of African descent.

He and the woman offered no more words, and at a loss, I turned and walked away. I was disappointed. I was also irritated and annoyed. Who was this guy and what was his capoeira lineage? Were his students Ghanaian or also foreigners? Did Africans qualify as people of "African descent"? Did his Ghanaian students share his views?

In her raw memoir of traveling the slavery routes in Ghana, historian Saidiya Hartman describes the loneliness and resentment she felt at being only ever called *obruni,* or "stranger," the label Ghanaians use for all foreigners. Hartman had hoped to feel a connection to West Africans through shared ancestry and history. But she discovered that the narratives Ghanaians had to tell about slavery were different from her own and in listening so intently for her own story, "had almost missed theirs."[7] My capoeira story is of course different from Hartman's story, yet at that moment of rejection her feelings resonated with me. Like Hartman, in my eagerness for my own capoeira story, I was missing the story in front of me.

This African American man had found something in capoeira different from what I found, and which didn't include me. Perhaps, while maybe never shaking the obruni label, he had forged a kinship through capoeira that had eluded Saidiya Hartman and other African American visitors. Perhaps his Ghanaian students discovered through an embodied expressive practice a connection to their diasporic kin that transcended complicated feelings about a shared and fraught history of slavery.

Being confronted again with my whiteness in Ghana reminded me that in its global circulation capoeira accrues new meanings and potency. For me, capoeira is a space to create fictive kin and find belonging across difference. For others, who live with a sense of nonbelonging because of the brutal displacement of their ancestors and their everyday experience of racism, capoeira is a place to find togetherness with others who have similar experiences—and to create kinship through exclusion of those who don't.

A year later on a belated honeymoon in Havana, Cuba, when I was seven months pregnant, I stumbled across more Global South capoeiristas. Walking one evening along Havana's Malecón, the oceanfront promenade that sweeps the length of the city, we heard berimbaus. Quickening our pace, we came upon a group of four or five teenage boys and one girl in T-shirts and shorts holding several rough-made instruments. They welcomed me enthusiastically, though not with much surprise, into their small circle and handed me a berimbau. They taught me the songs they knew, and I taught them others, the couples sitting on the seawall pausing their kisses to join in the chorus. Reminding me of the capoeiristas in Benguela, the Cuban capoeiristas told me they had no group or teacher and learned however they could. For a while an Italian had trained and shared knowledge with them.

Many Global South capoeiristas today learn not from Brazilians but from Global North capoeiristas. Ghanaians in Accra learn from African Americans, and Cubans learn from European foreign exchange students. Now, several decades after capoeira's introduction in these Global South locations, the practice has expanded with a proliferation of native instructors. Many of these native instructors, whether they have been to Brazil or not, are affiliated with global capoeira groups originating in Brazil, sometimes through pure happenstance or convenience (one Mexican capoeirista told me his group affiliated with a particular Brazilian mestre because he charged the least amount of money for visits abroad). Capoeira becomes a way, as I discovered in Angola in 2002, to connect to a transnational world.

Yet for many Global South practitioners, especially within the African diaspora, capoeira is also a means of connecting to local roots. Capoeira in Cuba has been a way for local practitioners to both discover their own Afro-Cuban history and connect to the larger world. Like the Angolan capoeiristas I met, Cuban capoeiristas feel that capoeira is something both within and beyond them.[8] Whether because of common ancestry or current life conditions, Global South capoeiristas of the African diaspora experience a distinctive capoeira convivência.

Eager to see how capoeira had developed in one Global South location where I had seen its implantation almost two decades before, I returned to Angola.

7

RETURN TO ROOTS

ANGOLA, 2019

I heard the drum from a mile away. Cabuenha hadn't specified the exact location of the roda on the Marginal, so I had gone early to walk its length and take in the city on my first day back in Angola after seventeen years. I was eager to see what capoeira, and what was touted as national reconstruction, reconciliation, and democracy, looked like in the city almost two decades after war's end.

On the surface, some things looked good.

A $350 million face-lift, inaugurated at the 2012 reelection of President José Eduardo Dos Santos, marking his thirty-three years in power, had transformed the dirty bayfront I remembered zipping by in Nzinga's jeep in 2002 into a wide esplanade with benches, playgrounds, and Miami-imported palm trees. Walking toward the ports, in the hot noon sun with not many people out, I looked to my left out across the bay to the Ilha and to my right across the multilaned Avenida 4 de Fevereiro. The worn-out colonial buildings lining the avenue in 2002 were crisply renovated and interspersed with new modern buildings including, fittingly, the Money Museum.

The "New Angola" ushered in with the war's end in 2002 has and has not changed the face of the country. The MPLA party continues in power but has shifted away from its socialist ideology toward a neoliberal agenda of development. As petrodollars and foreign investment began pouring into the country in the early 2000s, little changed for the population's majority. Nonetheless, still believing in the MPLA's promise of peace and development, Angolans overwhelmingly reelected Dos Santos. But by 2011, oil revenue began to tank, and it became increasingly difficult to ignore the fact that Dos Santos was heading one of the most corrupt regimes in Africa, ruling through a system of patronage for his family and political allies and dictatorial repression for everyone else. Angolans took to the streets in protest, and in 2017 Dos Santos reluctantly relinquished the reigns to João Lourenço, vice president of the MPLA. While repressive practices diminished, the jury was still out among Angolans as to whether President Lourenço would curb corruption, create jobs and public infrastructure, and address social inequality.

When I headed back down the Marginal, ears and eyes alert for a roda, the day had cooled and sunlight mellowed to a late winter tropical gold. The esplanade had filled with expat joggers and Angolan families with young children. The roda had begun at the far end of the Marginal, where a sun setting behind the São Miguel Fortress filtered through palm trees, splashed across eager faces, and illuminated the bay water beyond. Bodies popcorned across the roda in acrobatic solos. Unlike our closing roda in the dusty Independence Square in 2002, here capoeiristas outnumbered spectators—150, ranging in ages from five to forty and all in clean, white uniforms.

This section of the Marginal had been expanded into a large plaza in front of the incomplete Shopping Fortaleza. Celebrated in 2011 as Angola's future first mall that would rival those in Dubai and rebrand Luanda into a global city "like anywhere in the world"—eight years later it was a vacant shell.[1] Now with the local *kwanza* depreciated to an exchange of five hundred to the dollar, the city of the future had become a city of ghosts; a "haunted place" with a "hint of phantasmagoria," as anthropologist António Tomás describes his hometown.[2] If Luanda of 2002 was a city of concrete skeletons, decaying buildings waiting for the promise of independence, 2019 Luanda was a city of concrete ghosts, incomplete buildings waiting for the promise of neoliberal development. Yet, among these haunted spaces and concrete hulls, there was a vibrant street convivência in full display on a late July afternoon.

In contrast to the inanimate mall, the plaza was brimming with activity: a reminder that life in the tropics is better lived outdoors anyway. Next to the roda and in front of the Amore ice cream parlor, an attractive glass-fronted café with outdoor tables, male youth in hip-hop fashion and inline skates had set up orange cones. In between loop the loops and low bent-knee tricks, they made way for little kids in helmets to take scooter-runs at the cones as their parents looked on. Later, after the sun set, men and women gathered in the back corner of the plaza next to a big boom box to dance *kizomba,* the sensual couples dance that has become an international craze.

The roda, with its music and energy, dominated the plaza but did not command any more attention than the other activities. Passersby glanced over, and several mothers stopped to crouch next to their toddlers and point out the action through legs. Capoeira, it seemed, was no longer an unfamiliar or uncommon sight in this part of Luanda.

I felt strange and out of place not in uniform. Several of the capoeiristas glanced over as I joined the roda, only mildly surprised when I joined in the chorus. To them I was just another tourist or expat out for a Sunday stroll.

I felt a sense of loss knowing that if I had on my uniform they would have come over eager to greet me and hear my story. I had not brought my uniform on the trip, as I no longer identified as an active member of ABADÁ. After training *capoeira angola* in Italy, I was drifting away from the extreme athleticism, uniformity, and hierarchy of groups like ABADÁ. I had come to Angola to follow up on my research in 2002. But I was also eager to see if there were new developments and new groups. Had Angolans created an "Angolan" style that they had spoken of in 2002?

The crowd was young—children and teens, with two dozen advanced students in their twenties or early thirties. Only six girls and two female advanced students. I watched one young woman try to enter the roda and be bypassed repeatedly by male students. She finally gave up, reminding me of how hard it was for female students in Rio when I trained in the early 2000s, and how different things were now with so many more women in leadership positions. The solos were over, and the games had begun. Quality was high: clean and up-to-date technique and smoothly coordinated games; none of the nervous, aggressive energy I remembered from 2002. There was one flare-up between two players who started to throw punches, but who quickly got their emotions under control and returned to play.

As the sun set and a cool breeze kicked up, Cabuenha stopped the music. He called a boy, eight or nine years old, into the roda, handed him a berimbau, and instructed him to play different rhythms. The boy was extraordinarily skilled, faltering only a bit when Cabuenha asked him to also sing.

"My new student needs a nickname!" Cabuenha called out when the clapping died down.

"*Tocador* (instrument player)!"

"*Caxixi!*"

"No!" Cabuenha shouted. "It has to be in a native language!"

More nicknames were called out, Cabuenha asking for a translation and what language they were in. Nothing was decided and the music started again, capoeiristas eager to play.

"Gamba!"

Pleasure flooded over me at the call of my Angolan nickname from the grinning guy in street clothes who had taken over on the atabaque.

"Muxi!" He hadn't changed beyond a few additional pounds.

Leaning sideways, hands keeping the rhythm, Muxi received my double kisses and then spoke into my ear over the music: "I got here late because I'm an economics professor now at the Catholic University, and I have two kids so I don't have much time for capoeira."

Another young man approached whom I didn't recognize. When he told me his nickname, Segredo, I was relieved I had reread my 2002 field notes on the plane from Lisbon and could place him.

"And look who's also still in capoeira!" He pulled over another student who looked at me in disbelief.

"Is that really you Gamba!" I immediately recognized and remembered Índio. His face hadn't changed since boyhood.

"I still have a picture of the two of us at the Marítimo da Ilha," Segredo told me.

I was touched and saddened that I had not stayed in better contact with the Angolan capoeiristas. Capoeira convivência can be deeply felt but fleeting. I kept up with Nzinga on social media and had seen her several times in Brazil over the years. But I had stayed most in touch with Cabuenha, whom I had met not in Angola but in Brazil. Cabuenha was part of the new vanguard of capoeira instructors who had returned to Luanda after spending war years abroad. Not unlike the Brazilian capoeiristas I had traveled to Angola with in 2002, many of these returning Angolan capoeiristas were in search of capoeira's roots as a way to affirm their own *angolanidade* or "Angolan-ness."

Complicated and ambiguous, angolanidade began percolating in the mid-twentieth century during Angola's independence struggle. Influenced by the Negritude Movement in francophone African colonial struggles at the time, Angolan intellectuals called on angolanidade to develop an indigenous, national identity. Yet angolanidade was a decidedly cosmopolitan project of Luandan intellectuals, artists, and politicians. It would be embraced by the MPLA's postindependence creole politics of a multiracial, multicultural nation that seemed to continue the colonial concept of Luso-Tropicalism. Based on sociologist Gilberto Freyre's theory of Brazilian racial exceptionalism, Luso-Tropicalism had been used by the Portuguese to justify their continued colonial rule well after many African nations had gained independence. President Dos Santos continued this colonial narrative of racial harmony, claiming he grew up with Kimbundu spoken in the yard and Portuguese in the parlor, a rhetoric that reeks of Freyre's revisionist history of Brazil's benign slavocracy.[3] Angola, like Brazil, is a country built on racism under a shallow veneer of creole harmony. Nonetheless, diverse interpretations of angolanidade would continue to circulate among different actors in cultural arenas—music, dance, and now capoeira—as a quest for Angolan self-identification.

As Cabuenha told me, "In capoeira I found a vehicle to research, study, and express my own angolanidade; not who I am as a foreigner, but who I am as an Angolan."

Cabuenha refers to himself as part foreigner because, like many of the "new" Angolans in their thirties and forties, he spent many of his formative years living in Europe. And like many Luandans, Cabuenha speaks no local languages, and, until recently, had seen little beyond the capital. Angola is often described as two nations: the urban and rural, the modern and traditional, Luanda and the rest of the country. This division had, in part, driven the civil war: the MPLA party supported by a largely Luanda-based cosmopolitan, educated, and creole population and UNITA supported by the indigenous, rural populations.

For some of the new capoeira leaders who had returned to Angola after the war, many disillusioned by the government's corruption, capoeira was a way to discover their homeland and African identity.

The New Angolans

I had reconnected with Cabuenha at the 2009 World Games in Brazil. He was back living in Angola, teaching capoeira and researching local Angolan music and dance. He had brought some of his students that year to compete and to present a performance of Angolan combat games. I was drawn to Cabuenha's artistic and intellectual flare and to his distinctive afro so different from the uniform, shaven-head, athletic look of male ABADÁ capoeiristas.

Cabuenha told me, "I first saw capoeira in Luanda in 1996 when Mestre Camisa was there doing shows. It was love at first sight. I was young—an adolescent—but I learned quickly. Within two months I was playing berimbau. My friends saw my knack for capoeira, and they told me if I stuck with it, I could travel to Brazil. This became my dream, because you know, Angolans are fascinated with Brazil. But I had other influences as well. I grew up in a family that liked literature and art, and my older brother did theater. So, I identified not just with the fight and sport of capoeira, but with its artistic potential. Its poetics."

Cabuenha had spent the final years of the war in Europe with his mother and brother. He continued his capoeira training in Portugal, and in 2005 traveled to Brazil for eighteen months.

"It was marvelous, the best experience I've ever had, but also the hardest. I was alone without my family and my money ran out. I had to sleep for a while in that tiny, suffocating room in the CIEP were mestre keeps the instruments and mats and things. I hadn't imagined I would stay that long, but once I got there, I realized I had to if I really wanted to *conviver* (live; coexist) with capoeira and capoeiristas. But I also knew I had to go back to Angola. I had to return to help develop my country, to help shape its future."

Cabuenha moved back to Luanda in 2007 during what he called the country's "big bang." Oil money was flowing in, and the economy was growing, and he quickly found work teaching capoeira and doing presentations at all the new private schools and institutions that were popping up. He also began traveling around the country to research Angolan music and dance and created a performance company, Yakalakaya, the name of which comes from an Independence-era freedom cry.

Cabuenha's solo performances, which he has exhibited in Europe and Brazil and which have a large social media presence, mix spoken word, music, capoeira, and Angolan dance.

Other "new" Angolan capoeiristas I met in 2019 had similar stories to Cabuenha's. Nani, one of only three advanced female students in Cabuenha's group, balked when I asked for an interview.

"Camarão! I'm no capoeira expert! There are others you should talk too!"

"I am not interested in your expertise in capoeira, I am interested in your experience as a woman in capoeira."

"Ah, now that I can talk about! You know what we call the orange/blue cord? *A corda da feitiço*—the cursed cord! Girls get that cord and then disappear and never get their blue cord, which would make them an advanced student. They stop training because of one thing or another: family, pregnancy. Everyone jokes that it's time to buy diapers when a female student gets to orange/blue!"

Several days after the roda, Nani met me at the Amore ice cream parlor. Elegantly dressed in a pantsuit and discrete jewelry, she had just come from her job at the Ministry of Justice. Nani had received her law degree in Portugal. When she'd graduated from high school in the late 1990s, there had been no private universities in Angola, and it was near impossible to get into the one public university without bribery, so her parents sent her abroad.

"I went to Coimbra to study law and found capoeira," Nani laughed.

"I still remember my first class. It was so hard that the next day I was sore to the roots of my hair! But I went back and I kept training. My involvement's been kind of spotty over the years, but I always return because I feel something in capoeira that I don't feel anywhere else."

I asked, "What is it you feel?"

"I feel as if I am doing something my ancestors did. It's strange but what we have here in Luanda is not very African. Many Angolans are actually more European, but sometimes when we go abroad, we suddenly want to recuperate our African identity. At least that's what happened to me. I started wearing African cloth, and I stopped using chemicals to straighten my hair. I wanted to show people I wasn't just another immigrant fleeing Africa. I was in Europe only temporarily. I planned to go home. And I kept it up when I came home. Now I always wear African cloth to work on Fridays."

I pulled out the Murano glass bead necklace I had planned to give Nani until I'd seen her elegant jewelry. "Here, you can wear this on Fridays too."

Nani looked pleased and continued: "Capoeira helped me develop my Africanness by doing something my ancestors did. My great-great-grandfather was a slave in Brazil. But he was really rebellious, so they sent him back to Angola. When I started doing capoeira, my grandfather told me he was so happy because his great-grandfather fought with Zumbi dos Palmares! Of course, he made that part up."

Nani and I chuckled.

"He would have had to have lived over three hundred years ago for that! But we do know he was a slave who got sent back. We like to say in my family that our hair, which is not so course, is not a result of mixing with whites but with Indians from Brazil."

I asked Nani what it was like to live in Luanda during the war. Like most Angolans, she had stories of terror—an aunt who watched her husband get shot on the doorstep of their apartment when the fighting reached Luanda in 1992, and a cousin who ran off to join UNITA. But she also expressed nostalgia for the war years.

"During the war we supported each other because we were all suffering, and there was nothing else we could do. We would smile and laugh to give each other courage. And there was a greater sense of social responsibility. Sure, this may have come down from the Party, but we claimed it as ours. Now that we don't have a government telling us what to do, no one takes responsibility. For example, when I was a kid, I used to love Saturdays at my grandmother's apartment building because that was the day all the residents cleaned the building together. It was like a party, with water running down the stairwell! No one does that kind of communal work anymore. There are so many dirty buildings in Luanda now."

Nani's mixed feelings echoed sentiments expressed by Luandans in Jon Schubert's ethnography of the city. He writes of a certain "nostalgia for socialism" which, though "a time of wartime hardship and material scarcity, is now remembered as a bygone era of solidarity, social equality, and lost ideals that have today been swept away by economic inequalities produced by the national reconstruction drive."[4] A "culture of immediacy"—the seemingly limitless influx of petrodollars that created spectacular wealth overnight—left common Angolans impatient and frustrated when the trickle-down did not reach them. It is perhaps a nostalgia for a neoliberal future that was promised but never arrived, rather than loss of a paternal socialist state, as Nani suggested, that has in fact corroded work ethics and class solidarity.

We returned to talking about capoeira, and I asked what it was like to train in Luanda when she came back from Europe.

"It's so different here. The kids have a swing (*ginga do molejo*) that not even Brazilians have! And I didn't have it, even though I trained with an Angolan in Europe. Here you feel a vibration in the roda, and I say that's the angolanidade coming out. When I see capoeiristas in the roda getting aggressive, I say, hey, let the angolanidade speak!"

I asked what angolanidade meant to her.

"It's rebirth: recognizing and strengthening my identity and passing it on. Angola is where I was born, grew up, and where I hope to die. I don't condemn others for leaving, but this is where I want to be. Angolanidade shows the world that there is more to Angola than just war, and I am an ambassador to that. When I was in Brazil in 2013, I was playing in a roda and someone shouted out, "Look, there's an Angolan playing!" And everyone crowded around to see. I guess I have that swing now! And capoeira is angolanidade's ambassador. My friend was organizing an exposition on Angola to take abroad, and she asked me to organize a photo session with capoeiristas so she could include those. Brazilians might say that capoeira is theirs, but it was birthed here in Angola."

"But when Angolans see capoeira do they think it's Angolan?"

Nani shook her head no.

"That's why the work Cabuenha is doing to recuperate Angolan expressive practices is so important. He is showing how they contributed to capoeira."

Nani told me about the volunteer work she did with another female capoeirista in a girls' orphanage in Vania, a crowded suburb of Luanda disproportionately populated by women and children refugees from the war.

"We go every Saturday to teach capoeira, but we do more than that. We teach these girls that they haven't been forgotten, that they are productive members of society, and that they can be whatever they want to be—in capoeira and in the world."

I encouraged Nani in her work, wondering if one day Angolan women in capoeira would achieve what Brazilian female capoeiristas were accomplishing despite continued challenges.

Nostalgia in a City of Concrete Ghosts

"I live in a new apartment now Camarão. But I can take you around to see the old building when you come visit."

I had called Sylvia, Nzinga's mother, on my second morning in Luanda. I had hoped to see Nzinga—now an instructor and the only woman in Luanda teaching adults—but she was living outside the city and busy with her job, studying for medical school, and solo-raising her three-year-old son.

Following my phone map and Sylvia's instructions, I set out from Ingombota, the neighborhood where I was staying in a rented room, for her new apartment in Sambizanga. I was enjoying getting to know Luanda by foot. In 2002 I had almost always traveled by car and had never gotten my bearings. The city, in my memory, was a patchwork. Now, I was sewing the patches into a landscape. Sometimes memories jumped out, but more often, with the city's transformations they eluded me. That morning I passed right by Kinaxixi Square and Sylvia's old apartment building without knowing. The historic square and the statue of Queen Nzinga were gone, and the area was a massive construction site. Work on the Kinaxixi Business Area—a glass-encased, towering citadel of retail, office, and residential space surrounded by gardens and fountains—began in 2008. But like Shopping Fortaleza, all that was on display twelve years later was a ghostly concrete hull with massive immobile cranes marking time on the roof.

"It was terrible. We had really put a lot of work into the building."

Sylvia was filling me in on her recent housing history. I had found her brand new burnt umber, ten-story apartment building with breezy corridors, functioning elevators, and security guard ten minutes after unknowingly passing her old building. Sylvia looked much the same, her body softened with age and gray hair neatly pulled back from her smooth face. Ethan, Nzinga's three-year-old son, peered at me past his grandmother's legs, his large, doe eyes identical to his mother's. In striking contrast to her previous apartment with its decaying but homey clutter, Sylvia's new apartment was spacious and sparse. It looked barely inhabited even though she had been living there for three years. We were seated at a black glass dining table between the kitchen and living room. Ana, Sylvia's fourteen-year-old grandniece who also lived in the apartment with her mother, set out tea and bread and butter.

"We'd even won a city prize for the best clean up! And we had our own generators. I had put $25,000 into renovating my apartment. And then one of those cranes from the construction site fell on the roof. Luckily no one was hurt, but it put a huge hole in the roof and they condemned the building. They wouldn't even let us back in to get out stuff! I lost everything. And you know one of the worst things, Isabel is one of the investors in that building that destroyed mine!"

Isabel dos Santos. Daughter of ex-president José Eduardo dos Santos. Africa's first female billionaire. The construction craze—at one point as many as seventeen cranes had dotted the city's skyline—had made the wealthy wealthier.

"So they moved us here. The government had just finished this building, and we live here rent free but I don't own the apartment like I did before."

Suddenly I heard water running in the kitchen, and I asked Ana if she'd left the faucet on.

Sylvia chuckled.

"No, Camarão! It is just like in my old building! Water is erratic. That's our signal. Ana, go open the bathtub taps."

"How is it that a new building has water problems?"

"The building may be new, but Luanda's infrastructure is forty-five years old! We are still using the water system that the Portuguese built for a city of several hundred thousand inhabitants. We are six million now. The government doesn't care about improving services for the people. They just want to build fancy new things for the rich!"

The government had made some infrastructural concessions but the "disposable roads, Styrofoam bridges, and facade works" were already disintegrating.[5]

We went out for a city tour, Ana and Ethan coming along.

Suddenly a little voice started singing from the back seat:

Avante Angola!	Forward Angola!
Revolução, pelo Poder Popular!	Revolution through the power of the People!
Pátria Unida, Liberdade,	A United Country, Freedom,
Um só povo, uma só Nação.	One People, One Nation

"Sylvia, is Ethan singing the national anthem?"

She chuckled. "There was a television ad promoting Angola and the national anthem. It ran so much he memorized the song. Capoeira was in the ad! Cabuenha and some of his students, singing by the fort."

"What a change from 2002, when people were confused just by the name!"

"A lot has changed since you were last here, Camarão. Wait until you see the old building."

Prédio 5 had become a grimy facade of broken windows with a caved-in roof and mounds of garbage filling the arcade entries and spilling out onto the sidewalk. A group of youth sitting among the trash watched us. I asked Sylvia if I could take pictures and she nodded. One of the youth got up and sauntered toward the car. I got nervous, kicking myself for snapping pictures with my iPhone out the car window, and then immediately feeling ashamed when Sylvia warmly greeted the young man.

"Oh, my dear! So nice to see you! Why, you are all dressed up! Where are you going?"

The youth stepped back shyly to show off his fashionably ripped, stone-washed jeans, and tight, black, glittery T-shirt.

"I changed, because I'm going home, auntie. You know I got married."

"I heard. Congratulations."

Another young man in a red hoodie approached the car and Sylvia said, "Look! I have brought a friend to see the old building."

"Did you both live in the building as well?" I asked.

"No, Camarão, they were my *miudos!* They were good kids!"

The youth ducked their heads with pleasure and embarrassment.

Driving away I asked Sylvia what she meant that they were her "*miudos.*"

"They were street kids and did errands for me and others in the building. If we needed a new tank of gas for the kitchen, they would go and get it. I trusted them. They always came back with whatever I needed *and* the change. They were orphaned by the war and had nowhere to go. So, the building adopted them."

I remembered the war orphan who sells seashells and is adopted by the building in Ondjaki's novel.

Sylvia continued: "We would give the boys food or a little change, and Brenda gave them capoeira T-shirts. One of them even did capoeira with her for a while. And look now they are all grown up! They are still very attached to me. They brought their fiancées to meet me."

I remembered them now, young boys in 2002, hanging around the building. Nzinga and her mother would greet them with stern affection.

"Do they still live in the doorway?"

"No, most of them have families and houses out in the musseques. They just come here during the day to wash cars and make a little money."

It was a miracle that they were still alive—and even married. And yet their lives still revolved around eking out a living from the same doorway they had inhabited as kids, spitting distance from a luxury, skyrise construction project owned by an African billionaire nicknamed "princess." There would be no fairytale transformation from rags to riches for these youth or the two-thirds of Angola's population who live on less than two dollars a day.

Around the corner from Sylvia's old building is Miramar, a hilly neighborhood of mansions and bay views.

"The ex-president lives here now. And I think Isabel might have a house, too," Sylvia told me as we drove through.

From Miramar we headed downtown along the Marginal and then cut in to the Cidade Alta, which houses the government buildings. We drove up a wide sweeping road that curved around a new building styled like the older ones but quadruple in size.

"The new Assembly Building where they do so much hard work for us!" Sylvia's voice dripped with irony. Then she sighed and said, "My father taught me to drive on this hill."

Along with rose-tinted memories of socialism, some older Luandans are nostalgic for the orderly, clean, and efficient years of colonialism.[6]

Other Angolans express a different kind of nostalgia that stretches further back than the late years of colonialism and early years of socialism. Their nostalgia is rooted outside of the city in an imagined rural homeland.

Return to Roots

João was playing the berimbau with a cut-off bottle neck for a dobrão.

I was settled in his apartment just down the street from where I was staying. The three-story building, abandoned-looking on the outside, housed only two functioning apartments. Shortly after João moved in with his family, water started leaking through the ceiling. He went upstairs to investigate and discovered an old woman living alone with the roof caving in around her. She accepted João's offer to buy her apartment and move her to the empty one on the floor below. He fixed the roof and was hoping to buy and renovate the whole building one day.

I had met João earlier that afternoon downtown close to where he worked in a modern skyrise as an engineer for an oil company. We had been in communication through Facebook Messenger before my arrival in Luanda, and he had agreed to do an interview with me. Not my way of doing fieldwork—cold calling someone for an interview—but my time was short. João was one of two *capoeira angola* instructors in the city that now, according to one Facebook page, boasted over eighty groups.

I felt instantly at ease with João, with his dark-framed glasses and galloping speech that kept my synapses firing. In his early forties, João, like Nani, came from a family who had the means to send him away from Angola during most of the civil war. And like Nani, João had discovered capoeira while living abroad.

In a Starbucks-style café downtown that had a 5:00 p.m. crowd of mothers with young children, business men, and high school students, João told me his capoeira story. After greeting several people he knew, insisting on buying our espressos, and settling at a table, he eagerly spoke into my tape recorder for two hours.

"It was the music, Camarão, that called me. It was 1996, and I was going to University of Sussex, and this other student told me she was doing *capoeira angola*. And I didn't believe it. For nine months I ignored her, and she kept bugging me. 'Come on! It has to do with your country!' And I kept saying, 'No it's impossible!' But eventually I went. And they were playing old capoeira music—Mestre Traíra and Mestre Cobra Verde. And I had a flashback to Angola. To this TV reportage about Angolan tribes that used to play before the news. Capoeira music reminded me of the tribal music."

João's parents had sent their six-year-old son to live with relatives in Europe in the 1980s to escape the conscription raids—open-bed army trucks prowling the streets of Luanda for boys and men to send to the front. He had stayed in Europe, visiting his parents every year, to finish college and begin his career.

"You know I was Black in Europe." João chuckled as he told me about his decision to return permanently to Angola in 2009.

"I was head of the Black Student Union at the University of Essex! Here I'm a mulatto because my father is white, and I'm light-skinned. Though that changes when people see that my wife is very dark-skinned. But I came back because I was tired of being a minority; being told I was different, a foreigner."

Like Cabuenha, João also felt called to help his country.

"I came back because I wanted to help change things here, help develop my country. The war really limited opportunities here, and diminished Angolans' desire to fight for a better life. People's lives are so limited by their social conditions that they can't see a future beyond getting food in their stomachs. There is no ambition. I came back to Angola to help change that mentality. But it is going to take a long time, and the government has to create jobs. You can't liberate people if they are hungry."

Like Nani, João taught free capoeira classes in Vania on the weekends. Unlike other capoeira groups in Luanda, he was not affiliated with a Brazilian group, saying he didn't want that responsibility, preferring to be accountable to just himself and his students.

"I named my group Uavala, which is a Kimbundu word, my tribe's language. It means to stir up (*remexer*). Because for me, capoeira in Angola is a dry seed that we are now watering so that it will grow again. And I try to open the world up a little bit for my students and incentivize them—give them some hope that the future will be better."

João showed me pictures on his phone of a roda with his students. He pointed to a long wooden scraper, a large reco-reco, held between the legs of one of the seated musicians and resting on the floor.

"That's the *dikanza,* a local instrument. Most Angolan capoeiristas' only reference is Brazil. But I think it is important to reference Angola in our practice. I am going to Huíla in August to research n'golo."

"And will you incorporate some of the n'golo movement into your capoeira?"

"I'm not sure. I am a bit of a traditionalist when it comes to the movement. But the instruments for sure. I've been learning to play the berimbau with a piece of bottle neck. The Luandan musician Kituxi plays the hungu that way. He popularized the instrument when he began incorporating it into semba and electronic music. The hungu is pretty much the same as the berimbau—it's played vertically and with a wire. Not like the mbulumbumba in the south, which is played horizontally and uses animal gut for the cord. If you come home with me, I can show you how to play the berimbau with a piece of glass."

Night had fallen outside. Streetlights were almost as sparse as I had remembered in 2002, and I had to keep my eyes down to avoid tripping on black metal pieces sticking out of the sidewalks. They were for lampposts that never got installed, João told me with disgusted irony. At his apartment, I met João's smiley wife and their sweet seven-year-old son, who showed me his expert Floss and other globally popular dance moves. We tried to video call my seven-year-old son so they could dance together, but didn't get through. João and I continued our discussion.

"It's not just the instruments that are similar here. Some capoeira songs really resonate with Angolans. I was once in a market in Dombe Grande, near Benguela, and I had my berimbau and people stopped to ask what it was. So I started to play it, and I sang a *ladainha* that begins with:

Eu não vou na su casa	I don't go in your house
Pra você não vir na minha	So that you don't come to mine
Você tem boca grande	You have a big mouth
Vai comer minha galinha	You will eat my hen

And everyone started laughing, and one guy asked me if it was an Angolan song, and I said no, it was a Brazilian song."

"They identified with it!"

"Exactly!"

As an example of the intertextuality of capoeira music, this verse is actually from a "love" song popular in Brazil in the 1970s: the one-hit wonder, "Where the Cow Goes, the Bull Follows," by João da Praia "discovered" singing it with his one-string guitar while selling ice creams on a Rio beach. Perhaps the song was popular in Angola as well. Perhaps the verse was originally a proverb from Angola: the great flux and reflux of culture across the Atlantic.

João brought out his berimbau and placed a glass bottle neck on his thumb.

"I haven't gotten the hang of it yet, so it's not going to sound great."

He grasped the verga with his middle and ring finger, leaving his index finger free to hook around the wire. At the same time that he held his bottle-necked thumb against the wire, he pulled with his hooked index finger to create the closed note when he struck it with the baqueta. Then he released both for the open note. The sound was more muted than with a coin or stone.

Before I left that evening, we exchanged dobrões: I took home the bottle neck, and João was pleased with the old South African coin (I couldn't find an Angolan one) with an Impala on it that I had found in an antique shop in Venice.

Dancing in M'banza-Kongo

Sonia had on another fabulous outfit.

Her full-length, midnight-blue silk dragon kimono billowed over a low-cut tank, skinny jeans, and heeled cowboy boots. I looked down at the sweat-stained shirt, dirty skirt, and dusty sandals I'd been wearing since we left Luanda, and wished I had on *her* outfit.

My research trip had taken an unexpected turn when Cabuenha invited me north to FestiKongo in M'banza-Kongo the weekend before I was scheduled to fly home.

"M'banza-Kongo, capital of the Kongo Kingdom! It will be an *aventura* (adventure), but we need to go!"

In 2002 I had traveled five hundred kilometers south to Benguela; now I would drive five hundred kilometers north to the capital of the Angolan province of Zaire on the border with the Democratic Republic of Congo. The Kongo Kingdom, the largest constituted state in south-central Africa from the fourteenth through nineteenth centuries ruled by a powerful lineage of kings, holds a reverent place in the capoeira imaginary. While n'golo and other combat games from southern Angola are claimed as capoeira's physical ancestors, it is the Kongolese ontological system that many practitioners turn to for capoeira's philosophical underpinnings; the Kongo proverb, "hands build, feet destroy," for instance, is used to explain capoeira's emphasis on leg rather than hand strikes.

The Kongo Kingdom, and its ancient capital, are also celebrated by Angolans in search of authentic angolanidade. João had approved of my trip, telling me he'd had a "mystical" experience there, and had shown me a book of Kongolese ideographs and cosmograms, the latest in a genealogy of scholarship stretching back to the work of art historian Robert Farris Thompson. In *Flash of the Spirit: African and Afro-American Art and Philosophy,* Thompson made a strong, if somewhat conjectural, case for the extraordinary continuity and creative exchange of West and Central African artistic-religious traditions and similar practices in the Americas—particularly Brazil, Haiti, Cuba, and the southern United States. In a chapter on Kongo influences, Thompson traced everything from love charms in Cuba, religious symbols in Brazil, bottle trees in South Carolina, and the etymology of the words "jazz" and "funky," to the Kongo.[7]

But it is Kongo cosmology, and particularly the *kalunga,* that most attracts practitioners, especially of *capoeira angola.* According to Kongolese philosopher Bunseki Fu-Kiau, the universe came into being through a natural-divine mandate in which a fire-force, the kalunga, acted upon the empty space of the cosmos and birthed the earth. The earth's cooling produced water that half submerged the planet: terrestrial and temporal life above the water and submarine and spiritual life below.[8] Kalunga refers to life force, potentiality, water, and the communicative pathway between the terrestrial and spiritual-ancestral worlds.

The central cosmogram representing Kongolese worldview is a circle inscribing a cruciform. The horizontal line is the kalunga that marks the boundary between terrestrial and spirit realms, and the vertical line symbolizes the connection and passage between these two worlds. While there are many interpretations and variations of Kongo ontology, one consistency appears to be the belief, similar to Christianity, in a single divine power and an eternal human soul. In some interpretations there is even a judgment day for the soul.[9] Yet distinct from Christianity, the Bakongo soul can return to the land of the living. Movement, in fact, is continuous between the terrestrial and spiritual worlds; ancestors and spirits return to earth and affect the lives of the living, who thus must supplicate them through ritual leaders (*gangas*) and medicine (*nkisi*).

Practitioners and scholars of capoeira wishing to inflect their practice with greater spiritual and ancestral gravitas imbue the Kongo cosmogram with new meaning: for them, the kalunga also represents the Middle Passage and the potential to recross and reunite with the ancestors.[10] And the world below the kalunga is conceptualized as a mirror image of the world above, so ancestors, like capoeiristas, walk on their hands.[11]

Certain practices popular among capoeiristas may also be Kongo-inspired. Wearing a *patuá,* or amulet, usually a small pouch containing herbs, is thought to "close" and protect the body during play. While these herbal charms tend to be traced to the West African Mandinka in Brazil, famous for their witchcraft, they equally could be descended from the healing practices of the Bakongo. Another way to close the body deployed by angoleiros is to trace phantom marks on the ground in front of the orchestra before entering the roda. This abbreviated, improvised ritual evokes the *pontos riscados* (scratched points), or symbols drawn in chalk or fingered in sand during Candomblé rituals to summon the deities.

Perhaps capoeira's most famous ponto riscado is the emblem of Mestre Bimba's academy and *capoeira regional* style. A "star of solomon" with an R for *regional* inside it and a cross at the top, the symbol, according to one of Mestre Bimba's former students, is a refiguring of an old "Afro-Semitic-Christian hybrid" sign displayed by enslaved laborers and *capoeiras* on the streets of Salvador. According to Thompson, the symbol is a Candomblé ponto riscado for Pai Velho, a Kongo ancestor.[12] What all this should suggest is the rich and convoluted cultural influences on capoeira and the impossibility of finding one definitive source or meaning.

We can, however, trace the earliest instances of African and Christian religious syncretism, which would continue to evolve in Brazil, to the Kongo.[13] When Portuguese explorer Diogo Cão sailed up the Congo River in 1483 and encountered Nzinga a Nkuwu, the king of Kongo, the two recognized a mutually beneficial relationship. Within a few years, Nzinga a Nkuwu had converted to Catholicism, changed his name to João I (after the king of Portugal), baptized his children, sent Kongo nobles to be educated in Portugal, and opened a school that taught Latin and Portuguese. Meanwhile, the Portuguese established trade routes with the riches—ivory, metals, pottery, and cloth—the Bakongo had on offer.

By the early sixteenth century, with their new South American colony demanding labor, the Portuguese shifted all attention to the Bakongo's domestic slave trade. Impatient with the Bakongos' rule that only war captives could be enslaved, the Portuguese began plundering. King Alfonso I, who had converted the Kongo Kingdom to Christianity, died a broken man in 1542 after some of his own relatives were enslaved and sent to Brazil. Upon his death, the Kongo Kingdom plunged into civil war, and while the royal lineage of kings would continue until the 1950s, the kingdom would never regain its political strength and unity.

Designated a UNESCO world heritage site in 2017, M'banza-Kongo was hosting the First International Kongo Culture Festival with live music, theater, art, literature, and regional artisanal and agricultural vendors from provinces in Angola, the Democratic Republic of Congo, Gabon, and Congo-Brazzaville.

I hesitated, wondering if I was still up for this kind of travel. "Adventure" in Angolan Portuguese is code for roughing it. What if the car broke down and we didn't make it back in time for my flight to Lisbon?

"I have never been that far north," Cabuenha admitted.

My worries dissipated several days later as I sat in the passenger seat of Cabuenha's old SUV, his playlist—from the Independence-era semba of MPLA-supporter David Zé to the contemporary hip-hop of anti-government activist Ikonoklasta—in my ears. Hot air from the open windows blasted my face while flashing by my eyes were small villages of clustered huts, groups of women and children selling yams and fruit from colorful plastic buckets by the side of the road, and solitary, sylvan mammoths of the gnarled, expansive baobab trees. Grit and sweat on my skin and the stomach-tightening anticipation of the unknown gave me a rush of nostalgia for the backpack travel I had done in my twenties, and gratitude that just shy of fifty, I still had it in me.

We had left Luanda in the gray-yellow dawn along a massive multilane highway that cuts through the city's congested periphery already teeming with people rushing to the communal minivan taxis that would take them to work. By late morning, the weak winter sun finally struggled out, and the highway, now a two-lane road, began to climb into a terrain of red-orange earth, enormous boulders, and hanging cliffs. I took pictures of Cabuenha and Caetano, a friend and dancer who had tagged along, hitting poses on a domed rock for their social media feeds.

Cabuenha crouched and grabbed up dirt, "I love this red earth! I want to take buckets of it back to Luanda. This is the real Angola!"

When we pulled into M'banza-Kongo in the afternoon, I was disappointed. A midsized ordinary city of congested traffic and concrete buildings. Where was the mystical mountaintop village of thatched huts and swirling mists? We stopped at a traffic roundabout to ask directions to the festival from some moto-taxi boys who shrugged their shoulders.

We eventually found the historic center where things were beginning to look festive. Vendors and artists were arranging stalls to sell leather sandals, books, wood sculptures, paintings, kitchen supplies, and hair accessories. A temporary pavilion was filling with regional booths displaying everything from local foods to water purification systems. I snapped a selfie of Cabuenha and me next to side-by-side piles of dried cabuenha (sardine-like fish) and camarão (shrimp).

Beyond the plaza was a dusty bare field the size of two football pitches. An enormous stage was under construction at one end, and around the edges people were setting up tables and chairs, barrel barbecues, and coolers. Not far from the festival grounds, we found a restaurant and the Elinga Teatro actors.

Raul, one of the actors and also Cabuenha's capoeira student in Luanda, had told us about the festival. The theater group had been invited to perform a play about Beatrice Kimpa Vita, a seventeenth-century Kongolese noblewoman turned spiritual medium and prophet who was burned at the stake for leading a messianic movement to unite the Kongo Kingdom under a syncretic African Catholicism.

We joined the actors for a lunch of rice, chicken, and heaping piles of the local specialty: black, crisp *katato,* or tree caterpillars, that are nutty in flavor and high in protein and calories.

In the late afternoon Raul took us over to the oldest Catholic church in sub-Saharan Africa, built in 1491. It turned out that Raul, of Portuguese descent from Benguela, was a movie star celebrity, and our progress was hampered by young women asking for selfies with him. As we strolled, I began to see the charm, if not the spirituality, of M'banza-Kongo. The streets were crowded, but the energy was relaxed and welcoming. We passed a group of elders: thin, wrinkled men in khaki suits and peaked hats with wooden staffs and women in colorful skirts and elaborate head wraps.

"They must be going to the courtroom," Raul said. "After the war, they reinstated customary law here for settling local disputes. This is the real deal, Camarão. There is so much history here. Wait 'til you see the church and graveyard."

With its thick uneven walls of crumbling woven stone, arched entryway, and remnants of a narrow nave, we could have been standing among the ruins of a European Romanesque church. In the adjacent well-kept cemetery, we wandered among the neat rows of whitewashed tombstones inscribed with the kings' Christian and Bakongo names and dates of reign.

As we strolled back, the air had mellowed to a perfect temperature, and the streets were abuzz with dancers and musicians hurrying to the field where the performances would soon begin.

Raul took everything in with a leisurely appreciation and then thumped his chest and let out a long exhalation. "I am proud of being African. There is nowhere else I'd rather be."

On the last night of the festival, it wasn't just Sonia in a fabulous outfit. I had joined the actors in front of the stage. Relaxed after their performance, with faces painted like Shakespearean fairies, they were ready to party. Regional dances had preceded an appearance by Waldemar Bastos, a M'banza-Kongo native son and Angola's most well-known semba musician. Now the huge stage was empty and the spectacle had shifted to the young crowd churning up the dust on the field to loud, hard-driving electronic beats from enormous speakers. Sonia and the theater director's daughter, a dreamy twenty-something-year-old who carried around a juggling baton, started strutting and gyrating in a circle of young men and boys, the bravest jumping in the middle to dance with them.

The popping, rocking, bodies were mesmerizing. They were dancing in a style known as *kuduro*—a loose-limbed, solo competitive dance that accompanies the electronic music of the same name, which emerged in dance halls in Luanda in the 1990s. Kuduro translates as "hard ass," but refers not to anatomy but to the hard conditions of life in Angola. Similar to what Brazilians call "the fight that is life" that demands warrior tactics, Angolans refer to kuduro or "the tight place" one finds oneself in life and the "hard ass" one needs to get by.[14]

In fact, kuduro is anything but tight. Dancers were rag dolls, or as the expression has it, "bodies without bones."[15] They moved with fluid virtuosity, disarticulating their bodies in an uncanny reworking of the famous polycentric and polyrhythmic movement we'd seen earlier that evening with the regional dances. Eccentric fashion complemented creative movement. Sometimes just one item: a Russian fur cap on a tall, skinny man in faded jeans and dusty sneakers; a long-sleeved, buttoned-up floral shirt among a circle of boys in shorts and tank tops. Or a whole outfit: a gaunt youth in a cropped tuxedo jacket, skinny slacks, dark sunglasses, and a boxy hat over long Jheri curl—steamer punk meets Michael Jackson.

In his book on Black fabulousness and queer performance, cultural critic Madison Moore argues that "Fabulousness is creative labor, a type of 'self-couture' where our bodies become the site of artistic expression and creativity. . . . an enabling mode of performance that in particular allows people forced to the margins to assert themselves."[16] The youths' dancing and self-styling was born of the same creative impulse that gave rise to capoeira and so many African diasporic expressive practices. What if the angolanidade and "real Angola" that Raul, Cabuenha, and other urban dwellers look for outside the metropole is not in the "traditional" at all? What if instead it is in the improvised bricolage of a "vernacular modern"?[17]

Anthropologist Deborah Thomas argues that "modern blackness" needs neither a rooted past nor utopic future; rather it is "presentist and decidedly mobile." In its refusal of both past-tense "folk blackness" and future-tense "tamed blackness" of middle-class values, diasporic expressive culture is sonically and kinesthetically loud—and unapologetically Black.[18] Could an "Angolan capoeira" look to the past but take what is here in the present in a bricolage of assertive self-style?

"Capoeira is ours now"

The next morning before leaving town we stopped at a cafeteria with good coffee and pastries and a clean bathroom. I hadn't bothered with a bucket bath in the apartment without running water or electricity that we'd been staying in, and felt a little sheepish when the women working the counter glanced at me coming out of bathroom with a toothbrush and dampened down hair. A petite woman with a brown bob was sitting with Cabuenha. I had seen her around town, impressed by her own stylish tropical business couture—today a pale pink 3/4-length frock coat and matching capris paired with low, square-toed pumps. Cabuenha introduced her as an architect from a university in Luanda. They were comparing notes about the festival.

"We didn't have running water or electricity where we stayed either!"

My admiration for her sartorial freshness increased.

"M'banza-Kongo is just not ready for so many visitors! They will be better prepared next time."

She explained to me that she had come to the festival as she was part of a campaign to preserve cultural and architectural patrimony in Angola.

"We have so much rich history and culture that we need to present to the world. That means building tourist infrastructure."

I told her how I knew Cabuenha.

"Ah, capoeira! So beautiful. So important. It is part of our heritage now. We had a capoeira performance last year in Luanda for the International Day of the Abolition of Slavery."

Back in the United States, I was reminded of our conversation as I leafed through a glossy 2012 coffee-table book of the New Angola, a "country in the process of becoming."[19] In the "culture" section, photographs of capoeiristas were interspersed with semba dancers. What the young capoeiristas in 2002 were fighting for and which Cabuenha and João embrace in their mission to develop angolanidade is now nationally recognized: capoeira has become "native" in a nation becoming itself through diasporic belonging.

8

BRINGING IT ALL HOME

Joaninha is in a deep negativa: a sideways lunge, knee low to the ground between her hands, the side of her head grazing the floor, eyes trained on her partner, Calma. This defensive move is very different from the ones I've been teaching all semester.

"Now you give her a *rabo de arraia*," Mestre Cabello instructs Calma.

Calma glances at me.

"*Meia lua de compasso*," I say, using the name he knows.

Nodding, Calma places his hands on the ground and lifts his leg in a smooth, swift, rotating "half-moon" kick that arcs high over his partner.

"No, no!" Mestre Cabello says. "Aim for the head!"

Calma looks at me again, hesitant.

"Look," Cabello gestures to me. I sink down into a negativa.

"Her face is your target."

Mestre Cabello places his hands on the ground and swings his leg a few inches off the ground to execute a controlled "sting ray's tail" kick as the attack is known in *capoeira angola*. As he rotates his leg, his foot comes within an inch of my face, forcing me to shift my body low through a squat to a negativa on the other side.

My students take a collective in-breath as Mestre Cabello's kick passes a millimeter over my head.

"You've got to attack to make your partner react!" Mestre Cabello explains. "If you kick over your partner, she doesn't have to move, and the conversation ends."

It was 2016 and I had returned from a second stay in Venice. I was back teaching my popular capoeira course at Duke University in the Ark Studio, a creaky, white-clapboard house that stands apart from the surrounding colonial brick buildings. One of the university's oldest structures, the nineteenth-century gymnasium converted to dance studio has seen little change beyond a sprung floor, barres, movable mirrors, and a large fan to combat the humid summer heat of the American South that carries me back to Brazil. When I walk up the Ark's worn wooden stairs, I give thanks for the joy and honor of teaching in a space that holds a century of movement memories.

For a long time, I had resisted the idea of non-Brazilians teaching capoeira. But things had changed by the new millennium with a growing cadre of high-ranking foreign instructors and several American mestres. I knew that stepping into a full-time academic career would take time away from my physical practice, something too essential to my well-being and scholarship to squeeze in on the side. So, when I got to Duke, I designed a hybrid seminar-studio course. I was conflicted about teaching capoeira at an elite, predominantly white, institution built with money made on the backs of Black laborers in North Carolina's tobacco fields. I compensated somewhat by offering free classes at Durham organizations that worked with underserved youth.

But teaching capoeira at a place like Duke can also raise consciousness in students about how inequality and violence have produced their race and class privilege along with the creative, resistant strategies of those who are disadvantaged, or worse, by the system. By combining praxis and theory—movement and music in studio and sociohistoric context in seminar—I hoped to avoid both the transmittal of yet another deracinated, global trend, and the fetishizing of capoeira in the "neoliberal consumer culture that can glamorize racial difference."[1] I also hoped to challenge my students to step out of their customary ways of moving through the world and interacting with others.

The course was a hit. Students enjoyed the challenging workouts, learning about Afro-Brazilian history, and grappling with contemporary issues of globalization and cultural appropriation. I brought Brazilian capoeiristas to campus to teach workshops, and I created convivência beyond the studio with rodas on the lawn and feijoada dinners at my house. A student wrote on our course blog that when he saw other capoeira students around campus, he felt a "secret bond" to them that he never felt with students in his other classes.

After eight years, I began to stagnate in my body and teaching. ABADÁ's athletic style was becoming more taxing as I aged, but more significantly, I was experiencing a dissonance between what I taught in seminar and studio. In seminar, we focused on capoeira's African aesthetics, history of resistance, and liberatory potential. I brought these lessons into the studio through song, movement, and ritual:

vou dizer a meu senhor a	I am going to tell my master the
manteiga derramou	butter spilled
a manteiga não é minha, a	the butter is not mine, it belongs
manteiga é d'ioio	to the master's son

I interpreted this song for my students as an act of sabotage, the enslaved overturning the butter churn to slow production and waste time and resources; the benção, or "blessing" kick, I suggested, could symbolize Africans' refusal of forced religious conversion; and the roda like other African diasporic circle dances (the shout ring, the hip-hop cypher) is, in the words of Frantz Fanon, "a permissive circle: it protects and permits . . . by various means—shakes of the head, bending of the spinal column, throwing of the whole body backwards—. . . the huge effort of a community to exorcise itself, to liberate itself, to explain itself. There are no limits—inside the circle."[2]

Yet, the style I was teaching encouraged conformity and discipline over resistance and liberation. The athletic style required students to gain strength and flexibility before they could safely experiment with individual expression and playful improvisation. When they did get excited and spontaneous, I worried someone would get hurt, and found myself calling out "slow down!" and "be careful!" When several students dropped out early on because they found the class too physically challenging, I was bothered that it was catering to predominantly able-bodied students. I remembered the beautiful game I witnessed in Brazil by a capoeirista with legs atrophied by polio, or the deaf mestre who played with grace and elegance by feeling the drum vibrations through the ground and kinesthetically connecting to his partner.

My students were certainly diverse in race, gender, sexuality, and nationality (rural North Carolina, New York City, Colombia, Puerto Rico, Brazil, Bahrain, Mexico, Korea, China, Israel, Egypt, and Burundi). But for the most part, all were economically and educationally privileged. I tried to disrupt this by inviting my students to help me in my volunteer community kids classes and organized events that brought these youth and their families together with my Duke students. But how could I bring capoeira's political lessons into our embodied practice?

My answer came vis-à-vis a stylistic change to *capoeira angola* and my relationship with Mestre Cabello. I had first met Cabello and his wife Tisza in New York City in the 1990s when they were students in Mestre João Grande's academy. Originally from São Paulo and an adept player of another style, Cabello quickly absorbed the movement and ethos of *capoeira angola,* melding it with his virtuosic acrobatics and smooth ginga. Tisza, who had made a name for herself in the Senzala group in Rio in the 1980s when still just a teenager, developed into a beautiful and powerful *capoeira angola* mestra and musician. After twenty years of living and performing as capoeiristas and percussionists in New York City, Cabello and Tisza moved back to Brazil, settling on land near a small coastal town in southern Bahia where they run a capoeira school, cultural center, and farm. They are part of the most recent capoeira migration: mestres who have established their careers outside of Brazil and then return home with enough capital to buy land and build capoeira schools. They still travel extensively, their international workshops and affiliate groups supporting their work in Brazil. It was on one such trip that I invited Mestre Cabello for a week's residency at Duke.

Watching Mestre Cabello work with my students was ground-shifting. Within a week my students gained a deep appreciation and understanding of the game and music. The simpler, slower movement—though demanding strength and agility—can be modified to accommodate different physical abilities, allowing students to embody it and dialogue more quickly with their partners. Modeling my teaching on Mestre Cabello's, I began to develop a new pedagogy.

Pedagogy of Convivência

A pedagogy of convivência encourages connection, collaboration, and transformation.[3] It resonates with decolonizing projects that work to decouple knowledge production and practice from Eurocentric epistemology and settler-colonial systems of power, so as to encourage other ways of knowing and acting in the world. Decoloniality in dance studies and teaching has gained momentum in recent years, but may be traced back to a 1970 article by anthropologist Joann Kealiinohomoku that critiqued the assumption that Western dance is the universal standard by which to define and evaluate all dance. She argued that all dance, including ballet, is "ethnic dance," because all dance is created by specific people, in specific sociohistorical contexts— whether in a sixteenth-century royal French court or twentieth-century West African village—and conveys specific aesthetics, meanings, and values.[4] More recently, dance scholar Susan Foster argued that the term "world dance" that has replaced the label ethnic dance continues to "euphemistically [gloss] over the colonial legacy of racialized and class-based hierarchization of the arts."[5] World dance offers a multicultural menu stripped of the politics that have historically—and increasingly with global sharing—shaped dance everywhere.

Decolonizing dance must however go beyond nomenclature and increasing non-Western dance course offerings. We must also interrogate the ways in which technique and pedagogy uphold certain epistemologies and values.

Studio instruction reflects a history and approach to dance as presentational and performative rather than participatory and transformative. It privileges the evaluative gaze of the audience over the internal experience of the individual and community of movers. Capoeira aesthetics and practice—improvisational movement in a circle of participant-spectators—contrasts with the proscenium stage approach. Yet, in some ways, I was still teaching largely within that paradigm. Transforming my pedagogy would thus also transform the implicit values structuring my classes.

The first radical change was to teach in a circle. So obvious and necessary! Why would I teach a circular movement practice in rows facing a mirror? How could I expect students to feel comfortable playing in the roda if they were learning in a linear fashion? Organizing themselves in rows and looking at the mirror was doing my students a proprioceptive disservice. They were learning to see but not *feel* space. In a circle, my students gained a sense of themselves and others in space kinesthetically rather than visually.

Turning inward to feel movement rather than relying on exterior validation (and judgment in comparison to others) fosters a new relationship to the body. As one experienced dancer wrote on our course blog site: "the absence of mirrors requires us to learn how certain moves feel in the body, and to learn how to come back to that feeling." Developing muscle memory without recourse to an outside view meant, for this student, "developing a friendship with my body. What can I ask of my body, and how will it respond?" This new relationship suggests a shift away from the body as an object to be observed, disciplined, and evaluated, and toward the body as a subject and collaborator.

A circle also fosters horizontal, rather than vertical or top-down, learning: students are not ranked in rows (with the more confident or adept gravitating to the front), and I am working alongside rather than in front of them. In a circle we create a space, in which we see, not ourselves in a mirror, but each other. This seeing germinates connection, which prepares us for the roda.

Circle teaching presented new challenges, which led to new practices. Each student's perspective on the movement I am doing *with* rather than *in front* of them, is slightly different depending on their position in the circle. And from my position moving *alongside* rather than *leading* them, I cannot quickly scan them all, as I could in a mirror, calling out instructions. Instead, I must shift my attention more intentionally from one student to the next. Working my way around the inside of the circle, I play with each student, using my body, instead of words, for guidance and corrections: rather than calling out "lower your defense" or "switch sides," I drop the height or switch the direction of my attack, physically directing them to modify their response. This engagement ensures that my students are not simply memorizing movement sequences but understanding the logic of the game and encoding responses in their bodies. It also gives me a more immediate and playful (laughter shared when a student collides with my foot) connection to each student.

Working one-on-one with students models how they are to dialogue with each other, and the more limited vocabulary of *capoeira angola* quickens their road to fluency: rather than teach four different "escapes" for four different kicks, I teach one that serves as a defense for various attacks. I teach complexity through adding new moves, but also through seeing situations in new ways and adapting basic responses. Like learning a new language, memorizing vocabulary and grammar without using them in the world will not lead to fluency. Rather than waiting for movement proficiency in order to have conversations, my students master movement through dialogue and learn more quickly to be improvisational and playful. Students are less concerned with presentation and more focused on keeping the conversation going. As one student wrote, "capoeira demands a certain type of collective 'thinking' where responding to your partner's action is just as important as undertaking your own."

The absence of mirrors, reliance on interiority, and focus on dialogue and improvisation fosters individual creativity. In my previous classes I had encouraged uniformity: in rows facing the mirror, students stayed in sync, performing the ginga and combinations in unison. Now, in a circle I encourage each student to explore individual expression through the ginga. We shuffle, hop, spin, and break—the ginga becoming more than a side-to-side step connecting attacks and defenses; it becomes playful and strategic, a game in itself. We play with balance and gravity: standing with our feet rooted, we allow our bodies to sway front, side, and back, until we fall and catch ourselves in a deep negativa. Sometimes I begin class with a slow sweet samba or upbeat Afro-reggae tune, and we spread out solo to explore movement leveling up from floor to standing. Such exploration of space and unchoreographed movement is a common practice in many dance classes, yet I had never done it with capoeira.

I also incorporate more time for music. When I first began teaching, I downplayed the music, worried that my students would be embarrassed to sing together. Unless we are choir or church members, many of us in the United States stop singing with other people at around the time we leave kindergarten. I was thus surprised to learn that for many of my students, playing music and singing was their favorite part of class! I now allow for musical rodas without the distraction of games, so as to focus on the conjoining of voices.

Finally, I welcome self-reflection. We end class, still in the circle, with each person saying a word or two about how they feel. This encourages a body-emotional connection and builds convivência. At the end of the semester a student wrote: "Capoeira has recalibrated my view of movement as self-empowerment, establishing community, sharing history, and teaching accountability and respect. We've become movers in the classroom, but also in each other's lives, enjoying one another's company and playfulness."

My students weren't the only ones to benefit from my new style and pedagogy. I found myself doing things I hadn't done in years: watching capoeira games online; practicing berimbau and learning new songs; daydreaming about new moves I would master and games I would play. And I felt liberated to express myself in more playful ways. My years in ABADÁ allow me to feel grounded and protected, and I now use that confidence to explore freedom and creativity. Perhaps this excitement and liberation comes from being, in certain regards, at the beginning again: how often do we give ourselves license as we age to pick up new skills and develop new forms of self-expression? Perhaps something in my new ginga, which roots down through the legs but opens the chest and frees the arms, channels creative freedom through my body. Or maybe my new way of teaching and playing has pushed me to reevaluate my own goal-oriented, status-driven, and performative approach to capoeira and life.

As an academic, I have perhaps been most profoundly shaped by a lifetime within an American education system that values hierarchy and individual achievement over process and collaboration. Though I was attracted to capoeira for its communal and cooperative play, I was also drawn to its performative competitiveness; I, like many capoeiristas, wanted to excel and stand out in—not just be a part of—the roda. This need to achieve infiltrates every nook of my life. Toward the beginning of my graduate studies, I complained to Mestre Beiçola how stressed I was by the seemingly insurmountable goal of achieving a PhD. He chuckled and said, "That's because you Americans all want to become somebodies." Teasing as usual, Beiçola was also critiquing the drive to be the "best." Perhaps he was drawing on his experience growing up poor in Brazil, where life is a constant struggle and opportunities for becoming "somebody" are so few and far between that creating small moments of pleasure and convivência are achievements in themselves. Or perhaps he was drawing on his Hare Krishna training and lessons from the Bhagavad Gita: "through action without attention to results one achieves enlightenment."[6] It would seem that play with its "to-and-fro-movement which is not tied to any goal" is a route to enlightenment, or at least occasional peace of mind![7] Yet, like so many facets of my life, I had made capoeira into a drive for perfection. And that can distract from the ephemeral pleasures of playing with others.

In trying to make capoeira a space of play removed from the pressures of perfectionism, I tell my students that it is a course in which they have license to fail: their grade is not determined by mastery of content and individual performance—whether they can hold a handstand or backbend by the end of the semester—but by their learning process and interactions with others. This can be liberating, though challenging, to students at a competitive university like Duke. The need to excel has been driven into students their entire lives through an increasingly "standardized, surveillance-based" education system "requir[ing] that teachers abandon a personalized and context-sensitive approach to pedagogy."[8] A pedagogy of convivência is an attempt to let the subject, in this case capoeira, create the specific conditions of learning.

Giving my students permission to fail is, however, yet another indication of their privilege. Failure has become a hot topic in everything from social theory and educational practices to business strategies. In the *Queer Art of Failure,* Jack Halberstam argues that failure can critique heteronormative and capitalist measures of success and open up creative avenues for self-expression and knowledge production. Ironically, in the start-up world, failure is also now celebrated as an avenue to successful innovations; and in educational arenas, ideas circulate that "children occupy such risk-scrubbed environments that failure must be manufactured."[9] Celebrating failure implies a large enough safety net so that the failure will simply be a setback that with enough perseverance will transform into success. Not the case for someone like Tourinho whose failed shot at success through capoeira ended in death.

In her auto-ethnographic study of mixed martial arts training, dance scholar Janet O'Shea argues that failure in the fighting ring is sometimes just that—failure. Rather than setting up failures as only productive if they lead to future successes, O'Shea argues that martial arts training can cultivate an ability to humbly accept and withstand the emotional, and often physical, pain of failure. Accepting disappointment works against the cultural imperatives that failure is only acceptable if transformed into success, that every child athlete receive a trophy, and that we strive always to be optimistic and happy. Perhaps, O'Shea argues, allowing for introspection and doubt that failure's painful lessons incite "can produce a new kind of optimism, one that challenges self-importance and that links overtly to efforts toward equality."[10]

Rather than fabricating environments for "safe risks" and failures for our children and college students, which ultimately continue to reinforce race/class/gender privilege and individual achievement, perhaps we should emphasize relationality and responsibility through pedagogies of convivência: to be one of many voices in a chorus; to elevate group over individual achievement; to downplay winning; and to hold space for others, especially those for whom society does not allow room to express, expand, and succeed.

Durham Angoleirx

On the last Sunday of each month, I drive to Earthseed, a land collective by and for people of color in North Durham. A pretty, whitewashed barn with a weather vane stands against green pastures. On these Sunday mornings as I hear the familiar rise of a vocal chorus over berimbaus and my skin goose bumps, I remember the Candomblé priestess who warned me away from capoeira all those many years ago. What would Mãe Jorgina think now to see me entering this church-like space in gathering with others to share song and movement?

It was not just teaching, and my aging body, that inspired my capoeira transformation. I also missed convivência. I craved the continuity of a community of capoeiristas beyond my semester-long classes. When I first arrived in Durham, I had sought out the one established capoeira group. Similar in style to ABADÁ, the group also has a long-standing rivalry with ABADÁ in Brazil. I was disappointed to find that the American student-led group had transplanted this rivalry from Brazil to Durham.

There was also a small but growing *capoeira angola* group. Over the years the Durham Angoleirx group has ebbed and flowed. There are members with just a few years of training and little or no experience in Brazil, and others with over ten years in capoeira. What makes this group a bit of an anomaly is that it is not affiliated with any one group in Brazil; some members belong to different transnational groups, and others remain unaffiliated. Furthermore, in contrast to the hierarchical organization of most capoeira groups, there is no ranking or singular leadership: group decisions and actions are made though consensus, and teaching duties are shared. In-person learning and socializing is accompanied by a robust digital presence: videos of favorite capoeira games and songs, articles and websites, transnational events and gossip are shared along with birthday greetings, calls to local political actions, and appeals for support in crisis (house burglary) and transition (moving) that circulate on a WhatsApp group.

The Durham Angoleirx group reflects a decline in the international megagroups that exploded in the early 2000s. In the United States, capoeira is no longer restricted to these large groups or to cosmopolitan hubs such as New York City and the Bay Area. In out-of-the-way places, groups are often led by non-Brazilians, some with little experience, and sometimes (though rarely) having never traveled to Brazil. For some practitioners, financial or life circumstances do not allow for a robust relationship to Brazil; for others, capoeira is less a vehicle to connect to Brazil and the larger capoeira world as it is to create local ties, encourage individual transformation, and work toward collective actions.

Along with fostering inclusivity and horizontality, the Durham Angoleirx group promotes capoeira as a vehicle to raise consciousness and take action against social injustices such as racism, gender/sexual discrimination, food insecurity, and environmental degradation. The diversity of agendas can feel diffuse and at times create friction. After one mixed-age training in which we introduced our pronouns, a member of the group expressed his discomfort and offense on WhatsApp: man and woman were sacred in his religion, and while he respected the private choices of others, it offended him to have pronouns introduced as part of capoeira trainings, especially with children present. Though I did not agree with this student's beliefs, I could understand his expressed discomfort at assumptions of shared values. I was similarly uncomfortable at a discussion in which someone voiced the opinion that "whiteness has no place in capoeira." Not the majority view in the group, I continue to show up, accepting my minority status. If one day the group closes to all but BIPOC members, I will willingly, if sadly, leave.

Sometimes conflicting opinions cross oceans. At an event with an invited Brazilian mestre in 2019, trainings and rodas were interspersed with discussions addressing topics participants had written on large pieces of paper taped around the room: "concerns with exporting capoeira," "growing organic food," "black folk being killed, arrested, deported," "class and money access in capoeira," "role of white folks in capoeira," "addressing sexual and gender-based violence in capoeira," "amplifying presence of queer and trans folk in capoeira," "differently-abled bodies in capoeira."

During discussion, a female student raised a question about creating inclusive song lyrics in a gendered language like Portuguese.

The mestre interrupted: "How can you worry about language and gender when there are old mestres dying in poverty in Brazil? Don't you understand that tradition dies when they die? Shouldn't you be concerned with that!?"

The mestre was expressing a shared preoccupation in the capoeira world: older, predominantly Afro-Brazilian, mestres unable to retire because of a lack of pension or other financial security, are in danger of dying in poverty, just like Mestre Pastinha before them. Various international campaigns are raising money for them. By suggesting that the group's priorities were misguided, the guest mestre also raised another anxiety. With the era of international megagroups on the wane, will these new, small, groups no longer need or desire affiliation with mestres in Brazil? What happens when new generations of practitioners begin to question the practices and values of those before them? How, as one participant tearfully put it during our discussion, does one continue to respect ancestors and traditions when they clash with one's own politics, identities, and values?

The clashing of new and the old is nowhere more visible than in the growing number of women in capoeira, and the struggle to change what has long been a space that privileges heteronormative masculinity.

Women Warriors Redux

I offer two anecdotes.

The International Capoeira Encounter, San Francisco, 1995: over one hundred American and Brazilian mestres and students in attendance, the majority men. A "woman's roda" is announced as an opportunity to acknowledge and "empower" the growing number of female capoeiristas. Male attendees are invited to join in with clapping and singing, but not to play instruments or games. Most wander off to eat and chat among themselves. So, we are a small group of less than twenty women, almost all American, white, and mostly novices. Someone suggests we sing capoeira songs that mention women. The only songs we reluctantly come up with are "*eu sou homem, não sou mulher!*" (I am a man, not a woman!), "*O Doralice não me pegue não; não me pegue não, não me agarra, não me pegue não*" (Oh, Doralice don't grab me, don't grasp me, don't grab me, no), and *Dona Maria de Camboatá, levanta a saia e vamos deitar*" (Maria from Camboatá, lift up your skirt and let's lie down). The roda proceeds with tepid music and inexperienced games.

The Women's Capoeira Angola Conference, Washington DC, 2017: over one hundred female capoeiristas in attendance, less than a dozen men. The invited teachers and mestras from different groups in Brazil are all women and almost all Afro-Brazilian. At every roda, women play the instruments and lead the singing. Games are skillful and engaging to watch and the singing melodic and powerful. I get goose bumps moving with these strong, confident capoeiristas. I do not miss the men.

While much has been achieved in the last several decades, there is still work to do as female capoeiristas continue to negotiate a male arena. A debate about appropriate tactics to use in this struggle arose during a spontaneous pre-roda discussion at the 2017 event about what to do with songs that denigrate women. Representations of women in older capoeira songs generally operate in three ways: as a counterpoint to masculinity as in the example "I am a man, not a woman"; as an object of sexual desire as in the lyric, "raise your skirt and let's go lie down"; or to draw attention to nagging, groveling feminine characteristics as in the chorus line "Oh, Doralice don't grab me, don't grasp me, don't grab me, no." Such songs were at one time popular in rodas, sometimes used to taunt players performing poorly, an equivalent to a "throwing like a girl" insult.[11]

During the discussion, participants offered ways to transform lyrics so as to change the message but not the cadence: "*eu sou homem, não sou mulher*" can become "*é pra homem e pra mulher*" (it is for men and women). Others advocated permanently striking such songs from the repertoire, or writing new ones.

Mestra Gegê, one of the invited leaders of the weekend, interceded: "Look people, we can get rid of these songs or we can be capoeiristas about it. One time I was playing in a street roda, and my partner was closing in on me. He was blocking my moves and sweeping me left and right, and I was getting frustrated. I felt like he was mocking me, disrespecting me by not letting me play. No way would he have done that with a man of my level and experience. So, what did I do? I took him back to the foot of the berimbau and I asked permission of the gunga player to lead a song. And guess what I sang? '*Me leva moreno, me leva, me leva pra seu bangalô!*'"

The roda erupted in laughter. The song originally casts a brown woman ("*morena*") as an object of male desire, the singer insisting she take him back to her bungalow. Mestra Gegê had flipped the script—putting the male (*moreno*) in the place of the desired object of the female gaze.

"You should have seen him!" Gegê continued. "He got all flustered and had this goofy grin on his face, and when we entered the roda again, it was a totally different game! It was a good game!"

Mestra Gegê's story illustrated an approach to confronting macho attitudes and actions by deploying a common indirect capoeira tactic—delivering a message through song. By singing a song considered offensive to women, Gegê drew attention to her partner's disrespect of her; and by transforming the song she put the woman, and herself, in an agentic position. Her move was risky. Her partner may have gotten angry and aggressive—not an uncommon response by male capoeiristas who feel called out or shown up in a roda by a woman. But in this instance, for whatever reason (her partner accepted the message or was simply pleased-flustered with her public flirting), the tactic worked. Mestra Gegê achieved play between equals, at least for the duration of the game.

Discussing female members of a *capoeira angola* group in the interior of Bahia, ethnomusicologist Esther Kurtz reveals another indirect strategy or what she calls "sonic tactics of refusal." In rodas where men disproportionately lead the singing, women deploy what Kurtz calls "distuning," by refusing to respond in the male register, which is too low, or an octave above, which may be too high. Instead, they respond in a pitch that is comfortable to their range but which creates tonal dissonance in the chorus. At other times, Kurtz observed, their tactics involve silence, refusing to engage male capoeiristas in direct confrontation about sexism.[12]

Not unlike Brazilian discourses that simultaneously recognize structural racism and place the onus on individual achievement, debates around women in capoeira seem to oscillate between holding women responsible for "conquering their space" and insisting on removing sexist practices that keep women from achieving this. Some of the early pioneering women who struggled up through male-dominated trainings, rodas, and group hierarchies in the 1980s and 1990s complain that female capoeiristas have it too easy today. Others, like Mestra Gegê, suggest that women should use the tools of resistance that capoeira itself provides.

Sometimes the price for entering the roda, or taking one's place at the table, is very high indeed.

Black Death, Black Love

Foi no Rio de Janeiro	It happened in Rio de Janeiro
Num dia de quarta-feira	On a Wednesday
Mataram mais uma preta	They killed another Black woman
Mataram mais uma preta	They killed another Black woman
Mataram uma companheira	They killed a friend
Sua vida minah colega	Her life, my colleague
Sempre foi de muito risco	Was always risky
Pra quem luta toda dia	As it is for anyone who fights every day
Contra o machismo e o racismo	Against sexism and racism
Mas é na luta que aprendemos	But in the fight we learn
Vai a flor, fica a semente	The flower dies but the seed remains
Enquanto estivermos juntas	And when we are together
Marielle está presente	Marielle is present
Camaradinha	Comrade

—Ladainha by Mestra Janja

The year 2018 was sad for many in Brazil. On March 14, Rio de Janeiro city councilwoman Marielle Franco was executed by point-blank gun shots in her car in downtown Rio de Janeiro. Marielle was the first openly queer, Black woman from a favela to represent the people of Rio. Her mission was to fight police killings of Black people in favelas and to champion LGBTQ and feminist causes. Her assassins were former members of the military police with ties to then presidential candidate Jair Bolsonaro, who refused to condemn the assassination even though he was a running on a platform of heightening security in Brazilian cities.

Seven months after Marielle's assassination, on the evening of the first round of presidential elections, Mestre Moa do Katandê, a well-known master of capoeira and percussion, was murdered by a knife to his back in a bar in Salvador. A supporter of the Workers' Party candidate for president, Mestre Moa had gotten into a political dispute with his assassin, a supporter of the extreme right-wing and socially conservative Bolsonaro. A month later Jair Bolsonaro was voted into office.

These assassinations and the election of Bolsonaro came after a decade of political turmoil, corruption scandals, and economic recession in Brazil. For many, Bolsonaro's election is a giant step backward after sixteen years of governance by the progressive Workers' Party. Luiz Inácio da Silva (Lula), a passionate labor rights activist who had grown up poor in the poorest region of the country, was, after three attempts, elected president in 2002. He would go on to become Brazil's most popular president. During his two mandates, he launched social programs that helped lift forty million people out of extreme poverty and won bids to host the 2014 World Cup and 2016 Olympics. The new millennium was brimming with optimistic promises: hunger was reduced, a new middle class was on the rise, and increased spending on public universities and affirmative action programs promised to address racism and decrease the education and wealth gap; LGBTQ and Indigenous rights were on the move; and a flurry of World Cup and Olympic construction symbolized Brazil's arrival on the world stage.

But these promises dissipated into the dust left behind by the mega-event arenas that rapidly fell into disrepair. Like the copper pipes and new plastic seats ripped out and stolen from Rio's million-dollar renovated Maracanã football stadium after the Olympic closing ceremonies, the recent progress of the nation has been gutted. In 2016 Dilma Rousseff, Lula's predecessor, was impeached in what many believe to be an unjustified and unlawful process. And across the board, top politicians, including Lula, were embroiled in the most far-reaching corruption scandal in Brazilian history. The new middle-class prosperity was a chimera—like the glitter of carnival. Many Brazilians found themselves sliding back down the social ladder, burdened with debt.

On a trip to Rio a month before the Olympics in 2016, I ran into a capoeirista and fireman whom I had not seen in over ten years. He insisted on taking me home to visit his family, visibly pleased to show off his new truck and condominium in a newly constructed complex in a Zona Norte suburb. As we stood on his balcony looking out at the twinkling lights of a nearby favela, he said he appreciated the view because it reminded him of where he had come from.

And then with that dry Brazilian humor used to comment on life's precarity he added, "And it won't be far when I have to move back!"

My friend, along with all of Rio's policemen and firemen tasked with ensuring the safety of the city as millions of tourists flooded in for the Olympics, had not received his full salary in months. The state of Rio was bankrupt.

Infuriated with corruption and "politics as usual," Brazilians voted in the renegade, conservative, and foul-mouthed President Jair Bolsonaro. His administration, like Donald Trump's in the United States, unleashed unprecedented levels of partisan conflict and violence as he defunded social welfare programs, reversed laws protecting the environment as well as those supporting LGBTQ and Indigenous peoples, and championed extreme policing tactics.

The horror and pessimism that many Americans and Brazilians feel at what seems to be our nations' enormous steps backward has also been accompanied by a swell of on-the-ground mobilization. The morning after Marielle's murder, thousands of people gathered on Rio's city hall steps to cries of "*Marielle Presente!*" (Marielle is still with us!), which became a rallying cry at protests around Brazil and the world in subsequent days and weeks. And six months after Marielle's death, three of her former aids—Black feminist women—were elected as Rio state representatives, and São Paulo elected the first Black transwoman to state legislature. In the United States and around the world, the Black Lives Matter movement—the latest iteration in generations of Black freedom fighters—has galvanized and grown around the police killings of Black people. The movement was started by three Black women in 2013 in the aftermath of the killing of Trayvon Martin, Michael Brown, and Eric Garner. From a somewhat marginalized movement, it gained majority support by Americans after the police killing of Breonna Taylor and George Floyd in 2020. Mestre Moa's murder at the hands of a supporter of a president who publicly devalues Black lives outraged Brazil's capoeira community and Black Lives Matter movement.

In the face of so much Black death it is easy to slip into Afro-pessimism, a philosophical stance that Black life continues to be conditioned by death, loss, and mourning. Black feminist Jen Nash suggests an antidote to such pessimism and a way forward through a love-politics, which with its "dual commitment to *mutual vulnerability* and *witnessing*," can be "a strategy for remaking the self *and* for moving beyond the limitations of selfhood." Love-politics is a "radical embrace of connectedness."[13] Through moving together with vulnerability and accountability in spaces such as the ones capoeira rodas create, we can work toward that connectedness and fight for social justice and transformation.

Circle of Convivência

I am at a *capoeira angola* event in Birmingham, Alabama, a year before George Floyd's murder. I have never been to the Deep South and appreciate that the organizers have arranged the opening roda at the Civil Rights Memorial in Kelly Ingram Park downtown. It is an intimate event of about forty capoeiristas, mostly Americans from the southeastern United States, and a special visitor, Mestre Cobra Mansa, from Brazil. After the roda, we together take a guided tour of the park. It was here in May 1963 that hundreds of Black high school students and children gathered to peacefully protest Jim Crow and were met with firehoses and police dogs. The event sparked public outrage across the United States and helped catapult the country toward the Civil Rights Act of 1964. This opening to our event allows us to tie our *capoeira angola* practice to the historic and ongoing struggle for racial justice throughout the Black diaspora.

During the tour I keep catching the eye of a capoeirista about my age. Afterward he says he knows me. We run through recent events we have been to and nothing overlaps. Then he snaps his fingers:

"Berkeley! Mestre Beiçola's classes!"

I shake my head. He laughs.

"I had dreadlocks back then and a baby girl."

"And a brother! I remember you, Joseph!"

We hug and laugh and say we can't believe we are both still in capoeira.

Another American about our age who has recently been recognized as the first American mestre in his international group smiles: "There aren't so many of us that go that far back anymore. We're dinosaurs, man! But we are living history too. We were around when capoeira was just beginning in the U.S.!"

Later that year I go to Miami to Joseph's event. His baby girl, Gaby, is now in her twenties and an accomplished capoeirista. She has designed a beautiful shirt for the event—a goddess rising out of the water playing a berimbau—that is an inauguration of Joseph's new training space behind the house he shares with his Brazilian wife. It is an even more intimate group this time of about twenty male and female capoeiristas. We hold the closing event on a gorgeous Sunday afternoon at the beach. Myriam, who teaches in Atlanta, Georgia, and had been recognized recently as one of the first American instructors in the female-led Grupo Nzinga, leads us through a workshop. She spins in references to the speculative fiction of Octavia Butler, and we trace patterns in the sand and weave movement with our partners. As I gaze around the roda I think about the hybrid communities—gender, race, sexuality, ethnic, and species mixing—that populate Octavia Butler's alternative future worlds. Is capoeira such a space? It can be, I think, with work and convivência.

After the roda we fill a kayak with red, white, and yellow roses. With the ritual blessings of a local Brazilian Candomblé priest, Joseph, Gaby, and Myriam row the offering for Iemanjá out in the direction of Brazil as the sun sets, and the rest of us softly play berimbaus and sing. As the surf laps against my bare feet, I ask Iemanjá along with Xangô and Obaluaiê to continue guiding me on my capoeira journey.

"If I do not love the world," Paulo Freire writes, "if I do not love life—if I do not love people—I cannot enter into dialogue." And dialogue, he continues, "cannot exist without humility."[14]

In capoeira I have found love, dialogue, and humility. Entering the roda has allowed me to develop convivência with people I may otherwise never have come to know. Capoeira (and anthropology) has shown me a way to be in the world, in dialogue and movement, with others different from me; love and humility help me stick with it through difficult and demanding times. Love, like convivência, does not depend always on harmony or even positive feelings. Love, like convivência, is a "radical openness" that inevitably means these other hard feelings—anger, resentment, pain—can enter.[15] Sometimes I come to a roda not with my usual joy and excitement, but with other emotions weighing me down. And sometimes I leave with a bit of relief, a lightness in my body. Perhaps I receive a good rasteira that lands me on my butt, makes everyone laugh, humbles me, and returns me to the present. Perhaps I deliver a good sweep that makes me feel that I can act in the world to transform situations. Other times, the game itself creates frustration, anger, or resentment. When flow and dialogue evade, my partner and I may play at odds or even with aggression. But we return to the berimbaus and voices and try again.

I hope the stories I have told here can be an invitation to my readers to find a passion in something with others; others who may live and feel differently in the world from you. And let love and humility guide you in listening and responding to each other, and finding unity through movement.

Conclusions are difficult, especially when the story continues. But I have learned over the years that "a good capoeirista knows how to arrive well and to leave well."

I will end then, as best I can, in motion:

My heart races, and my stomach flutters. I squat-walk from my place in the roda to beneath the berimbaus. My partner-opponent approaches from the other side. We make eye contact and crouch facing each other at the foot of the gunga. The chorus has not yet begun, so I look down at the space between us and allow the thump of the atabaque, the ring of the agogô, the trill of the pandeiros, and the twang of the berimbaus flow down my body and into the ground beneath my feet. I push my knees out with my elbows to stretch my hips and wonder what kind of game it will be. I have not played with this capoeirista but know she outranks me and is better skilled, even though I am older and have more years in capoeira. Will we find fluidity and flow? Will the game be heightened with moments of tension or laughter?

A chorus of voices calls me back, and I look up. I touch my fingers to the bottom of the gunga and then to my forehead, chest, and ground. My ritual reminder to play with intelligence, love, and grace. My partner makes the sign of the cross, scratches on the ground, and then reaches across the space to me. We shake hands. I am new to this roda, and so opening moves are crucial. I will enter with an *aú de cabeça* to stay protected and gauge my partner. With my head on the ground, one leg in the air and the other low, I swivel my body toward the center of the roda. My partner accompanies me with a slow aú, knees tucked into her chest. My lower leg traverses the space between us, and then I quickly switch it with the one in the air when my partner ends her aú and comes in with a rabo de arraia, giving me just enough time to sink into a ground-hugging negativa. The game has begun: with bodies close and low we trace arcs and circles above and around each other as we ripple out from the foot of the orchestra to the center of the roda.

My partner slips under my circular kick and delivers a cabeçada to my ribs. The strike with her head is not hard, but I obey its signal. I roll out and away and then return on my head, my legs circling around me, pleased to have perfected this move enough to use it in the roda. She launches another circular kick, and I shoot out my foot for a sweep, which she easily lifts her leg over, sinking into a crouching position on her arms. We continue our *jogo de dentro,* or "inside game." I feel safe here, close together. But the gunga player has increased the rhythm in a command to rise from the floor and elevate our game in height and intensity. Once standing, my partner immediately sweeps my standing foot as I launch a kick. I manage to catch myself on my arms and rise from the floor with a straight kick from the ground and then propel myself into a handstand. She enters with a scissor movement on the floor, and I touch my knees to my chest and slide under her legs on the floor careful to avoid an attack.

I hold back, I am cautious. My partner throws a half-moon kick toward me. I lean away from it, and she throws another with the other leg, and then another and another. She arches her eyebrows at me. It is a test not a taunt; an invitation. If I don't respond, the game will slide into mundanity—banal for us to play and others to watch. Or perhaps my inaction will make my partner more assertive, taking advantage of my caution to showcase her own skill. She raises her leg once again, and before her kick reaches its apex, I crouch low and step forward into the opening of her body. Her leg thumps against my side as I strike with my head against her sternum, not hard, but firm enough to throw her off balance. She stumbles backward, surprised pleasure flits across her face, and hands from those seated in the roda push her back into the game. In an instant she is upside-down in a handstand. I am buoyed by the grin on her face and the laughter and claps from around the roda. The gunga player switches to a still faster rhythm and calls out a new song:

O facão bateu em baixo	The machete struck low
A bananeira caiu	The banana tree (handstand) fell

The chorus rises eagerly:

Cai, cai, bananeira	fall, fall, banana tree
A bananeira caiu	the banana tree fell

My partner claps her feet together in the air, showing off and letting all know this time the bananeira will not fall. I lunge forward, feigning another headbutt but keeping clear of her striking feet. She flips over and takes a volta ao mundo. I fall in step behind her as we "circle the world" inside the roda. The ball is in her court. By breaking off play she is acknowledging my momentary "victory," but will not allow it to go without a response.

We return to the foot of the berimbau. Crouch, touch palms, and together enter the roda.

The game begins again. . . .

ACKNOWLEDGMENTS

Capoeira cannot be played alone, and a book cannot be written alone.

I give thanks to my deep capoeira ancestors—mestrx and malandrx—whose perseverance kept this art alive so that it might be shared with later generations. *Salve!*

My more immediate capoeira ancestors are those mestrx with whom I have trained and who, in ways big and small, make up my capoeira-self today: Mestre Beiçola introduced me to the magic of capoeira; Mestre Acordeon showed me what a long, beautiful journey it would be; Mestre Touro, meu avô; Mestre Sardinha, Mestre Kinha, and Mestre Batata shared their Capoeira Besouro with me; Mestra Edna made me into a guerreira; Mestre Camisa welcomed me as a student and researcher and kicked my ass at every training; Mestra Márcia gave me her friendship and helped me develop as a performer and teacher; Contramestre Marquinho opened me up to the *capoeira angola* world; and Mestre Cabello and Mestra Tisza took me farther into that world. *Salve e obrigadão!*

Mestres are only some of a capoeirista's teachers. We learn in every training and every roda with each other. Far too many to name all, I offer as many as I can. My Capoeira Batuque/Narahari family: Mary, Victoria, Russell, Joseph, and George; my Capoeira Besouro family: Glayd, Bocoió, Jomar, Splynter, Heverton, Fernandinho, Cocada, Bate Bola, Guerreiro, Naja, Barra Mansa, Kipo, Pedra; my ABADÁ-NYC family: Gillian, Kto, Gafanhoto, Elvin, Comédia, Mosca, Flamengo, Gata, Guerreiro, Babushka; my ABADÁ-SF family: Sereia, Corrente, Vesper, Gafanhoto, Gaivota, Tulipa, Maria, Sucurí, Ciranda; my Venice capoeira family: Burano, Mariano, Pierangelo, Benedetta, Luigi, Lena, and Valentina; my Angola capoeira family: Cabuenha, Nzinga, Nani, Gindungo, Balú, Muxi, Philippe, Patrícia Sylvia, João; my Durham capoeira family: Santos, Courtney, Isa, Ade, Lucas, Amanda, Allison, J. P., Christian, Shayna, Cebola, Jason, Fabiano, Kathy; my Duke capoeira students who have been a joy to work and learn with over the years, especially Calma, Joaninha, Saeed, Pirilampa, Aristide, Isa(Bela), Gumbi. My deepest and longest capoeira convivência has been with ABADÁ-RIO: Maestrinha, Chá Preto, Bacurau, Sil, Tangerina, Dente, Naldo, Ana, Nathalia, Tourinho, Debora, Pirulito, Erik, Cafeína, Farofa, Albatroz, Cascão, Gavião, Lobisomem, Indae, Colibri, Asa Branca, Fala Mansa, Chocolate, Tavinho, Noresa, Coala, Apoador, Douglão, Nadinho, Prego, Sabujo, Cebolão, Pretão, Cobra, Cangaru, Morcego, Morceguinho, Mobília, Juma, Gigi, Genga . . . *e mais, muitos mais.*

To my fellow capoeira researchers with whom I have played in academic and capoeira rodas: Matthias Röhrig Assunção, Carlos Eugénio Líbano Soares, Clícea Maria Miranda, Daren Bartlett, Letíca Vidor Sousa Reis, Nestor Capoeira, Mestra Janja, Mestra Paulinha, Mestre Cobra Mansa, Greg Downey, Ana Paula Höfling, Santos Flores, T. J. Desch-Obi, Cabuenha Janguinda Moniz, and Fred Abreu. Katie Orenstein, Thad Dunning, Jennifer Bussell, Sarah Town, Kittiya Lee, Alain Pascal Kaly, Lisa Earl Castillo, and Carolina Sá, have been wonderful friends and intellectual interlocuters over the years and across coasts and continents.

My wonderful undergraduate professors at Reed College, especially my thesis advisor Ellen Stauder, instilled in me a love for the research, writing, and teaching that make up the academic life. Support in graduate school came from my professors in the Anthropology and Education Program at Teachers College, Columbia University: Charles Harrington, Hervé Varenne, George Bond, Lambros Comitas, and Lesley Bartlett; and my extended cohort, especially Mary Kenney, Olga Gonzalez, Paulette Young, Peter Cohen, and Allison Stratton. My mentor, Lesley Sharp, taught me that the "body is good to think with" and showed unswerving enthusiasm and compassion. Robin Nagle and Barbara Browning introduced me to Brazil through the lenses of anthropology, dance, and performance studies. Dissertation writing seminars led by Nancy Scheper-Hughes and Stanley Brandes at the University of California, Berkeley became my adopted intellectual home during the two years of writing. I am indebted to Nancy and Stanley for welcoming me in, and to all the participants, especially Jelani Mahiri and Seth Holmes, for our engaged discussions.

Thank you Julia Ilana, brilliant artist and my former capoeira student, for the frontispiece illustration created from a video still; and Raquel Costa (Graduada Gasparzinha) for permission to use two of her fantastic photographs. My research has been funded over the years by the Wenner-Gren Institute, Duke Brazil Initiative, and Duke Caribbean and Latin American Studies program (thank you Natalie Hartman for all your support!). Thank you John Collins and the Columbia University Seminars for a publication subvention for the cover art; Adriana Vendramini Terra at Copyrights Consultoria for her patience in helping me secure the rights for the Carybé drawing; and Haley Walton and Duke Libraries for fulfilling my dream through a TOME grant to make this book available for free around the world.

My anthropology, dance, and writing interlocuters at Duke University have been a joy to work with and get to know: Louise Meintjes, Charlie Piot, Anne Alison, Ralph Litzinger, Diane Nelson, Anne-Maria Makhulu, Harris Solomon, Lee Baker, Charlie Thompson, Rebecca Stein, Christine Folch, Kathryn Mathers, Márcia Rego, Tommy DeFrantz, Andrea Woods-Valdés, Ava Vinesett, Purnima Shah, Keval Kaur Khalsa, Michael Klien, Barbara Dickinson, Natalie Marrone, Tyler and Julie Walters, and Sarah Wilbur. A huge thank you to Ranjana Khanna and Sylvia Miller and all the participants in the Franklin Humanities Institute Manuscript Workshop: Deborah Thomas, Tommy DeFrantz, Ranjana Khanna, Sylvia Miller, Stephanye Hunter, Louise Meintjes, Márcia Rego, Ana Paula Höfling, Sarah Town, Gustavo Furtado, and Dasha Chapman. Thank you all for your generous attention and kindness and for pushing me in the right places. Additionally, Charlie Piot, Kathryn Mathers, Patricia de Santana Pinho, Lisa Earl Castillo, and Monica Wesolowska read chapter drafts. And a big thanks to my two reviewers, Barbara Browning and Gladys Mitchell-Walthour.

Louise Meinjtes has been a brilliant friend-colleague-chair and supporter of this project for so long—thank you for reminding me to keep the joy and love in sight! Márcia Rego, dear friend, colleague, and attentive line editor. John French and Jan Hoffman French have been enthusiastic fans of my work over the years and continents of our crisscrossing lives, thank you! Stilt-walking artivist and PhD student Courtney Crumpler was a wonderful research assistant, transcriber, reader, and friend. Thank you to my incredibly enthusiastic, supportive, and attentive editor Stephanye Hunter who found me at LASA, and to copy editor Elizabeth Detwiler and everyone at University of Florida Press who made publishing my first book a smooth and enjoyable experience. Mindy Spadacenta and Philip Spiro kept my body and mind together throughout it all.

Deep gratitude to my mother, Maureen Wesolowski, sister Monica Wesolowska, and brother Paul Kim who have supported me in all my endeavors (even when they caused worry), and with whom I have moved through sadness, anger, and pain, and come to a stronger place of love. Ray, Frances, Grandy, Grancie, Gretel, David, Miles, Ivan, Drina, Peter, Gabe, Eden, and Rafi, thank you for growing my family.

Finally, this book would never have seen the light of day without the unwavering love, support, and encouragement of my husband, Orin Starn. Every day and every moment my love, gratitude, and admiration deepen for Orin and my son, Lucien, fellow movers in the best convivência I will ever know: thank you for being on this journey with me.

CAPOEIRISTAS

With current ranking and group, listed in order of appearance.

Title and Nickname	Given Name	Group and Location
Mestre Pastinha (1889–1981)	Vicente Ferreira Pastinha	Centro Esportivo de Capoeira Angola, Salvador, Bahia
Mestre Touro	Antônio Oliveira Bemvindo	Corda Bamba, Rio de Janeiro
Mestre Nacional (1949–2011)	Adalberto de Souza Alvarenga	Capoeira Quilombo Nagô, Rio de Janeiro
Mestre Beiçola	Ronaldo de Sá	Capoeira Narahari, California
Mestre Kinha	Paulo Kinha Linhares	Capoeira Besouro Hawaii, Oahu, Hawaii
Mestre Sardinha	Paulo Fernando de Jesus	Capoeira Besouro, Rio de Janeiro
Mestre Bocoió	Antônio Campos Soares	Cordão de Ouro, Rio de Janeiro
Mestre Saci (Jomar)	Jomar Lino Dias	Centro Cultural Vera Cruz, Rio de Janeiro
Mestre Splynter	Neilson da Costa Abrahão	Escola de Capoeira Brasil Quilombola, Rio de Janeiro
Mestre DiMola (1952–2002)	Domingos André dos Santos	Capoeira do Mercado Modelo, Salvador, Bahia
Mestre Bimba (1899–1974)	Manoel dos Reis Machado	Centro de Cultura Física e Luta Regional, Salvador, Bahia
Mestre Curió	Jaime Martins dos Santos	Escola de Capoeira Angola Irmãos Gêmeos, Salvador, Bahia
Mestre João Pequeno (1917–2011)	João Pereira dos Santos	Academia de João Pequeno de Pastinha, Salvador, Bahia
Mestre Moraes	Pedro Moraes Trindade	Grupo Capoeira Angola Pelourinho (GCAP) Salvador, Bahia

Mestre Cobra Mansa	Cinézio Feliciano Peçanha	Centro Cultural Kilombo Tenondé, Valença, Bahia
Mestra Janja	Rosângela C. Araújo	Grupo Nzinga de Capoeira Angola, Salvador, Bahia
Mestra Paulinha	Paula Cristina da Silva Barreto	Grupo Nzinga de Capoeira Angola, Salvador, Bahia
Besouro Mangangá (1895–1924)	Manoel Henrique Pereira	Street capoeira, Santo Amaro da Purificação, Bahia
Mestre Medicina	Luís Oliveira Rocha	Grupo Raça, Muritiba, Bahia
Mestre Acordeon	Bira Almeida	United Capoeira Association, California
Mestra Edna	Edna Lima	ABADÁ-Capoeira New York, New York City
Mestre Camisa	José Tadeu Carneiro Cardoso	ABADÁ-Capoeira, Rio de Janeiro
Mestre André	André Luiz de Souza Pereira	Associação Cultural Arte Capoeira, Rio de Janeiro
Contramestre Jorginho	Jorge Bemvindo	Corda Bamba, Rio de Janeiro
Mestre Dentinho (1952–2011)	Alcino Oliveira Bemvindo	Capoeira Auê, Rio de Janeiro
Mestre Fatal	Cláudio Luís Alves Marinho	União das Raças, Rio de Janeiro
Mestre Hulk	Sidney Gonçalves Freitas	Terra Firme, Rio de Janeiro
Mestre Leopoldina (1933–2007)	Demerval Lopes de Lacerda	Capoeira Carioca, Rio de Janeiro
Mestre Artur Emídio (1930–2011)	Artur Emídio de Oliveira	Capoeira Artur Emídio, Rio de Janeiro
Mestra Sueli Cota	Sueli Cota	Cruzeiro do Sul, Rio de Janeiro
Mestre Biquinho	Adenilson Bemvindo dos Santos	Filhos da Corda Bamba, Rio de Janeiro
Mestre Zé	José Fernando Andrade	Capoarte, Rio de Janeiro
Mestrando Parafuso	Anderson da Silva	ABADÁ-Capoeira, Rio de Janeiro
Tourinho (1995–2015)	Matheus Bernado	ABADÁ-Capoeira, Rio de Janeiro
Professor Naldo	Ronaldo Cavalcanti	ABADÁ-Capoeira, Rio de Janeiro
Professor Dente	Paulo Braga	ABADÁ-Capoeira, Rio de Janeiro

Professora Cafeína	Ana Cristina Ferreira	ABADÁ-Capoeira, Rio de Janeiro
Graduada Maria Preta	Marina de Santos Reis	ABADÁ-Capoeira, Rio de Janeiro
Professora Maestrinha	Andréa Cristiane Alves da Cunha	ABADÁ-Capoeira, Rio de Janeiro
Professora Nzinga	Brenda Fortes	ABADÁ-Capoeira, Luanda
Instrutor Balú	Balumukeno de Lemos	ABADÁ-Capoeira Angola, Luanda
Mestre Charm	Jorge Gomes Martins	ABADÁ-Capoeira Goiás
Mestrando Cascão	Luiz Fernando Pereira Monteira	ABADÁ-Capoeira Portugal Guimarães, Portugal
Professor Bacurau	Anderson Lino	ABADÁ-Capoeira Tarragona Tarragona, Spain
Professor Chá Preto	Rodoval Angelo Ruas	ABADÁ-Capoeira, Rio de Janeiro
Instrutor Gavião	Luiz da Silva	ABADÁ-Capoeira Italia, Milan, Italy
Contramestre Marquinho	Marcos Albuquerque	Angola Center Italia, Sacile, Italy
Mestre João Grande	João Oliveira dos Santos	Capoeira Angola Center, New York City
Professor Cabuenha	Júlio Janquinda Moniz	ABADÁ-Capoeira Angola Luanda, Angola
João Reis	João Van Dunem Reis	Uavala Capoeira, Luanda, Angola
Mestre Cabello	Cabello Caobijubá	Centro de Capoeira Angola OuroVerde, Barracão D'Angola, Serra Grande, Bahia
Mestra Tisza	Tisza Coelho	Centro de Capoeira Angola OuroVerde, Barracão D'Angola, Serra Grande, Bahia
Mestra Gegê	Gegê Poggi	Florescer/Aluandê Capoeira Angola, Valença, Bahia
Joseph Watkins		Mosaic / FICA, Miami Florida
Mestre Moa de Katendê (1954–2018)	Romualdo Rosário da Costa	Salvador, Bahia

GLOSSARY

Abadá From the Arabic, the white prayer frocks worn by enslaved Muslims in Bahia who led a revolt in 1835. The stretchy white pants worn by capoeiristas. And the acronym for the Associação Brasileira de Apoio e Desenvolvimento da Árte Capoeira.

Acarajé Cooked and mashed cowpeas deep-fried in dendê oil and served with *vatapá* and *caruru* pastes made from shrimp, cashews, and palm oil. A street food and ritual food used in Afro-Brazilian religions like Candomblé.

Agarrar To grab as in grappling, wrestling.

Agogô Two-toned clapperless bell (or hollow Brazil nut husks attached to a stick) that is part of the capoeira orchestra.

Angolanidade Angolanness.

Angoleiro/a A practitioner of the style of capoeira known as *capoeira angola.*

Apelido Nickname.

Arame Wire cut from the inner side of a steel-rimmed car tire, used to string (*armar*) a berimbau in order to play it.

Arrastão To drag. Slang for a mass robbery.

Asfalto The asphalt or formal city, in contrast to the hills or favelas.

Atabaque A drum used in the capoeira orchestra.

Aú Cartwheel in capoeira.

Avô Grandfather.

Axé From the Yoruba term asë: life force; energy; potential; ability to make things happen. In capoeira, describes a roda or capoeirista full of positive, balanced energy.

Bagunça A mess.

Baianas Afro-Brazilian women from Bahia, may refer to those making and selling acarajé in the streets.

Baile funk Dance party in Rio favelas with loud Carioca funk music.

Baixada Fluminense The group of municipalities that make up the greater metropolitan area of Rio de Janeiro.

Bakongo People from the Kongo region of Angola (Zaire Province).

Bamba Someone extremely good at what he/she does, usually in the area of music, dance, or capoeira.

Bananeira Banana tree. A handstand in capoeira.

Baqueta Thin stick used to strike the wire of the berimbau.

Bassula A wrestling art from the Island of Luanda, Angola.

Bate papo Informal discussion; chitchat.

Bateria Percussive orchestra that accompanies a samba parade. Can also refer to the capoeira orchestra.

Batizado Baptism. A ceremony observed by some capoeira groups to mark a novice's induction into the group.

Batuque Colonial term for various African and Afro-Brazilian drumming and dancing practices.

Benção A forward kick delivered with a shoving motion of the leg and landing the flat of the foot on the chest or stomach of one's opponent.

Benguela Port city in Angola. A rhythm of the berimbau, and a style of game characterized by flowing movements close to the ground.

Biriba The wood used for making berimbaus from a tree indigenous to Bahia.

Berimbau Musical bow with a resonating gourd of African origin and the main instrument in the capoeira orchestra.

Boa aparência Good looks or appearance, light skin and European features often implied.

Brasilidade Brazilianness.

Briga Fight; brawl.

Brincar To play like children. Used in capoeira when a game is particularly playful.

Ca-puera Tupi-Guarani word meaning second growth forest; possible etymology of the name capoeira.

Cabaça Hollowed gourd affixed at the end of the verga of the berimbau, through which the sound resonates.

Cabeçada Headbutt. A characteristic strike in capoeira.

Caboclos Indigenous spirit who manifests in some Candomblé ceremonies.

Cachaça Distilled spirit made from sugarcane.

Caipirinha Brazil's national cocktail, made with cachaça, lime juice, and sugar.

Camarão Shrimp.

Camelôs Street vendors.

Candomblé Afro-Brazilian religion. Some branches syncretize African deities with Catholic saints.

Capoeira angola Term used since the 1930s to designate a style of capoeira associated with Mestre Pastinha.

Capoeira contemporânea Style of contemporary capoeira that blends elements from the *angola* and *regional* styles.

Capoeira regional *A luta regional da Bahia* (regional fight of Bahia). The name Mestre Bimba gave his style of capoeira in the 1930s.

Capoeiragem A nineteenth century term for capoeira.

Capoeiras The practitioners of nineteenth century capoeiragem.

Capoeiristas A contemporary term for capoeira practitioners.

Carioca A resident of Rio de Janeiro.

Carteira assinada Work papers.

Cavaquinho A small instrument with four strings used in samba and choro music.

Caxixi A woven rattle held in the hand while playing the berimbau.

Chamadas The ritual break in a game in which players momentarily touch and synchronize their movements while still guarding against attack.

Churrasco Barbecue.

Comprar o jogo To "buy the game": one capoeirista takes the place of another player in the roda so that the games continue without stop. Perhaps derives from *comprar a briga,* to "buy a fight," meaning to take a side in an argument or to defend someone in a confrontation.

Comunidade Community. A term for favela.

Concentração The gathering point before a Carnival parade.

Conjuntos Public housing.

Conscientização Consciousness or conscientiousness: a central concept in Brazilian educator Paulo Freire's pedagogy of liberation. Through conscientização people become aware of the conditions of oppression in which they live and learn to take action against them.

Contramestre In some capoeira groups the highest rank below mestre.

Convivência Connection; intimacy; cohabitation. An understanding of the life experiences of your companions.

Conviver To coexist or live together.

Corda Thick colored cord worn with abadá to indicate rank.

Cordel Another style of capoeira belt to indicate rank, made from thin braided cord.

Corpo fechado A closed, or protected, body.

Corridos Capoeira songs structured as a call-and-response.

Cruzeiros Brazil's currency from 1942 to 1986 and 1990 and 1993.

Dendê Thick, dark, reddish-orange, strong-flavored palm oil introduced to Brazil from West Africa and used in many Afro-Brazilian dishes and rituals.

Desabafar To vent; to expel or alleviate pent up emotions.

Dikanza An Angolan instrument similar to the Brazilian reco-reco.

Dobrão The coin or small stone used in playing the berimbau.

Dono da cabeça Main orixá in the configuration of all those that protect an individual.

Dono do morro The head of the drug traffic in a territory controlled by a drug faction.

Em obra(s) Under construction.

Favela Shantytown or informal settlement in Brazil.

Feijoada Black bean stew with beef and pork. Also an event where this dish is served.

Filhos e filhas de santo Sons and daughters of saints. Refers to initiates in Afro-Brazilian religions.

Flanar To wander.

Floreios Flourishes. The acrobatic moves in capoeira.

Fofoca Gossip.

Fundo de quintal Backyard.

Funkeiros Carioca youth who frequent baile funk parties.

Gamba A large shrimp.

Gindungo A small, spicy, red pepper used in Angolan cuisine.

Ginga Swing; hipness; cool. The most basic capoeira move, comparable to walking; a continuous swaying side-to-side step that keeps to the beat of the music and ties attacks, defenses, and acrobatics into a seamless circular whole.

Golpe General term for strike or attack in capoeira.

Graduada/o Graduate. Used in some capoeira groups to designate advanced students.

Gringa/o Foreigner. Can have affectionate or derogatory implications.

Guaraná A stimulant plant used by Brazilian indigenous people and included in many energy drinks, including a popular soft drink.

Guerreira/o Warrior.

Gunga The lead berimbau. Made with a large cabaça, the gunga has the deepest and loudest tone and keeps the rhythm with little variation.

Iúna Berimbau rhythm and a style of game characterized by elongated, graceful kicks and acrobatic movements. In some groups only advanced capoeiristas may play during this rhythm.

Jeitinhos "Little ways." Favors given to get around bureaucracy and other social restrictions.

Jeito Knack for something; habit; way of being.

Jogar To play, as in a game or sport.

Jogo A game in capoeira or other sports.

Jogo de búzios Divination using cowrie shells.

Jogo de dentro "Inside" capoeira game in which players stay close together.

Jogo duro Rough game or hard play. A more aggressive capoeira game.

Kalunga In Kongo cosmology, the communicative pathway between the terrestrial and spiritual-ancestral worlds.

Kikongo Bantu language spoken by the Bakongo people of Kongo.

Kimbundu Bantu language spoken by the Mbundu people around Luanda.

Kuduro Angolan music and dance style similar to Brazilian baile funk.

Kwanzas Angola's currency.

Ladainha Litany. The introductory solo that begins the song cycle in the *capoeira angola* style.

Laje An open rooftop terrace on houses in favelas.

Louvação "Praise." The short call-and-response that follows the ladainha in the *capoeira angola* song cycle. Also known as *chula* or *canto de entrada* (entrance song).

Mbundu People from from Luanda and Malanje Province.

Maculelê An Afro-Brazilian folkloric dance performed with sticks or machetes.

Mãe de santo A priestess in Afro-Brazilian religions.

Malandragem Cunning; deception; self-preservation. A tactic of malandros and capoeiristas.

Malandro/a Hustler; con artist; artful dodger.

Maldade Evil; wickedness. Malícia in its most negative manifestations.

Malícia Similar to malandragem, trickery, and deception. A capoeira tactic.

Malta Nineteenth-century capoeira gang in Rio de Janeiro.

Mandinga Magic and protection used in capoeira; derived from the Mandinka, the name of a West African people.

Manha Swing, as in the ginga and an approach to life.

Marginal Criminal.

Martelo Hammer. A capoeira kick similar to a roundhouse in other martial arts.

Médio A middle size berimbau that plays the inverse of the gunga rhythm when playing in the capoeira orchestra.

Meia lua Half-moon; circular front kick.

Mestrando/a In some capoeira groups the highest rank below mestre.

Mestre/a Master. The honorific title for a top ranking capoeirista.

Morro Hill. The term for a vertical favela used by residents.

Muqueca Brazilian seafood stew made with shrimp or fish and a base of dendê oil and tomatoes.

Musseques Shantytowns or informal settlements in Angola.

Negativa Negation; refusal. A defense in capoeira in which the body is held close to the ground to avoid an incoming kick.

N'golo "Zebra dance" of Southern Angola. A possible deep ancestor of capoeira.

Novela Brazilian soap opera.

Nzinga Seventeenth century Angola warrior queen; name of female led Bahian capoeira group.

Obaluaiê The orixá of healing and illness.

Obruni Akan word for foreigner in Ghana.

Ofertas Religious offerings.

Orixá Deity of major religions of the African diaspora; intermediaries between humans and the supreme being or god, Olodumare/Olorun.

Ovimbundu People from Benguela and the planalto region of Angola.

Pagode A style of pop samba played with electric instruments. Also refers to a gathering of musicians to play acoustic music, often accompanied by dancing.

Palmares The largest Brazilian quilombo that endured for most of the seventeenth century in the northern state of Alagoas.

Pandeiro A tambourine used in capoeira and samba, usually made from wood and animal skin.

Passarela A pedestrian overpass.

Patuá A talisman or lucky charm worn to protect the body.

Pelourinho The name of Salvador's historic center. The Portuguese word for "whipping post" found throughout colonial Brazil.

Ponteira A variation on the benção in which the strike is delivered with the ball of the foot in an upwardly thrusting motion.

Pontos riscados Signs used in ritual to invoke the orixás.

Povo People of the popular classes.

Puxada de rede A folkloric Brazilian dance performed to drumming and mimicking the collective rhythmic work of pulling in a fishing net.

Quadra An open-air court that is often used for samba parties and capoeira classes in favelas.

Quilombos Fugitive societies that existed throughout Brazil in urban and rural areas from the seventeenth century until abolition in 1888. Some quilombos still exist today inhabited by the descendants of former fugitives.

Rabo de arraia A stingray's tail. A characteristic capoeira kick in which the hands are placed near or on the ground and the leg swings up and backward in a circular movement as the torso lowers.

Rasteira Sweep. A capoeira counterattack that destabilizes an opponent's standing foot during a kick.

Real/Reais (pl) The current Brazilian currency.

Reco-reco A musical scraper of notched wood or bamboo used in the capoeira orchestra.

Roda Wheel; ring. The physical space in which capoeira is played; the event of bringing capoeiristas together to play.

Samba A musical and dance genre of central African origin found in various forms throughout Brazil.

São Bento Grande A berimbau rhythm, and a style of game characterized by high, fast kicks and takedowns.

Saudades Nostalgia; melancholy. An intense yearning or longing for something or someone.

Senzala The barracks for the enslaved laborers on sugar and tobacco plantations. The name of a capoeira group that formed in Rio de Janeiro in the 1970s.

Soba A chief in Angola.

Subúrbios Suburbs. The predominantly working class and poor neighborhoods on the peripheries of Brazilian cities.

Terreiro A Candomblé house of worship.

Toque de Angola A berimbau rhythm that accompanies slower, lower games.

Vadiação Idleness. Another name for capoeira, especially popular in the early twentieth century.

Vagabundo Vagabond; a "good for nothing." A derogatory term for someone unemployed.

Vale Tudos "Anything goes"/"no holds barred" fighting competitions.

Velha guarda Old guard. A term of respect for the older generation of samba musicians or capoeiristas.

Verga The body of the berimbau, made from a long stick about one inch in diameter and four to five feet long.

Viola The smallest berimbau that plays many rhythmic variations when in the capoeira orchestra.

Volta ao mundo Go around the world. A break in the action during a game in which the two players walk around the inside of the roda before commencing play again. Can be used to indicate that a "point has been scored" or to catch one's breath.

Xangô Orixá of thunder, lightning, fire, and justice.

Zona Norte North Zone. The working-class and poor industrial suburbs of Rio de Janeiro.

Zona Sul South Zone. The wealthy beachfront residential neighborhoods of Rio de Janeiro.

Zumbi The seventeenth century ruler of the quilombo of Palmares. Today a popular symbol of Afro-Brazilian pride and cultural resistance.

Zungueiras Female street vendors in Angola.

NOTES

Introduction: "Everything the Mouth Eats"

1. Mestre translates as "master" and is as an honorific title for an expert in a skill or trade. The feminine version is *mestra*. Portuguese terms can be found in the glossary.

2. The kula ring was the ceremonial exchange of shell armbands and necklaces among the Trobriand Islanders studied by Bronisław Malinowski. The exchange of these nonuse ornaments, Malinowski argued, enhanced prestige and social, rather than economic, capital ([1922] 1984).

3. Haraway 2016.

4. Favelas are informal settlements that have historically been translated as "slum" or "shantytown." Neither of these terms do justice to the complex and diverse neighborhoods that qualify as favelas in Rio, which can range in size from several hundred families to the largest, Rocinha, which has over 100,000 residents, several public schools, banks, and retail commerce. In total, there are an estimated 1,000 favelas in Rio that house 22 percent of the city's population or 1.5 million people. I use favela, rather than a translation, or at times, *comunidade* (community) or *morro* (hill), terms favored by favela residents.

5. Mauss (1925) 2016.

6. Meintjes 2017, 57.

7. For instance, brincar is used to refer to participation in carnival, the street festival that goes on for four days before Lent each year.

8. Cf. Gadamer 1975.

9. Huizinga 1955; Freud 1961, 11–17.

10. On flow see Csíkszentmihályi 1975.

11. Lewis 1992, 2.

12. Thompson 1984, xv.

13. Thompson 1979.

14. Fu-Kiau (1980) 2001, 11.

15. Gilroy 2004, xi.

16. Nyamnjoh 2017, 262.

17. Nyamnjoh 2012, 149.

18. Drewel 1992, xix.

19. Daniel 2005, 278.

20. Thompson 1973.

21. On play frames see Bateson 1972.

22. Savigliano 2009, 18.

23. Savigliano, 167.

24. Downey 2008.

25. Other capoeira scholar-practitioners have also noted the unlearned quality of the ginga: anthropologist Margaret Wilson writes, "the essence of the ginga cannot be learned, but is 'felt.' And this 'feeling' comes from the experience of one's self and one's ancestors: from poverty and struggle, from love, joy and despair" (2001, 23). For more on the ginga in capoeira and other Brazilian dance forms see Rosa (2015).

26. On finding ourselves and our potential for action in the world through movement, see philosopher Maxine Sheets-Johnstone's *The Primacy of Movement* (1999, 136).

27. Zora Neale Hurston also did fieldwork in the Caribbean that she documented in *Tell My Horse* ([1938] 1990). See Cotera (2008) for a feminist analysis of the work of Ella Deloria, Zora Neale Hurston, and Jovita González, an early twentieth-century Mexican-American folklorist.

28. Melville Herskovits, a leading anthropologist in the search for African "survivals" in the Americas, wrote a 1948 scathing review of Landes's ethnography in *American Anthropologist*. He critiqued her methodology as unobjective (she had an intimate relationship with her chief "informant," the Afro-Bahian folklorist, Edison Carneiro), her writing style as too personal, and her conclusions—that Candomblé was a living, dynamic practice and not simply an African "retention"—unfounded.

29. Landes 1986, 121.

30. Katherine Dunham studied with anthropologist Melville Herskovits at Northwestern and then Robert Redfield at the University of Chicago, whose lack of support of her as an intellectual eventually led her to abandon her academic studies (Dee Das 2017, 55–56). Pearl Primus, after much struggle and attempts to persuade her committee to let her "dance her dissertation," completed her PhD at New York University (Schwartz and Schwartz 2011, 159).

31. Dunham 1969, 10.

32. Particularly impactful on me for their ethnographic and writerly innovations in dance scholarship were: Taylor 1998; Browning 1995; Savigliano 1995; Ness 1992; Novack 1990.

33. Clifford and Marcus 1986.

34. Narayan 1993, 672. Aisha Beliso-De Jesús argues that debates over whether being a "native" bestows greater or lesser analytic insight are shaped by the topic of study. She points out that those who study religions of which they are practitioners are critiqued in ways that, for instance, anthropologists who study the law and are also lawyers are not (2015, 25).

35. Domínguez 2000, 388.

36. Nash 2019, 117.

37. See anthropologist Deborah Thomas's (2019) idea of Witnessing 2.0 as a combination of responsibility and a responsiveness—a response-ability—to others.

38. See Wesolowski 2012.

39. Stewart 1996, 34.

40. Bourdieu 1990.

41. Cf. Downey 2005.

42. Bourdieu 1977, 78–79.

43. DeFrantz and Gonzalez 2014, 11.

44. Geertz (1973) 1988, 23.

45. Cf. Conquergood 1991.

46. In his auto-ethnographic study of boxing in a Southside Chicago gym (2004), sociologist Loïc Wacquant refers to this methodology as "carnal sociology." Anthropologist Kathy Davis, in her study of tango (2015), uses the term "carnal ethnography" to self-reflexively acknowledge her place as a white privileged "insider."

47. Sally Ness notes in her ethnography of *sinulog* dancing in Cebu City, Philippines, "learning to identify and execute the movement of everyday practice attuned me to distinctive values implicit in the city's activity profile" (1992, 231).

48. Kabir 2020.

49. My idea of intercorporeality as a way to blur genre develops from ethnomusicologist Steven Feld's use of intervocality in his "memoir of encounters" of cosmopolitan jazz musicians in Accra, Ghana (2012).

50. On writing from a place of love, feminist anthropologist Virginia Domínguez writes: "loving does not mean (a) presenting only positive characteristics of people in our writing; (b) eliding conflict, violence, or debate; or (c) feeling so guilty about our own geopolitically defined position that we treat those we consult with kid gloves, both 'in the field' (i.e., when we are spending time with them) and in our published writings" (2000, 366).

51. Jackson 2017, 64.

Chapter 1. Entering the Roda: Rio de Janeiro, 1995–1996

1. Filho (1893) 1999, 101.

2. See Larkins (2015) for an ethnography of favela tourism.

3. In contrast to my experience, many researchers in Rio first come to stay in and know the South Zone before eventually moving out to the North Zone. See for instance the arrival stories of anthropologist Donna Goldstein (2003) and journalist Alma Guillermoprieto (1990).

4. Beliso-De Jesús 2015, 8. See also Feld and Basso 1996.

5. Lévi-Strauss 1981, 79, 89.

6. Carvalho 2013.

7. Karasch 1987.

8. Holloway 1989, 26.

9. A.P.D.G. 1826, 304–6.

10. For a complete history of Rio's capoeira maltas see Soares 1994.

11. Abreu 1886.

12. Holloway 1989.

13. Cavalcanti 2004, 201–2.

14. Soares 1994.

15. Almeida (1852) 1999, 57.

16. Azevedo (1890) 2000.

17. Freyre 1970, 11.

18. The first favela was established in the early 1900s on a hill near the War Ministry by a group of war veterans seeking compensation for fighting in the Canudos Campaign. The

veterans named their occupancy after Favela Hill, from which was launched the last assault on the religious community in the backlands of northeastern Brazil. The term favela subsequently came to refer to all informal settlements (Meade 1999, 71n61).

19. Filho (1893) 1999, 257; Holloway 1989, 669.

20. Quoted in Assunção 2005, 94.

21. Cf. Shaw 2018.

22. For a fictionalized biography of Madame Satã, see the 2002 film, *Madame Satã,* directed by Karim Aïnouz.

23. Ventura 1993.

24. Carvalho 2013.

25. Cf. Holston and Caldeira 1998.

26. A 2017 complaint filed against the Brazilian state with the UN Human Rights Council by Brazilian anti-racist organizations concluded that a Black youth is murdered every 23 minutes in Brazil, and that of all homicide victims in Brazil 53 percent are youth, 77 percent are Black, and 93 percent are male (see https://fopir.org.br).

27. Carnival is a Catholic festival that celebrates Lent. On Shrove, or Fat Tuesday, revelers say "goodbye to meat" as they enter the penitential six weeks before Easter.

28. The samba schools are social organizations and not actual schools, and "rehearsals" are gatherings to practice that year's samba song, dance, drink, and socialize.

29. Perlman 2010. Forced displacements continue in Rio, most recently, during the building of the Olympic Village in 2016.

30. A Russian man I trained with in New York City admired polar bears and took to wearing a medallion of one in hopes of picking up the nickname. Instead, the instructor, observing another sartorial quirk—the bandanna he wore to protect his bald head—and his nationality, nicknamed him Babushka.

31. Brandes 1975.

32. Holanda (1936) 2012, 118.

33. Cf. Yúdice 1994.

34. Schubert 2017, 54, 79.

Chapter 2. Authenticity and Loss: Bahia, 1996

1. For a comprehensive look at the Transatlantic Slave Trade including routes and estimated numbers, visit https://www.slavevoyages.org

2. On the "bahianization" of capoeira see Reis (2000) and Vassallo (2003).

3. Smith 2016.

4. The 2012 documentary film *Menino Joel,* written by Max Gaggino, tells the tragic story of Joel da Conceição Castro.

5. Landes 1994, 103, 106.

6. Assunção 2005, 105.

7. On twentieth-century politics in Candomblé see Capone 2010.

8. Lewis 1992; Downey 2005; *Lonely Planet Guide Book* 2002; see Griffith (2016) on the attitudes of foreign capoeiristas toward authenticity and street performers in Salvador.

9. Höfling 2019, 193n99.

10. Rego 1968, 35–36.

11. Höfling 2019, 100.

12. Williams 2013, 3, 5

13. Galm (2010, 20–22) presents some written evidence that suggests a link between capoeira and the berimbau in the 1800s.

14. Assunção 2005, 7.

15. See Acuña (2016) for a complete discussion of the berimbau's agency.

16. Almeida 1986, 69.

17. Quoted in Galm 2010, 5.

18. Almeida 1986, 72.

19. Foucault (1977) 1995.

20. See anthropologist Christen Smith's first experiences with official and nonofficial Pelourinho tours (2016, 53).

21. Smith, 53.

22. Collins 2015. See also Keisha-Khan Perry (2004) on the gentrification of Salvador.

23. *A Tarde,* August 5, 1980.

24. Cf. Abreu 1999.

25. Quoted in Höfling 2019, 87.

26. Höfling, 87.

27. Quoted in Acuña 2016, 388–89.

28. "'Mestre Bimba.' 'campeão na capoeira' desafia todos os luctadores bahianos." *A Tarde,* March 16, 1936.

29. *Camará,* short for *camarada,* or "comrade" here means fellow player or friend.

30. Downey 2005, 112.

31. See Höfling 2019.

32. See Pinho (2010) for a discussion of the Afroblocos and the reinvention of Blackness in Bahia.

33. Magalhães Filho, 2011, 112.

34. Reis 2000, 40.

35. According to Mestre Cobra Mansa, "the contribution of Ken Dossar, Daniel Dawson, John Lowell Lewis was really important because they were American intellectuals with radical Afrocentric ideas" (quoted in Magalhães Filho 2011).

36. Magalhães Filho, 2011, 135.

37. For a comparison of race and politics in Brazil, South Africa, and the United States see Marx 1998; for post-abolition mobilization against racism see Butler 1998; for ethnographies of the everyday experience of race in Brazil see Roth-Gordon 2017; Goldstein 2003; Sheriff 2001; and Twine 1998.

38. Gonzalez 1984, 225.

39. Pires 2002, 26.

40. Cf. Pinho 2018.

41. Collins 2015, 328.

42. Xangô's appearance is one of the film's many inaccuracies as Palmares was inhabited by Central Africans, and Xangô, a West African god, was introduced in Brazil much later.

43. Ochoa 2020, 280.

44. Browning 1995, 63.

45. Landes 1994, 92.

46. Collins 2015.

47. Collins, 311.

48. Guillermoprieto 1990, 41.

49. Cohen 2016, 652, 660.

50. Jackson 2005, 15.

Chapter 3. An Anthropologist in the Roda: Rio de Janeiro, 1997

1. On everyday violence in Brazil see Scheper-Hughes 1992.

2. *O Dia,* October 22, 1996.

3. Lacé Lopes 1999, 141.

4. Cf. Wesolowski 2012.

5. For more on the Central Station Roda and Rio's other historic street rodas see https://capoeirahistory.com.

6. Mauss (1934) 1973.

7. Capoeira 1992, 91.

8. Capoeira, 91.

9. Linger 1992, 3.

10. Cf. Williams 2001.

11. Holanda (1936) 2012, 107.

12. Taussig 1987.

13. Holston and Caldeira 1998.

14. Linger 1992.

15. Wacquant 2004.

16. On widespread acceptance of justified uses of violence in Brazil see Caldeira 2000.

17. Quoted in Soares 1999, 303 (my translation).

18. For what little documentation there is on Mestra Sandrinha (Sandra Eugênia Feitosa) visit https://capoeirahistory.com/mestre/master-sandrinha/.

19. *Revista Capoeira* 1, no. 1 (1998).

20. *Revista Capoeira* 1, no. 2 (1998).

21. Heywood and Dworkin 2003, 11.

22. Cf. Scheper-Hughes 1982, preface. Of course, the ethical question of including real names becomes more complicated when an ethnographer is documenting illegal activity. Yet even Philippe Bourgois and Jeffrey Schonberg included, at the behest of the subjects themselves, photographs of the homeless heroin users they worked with in their ethnography *Righteous Dopefiend* (2009). See their introduction for a discussion of the ethics of their decision.

23. Donna Goldstein describes a "tough ethics of care" among favela mothers as a tactic for "holding on" to their children to ensure they survive the violence and temptations of crime in the neighborhood (2003, chapter 4).

24. In the last several decades, these questions have become more urgent, inspiring "activist research" (Hale 2001), "engaged anthropology" (Ortner 2019), and "public anthropology" (https://publicanthropology.org), which call for ethnography to not only describe and analyze social problems but offer suggestions for change, often in collaboration with those experiencing the injustices. While "applied anthropology" has been a subfield since the 1940s, the often unethical ends to which anthropological methods and theory have been used to solve real world-issues (from European colonial expansion to the U.S. "war

on terror") has meant that activist anthropologists tend to distance themselves from the "applied" label.

25. I am, of course, not alone in this: most anthropologists have deep and complicated feelings for the people they work with, whether they choose to write about those feelings or not. Conveying affect, as I have attempted to in this book, is one characteristic of "engaged anthropology" (Ortner 2019).

26. It is also worth noting that the final line "look at Lampião's footstep" (not included in all versions of this song) is a shout-out to Lampião, the early twentieth century Northeastern bandit who gained a Robin Hoodesque reputation for stealing from rich land owners.

27. Clifford and Marcus 1986.

28. Lewis 1992; Browning 1995; Reis 1993.

29. Ortner 1995, 188.

30. Clifford and Marcus 1986.

31. Abu-Lughod 1990.

Chapter 4. "Only Intellectuals Like Misery": Rio de Janeiro, 2001–2004

1. Browning 1998, 184.

2. Edmonds 2010.

3. Caldeira 2000, 375.

4. Assunção 2005, 93.

5. Reis 1993, 103.

6. Cf. Roth-Gordon 2017.

7. Veloso 2010.

8. Live-in domestic workers are less common today. See Donna Goldstein's 2003 ethnography for an in-depth look at patron-domestic worker relationships in the last decades of the twentieth century.

9. Sansone 2003, 52–53.

10. Freyre (1946) 1963, 13.

11. Freire 1990.

12. DaMatta 1991, 168.

13. Julie Livingston, in her ethnography of an oncology ward in Botswana, argues that laughter is a way to socialize pain (2012, 147).

14. Cf. Goldstein 2003.

15. Cf. Caldeira 2000, 183.

16. Bartlett 2007.

17. See Bourgois (1995) on a similar attitude among Puerto Rican drug dealers in New York City.

18. "*Cafeína é guerreira: negra, favelada, suburbana, pobre, velha, mãe solteira mas batalha mesmo.*"

Chapter 5. Imagining Brazil in Africa: Angola, 2002

1. In ABADÁ, Mestrando is the title given to those who rank just below Mestre (the equivalent of the title Contramestre in other groups).

2. Wesolowski 2020; Pinho 2010; Holsey 2008; Ebron 2000.

3. Mbembe 1992, 22.

4. Hoffman 2017, 21.

5. Kaufmann 2017.

6. Ondjaki (2012) 2018, 178.

7. Hoffman 2017, 13.

8. Hoffman, 24

9. Ondjaki (2012) 2018, 282.

10. Piot 2010; Schubert 2017.

11. Pearce 2005, 10.

12. Tomás 2012.

13. Thornton, 1988, 364.

14. Heywood 2017, 12.

15. Thornton 1988, 364.

16. Heywood 2017, 249.

17. Heywood 2002, xi.

18. See Holsey (2008) for an analysis of the tensions between locals and tourists around the different meanings and expectations inscribed on the forts.

19. Schenck and Candido 2015, 225.

20. Ferreira 2012.

21. For a nuanced discussion of the challenges facing the memorialization of the Transatlantic Slave Trade in Angola see Schenck and Candido 2015.

22. Neves e Sousa 1974.

23. Neves e Sousa 1974.

24. Neto 2000, 39–45.

25. Assunção 2005, 58.

26. Kaufmann 2017.

27. Hoffman 2017, 23.

28. Mbembe 1992, 16.

29. Thank you, Kathryn Mathers for suggesting this interpretation.

Chapter 6. Global Convivência: Brussels, Venice, Accra, Havana, 2008–2018

1. Brodsky 1992.

2. The bridge battles were tolerated by the city's elite, who reasoned that they provided combat training and entertainment for the working classes, and an impressive display of aggression for any foreign ambassadors or princes with nefarious designs on La Serenissima (The Most Serene, as Venice was ironically known). Moreover, many of the city's law enforcers participated in the battles. See Davis (1998) for a history of the bridge battles.

3. In many groups contramestre is the title given to those ranked just below mestre (it is the equivalent to the title mestrando in ABADÁ).

4. Cf. Barros de Castro 2012.

5. Lefebvre 1991, 6.

6. Davis 2015, 9.

7. Hartman, 2007, 233.

8. Cuban capoeiristas told anthropologist Annie Gibson, "Let the world know that in

Cuba we practice capoeira. . . . Here we feel it because of what we have inside ourselves" (2014, 1).

Chapter 7. Return to Roots: Angola, 2019

1. Tomás 2012, 100n79.
2. Tomás, 52.
3. For a discussion of Luso-Tropicalism in Angola see Tomás, 275.
4. Schubert 2017, 77–78.
5. Marques de Morais 2011, 70.
6. Schubert 2017.
7. Thompson 1984, chap. 2.
8. Fu-Kiau 2001, 21.
9. Fu-Kiau, 36.
10. cf. Desch-Obi 2008, 3–4.
11. See Mestre Cobra Mansa's (Cinézio Feliciano Peçanha) 2019 dissertation on capoeira and the kalunga.
12. Thompson 1984, 115.
13. There is debate over the extent of the similarities between Kongo and Christian ontologies and how much these facilitated their confluence. See Sweet 2003.
14. Moorman 2008.
15. Moorman, 31.
16. Moore 2018, 44.
17. Piot 2010.
18. Thomas 2004, 13.
19. Galliani and Fernandes 2018, 7.

Chapter 8. Bringing It All Home: Durham, North Carolina, 2021

1. Gilroy 2004, 137; cf. hooks 1992.
2. Fanon 1963, 44.
3. Thank you Louise Meintjes for suggesting "pedagogy of convivência."
4. Kealiinohomoku (1970) 1983.
5. Foster 2009, 2.
6. Quoted in O'Shea 2019.
7. Gadamer 1975, 93.
8. O'Shea 2019, 170.
9. O'Shea, 170.
10. O'Shea, 123.
11. Cf. Lewis 1992, 171.
12. Kurtz (2020, 84–85) argues that this silence reflects Afro-Brazilian feminist strategies of maintaining silence in solidarity with Afro-Brazilian men against racism.
13. Nash 2019, 116, 118.
14. Freire 1990, 78.
15. Nash 2019, 116.

REFERENCES

Abreu, Frederico José de. 1999. *"Bimba é Bamba": a capoeira no ringue.* Salvador: Instituto Jair Moura.

Abreu, Plácido de. 1886. *Os Capoeiras.* Rio de Janeiro: Typ. Da Escola Serafim José Alves.

Abu-Lughod, Lila. 1990. "The Romance of Resistance: Tracing Transformations of Power through Bedouin Women." *American Ethnologist,* no. 17, 41–55.

Acuña, Mauricio. 2016. "The Berimbau's Social Ginga: Notes Towards a Comprehension of Agency in Capoeira." *Sociol.Antropol. Rio de Janeiro* 6 (2): 383–405.

Almeida, Bira. 1986. *Capoeira: A Brazilian Art Form.* Palo Alto: Sun Wave.

Almeida, Manuel Antônio de. (1852) 1999. *Memoirs of a Militia Sergeant.* Oxford: Oxford University Press.

A.P.D.G. 1826. *Sketches of Portuguese Life, Manners, Costume and Character.* London: R. Gilbert.

Assunção, Matthias Röhrig. 2005. *Capoeira: The History of an Afro-Brazilian Martial Art.* New York: Routledge.

Azevedo, Aluísio. (1890) 2000. *The Slum.* Translated by David H. Rosenthal. Oxford: Oxford University Press.

Barros de Castro, Maurício. 2012. *Mestre João Grande Na Roda do Mundo.* Rio de Janeiro: Editora Garamond.

Bartlett, Lesley. 2007. "Literacy, Speech and Shame: The Cultural Politics of Literacy and Language in Brazil." *International Journal of Qualitative Studies in Education* 20 (5): 547–63.

Bateson, Gregory. 1972. *Steps to an Ecology of Mind.* New York: Ballantine Books.

Beliso-De Jesús, Aisha. 2015. *Electric Santería: Racial and Sexual Assemblages of Transnational Religion.* New York: Columbia University Press.

Bourdieu, Pierre. 1977. *Outline of a Theory of Practice.* Cambridge: Cambridge University Press.

———. 1990. "Programme for a Sociology of Sport." In *In Other Words: Essays Towards a Reflexive Sociology.* Palo Alto: Stanford University Press.

Bourgois, Philippe. 1995. *In Search of Respect: Selling Crack in El Barrio.* Cambridge: Cambridge University Press.

Bourgois, Philippe, and Jeffrey Schonberg. 2009. *Righteous Dopefiend.* Berkeley: University of California Press.

Brandes, Stanley. 1975. "The Structural and Demographic Implications of Nicknames in Navanogal, Spain." *American Ethnologist* 2 (1): 139–48.

Brodsky, Joseph. 1992. *Watermark: An Essay on Venice*. London: Penguin Books.

Browning, Barbara. 1995. *Samba: Resistance in Motion*. Bloomington: University of Indiana Press.

———. 1998. *Infectious Rhythm: Metaphors of Contagion and the Spread of African Culture*. New York: Routledge.

Butler, Kim. 1998. *Freedoms Given, Freedoms Won: Afro-Brazilians in Post-Abolition São Paulo and Salvador*. New Brunswick, NJ: Rutgers University Press.

Caldeira, Teresa. 2000. *City of Walls: Crime, Segregation, and Citizenship in São Paulo*. Berkeley: University of California Press.

Capoeira, Nestor. 1992. *Capoeira: Os Fundamentos da Malícia*. Rio de Janeiro: Editora Record.

Capone, Stefania. 2010. *Searching for Africa in Brazil: Power and Tradition in Candomblé*. Durham: Duke University Press.

Carvalho, Bruno. 2013. *Porous City: A Cultural History of Rio de Janeiro (from the 1810s Onward)*. Liverpool: Liverpool University Press.

Cavalcanti, Nireu Oliveira. 2004. *Crônicas Históricas do Rio Colonial*. Rio de Janeiro: Editora Civilização Brasileira.

Clifford, James, and George Marcus, eds. 1986. *Writing Culture: The Poetics and Politics of Ethnography*. Berkeley: University of California Press.

Cohen, Adrienne. 2016. "Inalienable Performances, Mutable Heirlooms: Dance, Cultural Inheritance, and Political Transformation in the Republic of Guinea." *American Ethnologist* 43 (4): 650–62.

Conquergood, Dwight. 1991. "Rethinking Ethnography: Towards a Critical Cultural Politics." *Communication Monographs* 58 (June): 179–94.

Collins, John. 2015. *Revolt of the Saints: Memory and Redemption in the Twilight of Brazilian Racial Democracy*. Durham: Duke University Press.

Cotera, María Eugenia. 2008. *Native Speakers: Ella Deloria, Zora Neale Hurston, Jovita González, and the Poetics of Culture*. Austin: University of Texas Press.

Csikszentmihalyi, Mihaly. 1975. *Beyond Boredom and Anxiety: Experiencing Flow in Work and Play*. San Francisco: Jossey-Bass.

DaMatta, Roberto. 1991. *Carnivals, Rogues, and Heroes: An Interpretation of the Brazilian Dilemma*. Notre Dame: University of Notre Dame Press.

Daniel, Yvonne. 2005. *Dancing Wisdom: Embodied Knowledge in Haitian Vodou, Cuban Yoruba, and Bahian Candomblé*. Chicago: University of Illinois Press.

Davis, Kathy. 2015. *Dancing Tango: Passionate Encounters in a Globalizing World*. New York: New York University Press.

Davis, Robert C. 1998. "The Police and the *Pugni*: Sport and Social Control in Early-Modern Venice." *Stanford Humanities Review: Discipling Literature* 6 (2): 31–46.

Dee Das, Joanna. 2017. *Katherine Dunham: Dance and the African Diaspora*. Oxford: Oxford University Press.

DeFrantz, Thomas, and Anita Gonzalez. 2014. *Black Performance Theory*. Durham: Duke University Press.

Desch-Obi, T. J. 2008. *Fighting for Honor: The History of African Martial Art Traditions in the Atlantic World*. Columbia: University of South Carolina Press.

Domínguez, Virginia R. 2000. "For a Politics of Love and Rescue." *Cultural Anthropology* 15 (3): 361–93.

Downey, Greg. 2005. *Learning Capoeira: Lessons in Cunning from an Afro-Brazilian Art.* New York: Oxford University Press.

———. 2008. "Scaffolding Imitation in Capoeira: Physical Education and Enculturation in an Afro-Brazilian Art." *American Anthropologist* 110 (2): 204–13.

Drewel, Margaret Thompson. 1992. *Yoruba Ritual: Performers, Play, Agency.* Bloomington: Indiana University Press.

Dunham, Katherine. 1969. *Island Possessed.* Chicago: University of Chicago Press.

Ebron, Paulla A. 2000. "Tourists as Pilgrims: Commercial Fashioning of Transatlantic Politics." *American Ethnologist* 26 (4): 910–32.

Edmonds, Alexander. 2010. *Pretty Modern: Beauty, Sex, and Plastic Surgery in Brazil.* Durham: Duke University Press.

Fanon, Frantz. 1963. *Wretched of the Earth.* Translated by Constance Farrington. Middlesex: Penguin.

Feld, Steven. 2012. *Jazz Cosmopolitanism in Accra: Five Musical Years in Ghana.* Durham: Duke University Press.

Feld, Steven, and Keith Basso. 1996. *Senses of Place.* Santa Fe: School of American Research Advanced Seminar Series.

Ferreira, Roquinaldo. 2012. *Cross-Cultural Exchange in the Atlantic World: Angola and Brazil during the Era of the Slave Trade.* Cambridge: Cambridge University Press.

Filho, Mello Moraes. (1893) 1999. *Festas e Tradições Populares do Brasil.* Rio de Janeiro: Editora Itatiaia.

Foster, Susan Leigh, ed. 2009. *Worlding Dance.* New York: Palgrave Macmillan.

Foucault, Michel. (1977) 1995. *Discipline and Punish: The Birth of the Prison.* New York: Vintage.

Freire, Paulo. 1990. *Pedagogy of the Oppressed.* Translated by Myra Bergman Ramos. New York: Continuum.

Freud, Sigmund. 1961. *Beyond the Pleasure Principle.* New York: Liveright.

Freyre, Gilberto. (1946) 1963. *The Masters and the Slaves: A Study in the Development of Brazilian Civilization.* Translated by Samuel Putnam. 2nd edition. New York: Alfred A. Knopf.

———. 1970. *Order and Progress: Brazil from Monarchy to Republic.* Translated by Rod W. Horton. New York: Knopf.

Fu-Kiau, Kimbwandende Kia Bunseki. (1980) 2001. *African Cosmology of the Bântu-Kôngo: Principles of Life and Living.* New York: Athelia Henrietta Press.

Gadamer, Hans-Georg. 1975. *Truth and Method.* New York: Seabury Press.

Galliani, Francesca, and Walter Fernandes. 2012. *Portrait of a New Angola.* Milano: Skira editor.

Galm, Eric. 2010. *The Berimbau: Soul of Brazilian Music.* Jackson: University of Mississippi Press.

Geertz, Clifford. (1973) 1988. *The Interpretation of Cultures.* New York: Basic Books.

Gibson, Annie. 2014. "Rediscovering *lo cubano* through Capoeira in Cuba." *Postcolonialist* 2 (1): 1–11.

Gilroy, Paul. 2004. *After Empire: Melancholia or Convivial Culture?* London: Routledge.

Goldstein, Donna M. 2003. *Laughter Out of Place: Race, Class, Violence, and Sexuality in a Rio Shantytown.* Berkeley: University of California Press.

Gonzalez, Lélia. 1984. "Racismo e Sexismo na cultura brasileira." *Revista Ciências Sociais Hoje,* Anpocs, 223–44.

Griffith, Lauren Miller. 2016. *In Search of Legitimacy: How Outsiders Become Part of the Afro-Brazilian Capoeira Tradition.* New York: Berghahn.

Guillermoprieto, Alma. 1990. *Samba.* New York: Vintage Books.

Hale, Charles. 2001. "What Is Activist Research?" *SSRC Items and Issues* (1, nos. 1–2): 13–15.

Haraway, Donna. 2016. *Staying with the Trouble: Making Kin in the Chthulucene.* Durham: Duke University Press.

Hartman, Saidiya. 2007. *Lose Your Mother: A Journey Along the Atlantic Slave Route.* New York: Farrar, Straus, and Giroux.

Herskovits, Melville. 1948. "Review of *The City of Women.*" *American Anthropologist,* no. 50, 123–25.

Heywood, Leslie, and Shari Dworkin. 2003. *Built to Win: The Female Athlete as Cultural Icon.* Minneapolis: University of Minnesota Press.

Heywood, Linda M. 2017. *Njinga of Angola: Africa's Warrior Queen.* Harvard: Harvard University Press.

———., ed. 2002. *Central Africans and Cultural Transformations in the American Diaspora.* Cambridge: Cambridge University Press.

Höfling, Ana Paula. 2019. *Staging Brazil: Choreographies of Capoeira.* Middletown: Wesleyan University Press.

Hoffman, Daniel. 2017. *Monrovia Modern: Urban Form and Political Imagination in Liberia.* Durham: Duke University Press.

Holanda, Sérgio Buarque de. (1936) 2012. *Roots of Brazil.* Translated by G. Harvey Summ. Notre Dame, IN: University of Notre Dame Press.

Holloway, Thomas. 1989. "'A Healthy Terror': Police Repression of Capoeiras in Nineteenth Century Rio de Janeiro." *Hispanic American Historical Review,* no. 69, 637–76.

Holsey, Bayo. 2008. *Routes of Remembrance: Refashioning the Slave Trade in Ghana.* Chicago: University of Chicago Press.

Holston, James, and Teresa P.R. Caldeira. 1998. "Democracy, Law, and Violence: Disjunctions of Brazilian Citizenship." In *Fault Lines of Democracy in Post-Transition Latin America,* edited by Felipe Agüero and Jeffrey Stark, 263–96. Miami: University of Miami North-South Center Press.

hooks, bell. 1992. *Black Looks: Race and Representation.* Boston: South End Press.

Huizinga, Johan. 1955. *Homo Ludens.* Boston: Beacon Press.

Hurston, Zora Neale. (1938) 1990. *Tell My Horse: Voodoo and Life in Haiti and Jamaica.* New York: Perennial Library.

Jackson, John L., Jr. 2005. *Real Black: Adventures in Racial Sincerity.* Chicago: University of Chicago Press.

Jackson, Michael. 2017. "After the Fact: The Question of Fidelity in Ethnographic Writing." In *Crumpled Paper Boat: Experiments in Ethnographic Writing,* edited by Anand Pandian and Stuart McLean. Durham: Duke University Press.

Kabir, Ananya Jahanara. 2020. "Circum-Atlantic Connections and Their Global Kineto-scapes: African-Heritage Partner Dances." *Atlantic Studies* 17 (1): 1–12.

Karasch, Mary. 1987. *Slave Life in Rio de Janeiro 1808–1850*. Princeton: Princeton University Press.

Kaufmann, Andrea. 2017. "Crafting a Better Future in Liberia: Hustling and Associational Life in Post-war Monrovia." *Tsantsa,* vol. 22, 37–46.

Kealiinohomoku, Joann. (1970) 1983. "An Anthropologist Looks at Ballet as a Form of Ethnic Dance." In *What Is Dance? Readings in Theory and Criticism,* edited by Roger Copeland and Marshall Cohen. Oxford: Oxford University Press.

Kurtz, Esther Viola. 2020. "Guerreira Tactics: Women Warriors' Sonic Practices of Re-fusal in Capoeira Angola." *Women and Music: A Journal of Gender and Culture,* no. 24, 71–95.

Lacé Lopes, André Luiz. 1999. *A Volta do Mundo da Capoeira*. Rio de Janeiro: Markgraph.

Landes, Ruth. (1947) 1994. *City of Women*. Albuquerque: University of New Mexico Press.

———. 1986. "A Woman Anthropologist in Brazil." In *Women in the Field: Anthropological Experiences,* edited by Peggy Golde. 2nd ed. Berkeley: University of California Press.

Larkins, Erika Mary Robb. 2015. *The Spectacular Favela: Violence in Modern Brazil*. Berkeley: University of California Press.

Lefebvre, Henri. 1991. *The Production of Space*. Translated by Donald Nicholson-Smith. Oxford: Blackwell.

Lévi-Strauss, Claude. 1981. *Tristes Tropiques*. New York: Atheneum.

Lewis, John Lowell. 1992. *Ring of Liberation: Deceptive Discourse in Brazilian Capoeira*. Chicago: University of Chicago Press.

Linger, Daniel Touro. 1992. *Dangerous Encounters: Meanings of Violence in a Brazilian City*. Stanford: Stanford University Press.

Livingston, Julie. 2012. *Improvising Medicine: An African Oncology Ward in an Emerging Cancer Epidemic*. Durham: Duke University Press.

Magalhães Filho, Paulo Andrade. 2011. "'Jogo de Discursos': a disputa por hegemonia na tradição da capoeira angola baiana." PhD diss., Program in Social Sciences, Federal University of Bahia.

Malinowski, Bronisław. (1922) 1984. *Argonauts of the Western Pacific*. Prospect Heights, IL: Waveland Press.

Marques de Morais, Rafael. 2011. "The New Imperialism: China in Angola." *World Affairs* 173 (6): 67–74.

Marx, Anthony W. 1998. *Making Race and Nation: A Comparison of the United States, South Africa, and Brazil*. Cambridge: Cambridge University Press.

Mauss, Marcel. (1925) 2016. *The Gift*. Chicago: HAU Books.

———. (1932) 1973. "Techniques of the Body." *Economy and Society*. 2: 70–83.

Mbembe, Achille. 1992. "The Banality of Power and the Aesthetics of Vulgarity in the Postcolony." *Public Culture* 4 (2): 1–30.

Meade, Theresa A. 1999. *"Civilizing" Rio: Reform and Resistance in a Brazilian City 1889–1930*. University Park, PA: Pennsylvania State University Press.

Meintjes, Louise. 2017. *Dust of the Zulu: Ngoma Aesthetics after Apartheid*. Durham: Duke University Press.

Moore, Madison. 2018. *Fabulous: The Rise of the Beautiful Eccentric*. New Haven: Yale University Press.

Moorman, Marissa J. 2008. *Intonations: A Social History of Music and Nation in Luanda, Angola, from 1945 to Recent Times*. Athens: Ohio University Press.

Narayan, Kirin. 1993. "How Native Is a 'Native' Anthropologist?" *American Anthropologist*, no. 95, 671–86.

Nash, Jennifer. 2019. *Black Feminism Reimagined: After Intersectionality*. Durham: Duke University Press.

Ness, Sally Ann. 1992. *Body, Movement, and Culture: Kinesthetic and Visual Symbolism in a Philippine Community*. Philadelphia: University of Pennsylvania Press.

Neto, Salas. 2000. "Uma 'bassula' à Pescador/Bassula—Full-contact sport, fisherman style." *Austral, Revista de bordo TAAG*, no. 33, 39–45.

Neves e Sousa, 1974. *Da Minha África E Do Brasil Que Eu Vi*. Luanda: Oficinas Gráficas.

Novack, Cynthia. 1990. *Sharing the Dance: Contact Improvisation and American Culture*. Madison: University of Wisconsin Press.

Nyamnjoh, Francis B. 2012. "'Potted Plants in Greenhouses': A Critical Reflection on the Resilience of Colonial Education in Africa." *Journal of Asian and African Studies* 47 (2): 129–54.

———. 2017. "Incompleteness: Frontier Africa and the Currency of Conviviality." *Journal of Asian and African Studies* 52 (3): 253–70.

Ochoa, Todd Ramón. 2020. *A Party for Lazarus: Six Generations of Ancestral Devotion in a Cuban Town*. Berkeley: University of California Press.

Ondjaki. 2018. *Transparent City*. Translated by Stephen Henighan. Windsor, ON: Biblioasis.

Ortner, Sherry B. 1995. "Resistance and the Problem of Ethnographic Refusal." *Society for Comparative Study of Society and History* (7, no. 1): 173–91.

———. 2019. "Practicing Engaged Anthropology." *Anthropology of the Century* (25).

O'Shea, Janet. 2019. *Risk, Failure, Play: What Dance Reveals about Martial Arts Training*. Oxford: Oxford University Press.

Pastinha, Vicente Ferreira. 1964. *Capoeira Angola*. Salvador. Bahia.

Pearce, Justin. 2005. *Outbreak of Peace*. New York: David Phillip.

Peçanha, Cinézio Feliciano (Mestre Cobra Mansa). 2019. "Gingando na linha da Kalunga: Capoeira Angola, Engolo e a construção da ancestralidade." PhD diss., Federal University of Bahia.

Perlman, Janice. 2010. *Favela: Four Decades of Living on the Edge in Rio de Janeiro*. Oxford: Oxford University Press.

Perry, Keisha-Khan. 2004. "The Roots of Black Resistance: Race, Gender and the Struggle for Urban Land Rights in Salvador, Bahia, Brazil." *Social Identities* 10: 811–31.

Pinho, Patricia de Santana. 2010. *Mama Africa: Reinventing Blackness in Bahia*. Durham: Duke University Press.

———. 2018. *Mapping Diaspora: African American Roots Tourism in Brazil*. Chapel Hill: University of North Carolina Press.

Piot, Charlie. 2010. *Nostalgia for the Future: West Africa after the Cold War*. Chicago: University of Chicago Press.

Pires, Antônio Liberac Cardoso Simões. 2002. *Bimba, Pastinha e Besouro de Mangangá:*

Três Personagens da Capoeira Baiana. Tocantins: Fundação Universidade do Tocantins.

Reis, João José. 1993. *Slave Rebellion in Brazil: The Muslim Uprising of 1835 in Bahia*. Translated by Arthur Brakel. Baltimore: Johns Hopkins University Press.

Reis, Letícia Vidor de Souza. 2000. *O Mundo de pernas para o ar: A capoeira no Brasil*. São Paulo: Editora Publisher Brasil.

Rego, Waldeloir. 1968. *Capoeira Angola: ensaio sócio-etnográfico*. Coleção Baiana. Rio de Janeiro: Gráf. Lux.

Rosa, Cristina F. 2015. *Brazilian Bodies and Their Choreographies of Identification: Swing Nation*. New York: Palgrave Macmillan.

Roth-Gordon, Jennifer. 2017. *Race and the Brazilian Body: Blackness, Whiteness, and Everyday Language in Rio de Janeiro*. Berkeley: University of California Press.

Sansone, Livio. 2003. *Blackness without Ethnicity: Constructing Race in Brazil*. New York: Palgrave Macmillan.

Savigliano, Marta Elena. 1995. *Tango and the Political Economy of Passion*. New York: Routledge.

———. 2009. "Worlding Dance and Dancing Out There in the World." In *Worlding Dance*, edited by Susan Leigh Foster. New York: Palgrave MacMillan.

Schenck, Marcia C., and Mariana P. Candido. 2015. "Uncomfortable Pasts: Talking About Slavery in Angola." In *African Heritage and Memories of Slavery in Brazil and the South Atlantic World*. Edited by Ana Lucia Araujo. Amherst, NY: Cambria Press.

Scheper-Hughes, Nancy. 1982. *Saints, Scholars, and Schizophrenics: Mental Illness in Rural Ireland*. Berkeley: University of California Press.

———. 1992. *Death Without Weeping: The Violence of Everyday Life in Brazil*. Berkeley: University of California Press.

Schubert Jon. 2017. *Working the System: A Political Ethnography of the New Angola*. Ithaca: Cornell University Press.

Schwartz, Peggy, and Murray Schwartz. 2011. *The Dance Claimed Me: A Biography of Pearl Primus*. New Haven: Yale University Press.

Shange, Savannah. 2019. *Progressive Dystopia: Abolition, Antiblackness and Schooling in San Francisco*. Durham: Duke University Press.

Shaw, Lisa. 2018. *Tropical Travels: Brazilian Popular Performance, Transnational Encounters, and the Construction of Race*. Austin: University of Texas Press.

Sheets-Johnstone, Maxine. 1999. *The Primacy of Movement*. Philadelphia: John Benjamins Publishing.

Sheriff, Robin. 2001. *Dreaming Equality: Color, Race, and Racism in Urban Brazil*. New Brunswick, NJ: Rutgers University Press.

Smith, Christen A. 2016. *Afro-Paradise: Blackness, Violence, and Performance in Brazil*. Urbana: University of Illinois Press.

Soares, Carlos Eugênio Líbano. 1994. *A Negregada Instituição: Os Capoeiras no Rio de Janeiro*. Rio de Janeiro: Prefeitura da Cidade do Rio de Janeiro.

Stewart, Kathleen. 1996. *A Space on the Side of the Road: Cultural Poetics in an "Other" America*. Princeton: University of Princeton Press.

Sweet, James H. 2003. *Recreating Africa: Culture, Kinship, and Religion in the African-Portuguese World, 1441–1770*. Chapel Hill: University of North Carolina Press.

Taussig, Michael. 1987. *Shamanism, Colonialism, and the Wild Man: A Study in Terror and Healing.* Chicago: University of Chicago Press.

Taylor, Julie. 1998. *Paper Tangos.* Durham: Duke University Press.

Thomas, Deborah. 2004. *Modern Blackness: Nationalism, Globalization, and the Politics of Culture in Jamaica.* Durham: Duke University Press.

———. 2019. *Political Life in the Wake of the Plantation: Sovereignty, Witnessing, Repair.* Durham: Duke University Press.

Thompson, Robert Farris. 1973. "An Aesthetics of Cool." *African Arts* 7 (1): 40–43, 64–67, 89–91.

———. 1979. *African Art in Motion: Icon and Act.* Berkeley: University of California Press.

———. 1984. *Flash of the Spirit: African and Afro-American Art and Philosophy.* New York: Vintage Books.

Thornton, John. 1988. "The Art of War in Angola, 1575–1680." *Comparative Studies in Society and History* 30 (2): 360–78.

Tomás, António. 2012. "Refracted Governmentality: Space, Politics, and Social Structure in Contemporary Luanda." PhD diss., Columbia University.

Twine, France Winddance. 1998. *Racism in a Racial Democracy: The Maintenance of White Supremacy in Brazil.* New Brunswick, NJ: Rutgers University Press.

Vassallo Pondé, Simone. 2003. "Capoeiras e Intelectuais: A Construção Coletiva da Capoeira 'Autêntica.'" *Estudos Históricos,* no. 32, 106–24.

Veloso, Letícia. 2010. "Governing Heterogeneity in the Context of 'Compulsory Closeness': The 'Pacification' of Favelas in Rio de Janeiro." In *Suburbanization in Global Society,* edited by Mark Clapson and Ray Hutchinson. Bingley, UK: JAI Press.

Ventura, Zuenir. 1993. *Cidade Partida.* Rio de Janeiro: Companhia das Letras.

Wacquant, Loïc. 2004. *Body and Soul: Notebooks of an Apprentice Boxer.* Oxford: Oxford University Press.

Wesolowski, Katya. 2012. "Professionalizing Capoeira: The Politics of Play in 21st Century Brazil." *Latin American Perspectives* 183 (39, no. 2): 82–92.

———. 2020. "Imagining Brazil in Africa: Capoeira's Transatlantic Roots and Routes." *Journal of Latin American and Caribbean Anthropology* 25 (3): 453–72.

Williams, Daryle. 2001. *Cultural Wars in Brazil: The First Vargas Regime 1930–1945.* Durham: Duke University Press.

Williams, Erica Lorraine. 2013. *Sex Tourism in Bahia: Ambiguous Entanglements.* Urbana: University of Illinois Press.

Wilson, Margaret. 2001. "Designs of Deception: Concepts of Consciousness, Spirituality and Survival in Capoeira Angola in Salvador, Brazil." *Anthropology of Consciousness* 12 (1): 19–36.

Yúdice, George. 1994. "The Funkification of Rio." In *Microphone Fiends: Youth Music and Youth Culture,* edited by Andrew Ross and Tricia Rose, 193–217. New York: Routledge.

INDEX

Abadá, 35, 124

ABADÁ-capoeira, 85, 94, 97, 110, 121–25; in Angola, 165–68, 173; boycott of, 94; diversity, 124, 182; etymology of name, 124; foundation of group, 123; full name, 124; international growth, 123, 186–87; and professionalization of capoeira, 124, 139, 140, 143; style, 97, 143, 201, 228; in the United States, 85, 144, 182

ABADÁ European Games, 182–83, 186

ABADÁ World Games, 89, 121, 182, 186, 203; and gender inclusion, 89–90

Abu-Lughod, Lila, 13, 113

Achievement, 3, 133, 137, 226–27, 232

Acordeon, *Mestre* (Bira Almeida), 56, 70, 74, 107

Africa, 8, 158–80, 197–219; in Brazil, 44–45, 159; and Catholic or Christian syncretism, 215, 217; eroticization of, 164; and postcolonialism, 159, 161, 202; West, 45, 76, 82, 215; West Central, 6, 55, 170

African Americans: and culture, 73, 170, 214; and roots tourism, 46, 73, 170, 197

African cities, 173; as invisible and liquid, 160

African culture: and dance, 13, 46, 82, 113, 164, 171, 173, 202–4, 217–18, 222–25; and expressive practices, 4, 15, 206, 218; and music practices, 4, 46

Afro-Brazilian culture, 4, 6–7, 18, 23, 45–49, 159, 221; appropriation of, 57, 221; commercialization of, 111; commodification of, 47, 54–55, 58, 62, 82, 97; expressive practices, 4, 15, 17, 23, 49; and feminism, 72, 164, 234; preservation of, 49, 64, 69; religious beliefs and practices, 4, 6, 73, 75–78; repression of, 3, 49. *See also* Candomblé; capoeira; samba

Afrocentrism, 69–71, 259n35 (chap. 2)

Almeida, Manuel Antônio de, *Memoirs of a Militia Sergeant*, 22

Amado, Jorge, 49–50, 62, 64

Ancestry, 11, 37, 158, 197, 205, 214

André, *Mestre* (André Luis de Sousa Pereira), 86, 89–90

Angola, 158–80, 199–219; and Atlantic Slave Trade, 170; Benguela, 176–78; in capoeira imaginary, 158; civil war, 161, 205, 209; colonial history, 164, 166, 170, 202; division, 203; Dumbe, 178; expressive practices, 206; fascination with Brazilian culture in, 159, 203; history of slavery in, 170; memorialization of slavery in, 171, 174, 218; modernization, 199, 208; "New," 199; and origins of capoeira, 120, 169; post–civil war, 161, 176; postcolonial, 159; pre–civil war, 161; and racism, 202; *sobas*, 168, 179; struggle for independence, 161, 165

Angolanidade, 202, 206, 213, 218–19

Anthropology, 12–13, 16, 53, 113; anonymity in, 104; detachment in, 105, 112; and feminism, 13

Apelido, 29–31, 163, 258n30 (chap. 1). *See also* nicknaming

Assunção, Matthias Röhrig, 173

Authenticity, 44, 46–53, 55, 69–70, 81–83, 192, 196, 213; and tradition, 63–64; versus sincerity, 83

Avô, 28–29

Axé, 4, 6, 78, 174; etymology, 4

Axiluanda people, 166, 172–73

Azevedo, Aluísio, 22–23

Bacurau, *Professor* (Anderson Lino), 126, 181, 185

Bahiatursa, 47, 51

Baianidade, 62

Bailes de corredor, 38
Bailes funk, 37–38, 40, 92, 126, 130
Bakongo people, 173, 214–15, 217
Balú, *Instrutor* (Balumukeno de Lemos), 169, 172–73; *Terra Mãe,* 169
Bantu people, 6, 164
Bassula, 169, 172–73; and capoeira, 173; persecution of, 173
Batizado, 88–89, 134, 174–75
Beiçola, *Mestre* (Ronaldo de Sá), 9–10, 26, 36, 49, 52, 86, 90, 107, 111, 183, 226; background, 25, 28–29; as cultural mediator, 26, 71; inclusive capoeira, 71
Beija Flor (samba school), 27, 32, 140
Belisário, João, 167
Benção, 93, 106–10, 222
Berimbau, 4, 17, 54–60, 72–73, 83; African roots of, 55; construction of, 57, 59–60, 178–79; and identity, 57; importance in capoeira of, 55–56; legend of, 57; playing of, 60; rhythms, 143; and spirituality, 56, 179; varieties of, 60
Berkeley (city), xi, 8, 70–71, 129
Besouro Mangangá, 37, 73
Bimba, *Mestre* (Manoel dos Reis Machado), 62–65, 72, 215; academy, 123; background, 63–64; berimbau rhythms, 143; criticism of, 63–64; lineage, 74
Biquinho, *Mestre* (Adenison Bemvindo dos Santos), 106–8
Black: consciousness, 31, 37, 72; fabulousness, 218; feminism, 235; nationalism, 161; performance, 15; radicalism, 69
Black culture, 54; eroticization of, 54, 103; and music, 8, 69, 225
Black Lives Matter, 234
Blackness, 71–72, 129; modern, 218
Black power movement, 38, 69, 234; empowerment, 71
Black Rio (scene), 69
Black sisterhoods, 73. *See also* Good Death Sisterhood; Sisterhood of Good Death Museum
Boa aparência, 127–28, 130, 139
Boal, Augusto, 118, 136
Boas, Franz, 12, 48–49
Body, 16, 115–18; Black, 47, 54, 61; open and closed, 116–17; as unbounded, 117
Bolsonaro, Jair, 233–34
Boneco, *Mestre* (Beto Simas), 102

Bourdieu, Pierre, 15
Brasilidade, 62, 98, 139
Brazil: abolition of slavery, 23, 45, 49, 73; and Africa, 159, 169; colonial history of, 21–23, 46, 99, 170; hyperinflation, 24–25; indigenous cultural influence, 46, 205; individualism, 137; military dictatorship, 25, 69, 72, 79; national culture, 37, 98, 139–40; and plastic surgery, 117; politics, 233; as "racial democracy," 49, 72, 99, 130
Bridge battles, 190
Briggs, Frederico Guilherme, 61; *Negroes, Going to be Whipped,* 61
Buarque de Holanda, Sergio, 31, 99
Búzios, 78–80

Cabello, *Mestre* (Cabello Caobijubá), 220, 222–23
Caboclos, 76, 79–80
Cabuenha, *Professor* (Júlio Janquinda Moniz), 199, 201–4, 206, 208, 213, 216–19
Cachaça, 50–51, 58–59
Cafeína, *Professora* (Ana Cristina Ferreira) 141–45
Caldeira, Teresa, 117
Call-and-response, 4–5, 66, 189
Câmara Cascudo, Luís da, *Folclore do Brasil,* 171
Camisa, *Mestre* (José Tadeu Carneiro Cardoso), 85, 89, 97, 120–21, 137, 165, 167–68, 174, 203; background, 123, 158, 186; Camisa Roxa (brother), 123, 184; pedagogy, 121–22, 135–36, 140, 143
Candomblé, 46–49, 58, 64, 66, 75–78, 116, 215; and Catholicism, 67, 76, 83; and Gods, 76; parallels to capoeira, 78; tensions with capoeira, 81; and tourism, 49
Canjiquinha, *Mestre* (Washington Bruno da Silva), 68, 72; and homoeroticism, 68
Capoeira: and "aesthetics of cool," 7; African roots of, 6, 8, 11, 37, 44, 64, 120, 159, 165, 169–70, 206; Afrocentrism in, 70–71, 197, 205; Amazonas, 143; in Angola, 167–70, 173; and authenticity, 46, 49–51, 63–64, 81; Benguela, 143; as Black art, 39; boom, 119, 130; as camaraderie, 3, 125, 135; and class, 123, 130, 136–37; commercialization of, 97–98, 126, 140; *contemporânea,* 74; definitions of, 1–2; and elite universities, 221; and ethnic diversity, 9, 85, 121, 124,

222; etymology, 46, 169; female *capoeiris-tas,* 72–73, 84–85, 89, 100–104, 141–45, 182, 204–7; and feminism, 38, 72, 101, 103, 164, 230; feminization of, 65; first academies, 62–63; and folklore, 94, 97, 101, 140, 171; and food metaphors, 1–2, 6–7, 18; and gender inclusion, 8, 31, 35, 38, 56, 66, 72, 74, 89, 101–3, 140–45, 201, 204, 230, 232; and gifts, 3; group affiliation, 2, 27, 88; history of, 11, 22–24, 55, 62, 72–73, 85, 113, 120, 169; internationalization of, 8, 13, 17, 85–86, 94, 97, 113, 168, 181, 196, 213, 225; Iuná, 143; as kinship, 2, 11, 20, 173, 197; and legislature, 14, 23; legitimacy of, 64, 175; lineage, 11, 29, 52; in literature, 22; as lover, 54; as male-dominated space, 8, 54, 85, 130, 232; and masculinity, 66, 94, 104; modernization and corruption of, 63, 82, 94, 110, 140; and music, 56, 65, 225; mythology of, 22; as nourishment, 1–2; oral history, 73; origin narratives of, 73, 169, 173; and pedagogy, 9–10, 85–86, 192–94, 220–21, 223–24, 227; as a pan-African manifestation, 69, 197; as performance, 49, 51–52, 64, 184; as play, 3–4, 6; politicization of, 3, 64, 68–72, 118, 140, 173, 222; as popular education, 135–38; as practice, 1, 51, 64, 114; professionaliza-tion and institutionalization of, 14, 64, 81, 94, 113, 139–40, 184–85, 221; as protest, 3, 8, 48; and race, 130; *regional,* 11, 63–64; and reputation, 27; as resistance, 22, 112–13, 40, 232; São Bento Grande, 143; and social activism, 125, 130, 136, 206, 229; sexism in, 105, 201, 232; as source of cultural and ancestral identity, 140, 142, 173, 203–5; and spirituality, 159, 214; as transformative, 1, 123, 225; as threat to social order, 22–23, 49, 62, 100; and tourism, 25, 49, 74, 82

Capoeira angola, 11, 61, 63–64, 68–70, 118, 143, 171, 192, 195, 210–11, 218, 220, 225, 235; academies, 69; *chamadas,* 67; and folklore, 70, 171; and *kalunga,* 214; uniforms, 140

Carneiro, Edison, 49, 51, 64, 81

Carnival, 25–27, 99, 115, 258n27 (chap. 1); and *convivência,* 32; in Luanda, 172

Carybé (Hector Julio Páride Bernabó), 49, 62, 240

Cascão, *Mestrando* (Luiz Fernando Pereira Monteiro), 118, 167–68, 173

Catholicism, 67, 73, 76–78, 83, 164, 215, 217

Centro Cultural e Recreativo Marítimo da Ilha, 167

Chá Preto, *Professor* (Rodoval Angelo Ruas) 126, 183–85

Charm, *Mestre* (Jorge Gomes Martins), 165–66

Cigarra, Márcia, *Mestra* (Márcia Treidler), 144, 182

Classism, 129, 137; structural, 137

Cobra Mansa, *Mestre* (Cinézio Feliciano Peçanha), 69–70, 194–95, 235, 259n35 (chap. 2)

Cohen, Adrienne, 82

Collins, John, 61–62; *Revolt of the Saints,* 61

Colonialism, 62, 99, 170, 196, 202, 210, 215, 223

Compulsory closeness, 128–29

Conscientização, 136; and capoeira, 136

Convivência, 5–6, 10–11, 15–18, 32–34, 36, 39–40, 48, 76, 112, 173, 175–76, 181; and ABADÁ, 122, 124; in Angolan literature, 160; in Europe, 187–88; as fleeting, 202; and improvisation, 159; and language, 140; pedagogy of, 227

Conviviality, 6, 7; and improvisation, 159; laughter, 175; and postcolonial, 159, 175

Corda, 88, 124, 204

Cor-diality, 99, 116

Corruption, 24, 199, 203, 233–34

Curió, *Mestre* (Jaime Martins dos Santos), 65–70, 82; lineage, 65; and spirituality, 66–67, 72

Dance, ethnography, 13, 16, 196, 223; world versus ethnic, 223

Daniel, Yvonne, 6

Davis, Kathy, 196

Decoloniality, 223

Dendê, 7, 45, 57

Dentinho, *Mestre* (Alcino Oliveira Bem-vindo), 91, 97–98, 137

Desabafar, 7, 99

Diabo Branco, 177–79

Diaspora, African, 4, 15; and culture, 73; expressive practices of, 15, 17, 113, 218; and performance, 7, 15; and slavery, 21, 45, 47, 113, 164, 170, 205

DiMola, *Mestre* (Domingos André dos San-tos), 49, 51–52, 54–55, 57–61, 72, 76, 82–83

Displacement, xii, 47, 171, 186, 197

Douglas, Mary, 43
Downey, Greg, 9, 67
Duende, *Mestre* (Carlos Eduardo dos Santos e Silva), 158, 174, 176
Dunham, Katherine, 12–13, 256n30 (intro.); *Island Possessed,* 12
Durham Angoleirx, 228–30

Emídio, *Mestre* Artur (Artur Emídio de Oliveira), 96, 101, 123
Escola de Capoeira Angola Irmãos Gêmeos, 65
Ethnography, 13, 16, 99–100, 105, 113, 260n22 (chap. 3), 260n24 (chap. 3)
Europe, 181–96; Brazilian immigration to, 167, 183–84
Exoticism, 48, 54, 58, 182, 196
Exploitation, 47, 62

Fanon, Frantz, 136, 222
Fatal, *Mestre* (Cláudio Luís Alves Marinho), 91–92
Favelas, 19–20, 23–24, 29, 39, 87, 91–92, 119, 126–27, 130–32, 255n4 (intro.), 257n18 (chap. 1); and drug trafficking, 146; forced displacement, 28, 129, 258n29 (chap. 1); pacification, 92; and tourism, 24, 119; youths from, 135
Festa de Boa Morte, 73
Fieldwork, 12, 14, 16, 75, 84, 86–88, 125, 185; multisited, 14, 86
Flor da Gente, 118
Floreios, 3, 133, 144, 187, 188
Flow, 4–5. See also *Axé*
Foster, Susan, 223
Franco, Marielle, 232–34
Freire, Paulo, 136, 236; pedagogy of the oppressed, 136
Freud, Sigmund, 4
Freyre, Gilberto, 49, 99, 130, 202

Gardner, Howard, 135; eight intelligences, 135
Gavião, *Instrutor* (Luiz da Silva) 183–84
Geertz, Clifford, 16, 88
Gegê, *Mestra* (Maria Eugenia Poggi), 231–32
Gentrification, 24, 61
Gilroy, Paul, 6
Ginga, 10–11, 46, 56, 193, 256n25 (intro.); *do molejo,* 206
Globalization, 195, 221

Global South, 20, 196–98; *capoeiristas,* 198; versus Global North, 196
Gonzalez, Anita, 15
Gonzalez, Lélia, 72
Good Death Sisterhood, 73–74
Grupo Capoeira Besouro, 37, 39, 86, 107
Grupo de Capoeira Angola Pelourinho (GCAP), 69–71
Grupo Nzinga de Capoeira Angola, 72, 174, 236
Grupo Senzala, 123, 222
Guiamus, 96
Guillermoprieto, Alma, 32, 82; *Samba,* 32, 82
Gunga. See *berimbau*

Habitus, 15
Hartman, Saidiya, 197
Herskovits, Melville, 256n28 (intro.)
Heyward, Leslie, 103
Hoffman, Daniel, 159
Höfling, Ana Paula, 52, 65
Homophobia, 105, 144
Huizinga, Johan, 4
Hulk, *Mestre* (Sidney Gonçalves Freitas), 93–94, 110
Humor, 5, 7, 30, 36, 41, 48, 98, 138, 212, 234; and pain, 175; as agency, 175, 231
Hunger, 138, 142
(Hyper)heterosexuality, 196

Identity: local, 189; national, 98, 202; politics, 64; and racial, 83
Ilê Aiyê (carnival group), 69, 71
Imagined community, 6, 159
Improvisation, 4–5, 26, 40, 65–66, 159, 215, 218, 222, 225
Inclusivity, 71, 229
Inequality, 8, 14–15, 20, 24–25, 27, 61, 86, 166, 200, 205, 209, 221
Informal economy, 62, 129, 141
Integrated Centers for Public Education (CIEP), 120, 122, 124, 134, 186
Intercorporeality, 17, 257n49 (intro.)
Internet, 17, 145
Interracial social relationships, 129, 141
Isaac, Glynn, 8

Jackson, John L., Jr., 83
Jackson, Michael (anthropologist), 18
Jackson, Michael (singer), "They Don't Care About Us," 126

Janja, *Mestra* (Rosângela Costa Araújo), 72, 232

Jim Crow laws, 48, 71, 99, 235

João Grande, *Mestre* (João Oliveira dos Santos), 192–94, 222

João Pequeno, *Mestre* (João Pereira dos Santos), 69–70, 72

Jogar (play), 1, 5

Jogo (game), 1, 17

Jogo duro (rough play), 7, 26, 33, 37–38, 51, 98–100; and gender equality, 38; versus *briga* (fight), 99

Jomar (Jomar Lino Dias), 39–40

Kabetula, *Mestre* (António Joaquim Bento), 172

Kealiinohomoku, Joann, 223

Kimpa Vita, Beatrice, 217

Kinetoscape, 17

Kinha, *Mestre* (Paulo Kinha Linhares), 28

Kizomba, 200

Kongo Kingdom, 213; colonial history of, 215; as source of capoeira's philosophy, 213; worldview, 214

Kuduro, 218

Kula ring, 2, 255n2 (intro.)

Kurtz, Esther, 231–32

Ladainha, 66–67, 107, 169, 212, 232

Landes, Ruth, 12, 48–49, 51, 56, 81, 256n28 (intro.); *City of Women*, 12, 48

Language, 139–40, 168, 185; Angolan Portuguese, 170; Bantu, 173; and gender, 229; Kimbundu, 168, 172, 211; and otherness, 203; Tupi-Guarani, 34, 46; Yoruba, 4

Leopoldina, *Mestre* (Demerval Lopes de Lacerda), 95; lineage, 96; style, 96–97

Lévi-Strauss, Claude, 20; *Tristes Tropiques*, 20

Lima, *Mestra* Edna (Edna Lima), 84–86, 121, 144, 192; pedagogy, 85

Linger, Daniel, 99

Lourenço, João, 199–200

Louvação, 66–67

Loyalty, 14, 22, 86, 105; to place, 189

Luanda, 158–61, 200; colonial history, 166–67; and displacement, 161–62; Ilha de, 166–67, 169, 172; and inequality, 166, 208–9; Praça Kinaxixi, 162, 165, 207; São Miguel Fort, 170, 200

Luso-Tropicalism, 202

Machismo, 54, 102

Maculelê, 73, 83, 168, 179

Mãe Jorgina, 76, 78–81, 83, 228

Mãe Menininha, 75; and Gantois, 75

Mãe Stella, 75; and Ilê Axé Opô Afonjá, 75

Maestrinha, *Professora* (Andrea Cristiane Alves da Cunha), 144, 158

Magalhães, Antônio Carlos, 70

Malandragem, 7, 10, 27, 51, 96, 116; as hustling, 23–24, 58; as resistance, 113

Malhação (soap opera), 36, 126; and racism, 127–28

Maltas, 22, 30, 49, 118, 172; persecution of, 173

Mandinka people, 215

Marquinho, *Contramestre* (Marcos Albuquerque) 191–94; lineage, 194; pedagogy, 94

Masculinity, 230–31

Mauss, Marcel, 3, 95

Mbandi, Ngola, 164

Mbandi, Nzinga, 163–65, 207; and colonizer, 215

Mbembe, Achille, 159

Mbundu people, 161, 173

Medicina, *Mestre* (Luís Oliveira Rocha), 73–75

Megagroups, 97, 11, 229

Memoir, 12, 17

Memoirs of a Militia Sergeant (Manuel Antônio de Almeida), 22

Memory, 15, 17, 115, 207; in capoeira, 118; and movement, 221

Mercado Modelo, 49–51, 58, 61, 81, 83; as historic capoeira site, 50–51

Mestre or *mestra* (as titles), 17, 88, 255n1 (intro.); and *berimbau*, 56; and first *mestra* in Rio, 101; and lineage, 11; and proliferation of title, 95; and related titles, 261n1 (chap. 5); and remuneration, 2; -student relationship, 32

Miscegenation, 49, 99

Moa do Katandê, *Mestre* (Romualdo Rosário da Costa), 233–34

Mobility, 14; social, 139, 141; transnational, 159, 173, 198

Moore, Madison, 218

Moraes, *Mestre* (Pedro Moraes Trinidade), 69–70, 72; background, 69; racial politics, 70

Moritz Rugendas, Johann, 46; *São Salvador*, 46

Morro, 24; *donos do*, 92
Movement-vocabulary, 5, 9
Multiple intelligences, 135–36
Musical instruments: *agogô*, 4, 61, 121; *atabaque*, 4, 121; *cavaquinho*, 118; *caxixi*, 58; *dikanza*, 212; *hungu*, 212; *pandeiro*, 4, 121; *reco-reco*, 4, 211
Musseques, 162–63, 209

Nacional, *Mestre* (Adalberto de Souza Alvarenga), 2, 90, 101
Narayan, Kirin, 13
Nascimento, Beatriz, 72
Nash, Jen, 235
National Union for the Total Independence of Angola (UNITA), 161, 167, 178, 203; and Jonas Savimbi, 178; and witchcraft, 178
Native anthropologist (theoretical category), 13, 219, 256n34 (intro.)
Neale Hurston, Zora, 12, 256n27 (intro.)
Negativa, 46, 220
Negritude Movement, 202
Nenel, *Mestre* (Manoel Nascimento Machado), 72
Neoliberalism, 113, 137, 143, 161, 199–200, 205, 221
Neto, Agostinho, 120, 161
Neves e Sousa, Albano, 171–72; *Da Minha África e do Brasil Que Eu Vi*, 171
N'golo (combat game), 171–73, 212–13; as origin of capoeira, 171
Nicknaming, 29–31; and racism, 31
Nimomolo, 37, 39
Nô, *Mestre* (Norival Moreira de Oliveira), 72
Nossa Senhora da Penha (church), 19, 29, 86–87
Nostalgia, 5, 43, 159–61, 205, 210
Novais, Paulo Dias de, 166
Novela, 36
Nyamnjoh, Francis, 6
Nzinga, *Professora* (Brenda Fortes), 162–63, 207
Nzinga (queen), 163–65

Oakland (city), 9
Olinda (city), 33, 194–95
Ondjaki (author), 160
Only the Strong (film), 168
Orixás (living gods), 76, 78; Iemanjá, 76, 79, 236; Obaluaiê, 78–80; Xangô, 76, 78–80

Ortner, Sherry, 113
Os Transparentes, 160, 209
Otherness, 8, 13, 48, 211
Ovimbundu people, 161

Participant-observation, 11, 16, 32, 88
Pastinha, *Mestre* (Vicente Ferreira Pastinha), 1, 11, 62–64, 66, 69–70, 194; background, 63; *Capoeira Angola*, 63, 171
Patronage, 70, 82, 129, 213
Patuá, 214
Pau Brasil, 46
Pau elefante, 178–79
Paulinha, *Mestra* (Paula Cristina da Silva Barreto), 72
People's Movement for the Liberation of Angola (MPLA), 161, 167, 200–203
Piaget, Jean, 4
Place, 43; affects of, 40–44; loyalty to, 189; politics and poetics of, 16; sensations of, 20
Polar, *Instrutor*, 187
Popo, *Mestre* (Alcides de Lima), 73
Postcolonialism, 159, 161, 175
Poverty, 4, 11, 15, 33, 38, 62–63, 100, 137, 166, 211
Praia, João da, "Where the Cow Goes, the Bull Follows," 212
Primus, Pearl, 12–13, 256n30 (intro.)
Privilege, 13; social and racial, 141, 221, 227
Purity, 49, 64–65, 83, 169
Puxada de rede, 168

Quilombo, 22, 113; Palmares Quilombo, 79, 163
Quilombo (film), 78
Quintas, Alfonso, *Viva Noite*, 169

Race: politics, 71, 145; relations, 71, 129
Racism, 11, 13, 36, 54, 57, 71–72, 100, 127, 183, 198; structural, 137
Rank, 31, 37, 88–89, 121, 142, 158, 221, 224, 228
Re-Africanization, 69, 171
Recôncavo, 46, 72–74
Rego, Waldeloir, 50
Repression, 49, 69, 199, 234
Resgate de cidadania, 136
Rio de Janeiro (city), 14–15, 19–23, 257n3 (chap. 1); Baixada Fluminense, 19–20, 24, 88; Bonsucesso, 92; Catete, 117–20;

colonial history of, 21; Guanabara Bay, 20–21, 41; Irajá, 33–34; Penha, 19, 29–30, 100–101; Piscinão de Ramos, 40–41, 81; Quitungo, 28; race and class segregation, 41, 43, 129; urban development or renewal, 24, 43; Vila da Penha, 19, 28; Zona Norte, 19–20, 28, 41, 88; Zona Sul, 19, 24, 28, 41, 89

Roda (circle; capoeira event), 1–2, 4, 7, 48, 224; da Penha, 95, 197; and Central Station, 94; hosting, 2; and other African-diasporic circles, 222

Rooftops (film), 85

Roth-Gordon, Jennifer, 130

Rousseff, Dilma, 233

Salvador (city), 44–83; African influence, 45–49; colonial history, 46, 68; as cradle of capoeira; Forte de Santo Antônio, 68, 82; landmarks, 50, 68, 81; Pelourinho, 47–48, 61–65, 68–70, 72, 82

Samba, 7, 49; schools, 27, 258n27 (chap. 1). See also Beija Flor

Sandrinha, Mestra (Sandra Eugênia Feitosa), 101

Sansone, Lívio, 129–30

Santana Pinho, Patricia de, 158

Santos, João Francisco dos (pseud. Madam Satan), 24

Santos, José Eduardo dos, 161, 199

Santos, Isabel dos, 207–9

Santos e Silva, Ana Joaquina, 171; home of, 171

Sapo, Mestre (Humberto Ferreira de Mendonça), 194

Sardinha, Mestre (Paulo Fernando de Jesus), 34, 53, 91, 106, 107–10

Saudades, 5, 145–46, 186

Savimbi, Jonas, 158, 161; and US and South African support, 161

Scaffolding mimesis, 9

Schubert, Jon, 205

Segregation, 24, 40–41, 72; spatial, 43–44, 70–71

Sensations, 20, 25. See also place; space

Sex tourism, 54

Shange, Savannah, 70–71

Silva, Luiz Inácio da (Lula), 30, 176, 233

Sinhá Moça (soap opera), 168

Sisterhood of Good Death Museum, 74

Slavery, 47, 61, 113, 170, 215

Slavocracy, 44, 202

Smith, Christen, 47

Soccer, 28–29

Soul Train (television show), 8–9, 71

Space, 9, 15; affect of, 43; Black-controlled, 22, 70–71; hypermasculine, 94; male-dominated, 58, 62, 94, 100; sensations of, 43; urban, 16, 162

Styles, 63–65, 67, 70, 72, 74, 86, 96–97; corruption of, 94; versus group loyalty, 86; versus technique, 83, 85–86, 98, 187

Stewart, Kathleen, 14

Sueli Cota, Mestra (Sueli Cota), 101–4

Tabosa, Mestre (Hélio Tabosa de Moraes), 85

Tarde, A, 62

Terreiros, 48–49, 75; Gantois, 75; Ilê Axé Opô Afonjá, 75

Theatre of the Oppressed, 118. See also Boal, Augusto

Thomas, Deborah, 218

Thompson, Robert Farris, 215; Flash of the Spirit: African and Afro-American Art and Philosophy, 214

Tisza, Mestra (Tisza Coelho), 222–23

Tomás, António, 200

Toni Vargas, Mestre (Antonio César de Vargas), 174–75

Touro, Mestre (Antonio Oliveira Bemvindo), 1–2, 29–31, 84, 86–87, 90, 106–7; family, 90–91; folkloric style, 95, 97; critique of commercialization, 98; critique of megagroups, 97, 110; critique of racism, 137; lineage, 95–97; monthly roda, 107–10; nickname, 31; title, 95

Transatlantic Slave Trade, 170–71

Transnationalism, 17, 159, 198

Traumatic loss, 77–80, 83; and cultural identity, 173

Trinta, Joãozinho, 140

Troca de cordas, 88

Uniforms, 106, 138–40

US cultural imperialism, 140

Vadiação, 50–51, 81

Vale tudo, 93

Vargas, Getúlio, 64

Vasconcelos, Naná, 56

Velha guarda, 11

Veloso, Leticia, 128

Venice (city), 187–92; and bridge battles, 190; and *convivência,* 192; history of, 189–91; and labor, 189; and sensations of, 189

Verger, Pierre, 50

Violence, 91–93, 117, 138; in Angola, 161, 167, 178; in capoeira, 93–94, 100, 194; and carnival, 99; controlled, 100; and coping, 175; and drug trafficking, 128, 145–46, 185; gendered, 196; and masculinity, 65, 94; as motive for immigration, 184; political, 232–34; and race, 25, 38, 44, 47, 98, 258n26 (chap. 1); state, 234; systemic, 138

Wacquant, Loïc, 100, 257n46 (intro.)

Whiteness, 70–71, 127–28, 139, 197, 229

Williams, Erica, 54

Workers' Party, 70

Xuxa, 144

Yakalaya, 204

Yoruba people, 4, 76, 124

Zumbi (de Palmares), 163, 205

Zungueiras, 163

KATYA WESOLOWSKI (Camarão) is a lecturing fellow in cultural anthropology and dance at Duke University.

www.ingramcontent.com/pod-product-compliance
Lightning Source LLC
Chambersburg PA
CBHW031412270326
41929CB00010BA/1423